The
Jamestown
Brides

Also by Jennifer Potter

The Jamestown Brides

The untold story of England's 'maids for Virginia'

Jennifer Potter

Atlantic Books
London

First published in hardback in Great Britain in 2018 by Atlantic Books,
an imprint of Atlantic Books Ltd.

1 3 5 7 9 10 8 6 4 2

A CIP catalogue record for this book is available from the British Library.

Hardback ISBN: 978-1-78239-913-1
E-book ISBN: 978-1-78239-915-5
Paperback ISBN: 978-1-78239-916-2

Map on p. 197 by Jeff Edwards

Printed in Great Britain by TJ International, Padstow, Cornwall

Atlantic Books
An imprint of Atlantic Books Ltd
Ormond House
26–27 Boswell Street
London WC1N 3JZ

www.atlantic-books.co.uk

For Chris and Lynn with love

*and special thanks to Martha W. McCartney,
Helen C. Rountree and Beverly A. Straube.*

Contents

Citizens: daugter

Ciuis Londinensis Filia.

Wenceslaus Hollar, 1643

I looked at that wife, and of a sudden, the anger in my heart melted away. It was a wilderness vast and dreadful to which she had come. The mighty stream, the towering forests, the black skies and deafening thunder, the wild cries of bird and beast, the savages, uncouth and terrible, – for a moment I saw my world as the woman at my feet must see it, strange, wild, and menacing, an evil land, the other side of the moon.

Mary Johnston, *To Have and To Hold*

Witness

In the late summer and early autumn of 1621, a succession of ships set sail from England bound for Jamestown, Virginia. On board were fifty-six young women of certified good character and proven skills, hand-picked by the Virginia Company of London to make wives for the planters of its fledgling colony.[1] The oldest was twenty-eight (or so she claimed) and the youngest barely sixteen. All were reputedly young, handsome and honestly brought up, unlike the prostitutes and vagrant children swept off the streets of London in previous years and transported to the colony as cheap labour.

The Virginia Company's aim in shipping the women to Virginia was that of money men everywhere: to generate a profit by bringing merchantable goods to market. Since King James had abruptly suspended the Virginia lotteries on which the colony depended for funds, the company's coffers were bare. Importing would-be brides was one of four moneymaking schemes designed to keep the company afloat, and its leaders in London hoped to ensure the colony's long-term viability by rooting the unruly settlers to the land with ties of family and children. While the women travelled of their own free will, the company had set a bride price of 150lbs of tobacco for each woman sold into marriage, which represented a healthy return for individual investors. These were businessmen, after all, doing what they did best: making money.

But the women – what did they want from the enterprise? Why did they agree to venture across the seas to a wild and heathen land where life was hard and mortality rates were catastrophic? Had anyone whispered a word to them about the dangers they faced, or warned them how slim their chances of survival really were?

The Jamestown Brides sets out to tell the women's story: who they were, what sort of lives they led before falling into the Virginia Company's net, the hopes and fears that propelled them across the Atlantic, and what happened to them when they reached their journey's end. I have stuck as doggedly as I am able to what the 'evidence' tells us, but the record is worn as thin as a vagrant's coat, requiring a bold leap of the imagination to appreciate from the inside the shock of transitioning from one life to another, made all the harder by the four centuries that separate then from now.

Considered a mere footnote to Virginia's colonial history, the story of the 'maids for Virginia' first came to me in Colonial Williamsburg's John D. Rockefeller Jr. Library, where I was researching *Strange Blooms*, a dual biography of John Tradescant and his son (also called John), gardeners to the Stuart kings and early collectors of plants and curiosities. Distracted by guides in eighteenth-century costume who were visiting the library to check their facts or simply to escape the tourists, I chanced across David Ransome's scholarly article, 'Wives for Virginia, 1621'.[2] The story of these women shipped thousands of miles across the Atlantic to procure husbands has stayed with me ever since for reasons that are only partly personal. Then soon to be divorced myself, I could also be said to be looking for a husband, but how far would I travel to find one? (Answer: not far enough to find one.) Beyond that, I wondered what combination of faith, hope, courage, curiosity or just plain desperation might encourage me or anyone else – at any time – to journey into the unknown.

The starting point for my researches was a series of remarkable lists that survive at Magdalene College, Cambridge, among the papers of Nicholas Ferrar, a London merchant closely involved with the Virginia Company who would later retreat with his extended family to found an informal Anglican community at Little Gidding in the historic county of Huntingdonshire. Intended as a kind of sales catalogue for prospective husbands, the lists record the women's personal histories: name, age, marital status, birthplace, parentage, father's occupation, domestic skills, guarantors and testimonials from their elders and betters. Dry as they are, lists such as these quickly come alive as you make connections, chase after hares, interrogate possibilities, scramble into and out of dead ends like the 'Kremlinologists' identified by the Virginian historian Cary Carson – 'decoders of elusive clues' from the few surviving scraps of evidence, much of it buried underground.[3]

The Virginia Company's council had every right to take pride in the human cargo they had assembled at East Cowes on the Isle of Wight and later at Gravesend. Some one in six were the daughters of gentry or claimed gentry relatives, while the rest presented a microcosm of 'middling' England, with fathers, brothers, uncles working in respectable trades. They came recommended by the great and good of the City of London or by company investors and employees, from the lowliest porter to Sir Edwin Sandys himself, the effective leader of the Virginia Company and chief architect of the scheme to bring brides to the colony.

One of the maids jumped ship on the Isle of Wight, but miraculously the rest survived the Atlantic crossing and arrived in good health. A few were married before the ships left Jamestown, so we are told, but a little over three months later an Indian attack wiped out between a quarter and a third of the English colony. For the word purists among us, descendants of Virginia's indigenous people continue to call themselves Indians – and so I shall use the term throughout this book – but you must be careful how you refer to the events of that cataclysmic day. At the time it was invariably labelled a 'massacre', later an 'uprising' and now simply an 'attack' or the 'Great Assault', as a way of sharing responsibility for what

3

happened, after fifteen years of concerted land grabs by English settlers and barbaric acts committed by both sides.

Some of the Jamestown brides died in the slaughter, others clung tenaciously to life. Lists of the living and the dead compiled soon after the attack and two later censuses allow us to track what happened to around one third of the Jamestown brides, who also appear fleetingly in court records and the minutes of Virginia's general assemblies, held from 1619. However brief and apparently inconsequential, such records throw up snippets of everyday life: malicious gossip, misdemeanours, fraudulent land registrations and squabbles over property, the stuff of life that illuminates what became of the women and the kind of men they chose to marry.

In retelling the women's stories, I am trying to experience life as they found it and to participate in the choices and decisions they made. Inevitably this means slipping myself into the narrative, as unobtrusively as possible, especially when I go looking for the women on the streets of London, in the backwaters of rural England and the Virginian swamps and settlements to which they scattered. The histories I enjoy take me back into the past but also bring the past into the present, however dislocating the effect. And so I found myself sifting through the detritus of material culture, the post holes and broken pottery shards of Carson's Kremlinologists, looking for sites which the women may have seen and objects they may have held in their hands. I found them too, always with a heady rush of recognition: bodkins of silver and brass excavated at Jordan's Point on the Upper James where one of the brides settled, fragments of clay milk pans made by a potter known to another of the women, although she never found herself an English husband; hers is one of the most unsettling of all the women's stories.

No letter or journal survives from any of these women, nor should we expect any to surface. While girls from the middling classes might be taught to read along with sewing and knitting, writing was a skill generally reserved for boys and for the children (boys and girls) of the upper gentry or families exposed to humanist education. The task I have therefore set myself is to bear witness to the lives and stories of these women, whose voices have left no trace in the historical record. 'I WILL BE HER WITNESS' is how the narrator of Joan Didion's *A Book of Common Prayer* begins her story of the decline and fall of one Charlotte Douglas, who dreamed her life and died, hopeful, in the fictional Central American republic of Boca Grande. The story I am telling is fact not fiction, but like Didion's narrator I struggle to make sense of what happened.

Much of the book's textual detail comes from listening to the 'chatter' of the times: the sardonic musings of social commentator John Chamberlain; the nostalgic antiquarian John Stow writing about a London that was changing before his eyes; Virginia Company records, which you must read between the lines in order to disentangle factional truths and falsehoods; the bombastic but always lively writings of Captain John Smith on Virginia and seafaring topics; accounts and letters home from a variety of early settlers, whose viewpoints veer from the disaffected to the wildly propagandist; and one of the richest sources of all, the babble of voices from the street contained in contemporary ballads, once derided as a historical source but now valued as social texts.

My book falls naturally into two halves, divided partly by geography and partly by chronology. Part One, 'England and its Virginian Colony', tells the women's stories up to the moment they boarded their ships at Cowes and Gravesend. Early chapters delve into their social, economic and geographical backgrounds, grouping them according to the ships by which they sailed to Virginia. Crucially, this part looks also at how it felt to be a woman in early modern England. We need to know where the women came from, literally and metaphorically, to judge how far they travelled. The focus of Part One then switches to the Virginia Company's colonization of North America, refracting Virginia's early history through the experience of largely female settlers, although Chapter 6,

'La Belle Sauvage', examines the parallel narrative of Pocahontas's marriage to English settler John Rolfe, and the perplexing fate of the Virginia Indian women who accompanied the Rolfes to England in 1616.

A short 'Intermezzo' carries the women across the Atlantic and tacks with them slowly up the James River to Jamestown, where they arrive in the winter of 1621.

Part Two, 'Virginia', takes the story forward, setting out as forensically as I am able how the colony will have appeared to these young women fresh from England, and how they settled into their new lives. Here lies the heart of the book, which also provides a fresh perspective on the Indian attack and its aftermath. Where did the women stay? How did they choose their husbands? Where did they go and how did they adapt to their new lives? Who lived and who died? What happened to those who never married? Did investors in the scheme ever reap the rewards they were promised? These are some of the questions I try to answer as honestly as I can, looking also at the Virginia Company's inevitable decline and fall. Chapters 15 to 18 pick up the lives of four women who survived through the 1620s, three who married and one who was captured by the Indians. Tracking these four women through the records and on the ground has been a joy, linking the very English landscapes of their childhoods to the creeks and inlets of tidewater Virginia where they made their homes. Place matters in this book, as you will see.

In my acknowledgements I pay tribute to the enormous help I have received from many people and institutions in the UK and in Virginia. Here I would like to thank three women in particular who have generously shared with me their unique insights and helped to guide my researches in Virginia: historian Martha McCartney, anthropologist and cultural historian Helen Rountree, and curator Beverly (Bly) Straube. This is a book written by a woman about women's experiences, aided by women. Men have helped too, of course. I think of archaeologist Nicholas Luccketti giving up a bright but bitter Sunday morning to walk me over the ground of Martin's Hundred, and riverkeeper Jamie Brunkow taking me from Jamestown down to Burwell's Bay and back again, to experience the river as the women will have done, from the water. Thank you all: without your help this would be a far slimmer book.

Historians are taught not to judge the past by the standards of today, fair enough, but the fundamental question I am asking demands the exercise of judgement. I leave this task with you in the hope that you may find your own answers in the pages that follow. Were these women the victims of a patriarchal society, shipped overseas to serve the interests of others: investors who stood to gain from their 'sale', company officials who wished to tame male colonists with the carrot of female company, planters looking for female skills to aid their colonizing endeavours, English families wishing to dispose of unmarried daughters on the cheap? Or were they adventurers in the truest sense, women prepared to invest their persons rather than their purses in the New World?

A note on the text

Most quotations from primary sources retain the original spelling, although I have substituted 'u' for 'v' and 'j' for 'i' where relevant, and supplied missing letters from some abbreviations. Dates generally follow the old Julian calendar, realigned to start each new year on 1 January. Despite having originally intended to write this book without using notes, I believe that any claim to 'truth' must be open to challenge. I therefore supply references exclusively to indicate my sources; the text can happily be read without them. For readers unfamiliar with England's pre-decimal currency, twelve pennies made one shilling and twenty shillings one pound sterling, expressed as £ s. d. As well as the '£' sign, pounds could also be abbreviated to 'li' from the Latin word, *libra*. In 1620s Virginia, tobacco was the prevailing currency: one pound in weight of best Virginia tobacco was then officially valued at three shillings, or £19.73 at today's values.

PART ONE

England and its Virginian Colony

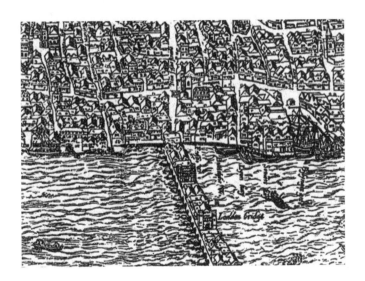

Come all you very merry London Girls,
that are disposed to Travel,
Here is a Voyage now at hand,
will save your feet from gravel,
If you have shooes you need not fear
for wearing out the Leather
For why you shall on shipboard go,
like Loving Rogues together,
Some are already gone before
the rest must after follow
Then come away and do not stay
Your guide shal be Apollo.

Lawrence Price, 'The Maydens of Londons brave adventures, /
OR, / A Boon Voyage intended for the Sea', London,
printed for Francis Grove on Snow-hill, 1623–1661

CHAPTER ONE

The *Marmaduke* Maids

Some time after Sunday 12 August 1621, thirteen young women gathered beside the burgeoning wharves and storehouses at East Cowes on the Isle of Wight, waiting for a lighterman to row them out to the *Marmaduke* anchored in the roads.[1] Already a month into their journey, they had travelled by boat from London to Gravesend and after a short stay had continued overland to Portsmouth then by boat across the Solent to Cowes on the island's northern coast.[2] The Virginia Company had commissioned the *Marmaduke*'s master, John Dennis, to pick up passengers and goods from the Isle of Wight, and here the women had stayed until the boat was loaded and the winds and the tide turned in their favour.

The hand-picked women travelled without family, apparently of their own volition, in response to the company's call for 'maydes for Virginia' – English women 'young, handsome and honestlie educated' willing to cross the Atlantic to marry planters in its colony of Virginia, then less than fifteen years old.[3] Promised a free choice of husband, the women doubtless remained ignorant of the financial nature of the operation: that they formed part of a 'magazine' or trading enterprise designed to bring much needed cash from individual investors to replenish the company's now empty coffers.

Among those whose fortunes we shall track is Catherine Finch from the small rural parish of Marden in Herefordshire, where she was baptized in the church of St Mary the Virgin, perched beside the sluggish River Lugg in a broad flood plain surrounded by gently undulating farmland. The long-distance footpath across the Welsh Marches runs through the straggling village, which remains deeply agricultural to this day, its old-world charm dislocated by shimmering rivers of polytunnels protecting the soft-fruit crops of the region's thriving agribusinesses and refrigerated lorries thundering through its narrow country lanes.

As parish records for Marden survive only from 1616, it has not been possible to check the age that Catherine declared to the Virginia Company (twenty-three in 1621), but you can still touch the fourteenth-century sandstone font where she was baptized and admire the fine brass plate commemorating the 'Pietie and Virtues' of a gentlewoman from Catherine's time: Dame Margaret Chute, who died on 9 June 1614 following complications in childbirth, the day after her infant daughter, Frances.[4] Clearly a member of the upper gentry, Dame Margaret is dressed in the court fashions favoured by Queen Anne of Denmark, wife of the Stuart King James: low neckline, tight bodice winged at the shoulders and pointed at the waist, cuffs and raised collar in expensive needlepoint lace, necklace of pearls and one visible dangling earring. Her children appear beside her, a surviving daughter dressed like a scaled-down version of her mother and the dead baby wearing a lace collar and bib over her swaddling clothes. The young Catherine will have seen the Chute family at church, seated according to their station in life, which placed her own family somewhere between the middle and the back.

From Marden, the orphaned Catherine Finch travelled to Westminster to live in service with her quarrelsome brother Erasmus Finch, crossbow maker to King James and later to King Charles I. Erasmus then lived on the less favoured 'landside' of the Strand, a wide thoroughfare connecting the two cities of London and Westminster where poor and middling sorts of people lived in tenements squeezed between the grander houses of aristocrats, courtiers and gentlemen's lodgings. Two other brothers lived close by: Edward, described variously as a goldsmith and a locksmith, a little way east along the Strand in the parish of St Clement Danes, and John, also a crossbow maker, in St Martin's Lane off the Strand, a winding thoroughfare running northwards from Charing Cross to the church of St Giles-in-the-Fields flanked by land only recently turned over to housing. Brother John would rise to be one of ten assistants in the newly formed Company of Gunmakers under Master Henry Rowland, the king's master gunmaker, outranking Erasmus Finch, who appears among the commonality of 'Skilful Artists'.[5]

One of Catherine's companions on the *Marmaduke* was Audry (Adria) Hoare, a shoemaker's daughter from the lace-making town of Aylesbury in Buckinghamshire. Baptized on 25 August 1604 at the parish church of St Mary the Virgin, Audry was the youngest child of Thomas and Julyan Hoare, aged barely seventeen when she sailed, two years younger than the age she gave to the Virginia Company. She had at least four older siblings, three sisters (Joan, Agnes and Elizabeth) and brother Richard, apprenticed to a fustian dresser.[6] Unlike many of her fellows, Audry Hoare had both parents still living when she was brought to the Virginia Company by her married eldest sister, Joane Childe, who was living in Blackfriars 'down in the Lane neer the Catherne wheell', which might refer to a tavern or to a tenement building.[7] Stretching north from the Thames, this lively neighbourhood was popular with gentry and much favoured by players, musicians, composers and artists. Shakespeare was a shareholder in the small, indoor Blackfriars Theatre and even bought a substantial house here in 1613, which he bequeathed to his daughter Susannah on his death just a few years later.[8]

On the face of it, neither Catherine Finch nor Audry Hoare had an obvious reason to join the shipment of young women willing to risk their futures on finding a husband in the New World. Audry Hoare had close kin living in London and well connected relatives who might have helped her attract a husband: one of her first cousins was a merchant, Master Thomas Biling, and another an upholsterer in Cornwall. Catherine Finch enjoyed even more advantages. She lived with her brother, a craftsman with royal connections, in one of the capital's most vibrant and fashionable neighbourhoods, within easy reach of the river and the open spaces of St Martin's Field, and she had other family living nearby. Surely her chances of finding a husband were better than most? But all three brothers commended her to the Virginia Company, either because they wanted to rid themselves of responsibility for their unmarried sister, or because Catherine herself was more than willing to adventure her life overseas. Perhaps the truth lies somewhere in between: that through his royal connections or neighbourhood gossip Erasmus Finch caught wind of the company's plan to ship marriageable women out to the colony and successfully convinced his sister to take up the challenge.

It is easy to see why a third Jamestown bride aboard the *Marmaduke* wished to travel to Virginia. Also considerably younger than the age she gave to the Virginia Company, Ann Jackson was bound for Martin's Hundred, some ten miles downriver from Jamestown, to join her bricklayer brother John Jackson, who had represented the new settlement as one of its two burgesses in Virginia's first general assembly held in 1619. Born within sight of Salisbury cathedral and baptized on 24 September 1604 in the parish church of Sarum St Martin, several years after two brothers, Ann Jackson came to the Virginia Company with the blessing of their father William, a man of 'known honesty and conversaton'.

By the time Ann sailed, William Jackson had moved from Salisbury to Westminster and was living in one of the overcrowded tenements squeezed into dingy alleyways between the grand houses of Tuttle (Tothill) Street inhabited by the nobility.[9] No mention is made of Ann's mother so I can only assume she had died and that Ann was keeping house for her father, who was attracted like many

The maids who sailed by the Marmaduke *left England from East Cowes across the Medina estuary from Cowes Castle, sketched here by the Dutch artist Lambert Doomer.*

others to the densely populated parish of St Margaret's to serve the courtiers and bureaucrats of Westminster. Since his name does not appear in the various tax assessments for the parish, he was either subletting or judged too poor himself to contribute towards the upkeep of paupers, but as a gardener William Jackson will have found plenty of work tending the large gardens running north and south from Tuttle Street.[10]

While account books and ledgers can tell you the names of the passengers taken on board, they cannot tell you what those passengers were thinking, or how the women viewed their prospects as they waited for the flat-bottomed barge that would take them out to the *Marmaduke*.

Already one of their number had jumped ship: the widowed Joan Fletcher, at twenty-eight one of the oldest in the group and by all accounts the best connected, born into a prominent family in Cheshire and Staffordshire that included members of parliament, viscounts, a lord chancellor and even an earl. Her paternal uncle, Sir Ralph Egerton Knight, may be identified as one of two Ralph Egertons of Betley in Staffordshire, either 'Radus [Ralph] Egerton de Betley, Armiger', who married his relative Frances Egerton in January 1577, or their first-born son Radus, baptized at Betley three years later.[11]

Perhaps the widowed Joan Fletcher had taken fright at her companions or at the cramped conditions and undeniable hardships of travel in early seventeenth-century England. It can only have been a last-minute decision as the trunk containing her personal possessions was loaded onto the ship before she changed her mind, or had it changed for her.[12] All we know is that she was 'turned back' at the Isle of Wight and her place taken by An[n] Buergen, who may have been of German or French origin since Buergen in all its variant spellings is not a local name.[13]

The ship's master, John Dennis, carried with him a letter from the Virginia Company to the governor and council in Virginia, clearly written before Joan Fletcher's hurried departure, as it includes among the ship's passengers 'one Widdow and eleven Maides for Wives for the people in Virginia, there hath beene especiall care had in the choise of them; for there hath not any one of them beene received but uppon good Comendacons, as by a noat herewth sent youe may perceive.'[14] In fact thirteen women sailed on the *Marmaduke* as part of the bridal shipment, according to a second note written by Nicholas Ferrar, merchant and younger brother to John Ferrar, who was then deputy to the Virginia Company – in effect its chief administrator – and the Ferrars' clerk, Tristram Conyam. The thirteen included eleven maids from the original dozen, Joan Fletcher's replacement Ann Buergen, and Ursula Lawson, who was travelling with her kinsman Richard Pace and his wife, on their return to the colony.[15] Just two of the *Marmaduke* women were

Londoners born and bred: twenty-year-old Susan Binx, raised outside the City walls in St Sepulchre's parish, and fifteen-year-old waterman's daughter Jane Dier, the baby of the group, brought by her mother, who lived among the drunken Flemish refugees, seamen, madmen and pestering tenements of the riverside precinct of St Katharine's by the Tower. The others were all born elsewhere.

Wherever their birthplace, most of the young women were living in London by the time they fell into the Virginia Company's net, working in service with family members or respectable citizens who could vouch for their honesty and industry. As was usual for the times, a good many had lost either or both parents, but socially these women were far from society's cast-offs. If we include Joan Fletcher among their number, as many as five of the original dozen were the daughters of gentlemen or counted gentlefolk among their relatives. The father of twenty-one-year-old Ann Harmer from Baldock in Hertfordshire was 'a gentleman of good means now lyvinge'. Londoner Susan Binx had a widowed maternal aunt, Mistress Gardiner, a gentlewoman living near the Finches in the Strand. Margaret Bourdman's maternal uncle was Sir John Gibson, knighted by King James in 1607 and holder of the patent to exploit alum in the North Riding of Yorkshire, a county he would later serve as sheriff.[16] Lettice King could even lay claim to two gentry relatives. One was an uncle dwelling in London's Charterhouse, then an almshouse for indigent gentlemen, soldiers or merchants, although he was later expelled for 'misprision of treason', a lesser form of treason or concealing the treachery of others.[17] The second was her cousin once removed, Sir William Udall, in all likelihood the popular courtier Sir William Uvedale or Udall, who had recently been nominated by the Earl of Southampton as member of parliament for the Isle of Wight.[18] Given Southampton's involvement in Virginia Company affairs – he was soon to take over as treasurer – he may have been the conduit for Lettice King's recruitment to the Jamestown brides.

While not of such elevated stock, the other *Marmaduke* maids had fathers, brothers, uncles or cousins who worked in respectable trades as saddlers, husbandmen, soldiers, wire drawers, grocers, printers, in addition to the merchants, gardeners, shoemakers, upholsterers, crossbow makers and fustian dressers already encountered. Even Jane Dier's dead father could claim his place among Sir Thomas Overbury's *Characters*, which painted the watermen as tellers of 'strange newes, most commonly lyes… When he is upon the water, he is Fare-company: when he comes ashore, he mutinies; and contrarie to all other trades, is most surly to Gentlemen, when they tender payment'.[19] Here was a microcosm of middling England under King James, independent tradesmen who worked for their living, trading with the products of their hands or with the skills in business or the professions for which they had trained.[20]

In putting together its prospectus for potential husbands, the Virginia Company took pains to enumerate the women's accomplishments. Provenance alone was sufficient guarantee of worth for most of the gentry daughters among them, while skills listed for the lower-status women were generally of two sorts: robust, practical skills in housewifery on the one hand, and more refined needlework or knitting skills on the other. Despite her more advanced age (not in itself a handicap), husbandman's daughter Allice Burges would have made a splendid planter's wife: 'She is skillfull in manie country works, she can brew, bake and make Malte etc'. The same was said of another husbandman's daughter, Ann Tanner from Chelmsford, who could 'brew, and bake, make butter and cheese, and doe huswifery', in addition to her ability to 'Spinn and sewe in Blackworke'.

Another four *Marmaduke* maids had rarefied needlework skills: Cambridge-born Mary Ghibbs could make intricate bone lace, which involved weaving linen thread around bobbins of bone. Brought up in the household of a seamstress, gentleman's daughter Ann Harmer 'can doe all manner of workes [in] gold and silks', while

Audry Hoare could 'doe plaine works and blackworks' and make all manner of buttons. As well as working in 'divers good services', Susan Binx was able to knit and embroider in white- and blackwork, a skill she may have acquired from her wire-drawer father, since blackwork embroidery was sometimes embellished with gold or silver-gilt thread. But the fashion for blackwork was almost over, and it is hard to imagine that its delicate ornamentation would prove a selling point for a planter's wife in Virginia.[21]

By the time the women reached the Isle of Wight, they will surely have got the measure of each other and begun to form natural alliances that would help them weather the long journey ahead. The man charged with seeing them safely aboard their ship was local merchant Robert Newland from nearby Newport, who had been largely responsible for bringing the Virginian trade to the island. It was Newland who had replaced Joan Fletcher with Ann Buergen, and given the delicate nature of his cargo, he will undoubtedly have wished to attend on them personally as they waited for the boat that would take them out to their ship, anchored in the choppy waters of the Solent.

Facing north towards the English coast, Cowes is a town in two parts – East and West Cowes – straddling the mouth of the River Medina. In Tudor times, ships had traded from Newport at the head of the estuary, but by 1575 a new customs house had brought maritime trade downriver to East Cowes, and now Newland was devoting his considerable energy to establishing a working port with storehouses and a quayside.[22]

He had come to the Virginia Company's attention two years before the women left for Jamestown, recommended by Gabriel Barbor in a letter to Sir Edwin Sandys, who had just wrested control of the company from wealthy City merchant Sir Thomas Smythe.[23] One of the overseers of the Virginia Lotteries, Barbor was personally connected to two of the women: *Marmaduke* maid

Mary Ghibbs, and Fortune Taylor who sailed shortly afterwards on the *Warwick*.

Newland was, said Barbor, 'an honest sufficient & a moste indevoring man for Virginia', who could further the colony's development by victualling the ships or providing manpower. Already he was 'so well reported of' by the Virginia Company of London's sister Plymouth Company, among others, and had helped Captain Christopher Lawne establish a Virginian plantation along the James River in what would later become Isle of Wight County. Indeed, Newland was one of nine associates who had invested in Lawne's plantation, earning praise as a 'ventrous charitable marchant'.[24] Newland would not only help prevent deserters from the company's ships, promised Barbor, but would 'victuall cheaper th[a]n Londoneres', surely his chief attraction for a commercial company perennially short of funds.

Sandys and his deputy, John Ferrar, had clearly taken Barbor's recommendation to heart and commissioned Newland to ship some 230 people and supplies by the *Abigail* from his base at East Cowes 'for the more comodiousnes and for procuringe of people the better'.[25] The operation was so successful that Newland was given five shares in the Virginia Company on condition that he did not sell them, recognizing the 'extraordinary paines taken in their service in taking care of Shipping their people in the Abigaile at the Ile of Wight'.[26]

That was in early May 1621, just three months before the *Marmaduke* set sail from East Cowes and right at the start of the port's brief decade of prosperity, when Robert Newland had a hand in much of the island's trading activity. 'All things were exported and imported at your heart's desire', wrote the islander Sir John Oglander, recording the port's rapid development from just three or four houses at Cowes to the magnificent sight of 300 ships riding at anchor in the roads, before European wars brought 'poverty and complaint' back to 'our poor Island' by the end of the decade.[27]

Although Newland drops out of the Virginia Company's story from late 1622, when he received a commission to transport people to Virginia on the *Plantacon* and to proceed on a fishing voyage,[28] he continued to play a leading role in island affairs as one of Newport's chief burgesses, rising to mayor in 1629 and again for three months in 1636. Just one month after the *Marmaduke* sailed for Virginia, he was entrusted with the town's 'Comon Box to receave and accompt for all the towne rents revenues and proffitts'.[29] But he was not considered a gentleman by the standards of the day, appearing simply as 'Newland' at the bottom of Sir John Oglander's list of new year's gifts received in 1622, the only donor denied a polite 'Mr', a 'Goodman' or even a Christian name.

Whatever talents he possessed for provisioning the Virginia Company's ships, Newland was not especially well lettered, judging from the only correspondence of his to survive among the company's records. The letter reveals his poor grasp of composition and punctuation and his erratic spelling, but if you read it aloud, his strong Hampshire voice rings through.[30] Its first paragraph concerns shirts, packed away in a chest in the ship's hold and therefore out of reach of the poor passengers, many of whom had endured a full month without changing their shirts. Newland's tone is defensive, as if he is responding to a complaint about his charges:

> Sr. Youers of the 18 of this instant I Recavd and you say that Capten Barwik had order to opene the Chest vher the shirtes is but thoues Chist ar stod in the ship and ar not to be Com by Some of youer pepell hath gon a month in a shirt so that of nesitie they most have Chaing I do for you as for my sell nothing but what Nesistie is done the fordrence paseger hath ben 2 times at the Coues to goe abord but the wind is Come to the wastward a gaine so now that be hear at Nuport and Capten Barwike will not leat his pepell Remane a bord befor the wind is faier.

Newland will have needed all his mercantile skills to provision the company's ships with sufficient food, fuel and general stores for the long sea crossing, and to sustain the new settlers during their first year in the colony. The *Marmaduke* maids were dispatched at such speed that they travelled empty-handed, without the usual provisions aside from clothes provided by the company and bedding: two trusses 'for use at sea' containing six bed cases and bolsters, six rugs, two psalters and twelve catechism books, the last two items to be delivered to the master's mate, Mr Andrews, for the maids' use.[31] A further half-barrel contained six pairs of sheets, six bed cases and six bolsters, intended perhaps for six of the maids when they arrived in Virginia.[32]

The thirteen maids were not the only settlers travelling to Virginia that summer. Also on board the *Marmaduke* were 'twelve lustie youths' and stores bound for Martin's Hundred,[33] where gardener's daughter Ann Jackson was joining her brother; forty more settlers for the plantation would follow in the *Warwick*. The Virginia Company's 'husband' or chief accountant dutifully recorded the goods loaded onto the *Marmaduke* destined for this plantation: four barrels of peas; two herring barrels of oatmeal; eight more barrels of meal; a ten-gallon cask of spirits ('aquavite'); a four-gallon cask of oil; six shovels and spades; a cask of tools containing eight axes, four hatchets, six broad and six narrow hoes; a dozen each of shirts, pairs of sheets, frieze suits and Irish stockings; two dozen falling bands (flat collars falling on the shoulders); and two dozen pairs of shoes.[34] Also travelling – three to a bed – were twelve boys, kitted out with canvas suits, shoes, stockings, garters, headbands, knives, points or fasteners for their clothes, plus two shirts apiece. Such a full load of passengers and cargo left little room for the passengers' personal belongings. Mary Ghibbs's 'small packe of cloaths' was confused with one belonging to a Mr Atkinson and left behind, to be sent on later in the *Tiger*.[35]

Keeping discrete accounts for separate ventures was another challenge that Newland did not always get right. Expenses incurred by the maids should have been charged to the magazine of named investors who had adventured the money for their passage and expected to share in the profits from their sale to prospective husbands, but Newland mistakenly charged them to the general company.[36] The £9 3s. he claimed to have laid out for the *Marmaduke* maids during their stay on the Isle of Wight suggests that they remained on the island for at least four weeks, since Newland himself would later receive 3s. 6d. per week for each Scottish soldier billeted on him in late 1627.[37]

They must have been relieved to be finally on their way – the thirteen maids no less than Robert Newland, his responsibility for their welfare finally acquitted. One imagines that hopes and fears conflicted as they set off from the shoreline towards their ostensible goal: finding a husband in a distant land, a goal that united and divided them at the same time. Now sisters-in-arms but soon they would be rivals, if not in love then at least in the marriage stakes.

Their situation set them apart from most women sailing to Virginia, who usually travelled as wives or as indentured servants. Ann Jackson's brother had in all likelihood married his wife in England before setting out for Virginia,[38] like five young men who married in the parish church of Sts Thomas at Newport, Isle of Wight, on 11 February 1621. 'Last fyve cupple were for Virginia,' reads a note in the parish register after their names: Henry Bushell and Alice Crocker, Christopher Cradock and Alice Cook, Edward Marshall and Marye Mitchel, Walter Beare and Anne Green, Robert Gullafer and Joan Pie.[39] They sailed to Jamestown on the *Abigail* so successfully provisioned by Robert Newland, who may even have persuaded them to go and will certainly have talked of their example to the *Marmaduke* maids, who followed just a few months later. However, such was mortality in Virginia that four years on, not one of the couples survived intact, although two of the men were living as servants, and one or other of the women may have been

The Marmaduke *maids' haunting last view of England can be imagined from this map of the Isle of Wight engraved by Jodocus Hondius and published by John Speed in 1611.*

widowed and married again.[40] The rest were almost certainly dead.

The thirteen young women now taking ship have no husbands as yet. Instead, they have agreed to sail across a treacherous ocean to marry men as yet unseen in a place of conflicting histories, part Eden, part savage wilderness.

Stay with them as they reach the *Marmaduke* out in the Solent and clamber as tidily as they can aboard the merchantman, stopping to take one long last look at the island, a gentle, very English landscape of trees, pastures and meadows, the wooded promontories on either side of the River Medina enclosing the natural harbour at Cowes like mittened hands.[41] Leaving home is hard at the best of times, and these women will have known they had little hope of ever returning. Would you have been brave enough – or foolish enough – to follow in their wake?

CHAPTER TWO

The *Warwick* Women

A few weeks after the *Marmaduke* sailed from East Cowes, a much larger group of around one hundred settlers – men and women – left Gravesend for Virginia in the good ship *Warwick* under Captain Arthur Guy and Master Nicholas Norburne.[1] Their instructions were to set sail from England 'with the first oppertunity of wynd and weather' after loading goods, provisions and passengers, taking the direct route to Jamestown 'according to their best skill and knowledge'. Piracy or attack by an enemy 'man of warre' was a distinct possibility, in which case their orders were to 'hinder their proceedinges or doe them violence' as far as they were able.

Among the passengers were another thirty-six 'Maydes and Younge Woemen' assembled by the Virginia Company as part of its money-making plan to supply brides for planters who could afford to pay for them.[2] Like the *Marmaduke* maids before them, they came with guarantees of provenance and personal recommendations from city and parish worthies, and each travelled with a bride price on her head.

Lying some twenty-two miles due east of London, or twenty-six miles if you travelled by the snaking River Thames, Gravesend and its sister parish of Milton had been a hythe or landing place for river traffic since the Domesday survey at least.[3] The heart of the City was only a flood tide away, allowing ships a quick passage upriver, while the Kent and Essex shores on either bank provided safe anchorage should they need it. The town's nightingales were much praised and its air was reputedly healthy, unlike Tilbury Fort directly across the Thames, whose inhabitants suffered constant agues from the 'effluvia' of the surrounding marshes.

For many foreigners arriving on these shores, Gravesend afforded their first sight of England and they were not always overly impressed. Visiting at the end of Queen Elizabeth's reign, Swiss medical student Thomas Platter noted that the town lacked walls, was not especially large and had 'very little to be seen', despite its many inns, where he stayed just one night before taking a small boat to London with the incoming tide.[4] More than a decade later, the Roman Catholic priest Orazio Busino came to England in the train of Piero Contarini, Venetian ambassador to the court of King James. They too stopped at Gravesend after a tempestuous sea crossing from France, dropping anchor as soon as they reached the Thames estuary since both wind and tide were against them. They went to the Post Inn, which was apparently accustomed to receiving ambassadors and foreign grandees, but found its charges exorbitant, 'namely 2 golden crowns per meal for each person', and so like Thomas Platter before them, they quickly hurried away.[5]

But Gravesend was in business to service ships and travellers on their way to and from the capital, not to keep them entertained, and its watermen clung to their ancient privilege of transporting His Majesty's subjects by the 'long ferry' that plied between Gravesend and London. They faced increasingly fierce competition from the owners of the smaller tilt boats, so-called because passengers sat on bales of straw under a 'tilt' or canvas that shielded them from the worst of the weather. The journey by public barge cost twopence per passenger, rowed by four men in fair tides and five in foul weather, plus a steersman at least. Fatal drownings were a fact of travel but thankfully rare. Tilt boats could carry up to thirty passengers for a maximum fare of fifteen shillings per boat, or sixpence per passenger, three times the cost of travelling by barge.[6]

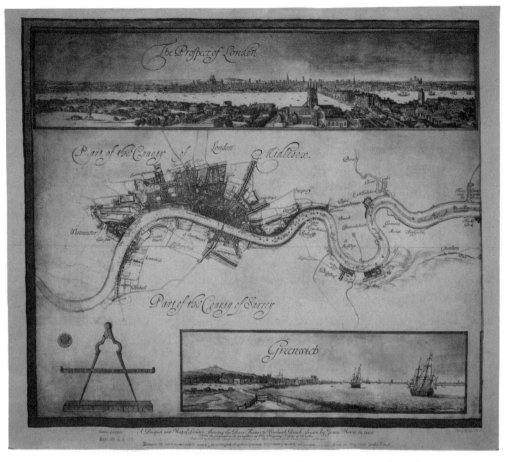

The journey for the Warwick *maids began at Billingsgate Quay, where they caught the long ferry to Gravesend.*

The long ferry and much of the river traffic from London to Gravesend set out from Billingsgate Quay just to the east of London's only bridge, which presented a hazard to smaller boats shooting between the piers, especially at low tide.[7] Here at Billingsgate the *Warwick* women will have started their long journey to Jamestown, having first gathered at the house of Deputy Treasurer John Ferrar in St Sithes Lane close to the City's pulsing heart. During the years when Sir Edwin Sandys effectively controlled the Virginia Company, its administration was centred here in the merchant household of the Ferrars.

Treasurer Sandys was the prime mover behind the plan to send brides to Virginia, determined to increase the colony's population by tying down its rootless male settlers with the bonds of family and children. He even provided the link to one of the women who gathered at Billingsgate, twenty-five-year-old Cicely Bray from Gloucestershire, her parents described as 'gentelfolke of good esteeme' and herself as being 'of kine [kin] to Sir Edwin Sandys'. Nicholas Ferrar inscribed her name first in his catalogue of thirty-six young women who sailed to Jamestown on the *Warwick*, giving her the prominence and flourish due to her rank, before handing the pen to his secretary Tristram Conyam to enumerate the other thirty-five.

Viewed as a group, the *Warwick* women were less illustrious than their *Marmaduke* sisters: just four out of thirty-six could claim gentry status. Immediately after Cicely Bray came Elizabeth Markham, one of only two sixteen-year-olds to sail on the *Warwick*. Tristram Conyam had corrected her father's first name from 'James' to 'Jervis', surely the writer Gervase Markham, whose books on husbandry and housewifery had already reached the colony, bound together and sent on the *Supply* in September 1620.[8] A younger son of a well connected but largely penurious branch of the Nottinghamshire Markhams, Gervase Markham was closely identified with Shakespeare's patron the Earl of Southampton, having dedicated a rather florid sonnet to him and fought alongside him in military campaigns led by the Earl of Essex. They may even have studied together at Cambridge, since Markham would later claim to have 'lived many yeares where I daily saw this Earle'.[9]

Both Markham and Southampton were lucky to escape the devastating consequences that followed the Earl of Essex's fall from grace. On 23 February 1601, two days before Essex was executed for treason, Gervase Markham married Mary Gelsthorp at the church of the Holy Cross in her home parish of Epperstone, Nottinghamshire, and retreated to the country, where he lived quietly as a tenant farmer with his rapidly expanding family before returning to London a decade or so later, perhaps to the parish of St Giles Cripplegate, where he would eventually be buried. We are told that young Elizabeth was 'by her father and mother presented', so both her parents were still alive by the time she left for Virginia. The year after her departure Gervase Markham proposed a bizarre wager to walk from London to Berwick on the Scottish borders without crossing any bridges or travelling by any sort of boat, claiming that he had 'groune pore' because of his 'many children and greate Charge of householde'.[10] Was this a penance, perhaps, for having encouraged or allowed his young daughter to travel to Virginia?

A third gentry maid was the orphaned Lucy Remnant from Guildford in Surrey, who claimed Sir William Russell as her maternal uncle. Lucy's father, Antony Remnant, had married Russell's sister Mary as his second wife on 13 January 1595 at the church of St Mary the Virgin, Worplesdon, and the couple settled at Pirbright on the outskirts of Guildford. Their union was blessed with a son just nine months later, followed by Lucy (baptized 1 May 1598) and at least two more daughters, all baptized at the ancient church of St Michael and All Angels, Pirbright, where their father was buried when Lucy was just twelve years old.[11]

All we know of the fourth gentry maid to travel on the *Warwick*, nineteen-year-old Elizabeth Nevill, is that she was born in Westminster, the daughter of a 'Gentleman of worth', and that her mother's name was Frauncis Travis, facts attested 'by divers of the Company on their owne knowledge', together with her 'good Carriage'. Information about the parentage of her companions is equally sketchy. Their fathers or kinsmen included clothworkers, a cutler, a draper, a baker, a victualler, a tailor, a hat maker and a plasterer from Oxford, but the father's occupation for twenty-three women was not recorded. Eleven of the *Warwick* maids were born in London, Middlesex or Westminster; seventeen came from elsewhere, while nothing is known about the birthplace of the other eight.

Parish records nonetheless survive for some of the non-gentry women who gathered at Billingsgate at the start of their long voyage to Jamestown. One whose footsteps we shall track is Bridgett Crofte, born in the Wiltshire parish of Britford (old name Burford) and a little older than the age she gave to the Virginia Company, turning twenty as she crossed the Atlantic.[12] The church where she was baptized still stands, fragments dating back to Saxon times, surrounded by ancient water meadows with fine views towards Salisbury cathedral. 'The City of *Salisbury* is made pleasant with waters running through the streetes,' wrote the Jacobean gentleman traveller Fynes Moryson, 'and is beautified with a stately Cathedrall Church, and the Colledge [of] the Deane and Prebends, having rich Inhabitants in so pleasant a seate.'[13]

From further north came Jennet Rimmer, aged twenty, 'borne at NorthMills [North Meols] in Lanckisher', a parish near present-day Southport, which was virtually waterlogged until its meres and marshlands were drained in the nineteenth century.[14] In the decade or so between November 1595 and February 1605 at least eleven male Rimmers in North Meols produced a host of children, despite a five-year gap in the records.[15]

Among the London-born maids, birth records survive for Sara Crose,[16] daughter of baker Peter Crose; a Peter Crosse was still living in the parish of St Margaret Lothbury in 1638.[17] And the records throw up two possible infant girls for nineteen-year-old Elizabeth Dag, born in Limehouse on the Thames between Ratcliff and Poplar: either Elizabeth Dage, daughter of Robert, baptized at the church of St Dunstan and All Saints in Stepney on 15 May 1603, or her namesake baptized at the same church on 26 September 1604, the daughter of John Dagg, 'mariner of Lymehouse'.[18] While the maiden name of Ann is unknown, her husband was surely the John Richards buried at St James Clerkenwell in the county of Middlesex on 20 June 1619, the very church whose parishioners gave Ann a glowing testimonial to send her on her way to Virginia.[19] The birthplace of the other two widows, Marie Daucks and Elizabeth Grinley, is unknown.

Information about the *Warwick* women's skills is also patchier than for those who sailed on the *Marmaduke*, although Tristram Conyam noted that Parnell Tenton 'cann worke all kinds of ordinary workes', that Ellen Borne was 'skilfull in many workes' and that Martha Baker was 'skillfull in weavinge and makinge of silke poynts'. Interest in the women's suitability as brides had shifted from practical skills to moral worth. Stock phrases recurred like a refrain; to be called 'honest' was the highest accolade. Ellen Davy was praised for her 'honest and Good Carriadge' and Alse Dollinges as a 'Mayde of honest Conversation'. Ann Parker, in service with a scrivener, was labelled an 'honest and faythfull servant'. Two maids – Ann Westcote and Mary Morrice – were described as 'honeste and sober', and three more praised for the honesty of their immediate family, echoing the advice of the pamphleteer Joseph Swetnam that 'in choyse of a wife, a man should note the honesty of the parents, for it is a likelyhood that those children which are vertuously brought up will follow the steps of their parents'.[20] Both parents of Londoner Frauncis Broadbottom were described as 'very honest people'. Alse Dauson was brought up by her mother, 'whom Mrs Ferrar reportes to be a verrie honest woman', and Mary Thomas by her grandfather Roger Tudor, clothworker, 'known for a verrie honest Man by divers of the Company'.

And here lies a clue to how the Virginia Company recruited many of its women: by word of mouth and personal acquaintance. Company personnel from the top downwards had clearly trawled among their relatives and friends for suitable brides, such as Treasurer Sandys' Gloucestershire kinswoman Cicely Bray and Alse Dauson, the daughter of old Mistress Ferrar's acquaintance. Their words of commendation reflect the chatter of the times, as those connected to the company spread the word about the kind of upright young women it was seeking, doubtless emphasizing the venture's opportunities for advancement. The Earl of Southampton's wide circle of patronage may have netted Gervase Markham's sixteen-year-old daughter Elizabeth as well as Lettice King, who travelled out in the *Marmaduke*.

Other company personnel who personally recommended potential brides include company secretary Edward Collingwood (Ann Westcote) and merchant William Webb,[21] whose post as the Virginia Company's 'husband' was created to increase investor confidence in the organization's affairs (Mary Morrice). 'Robert the porter' who introduced the orphaned Bridgett Crofte from Wiltshire was surely Robert Peasly, confirmed in his post only in May 1622 but already well known to senior officials. His appointment to the company's warehouse followed the sacking of the previous incumbent, James Hooper, who was caught with tobacco thrust up his hose. Robert's appointment went as high as the company's court, which discussed a motion to employ 'one Robert Peasly who was well knowne to divers of the Companie to be sufficient for the place and one that proffered good security for his truth upon wch good report and promise of Security the Companie have entertayned the said Robert Peasly for their Porter.'[22]

The two men charged with running the now defunct Virginia lotteries, Lott Peere and Gabriel Barbor, both had links to twenty-year-old Mary Ghibbs from Cambridgeshire, who had sailed on the *Marmaduke*: Peere was her maternal uncle, with whom she lived, and she was also known to Barbor. Barbor, who lived in East Smithfield, had similarly recommended eighteen-year-old Fortune Taylor, and he had a personal stake in the venture, having advanced twenty-four pounds to the subscription for the maids, three times the minimum investment allowed. Another investor was Christopher Marten, who recommended Elizabeth Dag and sank eight pounds of his own money into the enterprise. Mistress Cuffe, wife to company bookkeeper John Cuffe, could vouch for Mistress Gilbert of Holborn, who in turn commended the young daughter of a hat maker, Jeane Joanes. And so the gossip spread about the Virginia Company's intention to ship brides to its struggling colony.

As for those who were not personally known to the company, several came with the explicit commendation of City worthies – officials of London's great livery companies, such as Mr Hobson, an official of the Drapers' Company, who vouched for the 'honest Carridge' of Parnell Tenton and praised Ellen Borne as 'a sober and industrious Mayd'. Mr Spark, clerk of Blackfriars, recommended Jennet Rimmer, while the wife to the clerk of the Minories could vouch for Martha Baker, and the wife of the recorder of London's coachman recommended Margaret Bourdman, who travelled on the *Marmaduke*.[23] Jean Grundye and Barbara Burchens came with the backing of yeomen from the sovereign's bodyguard, or of their wives. So while the majority of these women lacked the social cachet of the best of the *Marmaduke* maids, they nonetheless came of honest stock and surely travelled with the good wishes of many in the City.

To anyone who witnessed the women's departure for Gravesend, they will have made an impressive sight as they gathered on Billingsgate Quay amid the cacophony of ships and boats unloading passengers and goods from many parts of the world: 'fish, both fresh and salt, shell fishes, salt, Orenges, Onions, and other fruits and rootes, wheate, Rie, and graine of divers sorts for service of the Citie, and the parts of this Realme adjoyning'.[24] I like to think they may have lingered in people's imaginations, re-emerging as a folk memory to inspire early street ballads such as 'The Maydens of London's brave adventures', which invited the brave and merry maidens of London to sail across the seas to start a new life in a land of plenty where the sun was hot and everything could be bought cheaply.[25]

Published some two or three decades after the women's departure, the ballad promises fun and adventure to those 'brave Lasses' and 'Loving Rogues' who are ready and willing to join the sisterhood of twenty named young women who have already dared to make the crossing, among them 'Fair Winifright, and Bridget bright,/ sweet

Rose and pretty Nany,/ With Ursely neat and Alice compleat/ that had the love of many'. Unashamedly upbeat in tone, it offers a stark contrast to the reality of life for Virginia's early immigrants. Even the food on board ship is praised as good strong fare: 'Bisket salt-Beef, and English Beer, and Pork well boyld with Peason'. The women who sailed on the *Warwick* would experience no such plenty, nor would they share in the supposed surfeit of victuals that awaited them at their journey's end: 'Pigs, Turkies, Geese, Cocks, Hens, and Ducks,/ and other fare most dainty/... A good fat Capon for a groat and eighteen eggs a penny.'

One essential difference distinguished the 'maydens' of the ballad from the real-life *Warwick* women and those who had travelled before them. The ballad maids mostly had sweethearts already, who hoped to join them later in the great plantation adventure, undeterred by jeering 'Jack Spaniard' and firm in their resolve to band together as Christians to subdue the infidels – a tub-thumping end to a stirring call to adventure that dangled a life of ease and plenty for those young women brave enough to take up the challenge. The *Warwick* women had no sweethearts or, if they did, they were leaving them behind to find husbands overseas. In this they more closely resembled the young women who appear in another set of ballads published later in the century, ballads ostensibly written for young men wishing to buy themselves brides. These read like bawdy versions of the Ferrar lists in their description of the women's charms. Choose, if you will, between 'Sweet Madam Mosella, who came from afar,/ With her white snowy Breast, most gallantly drest'[26] or another 'young Beauty', described as

> ... fit for Game,
> before you buy her,
> Young Nancy is her Name,
> take her and try her.[27]

'I love a ballet [ballad] in print, a-life, for then we are sure they are true,' declared Mopsa, the easily fooled country wench in Shakespeare's *The Winter's Tale*.

Regardless of whether they see themselves as brave lasses and loving rogues, or as young maids and 'graz'd Widows' to be sold at reasonable rates, the *Warwick* women are finally on their way, travelling downriver with the ebb tide, past the Customs House and adjacent Wool Quay, where wool entering the port of London was traditionally weighed, then a cluster of ships unloading their wares at Galley Quay against a backdrop of 'many fayre houses' built by merchants for storage, and on to the Tower of London, 'a most strong Palatine Tower, whose turrets and walles doe rise from a deepe foundation, the morter therof being tempered with the bloud of beasts'.[28] In Visscher's famous Thames panorama of 1616 it rises from the river like a tiered wedding cake, culminating in the turreted White Tower with which the Norman King William had asserted his royal power over his newly conquered kingdom. On they row, past the blackened mouth of Traitors' Gate – 'a draw bridge, seldome letten downe, but for the receipt of some great persons, prisoners'.[29] After the Tower come the tenements of seafaring St Katharine's, home to waterman's daughter Jane Dier who had sailed on the *Marmaduke*, and on to Wapping, where pirates and sea rovers were traditionally hanged on a short rope at the low-water mark, their bodies remaining until three tides had washed over them. On this stretch of the river, says the antiquarian John Stow, 'was never a house standing within these 40 yeares: but since the gallowes being after remooved father off, a continuall streete, or filthy straight passage, with Alleyes of small tenements or cottages builded, inhabited by saylors victualers, along by the river of Thames, almost to *Radcliff*, a good mile from the Tower,'[30] and from Radcliffe to Limehouse a mile to the east, once home to the great Elizabethan explorer Sir Humphrey Gilbert and graced with fine elms – all gone now.

At Limehouse the congested tenements give way to open country as the Thames loops down towards the royal naval dockyard at Deptford and the palace at Greenwich then up again through Blackwall Reach towards Bow Creek and the East India Company's shipyard.[31] Swiss student Thomas Platter visited Greenwich palace towards the end of Queen Elizabeth's reign, admiring its delightful fountain in an outer court and climbing the steep slope behind the palace. He even bragged about stealing a memento from Sir Francis Drake's *Golden Hind*, which had been pulled onto the shore, a theft he excused 'since it was rotten with age and now decaying'.[32]

And so the women continue their journey to Gravesend, observing perhaps how the Thames widens and flattens as it flows into the estuary, its banks 'wooded and gay with pleasant hamlets and homesteads',[33] past the settlements of Woolwich, Erith and Greenhithe, then up through Fiddler's Reach, so called because sailing ships must here tack backwards and forwards against south-westerly headwinds, and down again through Northfleet Hope. Two years later the waterman-poet John Taylor would pass the same way, taking every opportunity to stop off at the taverns of Deptford and Greenwich; and after Erith,

> we rows'd our selves and cast off sleepe
> Before the day-light did begin to peepe.
> The tyde by Gravesend swiftly did us bring
> Before the mounting larke began to sing.[34]

As they are rowed towards Gravesend the women cannot fail to notice the merchant ships on their way to and from the port of London, and the men-of-war headed for the naval yards at Deptford in what was fast becoming one of the busiest waterways in the world. Although England was nominally at peace with her traditional enemies of Spain and France, much of Europe was convulsed with

Like many travellers to Virginia, the Warwick *maids boarded their ship at Gravesend. The spire close to the waterfront marks St George's Church where Pocahontas was buried four years previously.*

religious conflict, and both piracy and privateering were rife. Only that spring King James' daughter Elizabeth and her husband Frederick had begun their lifelong exile in The Hague, having been ousted from the throne of Bohemia after reigning for less than a year.

Just like Cowes, the landing stage at Gravesend lies within sight of forts or blockhouses built by Henry VIII to ward off the threat of invasion from the sea, one fort at Gravesend, of which only a footing remains, and another at Tilbury across the river, close to the spot where Queen Elizabeth famously rallied her troops before beating off the Spanish Armada, aided by luck and bad weather. England must have felt well protected in contrast to the women's new lives, which are just beginning.

The Ferrars recorded the names of eight more young women who travelled to Virginia by other ships. Nicholas Ferrar himself added the few details that are known about them at the bottom of Tristram Conyam's *Warwick* catalogue. First to leave, in the *Charles*, was Joane Haynes, described as 'sister to Minturne the Joyner', presumably another company employee. Her ship sailed in July, a little before the *Marmaduke*.[35] Next came four maids who sailed in the *Tiger*, which departed Gravesend in September 1621[36] and after a tumultuous voyage, described in Chapter 8, limped into

Jamestown in late 1621 or early 1622. Only three of the four *Tiger* maids were actually eligible as brides: twenty-eight-year-old Allice Goughe, the daughter of 'Gentlefolke'; twenty-one-year-old Anne Gibbson, brought to the company by her guarantor, a Master or Mistress Switzer dwelling in the Blackfriars; and sixteen-year-old Elizabeth Browne, also from Blackfriars, whose parents were both still living. The fourth was described as 'Daughter to Mrs Palmer whoe w[i]th her husband went along in the Tiger'. Ferrar clearly knew very little about her, leaving blanks for her age and her Christian name. In fact she was called Priscilla and was probably aged no more than seven or eight when she left England, demonstrably too young to marry.[37]

Three more young women sailed in November aboard the 200-ton *Bona Nova,* a frequent carrier in the transatlantic trade. Nothing is known about Priscilla Flint, and all we learn of Allice Grove is her age (twenty-six). The third is more intriguing: Elizabeth Bluett, 'Daughter to Captayne Benjamin Bluett'. This was surely the Captain Benjamin Bluett who travelled to Virginia in 1619 with some eighty men to establish an ironworks for the Virginia Company.[38] Some reports suggest that he died at sea during the crossing, but a 'Mr Bluett' was appointed to Virginia's council in early 1620, and he is more likely to have survived the Atlantic crossing but to have died soon after his arrival.[39] By the time Elizabeth sailed for Jamestown, Bluett was definitely dead, since responsibility for establishing an ironworks in Virginia had passed to John Berkeley, who agreed to go 'upon the same condicons, as mr Blewett lately deceased',[40] concentrating his efforts at Falling Creek on the James River, now on the margins of the Virginia state capital at Richmond.

Elizabeth Bluett's decision to travel to Virginia becomes even more troubling if she can be linked to the Elizabeth Blewett, daughter of Benjamyne Blewett, who was baptized on 1 April 1605 at St Giles Cripplegate in London, the same parish where Gervase Markham would later be buried and one with strong seafaring connections.[41]

If this is the same girl, she was just sixteen years old at the time of her departure – the same age as Elizabeth Markham, whom she may conceivably have known.

Was Elizabeth Bluett travelling to Jamestown to secure her father's legacy and make a new life for herself overseas? Did she succumb to company propaganda or the blandishments of those who put God, king and company before the welfare of unprotected young women? Or was she travelling because she had no other options left?

CHAPTER THREE

A Woman's Place

Aside from their Virgin Queen, women who remained obstinately single and celibate throughout their lives in sixteenth- and seventeenth-century England faced a peculiar fate not shared by their married sisters. After death it was their lot to lead apes in hell, a proverb that fed on Protestant condemnations of celibacy – especially priestly celibacy – as a very Catholic evil that would dispose to debauchery and damnable defilements. Shakespeare slipped the apes into Kate's choleric mouth in *The Taming of the Shrew*, while lutenist William Corkine sang of the inevitable shame that befell those choosing to live and die as virgins, 'that dance about with bobtaile Apes in hell'. Far better, whispered Corkine seductively, to prostrate yourself to every passing peasant than undergo such shame: 'No tongue can tell, What injury is done to Maids in hell.'[1]

The best way to escape such censure, as the Jamestown brides well understood, was to find themselves a husband and subjugate themselves to his will. Society expected all women to marry, whatever they wanted for themselves, and those who remained single and owned no property of their own were pushed to the margins, required to remain dependent as daughters, sisters, kin or servants in other men's households.[2] 'All of them are understood either married or to bee married', declared the author of *The Lawes Resolutions of Womens Rights* of 1632.[3] 'I know no remedy', he added, 'though some women can shift it well enough.'

Contemporary guides to marriage laid equal stress on a wife's essential inferiority and her duty of obedience towards her husband. Take the eight treatises *Of Domesticall Duties* published by the Puritan clergyman William Gouge in 1622, the year after the Jamestown brides left for America. Gouge preached at the church of St Ann, Blackfriars, home to the maids Anne Gibbson and Elizabeth Browne, and to Audry Hoare's sister Joane Childe. A wife should refrain from ambition and abandon any notion that she was her husband's equal, insisted Gouge: 'by vertue of the matrimoniall bond the husband is made head of his wife, though the husband were before mariage a very begger, and of meane parentage, and the wife very wealthy and of a noble stocke'.[4] Even Gouge was forced to acknowledge that his sermons on female subservience frequently provoked a rustle of discontent among the women in his congregation.[5]

As for those 'masterless' women who remained unmarried by choice or circumstance, patriarchal society viewed them with alarm, fearing mayhem and social disorder. Successive acts of parliament regulating employment and vagrancy empowered local officials to hunt down never-married women between the ages of twelve and forty and force them into service 'for such wages and in such reasonable sort and manner as they shall think meet'.[6] Court records for many English towns bulge with orders to masterless persons to put themselves in service, their 'crime' of living without masters elided with other moral failings such as slack attendance at church. Those women who persisted in living on their own could be locked up in houses of correction, commonly known as bridewells after Bridewell Hospital on the Thames, an abandoned royal palace that was quickly branded a 'rogues' hospital', where the idle or disorderly poor could be confined, whipped and put to work for offences ranging from vagrancy, prostitution, adultery, swearing, dice-playing, drunkenness and slander, to running away from a master.[7]

To be born a woman subjected you to a flood of popular literature that sought to control what you thought and how you behaved, and made you the butt of countless ballads, proverbs, jokes and tales. These ranged from the relatively light-hearted, like Sir Nicholas Le Strange's origin myth collected in mid-century: 'When man and woman were first made, they had each of them a lace given to lace their Bodyes together, the man had just enough to lace himselfe home, so he left his Tagge hanging downe; the womans proovd somewhat too short, and seeing she must leave some of her body open, in a rage she broake of her Tagge, and threw it away.'[8]

Far more vicious were the anti-feminist pamphlets that vented their fury on women in general, and scolding, domineering and unfaithful wives in particular. One of the most popular was *The Araignment of Lewd, Idle, Froward [contrary], and unconstant women* by Joseph Swetnam, a Jacobean fencing master and pamphleteer who claimed to have formed his views during thirty years of travel. Published in 1615, Swetnam's diatribe against women was reprinted at least thirteen times during the century. He took his cue from Moses' claim that a woman was made to be 'a helper unto man, & so they are indeed: for she helpeth to spend and consume that which man painefully getteth'. Worse was to follow, as he described how women commonly spent 'the most part of the forenoone painting themselves, and frizling their haires, and prying in their glasse, like Apes to prancke up themselves in their gawdies; like Poppets, or like the Spider which weaves a fine web to hang the flie'.[9]

If men had to marry (and Swetnam did all he could to dissuade them), then his advice was to 'Choose not a wife too faire, nor too foule, nor too rich: for if she be faire, every one will be catching at her, and if she be too foule, a man will have no mind to love her which no body likes, & if too rich… thou shalt find her a commaunding Mistresse'. Widows were not to be trusted either, 'for if shee be rich, she will looke to governe, and if shee be poore, then are thou plagued both with beggery and bondage'.

The authors of broadsides and ballads were often as misogynistic as the preachers and pamphleteers. Carried around the country in pedlars' packs, broadsides delivered news to literate and semi-literate members of society, displayed in public places, nailed to church doors and trees on commons.[10] 'Fill Gut, & Pinchbelly', an illustrated broadside ballad of 1620, condensed society's condemnation of women into an image of two monstrous animals, one grown fat from its exclusive diet of good men, the other pitifully thin from its meagre fare of good women. John Taylor, the water poet, supplied verses to accompany the broadside's graphic portrayal of women as fractious, rebellious, power-hungry and discontented:

> Now full bellyed Fill gut, so Fat heere in show,
> Feedes on our good Men, as Women well know:
> Who flocke in great numbers, all weary of lives,
> Heere thus to be eaten, and rid from their Wives.
> …
> Heere Pinch belly starveth, for want of good meate,
> for Women untoward, he no way can eate:
> The good are his feeding, but hard to befound,
> The worst of them living, the best underground.[11]

Even King James threw himself into the anti-feminist fray, commanding the Bishop of London to order his clergy to 'inveigh vehemently and bitterly in theyre sermons against the insolencie of our women, and theyre wearing of brode brimd hats, pointed dublets, theyre haire cut short or shorne, and some of them stillettaes or poinards, and such other trinckets of like moment'.[12] The clergy duly complied, and London's pulpits thundered against 'the insolence and impudence of women', provoking a trio of pamphlets – all published in 1620 – on the theme of masculine women and womenish men, among them *Hic Mulier: Or, The Man-Woman*.[13] Playwrights also took women to task, as did the ballad singers 'so that they can come no where but theyre eares tingle'.[14]

Printed the year before the maids' departure, the broadside ballad 'Fill Gut, & Pinchbelly' projected the misogyny of clergy and pamphleteers onto these two monstrous animals, one near starved from its diet of good women.

Society's insistence that all women should marry nonetheless came at a price for those who conformed. As a woman, marriage created a place for you in society but it also gave your husband control over your rights at common law, notably the right to own property and sign contracts in your own name, since marriage converted your legal status from a *feme sole* (single woman) to a *feme covert*, a common-law term that lingered from Anglo-Norman and meant literally 'covered woman'.[15] All that you owned became your husband's, and even his gifts to you remained his in law. 'A wife how gallant soever she be, glittereth but in the riches of her husband, as the Moone hath no light, but it is the Sunnes.' A man could beat his wife (though not so much as to cause actual bodily damage), just as he could beat an outlaw, a traitor, a pagan or his villein, all 'dispunishable, because by the Law Common these persons can have no action'. In politics as in life, women were voiceless. 'They make no Lawes, they consent to none, they abrogate none.'[16]

Whatever disadvantages marriage might bring to them personally, each of the women gathering at Gravesend and Cowes knew that to gain society's approval their best option was to find themselves a husband. The Virginia Company's own record of their ages, status and accomplishments contains nothing to indicate why these women should have failed to secure a husband in England. As a group, they were all of marriageable age, ranging from fifteen or sixteen (the waterman's daughter, Jane Dier) up to a declared age of twenty-eight, producing a median age of twenty and an average of twenty years and six months.[17] Most middling women of the times married in their mid- to late twenties, while elite women tended to marry younger, as did London-born girls marrying for the first time, their families fearful perhaps of the capital's high mortality from plague epidemics.[18]

While most of the Jamestown brides had several years of courtship ahead of them, those approaching thirty may have felt their chances of finding a husband were fast slipping by. Allice Burges, one of three women to give her age as twenty-eight, had plainly lied when she presented herself to the Virginia Company. Parish records show that she was in fact thirty-one, having been baptized at the parish church of Linton in Cambridgeshire on 11 January 1590.[19] But why could the others not find husbands in the usual way?

Marriage statistics for the early 1600s provide a clear if unexpected answer. The women's experiences of life and courtship will have told them what the statistics would later prove: that securing a suitable mate was becoming increasingly difficult. Among individuals of both sexes born around the turn of the century, the proportion that never married rose sharply from a steady 4 to 8 per cent to almost one in four (24 per cent) at the very time the women responded to the Virginia Company's call.[20] For women raised to believe that marriage was their only option of gaining a foothold in society, this was little short of catastrophic.

As ever, economics were largely to blame. While each woman will have experienced financial pressures in different ways, the hard times that prevailed from the 1590s to the 1620s affected them all. Population growth was one factor: between 1540 and 1600, the population of England and Wales increased by almost 45 per cent from under three million to over four million, leading to inflated grain prices and declining real wages for those who worked for a living.[21] London, the city to which so many of the women had migrated, was growing especially fast, its population doubling during the sixteenth century and almost doubling again by the middle of the seventeenth.[22]

Depression in England's cloth industry added to everyone's misery, reaching disastrous proportions after the outbreak of war in Europe in 1618 and the failure of the Cockayne plan to bypass Dutch competition by changing the type of cloth exported.[23] Rising food prices and declining wages favoured wealthy landowners and merchants with the resources to tide them through the bad times, yet all felt the pinch: 'England was never generally so poore since I was borne as yt is at this present,' wrote John Chamberlain in February 1621, the very year the women travelled to Virginia.[24]

Hard times will also have affected the ability of each woman's family to contribute to her dowry or marriage portion, which all but the vagrant poor amassed in order to attract a husband. Love counted in many courtships, but approval of family and neighbours often counted even more, especially among the hard-working artisan class to which so many of the women belonged. Country gentry typically gave their daughters a dowry of between £500 and £1,000 on marriage. Between £50 and £100 was common for the daughters of prosperous yeomen, tradesmen and craftsmen, and between £10 and £50 for daughters born to the great bulk of yeomen, husbandmen and craftsmen, a group that included most of the Jamestown brides. Even the daughters of labourers expected to bring some money or goods to their marriage, although typically less than £5 in value.[25]

For families with small estates these were significant sums. And while wages and their purchasing power were in steady decline, dowries for all classes of women were subjected to significant and periodic hikes, especially severe for the daughters of aristocrats, but even the gentry experienced a three-fold rise in marriage portions between the sixteenth and seventeenth centuries.[26] This may partly explain why the handful of gentry parents chose or agreed to send their daughters overseas, thereby absolving themselves of the need to provide a dowry for them. Elizabeth Markham's father had grown poor from his many children, remember, and the mother of Westminster-born Elizabeth Nevill may have despaired of ever amassing a portion large enough to attract a suitable suitor for her.

Losing a parent may also have contributed to the women's decision to accept the Virginia Company's offer and try their luck in America. This was a common enough experience among the population as a whole: throughout the Tudor and Stuart age as many as one child in three had lost one or both parents by the age of twenty-one, and evidence suggests that at least half of all young women had lost their fathers by the time they married.[27] But the predominance of full or partial orphans among the Jamestown brides is nonetheless remarkable, and losing either or both parents undoubtedly made it harder for these young women to negotiate the perilous path from girlhood to the married state.

In all, just five of the fifty-six women definitely had both parents still living. The oldest of these at twenty years old was the wire drawer's daughter Susan Binx, who travelled on the *Marmaduke*, together with nineteen-year-old Audry Hoare. Two more sailed on the *Warwick*, both aged just sixteen: Gervase Markham's daughter Elizabeth, and tailor's daughter Elizabeth Starkey. The fifth maid with two living parents was sixteen-year-old Elizabeth Browne, who sailed on the *Tiger*.[28] At least twelve more women almost certainly had one or other parent still living, while eight women had definitely lost both parents by the time they sailed: three *Marmaduke* maids (Allice Burges, Catherine Finch and Margaret Bourdman) and five of the *Warwick* women (Ellen Borne, Lucy Remnant, Alse Dollinges, Christian Smyth and Elizabeth Pearson). For roughly half the women (twenty-nine out of fifty-six), including the four widows, we know nothing about their parents; the implication is that many of them were dead by the time the women sailed and no longer relevant to their daughters' lives.

As well as contributing to their dowries, parents could help their daughters in the delicate business of securing a mate, a protracted process in which mothers were almost as likely as fathers to be involved.[29] Daughters of the aristocracy and upper gentry were expected to follow their families' wishes since issues of property, succession and family standing were judged too important to be left to a young girl's heart. Lower down the social scale, daughters commonly conducted their own negotiations and expected to have a say in their choice of a husband,[30] but without parents or close family to guide them, many of the Jamestown brides will have floundered in London's more complicated marriage market, with its bewildering challenges and opportunities.

Altogether twenty-six out of fifty-six women came from counties outside London; fourteen were almost certainly born in London, while the other sixteen gave no details about their birthplace. Many of the incomers to London and several of those born in the capital worked in service in other people's households. Far from implying a drop in status, service was viewed as a natural stage in a young girl's lifecycle, usually undertaken from her

For all but the youngest Jamestown brides, living in service in the households of others marked their expected transition from girlhood to adulthood and marriage.

mid- to late teens until the time she married, sometimes with members of her extended family or with people known to her family. By living away from home, a girl gained a measure of independence from her parents while remaining firmly under others' control.[31] Fed and housed by her employers, she learned the skills of housewifery that would serve her well in married life – typically robust 'country' skills in cooking, baking, malting, brewing, dairying, running a household, sewing and embroidery, plus the specialist skills of a dairy maid, malt maker, washer maid and chambermaid. And crucially for a girl's marriage prospects, working in service allowed her to put her admittedly meagre earnings of between one and two pounds a year towards her marriage portion, a little more if she was very fortunate.[32]

But living in service had its downsides too. Servants worked long hours and some experienced ill treatment from their masters or mistresses. In early 1619 John Chamberlain wrote of a woman in Whitefriars who 'held her maides head so long in a tubbe of water, that she drowned her',[33] while ballads sang of the dangers young women faced from the amorous advances of their masters.[34] Living in service with relatives could also prove problematic. Catherine Finch's brother Erasmus was a hot-tempered fellow who could not have been an easy man to live with let alone serve, as Catherine was required to do. His name crops up twice in the Middlesex courts for 1616, standing bail in two neighbourhood disputes involving a motley group of men from the parish, including a labourer, a shoemaker and several gentlemen, some of whom switched sides between the quarrels. In the second incident Erasmus Finch and gentleman Alan Turner – both of St Martin-in-the-Fields – stood bail for one George Harper who had wrongfully accused the courtier and musician Sir Ferdinand Heyburne of fraud (the word used in the case was cozenage). The case was discharged at Sir Ferdinand's request, suggesting a quarrel in their cups.[35] Quarrelsome to the end, Erasmus Finch – by now appointed crossbow maker to Charles I – obtained a crown lease in 1631 to common meadows beside the River Frome in the Gloucestershire villages of Fretherne and Saul, and tried to stop the rest of the parish using the meadows as common land. The attempt failed at law when the villagers successfully rebuffed his claim.[36] By then of course his sister Catherine had been gone for ten years to make a new life for herself in Virginia.

Altogether, sixteen of the Jamestown brides came explicitly out of service, and it is likely that many of the others came recommended by their master or mistress, without the relationship being spelled out. Of the dozen or so *Marmaduke* maids, seven had definitely come out of service, plus possibly a couple more; while of the twenty-six *Warwick* women for whom we have information, nine had definitely come out of service, a further eleven probably came recommended by their employers, three were widows and two were sixteen-year-olds still living at home.

The young women who had migrated to London from the provinces on their own will have found life especially difficult. Good service positions were hard to come by and finding a husband was even harder. While London had a goodly pool of male apprentices, the large majority came from outside the city, and their conditions of employment enforced celibacy for the seven or eight years of their apprenticeship. By the time they were ready to marry, say between the ages of twenty-six and thirty, they favoured widows with capital or the daughters of master tradesmen who could help set them up in business or trade.[37] Migrant and possibly orphaned young women were pushed to the back of the queue, especially when they served in the households of strangers.

Economic hard times, losing one or both parents, migration to London and separation from kith and kin, the near impossibility of amassing a dowry fat enough to attract a good match and the reluctance of London's young men to marry unendowed maidens when they had the choice of richer widows or London-born girls: all these undoubtedly contributed to the decision taken by some or all of the women to gamble their future on sailing to America. A clutch of ballads published around this time underlined their plight: 'I can, nor will no longer ly alone,' sighs the heroine of 'A Maydens Lamentation for a Bedfellow' (*c.*1615).[38] Another ballad from a decade or so later begins:

The Maidens of London are now in despaire,
How they shall get husbands, it is all their care,
Though maidens be never so vertuous and faire,
Yet old wealthy widowes, are yong mens chiefe ware.
Oh this is a wiving age.
Oh this is a wiving age.[39]

Other ballads from the early 1620s echoed the maidens' complaints, or more coarsely reiterated young men's preference for widows over maids.[40]

A lifetime's training in habits of obedience may also have rendered the women susceptible to promises made by others about their prospects in America. Often criticized for glossing over the suffering endured by its colonists, the Virginia Company had felt obliged just the previous year to publish a broadside admitting the truth of the colony's shockingly high mortality, which 'this last yeere hath there wrought upon the People, to the consumption of divers hundreds, and almost the utter destruction of some particular Plantations'. After hastily acknowledging the 'just finger of Almighty God' in such bad news, the company proceeded to outline its plans for a better future and a healthier population, 'seing in the health of the People, consisteth the very life, strength, encrease, and prosperity of the whole generall Colony'.[41]

English administrator and intelligencer John Pory well understood how precarious life was in Virginia when he was offered the post of secretary there, vowing not to 'adventure my Carkase in so dangerous a business for nothing'.[42] But in its dealings with the women the company is unlikely to have dwelt on the hardships they might encounter in Virginia or their limited prospects of survival. Likewise the women's guarantors, whether connected to the company or to London's great and good, can hardly have painted a realistic portrait of what the maids might find in Jamestown. In truth, Virginia had little relevance to the daily lives of most Londoners. For all his gossiping, John Chamberlain writes of the colony but rarely, and Virginia makes few appearances in the tales or ballads likely to have reached the women's ears.[43] So they had little hard evidence to counter the propagandists who promised them a good life in America, or the ministers of religion who stressed their Christian duty to take part in the colonial adventure.

Since the colony's earliest days, English pulpits 'rang with praise of the infant colony on the banks of the James', and throughout its life the Virginia Company continued to pay preachers to deliver sermons to shareholders and others at significant departures or events.[44] Chamberlain himself commented on the rage for sermons delivered at specially convened feasts in hired halls, 'as likewise the Virginia companie had this weeke at Grocers Hall, where there have been three or fowre of this kind within these ten dayes'.[45] The date of this event is significant: 17 November 1621, by which time the last of the brides had departed for Jamestown. If the assembled company thought of them at all, the best we can hope for is that their recent dispatch was celebrated with a toast.

There is another reason why the Jamestown brides might have chosen to travel. At least one of the women (and how many more?) did so because she wanted to leave her old life behind. The evidence is indisputable. It appears in the one testimonial to survive among the Ferrar papers, for the widowed Ann Richards or Rickard, twenty-five years old and born in the parish of St Sepulchre on the western edge of London, just outside the City walls. Dated 13 December 1620, some nine months before Richards sailed from Gravesend on the *Warwick*, the testimonial comes from the churchwardens and parishioners of 'St James att Clarckenwell in the countie of Middlesex', who certified that she had lived in the parish for six years or thereabouts, during which time she had 'demeaned herself in honest sorte & is a woman of an honest lyef & conversation duringe the tyme shee hathe lyved amounges us'.[46]

Richards had requested the testimonial not because she had been approached by the Virginia Company – the dates do not tally – but because she was 'mynded & purposed to dwell elswhere'. Without such a testimonial she risked hounding by the authorities in any new place where she tried to settle. Such was the reality of life for any independently minded young woman of the times, even a respectable widow.

Would Ann Richards and the others fare any better in Virginia?

CHAPTER FOUR

Point of Departure

To appreciate the enormity of the step the women were taking, you need to cast a glance at the city they were leaving behind. London was then bursting at the seams, intent on transforming itself from a satellite of Antwerp's wool trade into a major port with trading links that stretched from the East Indies to the New World. By 1600 it contained some 200,000 souls, and when the *Warwick* and her sister ships left for Virginia, only Naples, Paris and Constantinople had larger populations. London's populace was increasing at almost twice the pace of England as a whole, doubling its share of the national total in each century: from about 2.5 per cent in 1520 to almost 5 per cent in 1600 and over 10 per cent by 1700.[1]

The maids who flocked to London from elsewhere were part of the problem. Among all the social and economic pressures that contributed to the capital's population explosion, one factor stands out: migration from other parts of the kingdom. Without the incomers, its numbers would have fallen in every quarter-century from 1550 to 1800. In plague years especially, London experienced significantly more burials than baptisms.[2] So the London experienced by the Jamestown brides – the minority born there and the majority lured like moths to a candle – was a city in transition, where inward migration increased competition for the bare necessities of life: a job, a roof over your head, a place to call your own, a husband.

The majority of non-Londoners among the brides came from counties in concentric circles around the capital: an inner ring of Hertfordshire, Essex, Surrey, Berkshire, Oxfordshire and Buckinghamshire, and an outer ring of Hampshire, Dorset, Wiltshire, Gloucestershire, Herefordshire, Worcestershire, Northamptonshire, Cambridgeshire and Suffolk. No one came from the south-western counties of Cornwall, Devon or Somerset, for which Bristol was the obvious port of embarkation to the Americas, and none came from either Kent or Sussex. Just five women came from further afield: Ann Holmes from Newcastle (which Newcastle is not made clear), Margaret Bourdman from the North Riding of Yorkshire, Jennet Rimmer from Lancashire, Mary Morrice from Derbyshire and Barbara Burchens from 'Denby' in either Derbyshire or Wales.[3] All these women will have carried a little of their homeland across the ocean, as well as memories shaped by the weeks, months or years they had spent in the capital, which would provide such a stark contrast to Virginia's vast and terrifying wilderness.

For all the brides London was a crowded place but especially for those who lived in the densely populated eastern suburbs, such as Mary Ellyott and Christian Smyth. Here the encroachment of 'filthy Cottages, and with other purprestures, inclosures and Laystalles [dungheaps]' drew howls of protest from the great Elizabethan antiquarian John Stow, whose *Survey of London* (1598) casts a humane if nostalgic eye on the city that was metamorphosing before his eyes.[4] Even Stow's tallow-chandler father had suffered from London's expansionist boom, losing part of his garden in Throgmorton Street to King Henry VIII's minister Thomas Cromwell, then intent on expanding his pleasure grounds.[5]

It was also a very dirty city. While English visitors to the Low Countries commented on the 'daintiness' of Dutch towns,[6] foreign visitors to London remarked on its filth, which Londoners may have taken for granted but others did not. The Venetian Orazio Busino writes of 'a sort of soft and very stinking mud, which abounds here at all seasons, so that the place better deserves to be called Lorda (filth) than Londra (London)'. London's water too was 'so hard, turbid and stinking that the odour remains even in clean linen'.[7]

Noise exacerbated the daily grind for London's beleaguered inhabitants, quite driving out the 'nastie, and loathsome sin of Sloth' if we are to believe playwright Thomas Dekker's satirical pamphlet *The Seven Deadly Sins of London*, 'for in every street, carts and Coaches make such a thundring as if the world ranne upon wheeles... Besides, hammers are beating in one place, Tubs hooping in another, Pots clincking in a third, water-tankards running at tilt in a fourth: heere are Porters sweating under burdens, there Marchants-men bearing bags of money.'[8] Westminster was scarcely any better, despite its status as the seat of royal power and justice: 'Yea, in the open streetes [of Westminster] is such walking, such talking, such running, such riding, such clapping too of windowes, such rapping at Chamber doores, such crying out for drink, such buying up of meate, and such calling uppon Shottes, that at every such time, I verily beleeve I dwell in a Towne of Warre.'[9]

But for all its faults, London was an astonishingly diverse city where every neighbourhood had its own character. Busino talks of one street crammed full of apothecaries' shops, besides others scattered about the city, and another street inhabited solely by booksellers who possessed not a single missal.

> Then there are the other streets of feather sellers, while certain mechanics make horn flowers and rosettes, as delicately wrought as if they were of the finest cambric. They paint them various colours. There is a suburb of gunsmiths; others only make bows and arrows. Some manufacture very handsome proof corslets, for the wear of the pikemen. There are several falconers' shops, whose proprietors do nothing at all but train birds of every sort for such as are fond of sport.[10]

London's diversity meant that each of the maids will have experienced the city in her own way, especially the fourteen or more who grew up here, if Westminster, Middlesex and Southwark are counted as parts of London. In Lothbury, home to cutler's daughter Frauncis Broadbottom and baker's daughter Sara Crosse, City bankers and merchants were slowly replacing the original cutlers and metal foundries that had occupied the street since medieval times, casting 'Candlestickes, Chafingdishes, Spice mortars, and such like' and making a 'loathsome noice' to passers-by, hence its name.[11] One of the streets running south off Lothbury was St Bartholomew's Lane, where another Londoner – Susan Binx – lived in service with a turner and his wife, Mr and Mrs Edward Patten, who had known her since infancy. Binx and the widowed Ann Richards had both been born in the parish of St Sepulchre, between Holborn and the City wall at Newgate, but five years separated them in age and Richards had moved to Clerkenwell with her husband, so their paths may not have crossed. Binx named Seacole Lane as the street where she was born, a winding lane just outside the City wall leading south from the Holborn conduit towards Fleet Lane and close to another lane 'called in record windagaine Lane, it turneth downe to Turnemill Brooke, and from thence back againe, for there is no way ouer'.[12] Captain John Smith would later be buried inside St Sepulchre's church, commemorated today by a plaque and a stained-glass window.

For his panoramic 'Long View of London from Bankside', the Bohemian artist Wenceslaus Hollar took his viewpoint from St Saviour's church in Southwark, where Suffolk-born Margaret Dauson lived in service with a leather seller's wife.

Central to the way Londoners, incomers and foreigners encountered the city, the River Thames provided a daily backdrop to the lives of three of the Jamestown brides who lived on its northern bank: Elizabeth Dag at Limehouse, young Jane Dier at St Katharine's by the Tower of London and sixteen-year-old tailor's daughter Elizabeth Starkey, who lived with her parents close to the Three Cranes in Vintry, so called 'not onely of a signe of three Cranes at a Taverne doore, but rather of three strong Cranes of Timber placed on the Vintrie wharfe by the Thames side, to crane up wines there'.[13] Ben Jonson knew the tavern well, and Samuel Pepys would later complain of having a bad dinner there.[14]

All the young women will have travelled by the wherries and small boats that plied their trade on the river, more than two thousand in all, carrying passengers and goods at terrifying speed.[15] Negotiating London Bridge at low tide was especially dangerous as the water level dropped by ten to twelve feet. 'Notwithstanding this the wherries shoot along so lightly as to surprise everyone,' commented the Venetian Busino, who likened the boats to 'so many mutilated gondolas, without prows or *felzi*, though they have seats aft with sundry convenient cushions'.[16]

Other places that were home to the families of the London maids include Newgate Market just inside the City walls (Jeane Grundye),

Westminster (gentleman's daughter Elizabeth Nevill) and St Martin's Lane, where Ann Westcote lived with her victualler father. London had three lanes of the same name, two feeding into the Strand and Thames Street, and the third running north from Cheapside, where the sound of shoemakers tapping on leather and cutlers clanging their wares would have accentuated the noise of 'cart wheels turning, horses clopping, and human feet shuffling'.[17] St Martin's Lane off the Strand is the most likely contender, since Mary, the wife of victualler John Westcott of St Martin-in-the-Fields – Ann's mother perhaps – was bound over to keep the peace here in 1614.[18]

Of the few incomers who lived within the City of London proper, Kidderminster-born Alse Jones had recently come out of service with a Mr Binneons dwelling in Bishopsgate Street, which continued northwards beyond the gate to the open fields around Shoreditch. Ann Parker and Ann Holmes, both aged twenty, were in service with a scrivener called Mr Emmons near the Exchange in the commercial heart of the City.[19] Allice Burges had served Mr Demer, a goldsmith, in Trinity Lane just north of Queenhithe, and had gone on to work for a silk weaver out at Whitechapel. Others had relatives or guarantors living within the City, with whom they may have lived in service. Ann Harmer had grocer cousins living close to the Ferrars in Bucklersbury, a street renowned for its grocers' and apothecaries' stores selling spices, confectionery, perfumes, wines and herbs.[20] Aldgate featured in two testimonials: that of Thomas Tanner, a saddler dwelling within Aldgate, who recommended his cousin Ann Tanner, and one from a Mr Gibson, 'dwelling near to the three Nunns without Algate', who recommended the well born Joan Fletcher.

Several maids – both London-born and incomers – had links to Blackfriars on the City's south-western edge, aside from Aylesbury-born Audry Hoare, who presented herself to the Virginia Company from her married sister's home down by the Catherine Wheel. Sailing on the *Warwick*, Jennet Rimmer came recommended by Mr Spark, clerk of Blackfriars, while the *Tiger's* sixteen-year-old Elizabeth Browne lived here with her parents, and twenty-one-year old Anne Gibson was brought by her guarantor, a Master or Mistress Switzer living in the Blackfriars. The area's theatrical tradition may have contributed in some small way to the women's decision to travel. Among the plays first performed at the small Blackfriars Theatre was Shakespeare's *The Tempest* with its magical new world opening up beyond the seas.[21] Just two and a half years before the women left, a group of churchmen and precinct officers had petitioned the City authorities to put a stop to the inconveniences caused by the multitude of coaches bringing patrons to the theatre, which clogged the surrounding streets so that 'the inhabitants there cannot come to their houses nor bring in their necessary provisions of beer, wood, coal, or hay, nor the tradesmen or shopkeepers utter their wares, nor the passenger go to the common water stairs, without danger of their lives and limbs, whereby also many times quarrels and effusion of blood hath followed'.[22]

More of the incoming women had found refuge outside the City's walls, from Westminster to the west, Moorgate and Moorfields to the north, and round to the eastern suburbs of Mile End and Whitechapel. For Catherine Finch from Herefordshire, living with her brother had brought her into the clattering world of Westminster, almost as far removed from rural Herefordshire as it would be from Jordan's Journey on the James River, where she eventually settled. The Finches' neighbours on the Strand included many luminaries of the Virginia Company and society generally, among them Sir John Danvers, the prominent parliamentarian and keen company investor, and Sir William Uvedale, whose name crops up in connection with other Jamestown brides.[23] Another Strand resident who would feature in Catherine's Virginian adventure was George Thorpe, one-time member of parliament for Portsmouth, a member of His Majesty's Privy Council and of the Virginia Company's council. Although Thorpe's main English residence was at Wanswell Court in Berkeley, Gloucestershire, attendance at parliament and court required him to keep lodgings in London.[24] His name appears among the parishioners of St Martin-in-the-Fields liable to pay poor relief in 1618, when he was living close to Catherine's brother Erasmus. Their difference in status can be seen from their assessed contributions: gentleman George Thorpe at 17s. 3d. and Erasmus Finch at 4s. 4d.[25] Also living on the Strand was Susan Binx's widowed maternal aunt, a gentlewoman and Inigo Jones, architect of Robert Cecil's New Exchange, which offered rare and exotic luxuries for sale in elegant surroundings on the waterside of the Strand.[26]

Only two maids located themselves south of the river: Lott Peer's niece, Mary Ghibbs from Cambridge, whose mother was alive and well and living in Deptford, and twenty-five-year-old Margaret Dauson from Suffolk, who had long lived as 'a good and faithfull servant' with Mistress Elizabeth Stevenson, the wife of a leather seller in Southwark. One of the most varied and vibrant of London's suburbs, Southwark contained more people and yielded more money in taxes than anywhere else in England aside from the City of London, or so claimed John Stow. A jumble of inns, prisons, prelates' houses, tenements, storehouses, granaries, theatres, brothels, bread ovens and a leather market (where Master Stevenson sold his wares, no doubt), Southwark was London's principal district for the more disreputable kinds of entertainment. Shakespeare's Globe theatre was located on the south side of Maiden Lane (now Park Street), and Stow writes of the district's two bear gardens, 'wherin be kept Beares, Buls and other beastes to be bayted. As also Mastives in severall kenels, nourished to baite them.'[27] The bear pits were 'scaffolded about for the Beholders to stand safe', but not everyone enjoyed the sport. Another Venetian visiting London, Alessandro Magno, found baiting bears with dogs '*not* very pleasant to watch', while for Thomas Dekker the very noise of the place put him in mind of hell, 'the beare (dragd to the stake) shewed like a black rugged soule, that was Damned… the Dogges like so many Divels inflicting torments upon it'.[28] Next to the bear gardens, said Stow, were the 'Bordello or stewes, a place so called, of certaine stew houses priviledged there, for the repaire of incontinent men to the like women, of the which priviledge I have read thus'.[29]

How many of London's many entertainments the Jamestown brides had experienced is impossible to gauge, although in the eyes of at least one Catholic visitor (Alessandro Magno), English women in general and serving girls in particular enjoyed considerable freedom to roam the city without their menfolk, running household errands:

> the women themselves carry the goods if they are poor, or make their maids do so if they have them, and they are free to buy whatever is needed. Many of these women serve in the shops. Many of the young women gather outside Moorgate and play with young lads, even though they do not know them. Often, during these games, the women are thrown to the ground by the young men who only allow them to get up after they have kissed them. They kiss each other a lot. If a stranger enters a house and does not first of all kiss the mistress on the lips, they think him badly brought up.[30]

Thomas Platter from Switzerland was also struck by the fact that women as well as men – 'in fact more often than they' – could be found in London's many taverns, enjoying music and dancing and drinking wine laced with sugar, 'and if one woman only is invited, then she will bring three or four other women along and they gaily toast each other'.[31] In 1634 the servant girl Joan Dessall testified to long periods spent working inside the Westminster home of her aristocratic employers intercut with visits to the market, taverns and a range of social contacts.[32] She even spent half an hour with

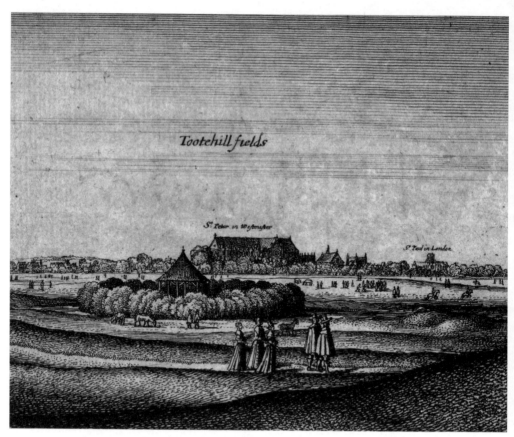

Gardener's daughter Ann Jackson lived close to Tothill [Tootehill] Fields in Westminster, its maze a magnet in summer for Londoners seeking entertainment.

her lady's maid and two fellow servants at the Cock tavern on the north side of Tothill Street, one of London's oldest drinking houses and surely known to gardener's daughter Ann Jackson, who lived on the same street.[33]

For the young Ann – not quite seventeen when she left for Virginia, despite the age she gave to the Virginia Company[34] – Westminster was a lively neighbourhood where the rich and powerful were daily thrown together with the thieves, pickpockets, vagrants and vagabonds crowding into Westminster Abbey's Broad Sanctuary at the bottom of her street. Close by was Tothill Fields, a marshy tract of mostly open country encircling the famous Tothill Maze, much frequented by Londoners seeking pleasure and recreation on fair summer evenings.[35]

But 'honest' William Jackson is unlikely to have allowed his daughter the same freedom as that enjoyed by Joan Dessall. Women who overstepped the boundaries of respectability risked a very public shaming, and popular ballads branded city women and those who had quit the country for the town as sexually loose, rapacious and prone to trickery. In one of these – 'Newes from the Tower-hill: or, a gentle warning to Peg and Kate, To walke no more abroad so late' – two young women are left to pay the tavern bill for their dainty supper of meats and sugared wine, supposedly offered by a man whom they had casually encountered on Tower Hill. Although the trickery seems evenly balanced on both sides, the ballad's moral dart is aimed squarely at the women who lead young men astray:

> It is a great abuse,
> in London at this day,
> Now in the street many nightly meet
> such wenches on the way.

> Which causeth many a Man,
> that would goe home in quiet,
> Upon such queans to spend his meanes,
> in filthinesse and ryot.[36]

As far as we know, no shame attached to any of the young women who heeded the Virginia Company's call to uproot themselves from one of the great cities of Europe – a raucous, stinking, intensely vibrant city that was rapidly gobbling up the fields around it. Some will have loved the excitements it offered; others may have felt overwhelmed by its size and diversity, and the ambiguities of a woman's life with its shifting boundaries between public and private space. Still more will have taken it for granted as home. But whether they liked London or longed for something different, nothing they had experienced to date could adequately prepare them for Jamestown or the life they would lead across the ocean.

CHAPTER FIVE

Of Hogs and Women

The Jamestown brides were by no means the first English women
to set foot on North American soil. That honour belongs to the
women and girls who accompanied John White, a gentleman artist
from London, on a colonizing expedition of 1587 masterminded
by Sir Walter Raleigh, after previous (all-male) attempts to establish
colonies had failed. White had himself sailed with at least one
of these earlier expeditions, recording native life in a series of
watercolours that capture in exquisite detail how early Europeans
viewed this strange new land and – to their eyes – its even stranger
inhabitants.[1] In 1587 he returned as governor with nearly 120 settlers
who included some fourteen families and kinship groups, among
them his own heavily pregnant daughter Elinor and her husband
Ananias Dare, who had married at St Clement Danes church in
Westminster on 24 June 1583, the same church that would later
include Catherine Finch's brother John among its parishioners.[2]
In all, seventeen of White's settlers were women, perhaps a dozen
wives and the rest single women who may have been servants.[3]
Also travelling with the group were nine boys and two male infants.

White's intended destination was the Chesapeake Bay, but the
Portuguese master of their flagship refused to take them any further
than Roanoake Island off the coast of what is now North Carolina,
where they found the melancholy remains of an earlier abandoned
English fort 'overgrowen with Melons of divers sortes, and Deere

within them, feeding on those Mellons'.[4] White's granddaughter was born soon after their arrival, on 18 August 1587, and christened the following Sunday. 'And because this childe was the first Christian borne in Virginia, she was named Virginia,' wrote White soberly in his journal.[5] Another child was born to Dyonis and Margery Harvie shortly afterwards, gender and Christian name unknown.

What happened to Virginia Dare and the others would come to haunt later colonists. At the settlers' behest, John White sailed reluctantly back to England towards the end of August to replenish the colony's dwindling supplies, leaving behind his daughter, granddaughter and the rest of the colonists. A succession of calamities delayed his return – the Spanish Armada, bad weather, French pirates and renewed Anglo-Spanish hostilities – and when White finally reached Roanoke, on his granddaughter's third birthday, the only trace of the settlers were the initials CRO chiselled on a tree and the word CROATOAN carved on a palisade, suggesting that the settlers had decamped to a nearby island. A storm was brewing and White's sailors refused to continue the search, although they did find three of his buried chests, which had been disturbed, 'my things spoyled and broken, and my bookes torne from the covers, the frames of some of my pictures and Mappes rotten and spoyled with rayne, and my armour almost eaten through with rust'.[6] White never saw his daughter or granddaughter again.

Virginia Dare has since become the stuff of folklore: comic-book heroine, postage stamp image, symbol of hope and new beginnings but also an icon of white supremacists; make of her what you will. The Virginia Company instructed sea captains and later colonists to search for Raleigh's lost company, who were fleetingly sighted but never found. An early Jamestown settler (George Percy) recorded seeing 'a Savage Boy about the age of ten yeeres, which had a head of haire of a perfect yellow and a reasonable white skinne, which is a Miracle amongst all Savages'.[7] Ben Jonson slipped the lost colonists into *Eastward Hoe*, his co-authored play of 1605,

Among the 'lost colonists' who disappeared from Roanoke Island were the first Englishwomen hoping to settle in North America, including Governor John White's daughter and granddaughter, Virginia Dare, the first English child born in America.

in which Captain Seagull solicits money for a voyage to Virginia: 'they have married with the Indians,' says Seagull, 'and make 'hem bring forth as beautifull faces as any we have in England.'[8] Another rumour surfaced in an early travel book about Virginia written by William Strachey, who served for a time as secretary there: that an Indian chieftain kept seven English settlers alive to labour in his copper mines, 'fower men, twoo Boyes, and one young Maid, who escaped and fled up the River of Chaonoke.'[9]

England's next attempt at colonizing North America was a strictly masculine affair, following the royal charter granted in 1606 to the Virginia Company of London, permitted to settle around the Chesapeake Bay area of modern-day Virginia, and to its sister Plymouth Company, granted rights further north.[10] Guiding the

London company as treasurer was the wealthy merchant and City dignitary Sir Thomas Smythe (or Smith).[11] Like many of his fellow adventurers, private profit was his primary aim, fortified by the belief that his colonizing endeavours would prosper if he 'zealously promoted the Lord's work'.[12] God and colonization evidently made powerful allies. Joining Smythe on the Virginia Company's governing council were two men who would play a leading role in sending brides to Jamestown: Sir Edwin Sandys, lauded as 'one of the ablest parliamentarians of seventeenth century England',[13] and Henry Wriothesley, third Earl of Southampton, the dedicatee of Shakespere's *Venus and Adonis* and popularly identified as the 'fair youth' of Shakespeare's sonnets.

No women accompanied the first group of settlers who arrived in the Chesapeake Bay in April 1607 and chose Jamestown as their primary settlement, a small swampy peninsula some two and a half miles in length and three quarters of a mile across, overgrown with pine, gum, hickory and oak and connected to the mainland on the north side of the James River by a narrow isthmus.[14] Easy anchorage was its main advantage: 'our shippes doe lie so neere the shoare that they are moored to the Trees in six fathom water', wrote the aristocratic colonist George Percy.[15] But however convenient for trading purposes, their chosen site would prove fateful for the colonists' survival, especially in the deadly summer months, when the waters of the James River become heavily contaminated with salt and sediment, and at low tide 'full of slime and filth'.[16] Even company propagandists were forced to concede that Jamestown was a 'marish seate',[17] an opinion shared by William Strachey, who perceptively identified its unsavoury water supply as the source of the many 'Fluxes and Agues' that afflicted the colonists,[18] and the colonists' initial delight at the Edenic nature of the Virginian landscape quickly turned to horror as the litany of dying began. By the time Captain Newport returned in early 1608 with supplies and a further seventy-three settlers, all male, nearly two thirds of the original group were dead.[19]

The first English women to arrive in the new colony – and then only two of them – came with Captain Newport's 'Second Supply' in October 1608, eighteen months after the first contingent had made its way warily up the James River looking for a place to settle. Mistress Forest, who was accompanying her husband Thomas, a Virginia Company adventurer, disappears immediately from the historical record, a casualty perhaps of Jamestown's lethal brew of typhoid, dysentery and salt-water poisoning. Her maidservant, Anne Burras, lived on and married within three months, which would have been unthinkable had her mistress still needed her services. By then the noisy and charismatic Captain John Smith had taken over as president of the council, and during a difficult winter he recorded 'a marriage betwixt John Laydon and Anne Burras; which was the first marriage we had in Virginia.'[20]

How the union was arranged can only be imagined. As the English settlement's sole marriageable woman Anne Burras will have sorely needed male protection, and most of the single settlers will surely have wanted a wife, or at least a pair of female hands to carry out the household tasks then considered women's work. Her chosen husband had arrived with the original group of settlers and survived the first winter when so many of his companions had perished. Classed as a labourer rather than a gentleman, Laydon lacked the specialist skills of some of his fellows, who are variously identified as carpenter, surgeon, blacksmith, sailor, barber, bricklayer, mason, tailor and a drummer.[21] But however they made their choice, the pair chose wisely. Remarkably for the times, both were still alive more than sixteen years later, living in 'Elizabeth Cittie' (present-day Hampton) along with four daughters all born in Virginia.[22] They will resurface in the story of the Jamestown brides as close neighbours to one of several Elizabeths among the *Warwick* maids who had successfully found herself a husband.

Anne Laydon's example proved that women could survive the harsh Virginian climate, adding weight to the Virginian proverb 'That hogs and women thrive well amongst them.'[23] Sir Francis Wyatt, the governor who would later welcome the brides to Jamestown, even suggested that 'the weaker sexe' were better constituted to survive Virginia's unhealthy climate than men, 'either that their worke lies chiefly within doores, or because they are of a colder temper.'[24] And so from early 1609 the Virginia Company actively encouraged women as well as men to join its colonial adventure, adding them to its lists of people required for Virginia, their trades advertised on broadsides posted in places where people congregated such as church doors and street corners,[25] and in pamphlets sold by the printers and booksellers around St Paul's Churchyard in London. Smiths, carpenters, coopers, shipwrights, turners, planters, vine growers, fowlers, fishermen, metalworkers of all kinds, brickmakers, bricklayers, ploughmen, weavers, shoemakers, sawyers and spinners were in demand, 'and all other labouring men and women that are willing to goe to the said Plantation to inhabite there.' New recruits were instructed to repair to Philpot Lane in the City to the house of Sir Thomas Smythe. In return, they were promised 'houses to dwell in, with Gardens and Orchards', food and clothing provided by the joint stockholders, a single share in the enterprise valued at £12 10s., their dividend in land and a share in the fruits of their labour.[26]

The broadsides had the desired effect, and more women followed in the next wave of migration, known as the 'Third Supply', which accompanied the colony's new leaders, who left Plymouth in early summer 1609 in a fleet of nine ships under Captain Newport, bringing upwards of five hundred new settlers to the colony.[27] Travelling with Newport in the fleet's flagship, the *Sea Venture*, were the colony's two deputy leaders, Sir Thomas Gates and Sir Thomas Dale, and the admiral of the Virginia Company, Sir George Somers. The Spanish ambassador in London reported to King Philip III of Spain that as many as one hundred of the settlers would be women (almost certainly an overestimate) and that Virginia's governor general, Lord Delaware, would follow with a further six or seven hundred men 'and a few women.'[28]

The exact number of women who sailed with the Third Supply is not recorded, but they included a fourteen-year-old maidservant nicknamed Jane by archaeologists at Jamestown and the young Temperance Flowerdew, who would later claim to have sailed on the *Falcon* under Captain John Martin and who reappears in Virginia a decade or so later as the wife of the new governor, Sir George Yeardley. Born into a prominent Norfolk family, Temperance was the daughter of Anthony Flowerdew and his wife Martha Stanley, and distantly related to the Earls of Derby and Romney.[29] Perhaps as many as ten women and children sailed with the colony's new leaders on the *Sea Venture*, among them the pregnant first wife of settler John Rolfe, who would later take Pocahontas as his second wife; a Mistress Horton and her servant Elizabeth Persons; and Edward Eason's wife.[30] West of the Canaries, a terrible hurricane dispersed the fleet. One ship was lost and the *Sea Venture* was driven off course then scuttled in the Bermudas to avoid loss of life. The remaining ships of the leaderless fleet limped into Jamestown in August 1609, bringing sickness and mutiny into the colony. Survivors of the shipwrecked *Sea Venture* would not arrive for another ten months, including several husbands who had travelled separately from their wives.[31]

Captain John Smith returned to England early that October after accidentally blowing himself up with his own gunpowder. He left behind nearly five hundred settlers living in fifty to sixty houses within Jamestown's palisaded fort plus a handful of forts and plantations elsewhere.[32] Nominally in charge was the gentle if ineffectual George Percy, who had recorded the colonists' first landing and whose brother languished in the Tower of London, suspected of complicity in the Gunpowder Plot to blow up England's House of Lords and King James with it.[33]

Then began the toughest winter the colonists had yet experienced: the Starving Time they called it, when dwindling food stocks and a tight siege by Powhatan Indians reduced their numbers to sixty at most, surviving on a diet of roots, herbs, acorns, walnuts, berries, a little fish now and then, the skins of their horses and a gluey porridge made from boiling their starched ruffs. It was rumoured that the poorer settlers even resorted to cannibalism, digging up a dead Indian and boiling body parts with roots and herbs. Those who spent the winter marooned on Bermuda had a far easier time despite mutinies, murder, execution, births and deaths, including that of the Rolfes' infant daughter, christened Bermuda, who lived for a few weeks only.[34]

When Sir Thomas Gates and the other shipwrecked survivors reached Jamestown in May 1610 on ships they had built themselves from salvaged timber and native cedar they found the colony close to collapse: the palisade fence torn down, the gates fallen from their hinges, the houses left empty by the death of their owners and many burned 'rather th[a]n the dwellers would step into the Woods a stones cast off from them, to fetch other fire-wood'. After two wearisome weeks attempting to put the colony back on its feet, Gates gave the order to abandon Jamestown and evacuate the settlers to Newfoundland, commanding every man and woman 'at the beating of the Drum' to repair to their allotted ships.[35] The evacuation was halted only when news of Lord Delaware's arrival reached the colonists as they sailed down the James River past Hog and Mulberry Islands. Delaware had brought more new recruits for the colony, far fewer than intended, but news of the disasters had reached England and deflated the enthusiasm provoked by the previous spring's propaganda campaigns.[36]

Although forced to acknowledge the truth of reported food shortages and disorder, the company could not allow reports of cannibalism to go unchallenged. In a version of events attributed to Sir Thomas Gates, one of the settlers had 'mortally hated his Wife', killed her and hidden her body parts about the house. When the husband was suspected of his wife's disappearance, the house was searched and her body parts discovered. In his defence, the man claimed that his wife had died and that he had hidden her body 'to satisfie his hunger'. 'Now whether shee was better roasted, boyled or carbonado'd [grilled over coals], I know not', wrote John Smith slyly, 'but of such a dish as powdered [salted] wife I never heard of'.[37] The husband's story was supposedly disproved when a subsequent search of his house uncovered good stores of 'Meale, Oat-meale, Beanes and Pease. He thereupon was arraigned, confessed the Murder, and was burned for his horrible villany'.[38]

While the newly married Anne Laydon survived the Starving Time, and Temperance Flowerdew may have returned home to England before it even began, the young English woman later nicknamed Jane was not so fortunate. Working within the fort area in 2012, archaeologists first uncovered fragments of her teeth, buried not in an obvious grave but rather among the detritus of everyday life – broken pottery, discarded weapons, butchered animal bones and mollusc shells – in an L-shaped cellar that had functioned as a kitchen for one of Jamestown's earliest buildings.[39] Further excavations revealed half of a human skull apparently chopped in two, plus other cranial remains and a section of shin bone. The objects surrounding these human remains held a clue as to their date. Senior Curator Beverly Straube of the Jamestown Rediscovery archaeological project was able to match a ceramic medallion from the cellar to a German stoneware jug found in a nearby well that had been filled with trash in 1610, suggesting that the cellar was backfilled soon after Delaware ordered a clean-up of the colony in June 1610.

The bones tell the story of who Jane really was and what had happened to her. Close examination of the split skull revealed further chop marks to the forehead and back of the cranium. Experts from the Smithsonian Institution carried out extensive tests to determine the sex, age and probable origin of the remains. Skeletal examination, radiography of the jaw and isotopic testing of the bones all pointed to a middle- to upper-class young woman of about fourteen years old, born along the coastal plains of southern England and recently arrived at Jamestown. Like the Jamestown brides, she may have been the daughter of gentry or a maidservant eating the same food as the family she served.

Despite the company's vigorous efforts to suppress reports of cannibalism, the chop marks on Jane's skull and leg bone show where the truth lies. Although they cannot tell us precisely how she died or when, they do recount what happened to her body after death. Under magnification, her jaw revealed many cuts made with quick sawing motions using a sharp knife – altogether more tentative than the chops aimed at dog bones from the Starving Time – together with nearly imperceptible knife jabs to dislodge the flesh. Her skull and leg bone had also undergone sustained blows, reflecting a concerted effort to separate bone from the brain and other soft tissue, including cheek muscles and material from both the inside and outside of the lower jaw, and attempts to prise out the marrow from her right tibia, which was chopped halfway through.

Jane's pensive face gazes back at you in Historic Jamestowne's small museum, her features reconstructed in resin then remodelled in clay. She looks shockingly young, her hair swept into a modest coif handmade by a costume researcher specializing in early seventeenth-century dress. The coif is decorated with blackwork embroidery, one of the skills brought to the colony by shoemaker's daughter Audry Hoare and Londoner Susan Binx.[40]

The Starving Time undoubtedly represented a low point in Jamestown's early history for all the settlers, men and women. Accustomed to dealing with Ireland's English colonists, who mostly came from the poorest elements of society and were deemed incapable of self-discipline, Jamestown's new leaders imposed strict rules, set out in the *Lawes Divine, Morall and Martiall* introduced from 1610.[41] All settlers were required to attend twice-daily church services; and punishments for transgressing any of the laws were severe, including whipping, public shaming, burning of hands, loss of ears and hard labour. Colonists were sentenced to death for many offences, from repeated non-attendance at church to killing cattle, hogs, goats, poultry or dogs.[42]

The laws gave some sexual protection to women, ordaining that 'No man shall ravish or force any woman, maid or Indian, or other, upon pain of death'. Other proven acts of fornication by men or women were punishable by escalating sentences of whipping, while 'he or she that can be lawfully convict of Adultery shall be punished with death'. Several laws concerned public hygiene, forbidding anyone ('man or woman, Launderer or Launderesse') to wash dirty linen in the open street, within the fort's palisade fence or forty feet outside of it, or to clean pots and pans within twenty feet of the old well or the new pump. Nor were colonists to perform the coyly phrased 'necessities of nature' within a quarter-mile radius of the fence, 'since by these unmanly, slothfull, and loathsome immodesties, the whole Fort may bee choaked, and poisoned with ill aires'. Even privies, it seems, were lacking.

The colony's longest-surviving female settler, Anne Laydon, reportedly suffered a severe whipping during the time of Sir Thomas Dale's government, together with Jane Wright, the first Virginia colonist to be accused of witchcraft.[43] The pair were among a group of women ordered to make shirts for the company's servants and since neither had enough thread to finish the job properly, they unravelled the bottom of completed shirts, making all their shirts shorter than the other women's, 'for wch fact the said Ann leyden and Jane Wright were whipt, And Ann leyden beinge then wth childe (the same night therof miscarried)'.[44]

However unpleasant for the settlers, Sir Thomas Dale's rigorous execution of the Lawes helped to bring stability to the colony.[45] Persuading potential investors to part with their money – and potential colonists with their lives – was another matter. A dual narrative developed in which company propagandists sought to counter the 'vile and scandalous reports' spread by disaffected settlers, painting Virginia as a promised land flowing with milk and honey and reserved exclusively for Englishmen, a tactic that made matters worse when the reality of Virginian life proved less than ideal for investors and colonists.

John Rolfe's introduction of a sweeter strain of tobacco, using Spanish seeds from the Orinoco, at last gave the colonists a cash crop they could actually sell and put them on the road to profitability, but investors remained wary.[46] As John Chamberlain remarked, many gentlemen rushed to invest in the adventure when Virginia fever was at its height, but when the time came for them to meet their obligations, especially the second or third time around, 'theyre handes were not sot so redy to go to theyre purses as they were to the paper, and in the end flatly refused, wherupon they are sued by the companie in the Chauncerie'.[47] A few years later, his prognosis of company fortunes was hardly more sanguine: 'I heare not of any other riches or matter of worth, but only some quantitie of sassafras, tobacco, pitch, and clap-board, things of no great value unless there were more plentie and neerer hand. All I can learne of yt is that the countrie is goode to live in, yf yt were stored with people, and might in time become commodious, but there is no present profit to be expected'.[48]

The company's financial performance bore him out. When the dividend on its 1609 stock fell due in 1616 there were no funds to divide between its many stockholders and so the company declared instead a dividend of land, not the 500 acres per share confidently predicted in 1609, but a more modest 50 that might rise to an ultimate total of perhaps 200 acres per share as the company's landholdings increased.[49] But from 1612 the company had enjoyed a new source of funding that would develop into its mainstay: the Virginia Lottery, permitted under its third royal charter and considered newsworthy enough for John Chamberlain to communicate to Sir Dudley Carleton: 'There is a lotterie in hand for the furthering of the Virginia viage, and an under-companie erecting for the trade of the Bermudes'.[50]

Just one copy survives of this Virginia Company's broadside of 1616 promising silver cups and sacks of coin to winning ticket holders in its Virginia lottery.

The company's first three lotteries held in London were not especially successful, despite the fanfare that accompanied the good fortune of tailor Thomas Sharplisse, who drew the chief prize of £4,000 'in fayre plate, which was sent to his house in a very stately manner'.[51] Far more popular were the running lotteries held from 1616, which travelled from town to town throughout England. Norwich and Leicester certainly played host, as did Salisbury in Wiltshire, birthplace of Jamestown bride Ann Jackson and close to where Bridgett Crofte was born. Other probable host cities included Manchester, Reading and Exeter.[52] Everyone was encouraged to take part, even women seeking a husband, according to the popular ballad 'Londons Lotterie':

> You Maydes that have but portions small
> to gaine your Mariage friend,
> Cast in your Lottes with willing hand,
> God may good fortune send.
> You Widowes, and you wedded Wives,
> one litle substaunce try:
> You may advance both you and yours,
> with wealth that comes thereby.[53]

Not everyone approved, however. The success of the running lotteries provoked complaints that they sucked money out of local economies at a time when trade and agriculture were depressed across the nation; and critics maintained that they appealed to a very English addiction to gambling.[54] There were rumours, too, that they swindled people who could ill afford the price of a ticket. While at least two early lottery managers were taken to court for fraud and theft, the men responsible for managing the running lotteries emerged with their reputations intact: Lott Peere and Gabriel Barbor, who between them brought two young women to the company as Jamestown brides, Mary Ghibbs and Fortune Taylor.

The Virginia Lottery played a vital role in the plan to send shipments of brides to Jamestown. Since profits from the lottery were helping to plug the gap in the Virginia Company's finances to the tune of some £7,000 to £8,000 a year,[55] its leaders could turn their attention to developing a viable and thriving colony, which required a constant supply of new settlers to tame the wilderness and transform Virginia's raw resources into profit. Now was the perfect time to heed the advice of one of the company's founding members, the English statesman and philosopher Sir Francis Bacon: 'When the plantation grows to strength, then it is time to plant with women as well as with men; that the plantation may spread into generations, and not be ever pieced from without.'[56]

To flourish, Jamestown needed two sorts of women: on the one hand honest wives, giving male settlers a reason to put down roots in the colony, and on the other hard-working women from the serving classes able to undertake the drudgery of housewifery and lend a helping hand in the tobacco fields.[57] From 1608 both sorts of women had been coming to the colony, although not in numbers large enough to stabilize its economy, either as wives or servants, and the ratio of women to men remained stubbornly low in the colony's early years, rarely exceeding one woman to every six men.

Since too few colonists – women or men – were willing to put themselves forward, the authorities had looked to coerce those who had little choice but to obey. The great Elizabethan promoter of colonization Richard Hakluyt provided the moral underpinning for this policy by drawing attention to 'the multitude of idle and mutinous persons' who stuffed England's prisons, recommending that petty thieves might be employed to fell and saw timber and plant sugar cane on the country's western plantations.[58] Decanting felons to the colonies remained official policy throughout Virginia's early days, despite Sir Francis Bacon's warning against planting with 'the scum of people and wicked and condemned men'. Equally popular as public policy was clearing England's city streets of vagrants of both sexes and shipping them to Virginia, thereby solving the labour shortage of the one with the unwanted population of the other. Sir Thomas Smythe's son-in-law Robert Johnson used a horticultural metaphor to describe the benefits that would flow from ridding England of its superfluous population: 'as with plants and trees that bee too frolicke, which not able to sustaine and feede their multitude of branches, doe admit an engrafting of their buds and sciences into some other soile, accounting it a benefite for preservation of their kind, and a disburdening their stocke of those superfluous twigs that suck away their nourishment'.[59]

As early as 1609 the Privy Council had taken the view that 'all the ills and plagues' affecting the City of London were caused by the number of poor people cluttering its streets. The council therefore recommended to the lord mayor that the corporation should join forces with the City livery companies and City wards to raise sufficient funds to ship vagrants to Virginia. The Merchant Taylors' Company offered £200 and its members a further £300, while the Ironmongers advanced £150. In total the City raised some £18,000 to help sweep the vagrant poor off London's streets.[60] King James took a personal interest in this endeavour, writing to Sir Thomas Smythe about 'divers idle young people' who continued to plague the court, despite being twice punished. 'His Majesty, having no other course to clear the Court from them, had thought fit to send them to [Smythe], that at the next opportunity they might be sent to Virginia, and set to work there.'

But as Bacon predicted, the unruly adults enticed to the colony by these means were not the answer to its prayers, 'for they will ever live like rogues, and not fall to work, but be lazy, and do mischief'. And so from 1618 the company increasingly called for vagrant children to work as servants in the colony, girls as well as boys, considering them to be less confirmed in their delinquency and more pliable than adults.[61] Smythe's original plan was to round up a hundred children aged between eight and sixteen who had 'no means of living or maintenance' and to ship them over to Virginia, where they would be educated and taught a trade or profession. The calculated cost per child was five pounds, which was to be collected from parish ratepayers like Erasmus Finch in Westminster, who contributed to poor relief.

Catching the children was easy. On the orders of the lord mayor, aldermen instructed their constables to walk the streets and apprehend 'all such vagrant children, both boys and girls, as they shall find in the streets and in the markets or wandering in the night', and commit them to Bridewell to await shipment overseas. Another instruction to the deputies and churchwardens of London's parishes quickly followed, requiring poor inhabitants 'that are overcharged and burdened with poor children' to agree to send any surplus children aged ten and upwards to Virginia, 'thereby to ease them of their charge'. Parents were to be reassured that their children would be 'well used' and provision made for their education and maintenance.

The plan clearly worked. As John Chamberlain reported in October 1618, 'The citie is now shipping [to Virginia] an hundred younge boyes and girles that lay starving in the streets, which is one of the best deeds that can be don with so litle charge not rising to above 500[li].[62] A quarter of the children were 'wenches' (twenty-four out of ninety-nine),[63] and the children left for Virginia in the late winter of 1618 and early spring of 1619, some travelling by the *Jonathan*,[64] others in the *George* and the *Neptune*. The Virginia Company let out a collective sigh of relief, thanking the City of London for the children sent to the colony over that year, 'wch by the goodnes of God ther saffly Arived, (save such as dyed in the waie) and are well pleased wee doubt not for their benefitt'.[65] Those who died on the journey will not have been so sanguine.

The company asked the City to send out a further hundred children in the spring but this time wanted them to be a little older: twelve years and upwards. Those impoverished parents who refused to send their children to Virginia were to be threatened with the loss of poor relief. The City agreed to pay three pounds per child for transportation and a further forty shillings a head towards clothing, stipulating that each should receive twenty-five acres of land after they had served out the terms of their apprenticeship. 'They shall be Apprentizes the boyes till they come to 21 years of Age the Girles till the like Age or till they be marryed and afterwardes they shalbe placed as Tennantes uppon the publique Land with best Condicons wher they shall have houses with Stocke of Corne & Cattle to begin wth, and afterwards the moytie of all encrease & pfitt what soever'. The children had no say in the matter. Any who were 'obstinate' or disobeyed could be imprisoned, punished and disposed of, 'and so to Shipp them out to Virginia with as much expedition as may stand with convenience'.[66]

The constables appear to have experienced increasing difficulties in apprehending girls. In the thirty days between 24 December 1619 and 22 January 1620 they brought to Bridewell just eight girls among more than one hundred young vagrants. These included Ann Momford, 'an ould guest that will take no warning', incarcerated on the orders of Mr Recorder for leading 'an incontinent life', and Mary Nicholls, apprehended as a 'lewde va[grant]'.[67] Whether the constables targeted boys or the girls had taken fright is not made clear. Outside London reports of maidens being 'pressed' or forced to travel to Virginia circulated wildly. In Somerset a justice of the peace ordered the arrest of one Owen Evans, accused of fraudulently raising money by claiming authority to entrap or press young maidens for Virginia and Bermuda. He had given one constable four shillings to press four maidens for Virginia, threatened to hang another constable unless he helped to press girls for him, given one shilling to Jacob Cryfe to press his own daughter, and had received ten shillings in protection money from another parish to stay away. Such was the terror he engendered in young women 'that forty have fled from one parish to obscure places, and their parents do not know what has become of them'.[68]

Evans was not alone in his trickery. Shortly afterwards, a clerk in chancery by the name of William Robinson was hanged, drawn and quartered at Charing Cross for trying to extract money from alehouse keepers and country moneylenders by counterfeiting the sovereign's Great Seal. One of his schemes involved sending young women to Virginia, claiming to have royal authority 'to take up rich yeomens daughters (or drive them to compound) to serve his Majestie for breeders in Virginia'.[69]

The plight of entrapped or 'trapanned' girls sent to Virginia entered the public's imagination as a fate to avoid at all costs. A popular ballad of the late seventeenth century tells the story of 'The Trappan'd Maiden: Or, The Distressed Damsel':

> Give ear unto a Maid,
> That lately was betray'd,
> And sent into Virginny O:
> In brief I shall declare,
> What I have suffered there,
> When that I was weary,
> weary, weary, weary O.

When that first I came
To this land of Fame,
Which is called Virginny, O;
The Axe and the Hoe
Have wrought my Overthrow,
When that I was weary,
weary, weary, weary O.[70]

Another ballad recounts a cautionary tale of a weaver's wife, 'witty and fair', who turned her wit against her husband once too often. When she fell for a 'lusty Lad', her husband exacted his revenge by selling her for ten pounds to a captain bound for Virginia, explaining,

The Times are very hard,
Ill sell my Wife for Mony
She is good Merchandize you know,
when you come to Virginny.

The captain agreed, and once the husband had tricked his wife into accompanying him on board ship, he abandoned her to her fate and rowed hastily back to shore. After they had crossed the Atlantic the captain sold her as a maiden 'for fifty pounds in Money,/ And she another husband had/ when she came to Virginny'.[71]

Sending women and girls to the colony against their will was ultimately self-defeating, however. The poor quality of women transported to the colony during his leadership was one of many complaints later levelled at Sir Thomas Smythe by his enemies, and specifically that he had sent 'but few women thither & those corrupt'.[72] Another critic complained that the few dispatched from Bridewell were of 'soe bad choyse as made the Colony afraide to desire any others'.[73] Smythe's ally Sir Nathaniel Rich came to his aid, suggesting that he sent out 'a great many [women]… the best hee could get', even claiming that one of the women he dispatched went on to marry a future knight and governor, surely an oblique reference to Temperance Flowerdew.[74]

But women settlers were needed for more than their labour alone. When Sir Edwin Sandys took over the reins of the company in the spring of 1619 he was determined to make the colony more attractive for colonists and investors alike, and to increase its population. This called for wives as well as workers, and so in early November that year the idea was mooted of sending shiploads of young marriageable women to the colony. As the company's finances were in a reasonable shape thanks to the lottery, these women were to be offered free to the company's own public tenants; any private planter taking one as his wife would simply be asked to reimburse the cost of her transportation.

Sandys was looking for 'a fitt hundreth' of women,

> Maides young and uncorrupt to make wifes to the Inhabitanntes and by that meanes to make the men there more setled & lesse moveable who by defect thereof (as is credibly reported) stay there but to gett something and then to returne for England, wch will breed a dissolucon, and so an overthrow of the Plantacon… and it was never fitter time to send them then nowe. Corne being here at home soe cheape and plentifull, and great promises there for the Harvest ensuing.[75]

A much larger general court discussed the plan two weeks later, when Sandys reiterated his determination to remedy the 'mischiefe' of planters who stayed in Virginia for a few years only, 'not setled in their mindes to make it their place of rest and continuance'. Ever prudent with company finances, Sandys did not intend to commission special ships to take the maids and the other new colonists to Virginia, but rather to put them on ships trading with Newfoundland, at six pounds a head, promising 'not to leave the Company one penny in debt for any thing in his yeare to be performed: And moreover that he would discharge 3000 li of former debts and reckonings according to the Stock left in the Lottaries at his coming to this place.'[76]

Unlike the brides who travelled to Jamestown in 1621, no list of these women has survived. Perhaps there never was one. As London adventurers were not seeking to make a profit from these earlier shipments, the company had less need to advertise its wares, but in February and March 1620 it dispatched a total of ninety women by the *Jonathan* and the *Merchant of London*,[77] perhaps by other ships as well, and shortly afterwards announced its intention to send one hundred more, although no more bridal shipments took place that year.

Sifting through the muster or census undertaken throughout the colony in 1625 throws up a small number of women who travelled by either the *Jonathan* or the *Merchant of London* in 1620, and who went on to marry men who had reached the colony at an earlier date or by different ships. These women may have travelled to Virginia in search of husbands, but they may equally have gone as indentured servants or as married women who subsequently lost their husbands and remarried.

Reviewing its achievements for 1620, the Virginia Company applauded itself for transporting ninety young maids 'to make Wives for so many of the former Tenants'[78] and for dispatching 1,200 'choise men borne and bred up to labor and industry', stout men from Devonshire, Warwickshire, Staffordshire and Sussex to join the 'neere one thousand' remaining from before. While freely admitting that 'many disasters' had struck Virginia in previous years, the company was determined to quell the 'false and malicious' rumours spread abroad about the state of the colony. Instead, it painted Virginia as a country 'rich, spacious, and well watered; temperate as for the Climate; very healthfull after men are a little accustomed to it; abounding with all Gods naturall blessings… In Summe, a Countrey, too good for ill people.' Here was a colony on the cusp of reaping great rewards. The future could only get brighter, or so the company thought.

CHAPTER SIX

La Belle Sauvage

While the Virginia Company busied itself with finding suitable English brides for its colonists, it turned its back on a source much closer to hand: the many native women living around the James River, who mostly belonged to Algonquian-speaking Indian tribes under their paramount chief, Powhatan.[1] The first seventeen years of Virginia Company rule over its colony produced just one recorded marriage between the settlers and the native community: that of tobacco planter John Rolfe and Powhatan's daughter, best known to Europeans by her nickname of Pocahontas. Why did the English keep themselves aloof when intermarriage would have solved the colony's chronic shortage of women, whether as wives, mothers or female labour?

John Rolfe supplies many of the answers in a deeply troubled letter he wrote to Virginia's then governor, Sir Thomas Dale, when he was agonizing over the dangers of marrying 'strange wives' and falling in love with one whose 'education hath bin rude, her manners barbarous, her generation accursed, and so discrepant in all nurtriture from my selfe'. His letter reveals much about how English men viewed themselves in relation to Indian women, and especially their reluctance to take heathen brides, a dilemma that Rolfe neatly resolved by turning his bride's barbarism to his advantage. By labouring in God's vineyard, he reasoned, he would bring this 'unbeleeving creature' into the Christian fold, pointing to 'her desire to be taught and instructed in the knowledge of God, her capablenesse of understanding'. Had he wished simply to slake his lust, he would surely have satisfied his desires 'with Christians more pleasing to the eie'.[2] What the spirited Pocahontas thought of this unintended slight, and what Indian women generally thought of these blundering, bearded, smelly, overdressed, hapless and intermittently helpless European men can only be imagined.

English colonists, by contrast, were forever recording their impressions of Indian women. One of the first to write about Virginian women in any detail was the astronomer and mathematician Thomas Hariot (or Harriot), who had sailed to Virginia with the watercolourist and future governor of Roanoke's lost colony, John White, on Sir Walter Raleigh's expedition of 1585 led by Sir Richard Grenville. Hariot and White were the expedition's recorders, charged with noting and drawing everything that might interest present and future colonists.

Writing of the Indians they encountered in their wanderings, Hariot noted their surprise that the settlers had brought no women with them, 'neither that we did care for any of theirs'[3] – a puzzling remark since Hariot himself showed a keen interest in Indian women, and must have inspected them at close quarters: 'They have small eyes, plaine and flatt noses, narrow foreheads, and broade mowths', he wrote of the women of Secotan village, describing in elaborate detail their hairstyles, their tattoos, their adornments, the colour of their eyes ('reasonable fair black') and their bearing. Unmarried girls of good parentage often covered their naked breasts 'in token of maydenlike modestye', he noted approvingly, but perhaps he was simply standing too close. Indian dress clearly fascinated him, as it did most early settlers used to judging rank from a person's attire,[4] from the fringed deerskin worn like an apron by the wife of an Indian chief from Pomeiooc, leaving her almost naked behind, to the moss or milkweed pad held by a cord to cover the 'priviliers' of her young daughter, who waves an expensively dressed European doll in White's original watercolour, to which his engraver Theodor de Bry has added a European rattle. Most of the women Hariot inspected were the wives and daughters of chiefs, whose apparent delight in walking in the fields and by the riverside he misinterpreted as leisure, when the business of gathering, growing or preparing food would have left them precious little time to spare, however high their status within the tribe.[5]

Another who recorded his impressions of Indian women was William Strachey, the chronicler of the *Sea Venture*'s shipwreck in Bermuda and briefly secretary to the Jamestown colony. Strachey describes Indians generally as 'most voluptious' and their women as willing, with their husbands' permission, to 'embrace the acquaintance of any Straunger for nothing, and yt is accompted no offence, and uncredible yt is, with what heat both Sexes of them are given over to those Intemperances'.[6] You might reasonably wonder if he had first-hand experience of their embraces. 'The women have handsome lymbes, slender armes, and pretty handes,' he tells us, 'and when they sing they have a delightful and pleasant tang in their voices'. Some of these songs were '*errotica carmina* or amorous dittyes... which they will sing tunable ynough'. Strachey's dictionary of more than 800 Algonquian words and phrases provides much helpful material for would-be suitors, from the hesitant 'What is your name?' (*Cacutterewindg Kear*) to the bolder 'I love you' (*Nouwmais*), and from the act of lying with a woman (*Saccasac*) to the resultant cuckolded husband (*Winpeton* or *Wimpenton*). Here too were words for a woman's breast (*Otaus*), a woman's 'Secrett' (*Muttusk, Mocosiit*) and a whole host of body parts, including hand, hair, head, eyes, nose, ears, thighs, arse and tongue.

Strachey also reveals that Indian women were part of the entertainment offered by Indian chiefs to honoured guests. First the Indians would spread a mat 'as the Turks doe a carpett', then bid their guest welcome with 'a tunable voice of showting', and such vehement and passionate orations testifying to their love that 'a Straunger would take them to be exceeding angry or stark mad'. After much feasting they would bring their guest at night to his appointed lodging then 'send a young woman fresh paynted redd with *Pochoe* and oyle to be his bedfellow'.

The settlers' close encounters with native women were not confined to feast days and celebrations. When Jamestown's food supplies ran low in early 1609, groups of settlers were sent elsewhere: some to fish at Point Comfort on the extreme tip of Chesapeake Bay, others to the falls upriver, where 'nothing could bee found but a few berries and acornes', while several more were billeted among the 'Salvages' and so were able to glean much useful information about Indian fields, pathways and habitations, and 'howe to gather and use their fruits'. Preferring life with the Indians to the rigours of Jamestown fort, a number of these billeted soldiers ran away, but an Indian brought them back to Jamestown in recognition of the good treatment he had received when he himself was a prisoner of the colonists.[7] Captain John Smith meted out exemplary punishments to the deserters as a warning to others who might be tempted to follow their lead, ensuring that they were 'rather contented to labour at home, then adventure to live Idle among the Salvages'.

Ever on the alert for news of how the English were extending their toehold on American soil, Spanish spies picked up rumours of such interminglings between the English colonists and the native population, and inevitably drew the wrong conclusions. 'I have been told by a friend, who tells me the truth, that some of the people who have gone [to Virginia], think now some of them should marry the women of the savages of that country', wrote the Spanish ambassador at the court of King James in a coded letter to King Philip III of Spain, 'and he tells me that there are already 40 or 50 thus married, and other Englishmen after being put among them have become savages, and that the women whom they took out, have also gone among the savages, and they have received and treated them well'.[8]

A handful of later colonists would regret the missed opportunity that intermarriage presented. The planter Robert Beverley believed that Indian hostility was provoked by the English refusal to marry

Indian women, and that 'the Colony, instead of all these Losses of Men on both Sides, wou'd have been encreasing in Children to its Advantage.'⁹ Such was the way of French colonists in Canada, thought Alexander Spotswood, an early eighteenth-century governor of colonial Virginia, who credited the strength of French colonization in large measure to their intermarriage with the Indians. But as Spotswood quickly discovered, 'the inclinations of our people are not the same with those of that Nation, for notwithstanding the long intercourse between ye Inhabitants of this Country and ye Indians, and their living amongst one another for so many Years, I cannot find one Englishman that has an Indian Wife, or an Indian marryed to a white woman'.¹⁰

It was a reluctance reinforced by English preachers, who for the most part ardently supported colonization as a means of bringing God's word to barbarous peoples but drew the line at intermarriage with heathens. 'Then must Abrams posteritie keepe them to themselves', thundered the preacher William Symonds to an audience of Virginia Company adventurers and planters assembled in April 1609 to the east of London at Whitechapel, where Jamestown bride Allice Burges would enter service with a silk weaver. Drawing inspiration from the biblical account of Abraham's journey into the Promised Land, Symonds likened the company's colonizing ambitions to Abraham's God-given mission to leave his country, his kindred and his father's house, and to found a great nation in the land of the Canaanites. Just so would the English in Virginia, he promised, providing they followed the rule laid down for Abraham's descendants: 'They may not marry nor give in marriage to the heathen, that are uncircumsised. And this is so plaine, that out of this foundation arose the law of marriage among themselves. The breaking of this rule, may breake the neck of all good success of this voyage.'¹¹

Such a clear prohibition explains why the prospect of taking Pocahontas as his wife so deeply troubled John Rolfe, and how her conversion to Christianity might have eased his conscience. Why

Pocahontas agreed to throw in her lot with the foreigners is more puzzling. Indian marriage was a working partnership dependent on each partner's labour, and English settler men had proved themselves spectacularly inept at meeting even the most basic human needs for food and shelter. Far from demanding a dowry from the bride's family, Indian custom expected the husband's family to negotiate a male equivalent, the 'bridewealth', which was paid to the bride's family to compensate for the loss of her labour.[12] Unlike the English, Indian men did not regard their women as weak and therefore inferior, but at least in accepting the advances of John Rolfe, Pocahontas was allying herself to one of the more successful English planters.

Pocahontas had been a familiar sight to the early colonists since girlhood, striding into the fort at Jamestown and persuading the boys to perform cartwheels in the market place then following them with cartwheels of her own, 'naked as she was all the Fort over'.[13] Living up to her nickname of Pocahontas, which Strachey tells us means 'little wanton', she brought a gust of fresh air to the bleak reality of lives lived on the edge of extinction within the confines of the palisade fence. She doubtless used her playfulness and high spirits to catch the attention of her powerful father, Powhatan, and so earned her reputation as his favourite daughter, although she too would have been required to work the fields and carry out all the other tasks reserved for women and children.

As a young girl, Pocahontas played a bit part in the narratives of early Virginia, aiding the settlers through her friendship with Captain John Smith, for whom she braved the 'darke night' and 'irksome woods' to warn of imminent dangers, or so he later claimed.[14] But for all Smith's mythologizing of the young girl's role in apparently saving his life when he was taken before her father and subjected to a form of initiation he had clearly misunderstood, there can be little doubt that genuine affection grew up between the swashbuckling settler and Powhatan's daughter. After Smith left the colony in 1609, relations between the settlers and Virginia's native

In a kidnap plot engineered by Captain Samuel Argall, the Indian Iopassus and his wife entice Pocahontas to board Argall's ship, which will take her back to Jamestown.

inhabitants deteriorated into warfare and Pocahontas drops from sight, married not to some tributary chieftain as one might expect but to a simple captain named Kocoum.[15]

There she might have stayed had not Captain Samuel Argall chanced upon her in 1613 while trading for corn with the Patawomeck Indians on Passapatanzy Creek, which feeds into the Potomac River. Enlisting the help of an old Indian friend, whom he bribed with a copper kettle, Argall enticed Pocahontas on board his ship and took her as a hostage back to Jamestown, hoping to force Powhatan to give up captured English booty and prisoners in return for his much loved daughter.[16]

News of the kidnap even reached England. 'They have taken a daughter of a king that was theyre greatest ennemie,' reported John Chamberlain, 'as she was going a feasting upon a river to visit certain friends.' The settlers laid down three conditions for Pocahontas's release: that Powhatan should deliver up English fugitives, hand back any English weapons or arms, and supply 300 quarters of corn. 'The first two he performed redilie, and promiseth the other at theyre harvest, yf his daughter may be well used in the meane time,' said Chamberlain. 'But this ship brought no commodities from thence but only these fayre tales and hopes.'[17]

Powhatan's delay in securing his daughter's release may have contributed to Pocahontas's growing estrangement from her own people and her acceptance of Rolfe as a suitor. No one mentioned her Indian husband, Kocoum. Rolfe presented his relations with Pocahontas as a love match, admitting to Governor Dale that his 'hartie and best thoughts' were lodged with her, and that for a long time they had been 'so intangled, and inthralled in so intricate a laborinth, that I was even awearied to unwinde my selfe thereout'. Pocahontas in turn showed her 'great apparance of love to me', as well as her desire to be taught and instructed in the knowledge of God, 'besides her owne incitements stirring me up hereunto'.[18] And so they were married in early April 1614, presumably in the church at Jamestown.[19] Governor Dale approved the marriage, as did Powhatan, who sent an uncle and two of his sons to witness the event. She bore Rolfe a son, Thomas, and relations between the settlers and the Indians improved.[20]

On putting her faith in Rolfe's Christian god, Pocahontas abandoned her given name Amonute and her secret name Matoaka, rarely revealed in case it was used by malevolent people seeking to lay a curse on her, taking instead the name Rebecca. In the Old Testament Rebecca is the wife of Abraham's son Isaac, chosen in accordance with Abraham's wish that Isaac should marry one of his own people rather than any of the indigenous Canaanites among whom they lived.[21] The implication of her new name is plain to see. Rolfe was marrying a Christian, not a heathen, and so escaped the prohibition on intermarriage handed down to Abraham's posterity.

A curious episode followed, in which the already married Dale dispatched an envoy to Powhatan asking the chief to give him his youngest daughter as wife, bedfellow and 'nearest companion', having heard of her 'exquisite perfection'. The envoy was Ralph Hamor, accompanied by the boy interpreter, Thomas Savage. At the start of their meeting Powhatan enquired after Pocahontas's welfare, 'her mariage, his unknowne sonne, and how they liked, lived and loved together'. Hamor told him that his daughter was 'so well content that she would not change her life to returne and live with him, whereat he laughed heartily, and said he was very glad of it'. But the interview went badly, and Powhatan rebuffed Dale's request for Pocahontas's younger sister, saying that he had sold her a few days previously to a great chief for two bushels of Roanoke beads made from oyster shells, which the Indians used as currency. Hamor tried unsuccessfully to persuade Powhatan to recall his daughter and pay back the beads, offering him three times the price for the girl, who was anyway 'not full twelve yeeres old' and therefore not officially marriageable. Still Powhatan refused, berating Dale for his desire 'to bereave me of two of my children at once'.[22]

Despite her change of name, Mistress Rebecca Rolfe remained Pocahontas to English eyes, the exotic Indian princess who had captured the heart of a native Englishman. Intent on deriving as much propaganda value as possible from her conversion to Christianity and her evident gentility (she learned to speak English fluently and became 'very formall and civill after our English manner'),[23] the Virginia Company arranged for the Rolfes and baby Thomas to accompany Sir Thomas Dale back to England with a retinue of Virginia Indian attendants, men and women. They arrived in Plymouth in June 1616 and travelled on to London, where the Rolfes lodged initially in the Bell Savage Inn on Ludgate Hill between St Paul's Churchyard and Fleet Street. The news was of sufficient interest for John Chamberlain to inform Sir Dudley Carleton about the Virginians' arrival, 'among whom the most remarquable person is Poca-huntas (daughter of Powatan a kinge or cacique of that countrie) married to one Rolfe an English man'.[24]

The Rolfes stayed on into winter, moving from the Bell Savage Inn into a house in Brentford close to the River Thames, convenient for court and blessed with better air. Economy may also have dictated the move, for as Chamberlain confided to Carleton early in the new year, 'you might thincke her and her worshipfull husband to be somebody, yf you do not know that the poore companie of Virginia out of theyre povertie are faine to allow her fowre pound a week for her maintenance'.[25]

For all Chamberlain's sneering, Pocahontas was accepted into high society and caused a considerable stir. The Bishop of London hosted a dinner in her honour at Lambeth Palace, where she was treated with 'festival state and pomp';[26] the Reverend Samuel Purchas was one of the dinner guests. Invited to court by King James, she was 'graciously used' by court officials and 'well placed' at the masque performed to celebrate Twelfth Night, a singular honour that showed she enjoyed the king's favour. Later accounts suggest that she was frequently admitted to wait upon Queen Anne, having been introduced by the Lady Delaware, and was 'carried to many plays, balls, and other public entertainments, and very respectfully received by all the ladies about the court'.[27] Her behaviour throughout was impeccable, and those who met her generally concluded that 'God had a great hand in her conversion, and they have seene many English Ladies worse favoured, proportioned and behavioured'. John Smith eventually went to visit her in Brentford 'with divers of my friends', but the meeting did not go well; she was angry with him for the way he had mistreated her father, and because she had thought him dead all this time and he had not bothered to make contact with her.[28]

Engraved during her visit to London in the winter of 1616, Simon de Passe's fashionable portrait of Pocahontas attests to her contemporary celebrity.

As a mark of her celebrity, she had her portrait engraved by the Dutch artist Simon de Passe, who had established a highly successful engraving practice in London. Portraits of noblemen, scholars and royalty were his speciality.[29] John Chamberlain called it 'a fine picture of no fayre Lady', poking fun at Pocahontas's 'tricking up and high stile and titles'.[30] This is the only known portrait of her taken from life, and it apparently sold well. Ignoring her popular nickname, de Passe introduces her as Matoaka alias Rebecca, daughter to the mighty Prince Powhatan, Emperor of Virginia, converted and baptized in the Christian faith and wife to the worshipful Mr John Rolff. Clutching a fan of ostrich feathers, she wears the embroidered velvet mantle of the early Stuart court and a mannish beaver hat of the sort favoured by Queen Anne but denounced by King James, her neck and wrists encased by a starched white ruff and cuffs.[31] Her solemn expression is hard to read: does she feel trapped by her English finery or is she rather projecting the dignity of her position?

By mid-January 1617 Mistress Rolfe was set to return to Virginia, 'though sore against her will', according to Chamberlain. The man charged with taking her back was her kidnapper, Captain Samuel Argall, then returning to Virginia to take over as lieutenant governor and to found a private plantation of his own. She was still apparently in good health, and while they waited for a favourable wind, the Rolfes received a grant of £100 from the Virginia Company to found a mission for native children, perpetuating Pocahontas's propaganda value. The warrant drew attention to her 'godly and virtuous example' and to the couple's promise to 'employ their best endeavors to the winning of that People to the knowledge of God, and embracing of true religion'.[32]

They sailed as far as Gravesend, where the Lady Rebecca's health suffered an unexpected decline. Taken off the ship, she died and was buried on 21 March 1617 in the chancel of St George's church, her husband's name wrongly recorded in the parish records, which describe her as 'Rebecca Wrothe wyff off Thomas Wroth gent A

Virginian Lady'.[33] No one thought to record the cause of her death at little more than twenty years old, but it may have been a form of dysentery known as the bloody flux, which infected the convoy of ships on which she sailed. Chamberlain duly sent notice to Sir Dudley Carleton that the 'Virginian woman (whose picture I sent you) died this last weeke at Gravesend as she was returning homeward'.[34] John Rolfe sailed on to Virginia, leaving their son Thomas in the care of Sir Lewis Stukely, Vice-Admiral of Devonshire, until Rolfe's brother could take him.[35] Clearly a man who felt the need to justify his actions to escape public censure, he later explained to Sir Edwin Sandys that baby Thomas was dangerously sick and the child's attendants 'hadd need of nurses themselves', adding a postscript that asked Sandys to remember him for some command and some estate of land to be confirmed 'to me and my childe'.[36]

In a curious parallel to the story of the Jamestown brides, at least two and perhaps three of Pocahontas's female attendants stayed on in London under the overall care of the Virginia Company.[37] One of the maids went into service with a mercer in Cheapside but by May 1620 had developed consumption and was taken in by a Mr Gough living in the Blackfriars, close to the Bell Savage Inn where the Rolfes had first lodged. This was probably the Reverend William Gough, cousin to the Virginian minister Alexander Whitaker who had presided over Rebecca Rolfe's conversion to the Christian faith. Gough took great pains to comfort the maid in body and soul, and the company agreed to contribute twenty shillings a week for two months towards the 'Phisick and Cordialles' necessary for her recovery. As ever the company was slow to pay, forcing one of its heaviest investors, Sir William Throckmorton, to reach into his own pocket.[38]

Later that same year the company appointed a four-man committee to take care of the two Virginian maids remaining in the custody of accountant William Webb. The committee hoped to place the women 'in good services' where they might learn 'some trade to live by hereafter'. [39] Since Webb personally vouched for Mary Morrice, one of the Jamestown brides, she would surely have come into contact with either or both of the surviving Virginians, now christianized as Mary and Elizabeth.

Anxious to free the company from the weekly expense of their maintenance, Webb proposed in June 1621 that some course might be found to 'dispose' of the two Indian maids. The sums were quite significant: five pounds for Elizabeth's board for eight months with a Captain Maddison, and up to twelve shillings a week on medical care for Mary at the height of her sickness. [40] Yet given that the company was at this time busy putting together its shipments of brides for the Virginian planters, the solution adopted was a curious one: the pair were to be kitted out and sent overseas with a servant apiece, not to their homeland but to the Summer Isles, as Bermuda was then called, 'towards their preferment in marriage with such as shall accept of them with that means'. [41] Although the Virginia Company had happily employed Pocahontas as an instrument of propaganda, it seems that including two of her attendants in the bridal shipments to Virginia was a step too far.

So Mary and Elizabeth sailed to Bermuda on the *James* with two boys each, to be married to whoever would have them. [42] With them went ample stores of oatmeal, brandy, vinegar and oil, and a trousseau that was far more generous than that provided for the Jamestown brides, comprising coifs, cross cloths, neckcloths, material for smocks, a gown and a petticoat each, sletia (a kind of cloth), blue aprons, stockings and shoes, trunks, a bible and a psalter, soap and starch, thread, girdles, pins, laces and needles, as well as beds, rugs and plentiful clothes for the boys. Altogether, William Webb's charges for equipping and transporting the two Virginian maids and their boys amounted to £71 4s. or £35 12s. per maid, three times the outlay on each of the Jamestown brides.

After the two Virginians were converted and married, it was hoped that 'they might be sent to their Countrey and kindred to civilize them'. At least one survived the voyage and found 'a husband fit for her', a union celebrated by more than one hundred guests 'and all the dainties for their dinner' that could be provided.[43] Like so much of their tantalizing story, precisely who they married or what happened to them is unknown.

CHAPTER SEVEN

Maids to the Rescue

The precarious state of the Virginia Company's finances, clearly seen in its dealings with the Indian maids, exacerbated tensions between the different factions on its governing council, which erupted into open warfare a couple of years before the maids left for Jamestown. Of the two principal camps, one-time Treasurer Sir Thomas Smythe headed the 'old guard' of rich City merchants whose many commercial interests enabled them to ride out the colony's lean early years. Bequeathed an enormous inheritance by his merchant father, Smythe belonged to two of the twelve great livery companies of London, the Skinners and the Haberdashers, and his fingers reached into virtually every overseas pie baked by the Merchant Adventurers, Muscovy and Levant Companies, the Somers Isles (Bermuda) Company and the East India Company, several of which he served as governor.[1]

Leading the other faction was Sir Edwin Sandys, a noted parliamentarian from the landed gentry and the man chiefly responsible for the plan to send marriageable women to Virginia. The Sandys faction included country gentlemen caught up in the adventure of the New World, lesser merchants and citizens infected with the 'microbe of speculation'[2] who needed a more immediate return on their investment, and a sprinkling of great lords who directed their patronage at Virginia much as they supported charities and the arts. Chief among these was the

By the time the maids left for Virginia, Sir Thomas Smythe's reign as treasurer of the Virginian Company had come to an end.

handsome, impetuous and much-lauded Henry Wriothesley, third Earl of Southampton, who invested heavily in the company and in the scheme to bring brides to Jamestown. Like Smythe and his backers, making a profit mattered to both Sandys and Southampton, but 'the well carrying of the publick is of more importance'.[3] Holding the balance of power on the company's increasingly splintered council was a third faction led by Robert Rich, the second Earl of Warwick, who was principally interested in using Virginia as a base for piracy and privateering against the Spanish further south. For the moment Warwick gave his support to Sandys, but he would later switch sides with disastrous consequences for all concerned.

Portraits of the two principal players throw into relief the differences between them. Like Pocahontas, Sir Thomas Smythe had his portrait engraved by Simon de Passe, dressed in a fashionable beaver hat that declared his status and his wealth. Clasping a navigational chart in his right hand, he wears the furred robe of a City alderman over a brocaded doublet, his neck and wrists encased in starched white ruffs. Icons of overseas trade complete the image of a man of global affairs: anchors, a ship, barrels and sacks of merchandise.[4] For all the accusations of mismanagement and profiteering that his opponents would later sling at his head, his features are sympathetically drawn – firm, practical and energetic certainly, but kindly too; like his father and mother before him, he was celebrated for his charity.[5]

Altogether sparer in tone, the portrait of Sir Edwin Sandys hangs in the wood-panelled dining room of Graythwaite Hall, Cumbria, still in the hands of the Sandys family, next to portraits of his father, mother and youngest brother George, who sailed to Virginia shortly before the Jamestown brides. Hatless and soberly dressed, Sir Edwin holds himself aloof, a man of reason and undoubted intelligence, who calmly returns your gaze, his small pointy beard distinctly Jacobean in contrast to Smythe's Elizabethan finery.[6]

The discontent that had long rumbled among members of the Virginia Company's governing council came to a head at its quarter court of 28 April 1619. Having led the company as treasurer since its inception, Smythe stepped down from the post, claiming the pressure of other business, and Sir Edwin Sandys was elected in his stead with the aid of a 'ballatinge box' brought in for the occasion. Sandys won the election by a clear majority: fifty-nine balls cast in his favour, compared with twenty-three for his nearest rival, the merchant Sir John Wolstenholme, whose wife's brother was married to

Sir Edwin Sandys supplanted Sir Thomas Smythe as treasurer of the Virginia Company and masterminded its plan to send the Jamestown brides to Virginia.

Smythe's sister, and eighteen for Smythe's son-in-law Alderman Robert Johnson.[7]

In choosing Sir Edwin Sandys as its new leader, the company also needed a new venue for its meetings and day-to-day business, for reasons both practical and political. Throughout his long regime Sir Thomas Smythe had housed the offices of the Virginia Company and the other companies he directed on the ground floor of his spacious house on Philpot Lane, a narrow street close to Billingsgate in the commercial heart of the City running north from Little East

Cheap up to Fenchurch Street. As befitted an active merchant, he had installed a strongroom to house documents and company assets, while upstairs he displayed a collection of curiosities brought home by his ships' captains from voyages around the globe; his suitably multiracial household included two Virginian Indians and a homesick boy from the Cape.[8]

The London home of Sir Edwin Sandys was better suited to his life as a leading member of the gentry than as the director of a great trading enterprise. It lay on fashionable Aldersgate Street just outside the City gates, said to resemble an Italian street more than any other in London on account of its straightness and the spaciously uniform houses that lined both sides. Others who took up residence here included the Earls of Westmorland, Pembroke and Shaftesbury, and the poet John Milton.

Better equipped as a place of business was the home of Sandys' deputy, the merchant John Ferrar, who lived with his extended family on St Sithes Lane (now the tiny Sise Lane) in the geographical heart of the City between Budge Row and St Pancras Lane. Heading the Ferrar household until his death in 1620 was John's father Nicholas, another respected merchant adventurer, who 'kept a good table' at which he entertained many of the great Elizabethan adventurers, among them Sir John Hawkins, Sir Francis Drake and Sir Walter Raleigh.[9] Nicholas had married Mary Woodnoth from Cheshire, who gave him seven children and survived well into her eighties: this is the Mrs Ferrar who commended the mother of the Jamestown bride Alse Dauson as 'verrie honest'. She sounds a remarkable woman, the sort to fill the gut of Pinch Belly in the broadside ballad of 1620. 'We are told that she was beautiful, bright-haired, and fair,' wrote a Victorian divine, 'upright even to her eightieth year; highly educated, of a strong judgment, a wise and even temper, so that her choleric husband declared that in their five-and-forty years of marriage she had never given him cause for anger.'[10] Also living in the household was John Ferrar's troublesome second wife Bathsheba, daughter of merchant Israel Owen; his young son Nicholas; his mother and his niece Mary Collet; and two unmarried brothers, Richard and Nicholas, as well as servants, apprentices and visitors.[11]

After Sandys took over as treasurer in the spring of 1619, the company met for the most part at St Sithes Lane and occasionally at Southampton House in Holborn, home of the Earl of Southampton, or at Sandys' house on Aldersgate Street when the elder Nicholas Ferrar lay dying.[12] Philpot Lane continued to be used occasionally, provoking several bad-tempered exchanges between the different factions. Soon after the transfer of power, Smythe's son-in-law Robert Johnson requested that the adventurers in the separately funded general magazine should be allowed to meet there, arguing that Smythe was 'one of the greatest and principall Adventurers and not able to goe to any other place'. The magazine was the monopoly supplier of essential provisions to the colony, and as its principal investors, Smythe and Johnson were suspected of milking the profits for their private gain. Sandys snapped back that if the adventurers paid back to the Virginia Company the £800 they had invested in the magazine, 'they might meete in what place they pleased'.[13]

In September of that year (1619) Sandys wrote privately to Southampton about the 'malignancie' of Smythe and Johnson his deputy. 'I had thought that no man, carrying the face of an honest man, could have been displeased with beeing called to an Account: beeing the onlie justification & discharge of a true man. But it hath fallen out otherwise.'[14] To be fair, the company minutes document only Sandys' version of events. No records survive from Smythe's period of office, and those kept by the ever-faithful John Ferrar may be partial in their account. Determined to blame the colony's current privations on Smythe's stewardship, Sir Edwin Sandys reminded the council that in April 1618 – one year before he took office – the colony had numbered just 400 men, women and children, of whom at most 200 men were able 'to sett hand to husbandry and butt one Plough was goinge in all the Country'. All this was the fruit of twelve years' labour and 'above one hundred thousand marks expences' paid out of the public treasury, not counting the £8,000 to £9,000 of company debt and the investments made by adventurers in their own private plantations. Despite all the land, men, provisions and livestock delivered to Captain Argall at the start of his deputy governorship, by the time Sandys took over as treasurer of the London company in May 1619, everything was 'gone and Consumed ther beinge not lefte att that time to the Company either the land aforesaid or any Tennant, Servant, Rent, or Trybute Corne Cowe, or Saltworke and butt six Goates'.[15]

Sandys' plan to turn the company around was to send out more people and to diversify the colony's economy, thereby making it more self-reliant and less dependent on tobacco. Reasoned and methodical as ever, he prepared a comprehensive plan to enlarge the plantation and to restore the company's land in Virginia, 'now lately decayed'. After preliminary discussions, it was approved unopposed at the company's great court of 17 November 1619, at which neither Smythe nor his son-in-law was present.[16] The proposal to transport one hundred potential brides – described in Chapter 5 – appeared as the third item of Sandys' plan, after raising the number of men to be sent out as public tenants and dispatching one hundred young people to become their apprentices. Sandys even came to the meeting with the draft of a broadside seeking 'Laborers and Husbandmen, Artificers and manuall Trades' as public tenants, which was read to the meeting and approved by public vote.

On the surface Virginia looked set to prosper. The council was much preoccupied with implementing the Sandys' plan and with various proposals to educate and bring up 'the Infidells children to the true knowledge of God & understanding of righteousnes' by establishing a college at Henricus (or Henrico) and taking children into settlers' homes.[17] Yet for all his energetic leadership, Sandys' formal role as treasurer was unexpectedly short-lived. When he stood for re-election at the quarter court of 17 May 1620, after just one year in office, the king intervened, sending word to the meeting that he wanted the council to choose its next treasurer from just four names he put forward: Sir Thomas Smythe, Alderman Robert Johnson, the diplomat Sir Thomas Roe, the merchant Mr Maurice Abbott 'and noe other'.[18] The intention was clearly to exclude Sandys, whom the king had reviled ever since 1604, when Sandys' speeches to parliament had disrupted his royal plan to unite the two kingdoms of England and Scotland, calling instead for a period of calm reflection.[19]

The king's intervention put the council 'att an exceedinge pinch'. While they did not wish to appear disloyal towards their sovereign, his message breached their privilege of free elections. In the end, they decided to delay their choice until the following quarter court. A committee would meet at Southampton House to draft a letter to King James, while Sandys was asked to remain as treasurer until the king's pleasure was known.[20]

Although the king remained adamantly opposed to the re-election of Sandys as treasurer, he withdrew his insistence that they should choose one of his nominees, claiming merely that he wanted them to elect 'such a one as might att all times and occasions have free access unto his royall personn',[21] which obviously excluded Sandys. 'Choose the Devill if you will, but not Sir Edwin Sandys' was his reputed reaction,[22] and after much toing and froing a compromise was reached at the quarter court of 28 June 1620. Sandys' close ally the Earl of Southampton was nominated for the post of treasurer 'with much joy and applause' and elected unopposed by the simple raising of hands, winning the dispensation that he would be allowed to involve himself in court business no more than 'his owne more waightie buisinesses did permitt'. Despite the change in titular leadership, Sir Edwin Sandys remained in effective control of the company, with John Ferrar returned as deputy by a secret ballot.

Bad feeling between the different factions was not the company's only flashpoint, however. Just as the 'weed' tobacco triggered dependency among smokers and Virginia's fledgling economy, so the company found itself utterly dependent on the running lotteries for funds despite public disquiet over their effects and the company's own efforts to find other sources of income. During Southampton's term as treasurer, Sandys proposed to continue the lotteries until the end of 1620, 'if there may be found places so many where to keepe them', and to collect the subscriptions owed by lords, knights, gentlemen, merchants and other citizens.[23] Just four months later, in November 1620, the council admitted that the lottery was 'now of late very much disgraced', and they sought ways of delivering it from the 'many fowle aspersions unjustly cast uppon itt by malignnant tounges', noting that it had already sent 800 people to Virginia to 'the great advancement of that Plantacon'.[24] But realistically the company had no other reliable source of income. Just under half the estimated £18,000 needed to finance the Sandys plan for the colony was scheduled to come from the lottery (£8,000), the rest from calling in debts and reckonings (£9,300) and a mere £700 from donations to the college at Henricus.[25] So when the king abruptly ordered the lottery to be closed down, early in 1621, company finances were thrown into disarray.

The request to suspend the lottery had in fact originated with parliament, summoned by James to relieve his own financial difficulties. But the prime parliamentary mover against it was the king's man Lord Cranfield, and debate was 'spirited, even acrimonious', with one member claiming that 'these lotteries do beggar every country they come into. Let Virginia lose rather than England'.[26] The king was only too happy to concede to parliament's request, declaring that he had never liked the lottery, suspecting that it would prove 'hurtfull and distastefull', and that he had agreed to it only 'upon information that the plantation could not subsist without it'. The speed with which the running lotteries were suspended was nonetheless dramatic. The king's reply to parliament was delivered on 26 February. On 4 March the Privy Council drew up instructions to suspend the lotteries and a proclamation was issued four days later, commanding the Virginia Company to end all its lotteries 'untill such time as Wee shall declare Our further pleasure therein'.[27]

The effect on poor John Ferrar's accounts was instantaneous. Not only did the proclamation dramatically reduce the flow of money into the company's coffers but it also left it with a stock of prize plate that could not be 'turned into money, wthout to[o] great losse'. Public confidence in the Virginia Company was also declining fast. Shares nominally valued at £12 10s. were changing hands for as little as forty or fifty shillings, thereby depriving the company of fresh revenue and discouraging those who had paid the full share price.[28] Debts were mounting and new proposals put on ice, including one from a gentleman 'of good Account and sufficiency' who claimed he could procure and transport to Virginia 'at an easie rate' a number of young men and maids as company employees. The court thought the proposition worthy of thanks but found itself 'unhable in Cash to goe through with so great a charge'.[29] Even small sums needed to be pinched where they could, such as the weekly maintenance charge to support the two Virginia Indian maids who had stayed on in the capital;[30] and the company found itself unable to finance the deal it had struck with Captain Norton to set up a furnace making glass and beads for trading with the Indians. Norton's bill for personnel and materials was £80 higher than the £150 originally envisaged, and 'ther was nothinge left in Stocke to discharge so great a Sume'.[31]

The company's coffers were completely bare. It needed a solution to its cash crisis, and it needed it fast if the colony was to survive.

The company's response was commendably swift. The extraordinary court called for Thursday 12 July 1621 had discussed just two issues: where to obtain Europe's best silkworm seed (Valencia in Spain, apparently) and how to avoid settling Captain Norton's larger-than-expected bill to establish his glassworks in Jamestown. The company's solution was to 'release' Norton from his contract with them, or more truthfully to release the company from its obligation to pay him, by allowing individual adventurers to trade with him directly.

Four days later, at its general court of Monday 16 July 1621, this proposal developed into a much more ambitious plan to restore the company's finances by setting up four individual joint-stock ventures or 'magazines'. Each would solicit subscriptions from individual adventurers who would share the risks of the enterprise and also, crucially, the profits. Captain Norton's glassworks was one such enterprise, as was shipping marriageable women to the colony – a commodity that had its price like any other.

The glassworks trade set the blueprint for the others. As the senior official present, it will have fallen to deputy John Ferrar to remind those present that the expense of transporting Captain Norton's Italian workmen together with servants, wives and children (eleven people in all) plus furnishing the necessary clothing, food, tools and material was far more than originally agreed, and that the company's stock was 'no way able to undergoe the burthen of this new charge'. So private adventurers would be allowed to finance the operation for profit and Captain Norton discharged of his contract with the company. Although the record maintains that the adventurers did not wish to exclude the company altogether, since glass beads were likely to prove 'the Verie Coyne of that Country', the company clearly wished to share in any potential gains. So the proposition put to the meeting was to raise a joint stock of at least £400, the company bearing one quarter of the charge and thereby entitled to one quarter of the profits.[32]

The court also discussed the conditions under which the glassworks would operate: the patent granted the venture a monopoly to manufacture glass and beads for seven years. For each person transported, the adventurers would receive from the company fifty acres of land, and Lieutenant Jabez Whitaker would make available his recently constructed Jamestown guesthouse for the 'entertaynmt of their people some two monneths after their first landinge yt they may be able to build theire houses, and this may be specially recomended to the care of the Gouvernor to see itt done'. Nicholas Ferrar was appointed treasurer to the glassworks magazine, overseeing a committee made up of two company nominees and six adventurers. As the venture was already well advanced, investors were urged to pay their subscriptions by the following Thursday, 'for the more speedie dispatch away of Captaine Norton and the said Glassmen'.

Four separate rolls were then read out to the meeting in order to solicit subscriptions. The first was for a 'Magazine of Apparrell, and other necessary provisions such as the Colony stood in great need of', replacing the one wound up the previous year, its finances still under investigation. The second trade was for 'sendinge of 100: mayds to be made wives'; the third for advancing the glass furnace; and the fourth for equipping 'a Voyadge to trade with the Indians in Virginia for Furrs', aping the great fur trade established by the French and the Dutch further north. While few practical details were discussed, enthusiasm ran high, and these 'good undertakings were generally approved of and moved many then present to underwrite in the said Rolls'.

The court also discussed the appointment of a new doctor for the colony to replace Dr Lawrence Bohune, killed in a skirmish with the Spanish in the West Indies.[33] The new man was Dr John Pott, who would play a shabby role in the story of the Jamestown brides. Described as a master of arts 'well practised in Chirurgerie and Phisique, and expert allso in Distillinge of waters', he claimed to possess 'many other ingenious devices' which would – in his own estimation – render his service 'of great use unto the Colony'.

Already a master at advancing his own interests, Dr Pott asked to be released from the clause in Dr Bohune's contract requiring him to replace at his own cost any of his tenants who should die after their first year in Virginia. Unable to grant Dr Pott's request, since only quarter courts could confirm contractual changes, the court nonetheless awarded the doctor a 'Chest of Phisique' worth twenty pounds and ten pounds in physic books, both charged to the company and to remain in their possession. The company would pay his passage together with that of his wife, a man- and a maidservant, and any surgeons who accompanied him. Also discussed at the meeting was a plan to create monopolies of products such as sassafras, limiting their export in order to raise prices, bearing in mind 'the p[re]sent State of the Companies Stocke', which was 'utterly exhausted'.[34]

The parchment rolls soliciting subscriptions for the various magazines were opened at once; those for the maids and furs would remain open for at least six months.[35] Written by the clerk Tristram Conyam, the maids' subscription appealed to potential investors' Christian duty as well as to their commercial interests, framing the venture in compassionate – even biblical – terms: 'Wheras by long experience wee have founde that the Mynds of our people in Virgenia are much dejected, and ther hartes enflamed w[i]th a desire to returne for England only through the wants of the Comforts of Marriage without w[h]ich God saw that Man could not live contentedlie noe not in Paradize'.[36]

But the lack of women in Virginia had unfortunate economic consequences as well. Without home comforts, the company's planters looked on the colony as a place of short stay rather than a permanent residence, and so directed their labours towards short-term profits to the neglect not only of 'Staple Com[m]odities, but even the verie necessities of Mans liffe'. Supplying maids 'young, handsome, and honestlie educated' would change all that, declared the roll, 'judginge itt a Christian charitie to releive the disconsolate mindes of our people ther, and a speciall advancement to the Plantacon, to tye and roote the Planters myndes to Virginia by the bonds of wives and Children'. Those who subscribed to the

*In the Virginia Company's coat of arms, a maiden queen – her hair
dishevelled and wearing an eastern crown – proclaims the colony's
status alongside the Crown's other dominions of England and France
(a heraldic fiction), Scotland, and Ireland.*

joint-stock venture were to pay their subscriptions to Mr Thomas
Gibbs and his assistants, advancing a minimum £8. The cost of
those who died en route (or 'faile through Mortallytie' as the roll
delicately put it) was to be added to those who survived. The
women were to be disposed in marriage 'to the most honest and
industrious Planters who shall defray and sattisfie us the Charges
of their passages and provisions att such rates as they and our
Agents shall agree'.

The intention was that the stock raised from individual investors
would pay for the brides' clothing and transport to Virginia, estimated
at £8 each in the original subscription but later increased to £12
per woman.[37] Adventurers would reap their profits by 'charging'

the men who married them in the colony's prevailing currency of tobacco – initially 120 pounds in weight of tobacco for each bride but raised to 150 pounds by the time the *Warwick* departed for Jamestown because of 'the great shrinkage and other losses uppon the tobacco from Virginia.'[38] Not surprisingly, the company insisted that the price should be paid in 'the best leafe Tobacco', which was then valued at three shillings per pound.[39] At a bride price of 150 pounds of tobacco, this represented a profit of ten guineas (£10 10s.) on an outlay of £12, a generous rate of return. The company had no wish to repeat the fiasco over the charges for boy apprentices, for whom the planters had paid just sixty-six pounds in weight of tobacco. This should have raised £10 per boy, but the planters had paid in tobacco of the 'worst and basest' kind, raising just £5 per boy at a tobacco price of 1s. 6d. per pound.

Cash was not the only incentive on offer to investors. Under the headrights system of land distribution, each person who paid another's passage to the colony (ultimately the women's future husbands) would expect to receive fifty acres of Virginian land. But as London explained to the governor and council in Virginia, 'the Company for some weighty reason too long to relate, have ordered that no man marryinge these weomen expect the proportion of Land useually alotted for evry head: wch to avoid clamor or troble hereafter you shall do well to give them notice of'.

The 'weighty reason' referred to was that the adventurers who invested in the maids wanted the land for themselves. For each woman transported, the collective magazine was to receive fifty acres of Virginia at the first division of land, and a further fifty acres per head at the second.[40] Mr Gibbs, treasurer for the maids' magazine, would later propose to the company's council that the land owing for the maids (some 2,850 acres in the initial shareout) should be laid out together and called Maydes Towne, a proposal enthusiastically endorsed at the quarter court held on the afternoon of Wednesday 22 May 1622, a full two months after disaster had struck the company's well laid plans but before the company caught wind of the changed landscape in Virginia.[41]

The lists of subscribers are incomplete but at least forty-four men put themselves forward, about two thirds (twenty-nine) for the lowest amount of £8. Nine investors subscribed £16, including Nicholas Ferrar, accountant William Webb and the venture's treasurer Thomas Gibbs. Four men advanced £24, including deputy John Ferrar, and Gabriel Barbor, who had managed the Virginia lotteries. Among the most generous, Sir Edwin Sandys adventured £40, while the Earl of Southampton topped the list with £48.[42] The total volunteered was £560, a little short of the £672 needed to finance the transport and clothing of fifty-six women, assuming a cost per head of £12. But the rolls remained open and by its quarter court of 21 November 1621, the company claimed that £800 had been raised and some sixty maids dispatched to the colony. Compared with the other magazines, women were a more popular commodity than glass (which raised just £500 in joint stock) but less popular than furs (£900 raised) and the general magazine of clothing and other necessities (£1,800 raised and expected to 'returne good proffitt').[43] No women invested in the maids' magazine, but only *femes soles* had rights in law over their own property, and only a handful of women invested in the Virginia Company as a whole.

The company's ruling body would not concern itself with the maids for the rest of the summer. A final court held in late July heard from deputy John Ferrar that the Earl of Southampton and Sir Edwin Sandys had each subscribed £200 to the four magazines and a fifth one added for sending out to the colony shipwrights and other essential workers.[44] But attendance was dwindling, and court meetings were suspended until the end of September, 'as divers gentlemen were gone into the Country (according to their usuall manner att this time of the yeare)'.

Behind the scenes, however, finding, equipping and dispatching so many marriageable women to the colony required frenetic preparations. The speed with which this was achieved was truly astonishing: just four weeks elapsed between the court's decision to send the women as a self-financing trade (16 July) and the letter written to accompany the *Marmaduke* women to Virginia, addressed to the governor and council in Virginia and dated 12 August, setting out how the women were to be entertained in the colony before they might be 'provided of husbandes'. Even the company had to admit that one month was not enough time to do the job properly, 'for such was the hast of sendinge them away, as that straightned wth time we had no meanes to putt provisions aboard', promising to remedy the defect by sending supplies with the magazine ship that would follow shortly.[45]

It seems likely that preparations for these latest bride shipments to Virginia were at least nominally under way, since the idea of dispatching '100 young maydes to make wives as the former 90 lately sent' had been an explicit part of Sir Edwin Sandys' plan – discussed in July 1620 – for revitalizing the colony by sending and supporting more public tenants.[46] The difference was that these new women were to be encouraged to marry husbands who could afford them, independent planters rather than company tenants, and the marriages were to take place as quickly as possible to give the adventurers a swift return on their investment.

Sandys' earlier plan of 1620 had sought to reach potential recruits (tenants, wives and servants) in two ways: by printing details of the kind of people the company wanted and the conditions under which they would volunteer, and by word of mouth, or as the company put it, 'partly by help of such noble frends and others in remoter parts as have formerlie given great assistance beinge desyred in the like kinde'. A broadside had been duly published on 18 July 1620 detailing the kind of tradesmen it wanted and the terms it was offering, but saying nothing of potential brides.[47] Anyone wishing to respond to the company's call to 'good men' and 'such of those as shall be commended for their honest conversation' was asked to repair to the 'Citie of London, to Mr. Ferrar, Deputy to the Company, his house in St Sithes lane', where they were to be entertained at the company's expense 'til such time as they be shipped for Virginia'.

The women now being sought were part of a money-making venture, and Sandys hoped that the whole experiment would be so successful that more women would flock to the colony.[48] His officials needed to hand-pick only the very best, sifting through names already known to the company and calling on contacts in London and elsewhere to draw in women who were handsome enough in their person or wifely accomplishments to attract planters able and willing to pay the premium placed on their heads. As we saw in earlier chapters, they were remarkably successful at drawing in the daughters of the lower and middle gentry, helped no doubt by Sir Edwin Sandys' wide network of contacts throughout England, and at trawling for personable young women among London's great and good and those with close company connections.

The Ferrar household will have been a hive of activity throughout the normally quiet summer months. Assembling suitable women was just one of John Ferrar's organizational headaches. He also had to find ships ready and able to take the women on board, and to furnish them with the clothes and provisions they would need in their new life – the cause of 'exceedinge troble and labor unto us, being but a very few on whom so great a burthen hath lien'.[49] Simply keeping track of all the arrangements was a challenge. Christopher Martin, who adventured £8 in the enterprise and personally recommended Elizabeth Dag among the *Warwick* maids, submitted a bill of £8 for providing clothing for four named maids, only one of whom (Sandys' relative, Mistress Cicely Bray) is known to have travelled. Was this a scam to recoup his investment, or were several Christopher Martins involved? This one anyway promised 'that theese maydes shall proceede there voyadge or otherwyse he will repay the mony'.[50]

The task of recording the clothes provided for each of the *Marmaduke* maids fell to John Ferrar's brother Nicholas.[51] His list is modest but practical for a woman expecting to enter into a working partnership with her future husband: one petticoat, one waistcoat, two pairs of stockings, one pair of garters, two smocks, one apron, two pairs of shoes, one towel, two coifs and one cross cloth, as well as worsted wool for darning and yarn for knitting stockings. Made of linen or wool, the clothes seem scarcely adequate for Virginia's violent extremes in temperature. But there were touches of luxury in the dozen 'white Lambe gloves' supplied to the *Marmaduke* maids by perfumer William Piddock at a total cost of 4s.,[52] and twenty-eight hats with bands supplied by hatter Rowland Sadler at 3s. 6d. each, plus a further 1s. 6d. for nine pairs of strings.[53] Poor Sadler had to wait four months for payment, as doubtless did many other suppliers.

Altogether the cost of clothing each woman amounted to some £2, less than half the amount spent on clothes for each of the two Virginian maids, while sheets, canvas beds, bolsters and rugs added several pounds more.[54] Wearing clothes supplied by an employer would have seemed natural to anyone who had worked in service, although some of the gentry women might have found the uniformity unsettling. A few also took small chests or bundles with their own belongings, but either the records are incomplete or the number of women consigning their possessions to the hold was pitifully small. These included Mary Ghibbs's 'small pa[c]ke of cloaths', mistakenly left behind, and a box each for two maids living in Blackfriars, Anne Gibbson and Elizabeth Browne, who both sailed on the *Tiger*.[55] The *Marmaduke*'s bill of lading names items for just two individual maids: a trunk for the widowed Joan Fletcher, who travelled only as far as the Isle of Wight before turning back, and a 'Small boxe of linnen' for the young Jane Dier.[56]

The *Marmaduke's* bill of lading is one of several documents I request to view one freezing December morning at the Pepys Library of Magdalene College Cambridge, intrigued that apparently so few of the maids should have taken anything of their own to Virginia. I remember how cold I felt as I glanced at the nondescript items taken on board.

Before consigning your trunks or boxes to a ship's hold, the purser would ask you to acknowledge your belongings by signing the manifest, but in an age when writing was a skill determined by class and gender, most ordinary passengers simply made a mark of their initials. Among the twenty or so names on the *Marmaduke's* bill of lading, male and female, only one passenger had actually produced a signature: the widowed Joan Fletcher, whose writing is confident, even bold, each rounded letter inscribed with care. Young Jane Dier – and all the men entrusting their goods to the hold – could only manage a mark, in Dier's case a slightly shaky crossed 'I' and a capital 'D'.

It takes a moment for the significance of their different hands to register. Joan Fletcher's kin were upper gentry, the Egertons of Cheshire and Staffordshire, who had naturally taught their daughter to write. Jane Dier, on the other hand, was merely a waterman's daughter from the liberty of St Katharine's by the Thames, at best taught to read but not to write. Of all the Jamestown brides, the one woman who might definitely have recorded her experiences never travelled to Virginia.

For the others, I must rummage through what few records survive to piece together what happened to Catherine Finch, Audry Hoare, Ann Jackson and their fellows gathering on the quayside at East Cowes and the much larger cohort who sailed from Gravesend, among them Bridgett Crofte from Wiltshire, recommended by a lowly porter, and clothmaker's daughter Barbara Burchens. Although some of the gentry maids who travelled with them will surely have learned to write – Gervase Markham's daughter Elizabeth, for instance, and Sir Edwin Sandys' kinswoman Cicely Bray – nothing has yet come to light and probably never will. And so I must patiently retrace their steps wherever I can, sifting through the detritus of lives lived nearly four hundred years ago, the cracked pots and lost earrings that belonged to women just like them, searching for clues that might tell us what became of them in their new lives.

Maidens' Voyage

Sometimes [on] Neptunes bosome
Our ship is tost with waves
And every minite we expect,
The sea must be our graves
Sometimes on high she mounteth,
Then falls againe as low:
with waves:
with waves:
When stormie winds do blow.

Then with unfained prayers,
As Christian duty bindes,
Wee turne unto the Lord of hosts,
With all our hearts and minds,
To him we flee for succour,
For he we surely know,
can save;
can save,
How ere the wind doth blow.

*Martin Parker, 'Saylors for my money./ A new Ditty
composed in the praise of Saylors and Sea affaires',
London, printed for C. Wright, 1630?*

CHAPTER EIGHT

When Stormie Winds do Blow

Even a maid such as Ann Richards seeking new horizons will have felt more than a touch apprehensive as she stepped onto the ship that would carry her across the Atlantic. Fear of the sea burned deep in the national consciousness, stoked by dramatists and balladeers and the tempest narratives which the Virginia Company sought to suppress with only varying degrees of success. 'Upon the Seas are dangers cruel,' sang the valiant soldier to his sweetheart Betty in the popular ballad 'A Voyage to Virginia,' 'and many storms do there arise:/ To stay at home then be contented,/ whilst I do fight against my foe.'[1] But now the women were set on leaving, entrusting themselves to wooden troughs of ships that were 'but Tennis Balles for the windes to play withall… Tost from one wave to another; Nowe under-line; Nowe over the house; Sometimes Brickewal'd against a Rocke, so that the guttes flye out again; Sometimes strooke under the wide Hazzard, and farewell Mast(er) Marchant.'[2]

In the face of such dangers, real or imagined, it was customary for passengers and crew to pray for God's blessing and a safe delivery before embarking on their journey.[3] The *Warwick* women and all who sailed from Gravesend will have called at the parish church of St George, where Pocahontas lay buried in the chancel, and continued from there the short distance to the port, cutting their way as best they could through the frenzied coming and going of goods and people on the quayside.

You catch a sense of the operation's complexity from William Webb's jumbled accounts to the Virginia Company of monies disbursed on goods to be shipped to Virginia in the *George*, the *Charles*, the *Marmaduke*, the *Warwick* and the *Tiger*.[4] In June 1621 he was organizing porters and lightermen to convey casks of oatmeal, pease, cider and nails, as well as loads of coal, ironware, mounted guns, wooden planks and masts, bed cords, rabbits and straw for the oven. Onto the *George* went goods belonging to the colony's new governor Sir Francis Wyatt and its new treasurer George Sandys, Sir Edwin's youngest brother, both sailing on her to Jamestown. Webb's expenses for July and August extended to loading ship's biscuit onto the *Charles*; purchasing a selection of baking pans, pudding pans, porridge pans, chamber pots, pipkins and pots for rabbits and pigeons; salt; a book and ink; a chest for Mr Bowlton the preacher; a bed and rug for Dr Pott's servants; building cabins in the *Warwick*; an assortment of grindstones, woad seed and clothes for planter Myles Prickett; plus 'wharfidge & cranidge' fees for the *George*, *Charles*, *Marmaduke* and *Warwick*. That left just the *Tiger*, which departed a little later in September.

Throughout the summer months a certain James Hooper crops up repeatedly by name, presumably a trusted overseer of these many activities; his daily rate was 1s. 6d., plus the expense of dispatching him to Gravesend in July. Porters scurried about London, picking up loads from the Ferrars in St Sithes Lane, from Newgate Market, Houndsditch and Tower Street, while boats came and went to Blackwall, Galley Quay and out to the various ships; 'ferridg by water divers tymes' appears like a refrain. Here too, recorded on 21 July 1621, are expenses incurred transporting the *Marmaduke's* passengers and goods to Portsmouth and over to the Isle of Wight.

By the time the ships were ready to receive their passengers, most of the cargo will have been hoisted aboard and stowed away, much of it tightly packed in the inky-black hold at the bottom of the ship. Seasoned Virginia hand Captain John Smith explains how cargo is best stored: the heaviest casks loaded first, next to the ballast of gravel, stones or lead distributed around the sides of the ship, wedged in with short pieces of wood to prevent them rolling about in heavy seas.[5] Anything stored in the hold could not normally be accessed during the voyage, which might last two, three, even four months travelling westwards across the Atlantic. Aside from the clothes they were wearing, the women will have had with them at best a small bag of personal effects, leaving them without a proper change of clothes for the long voyage.

The Virginia Company's orders to the *Marmaduke*'s master, John Dennis, will have mirrored its covenant with William Ewens, master of the *George*, drawn up at the same time. Ewens promised that, before departing from the River Thames, the *George* would be 'stronge and staunch and in all thinges well fitted and provided', a promise that extended to furniture, mariners and seamen 'fitt and sufficient for the safe and good performance of the voyage'. He further promised that at the first opportunity of wind and weather he would set sail for the port of Cowes on the Isle of Wight, 'there to receauve and take into the said Shippe such Passengrs and goodes' as the company would direct.[6]

The covenant for the *Warwick* was clearer still, agreed on 24 August 1621 between the company and the ship's master, Nicholas Norburne, and its captain and co-owner, Arthur Guy. The ship was to arrive at Gravesend by 4 September and remain there for four days to receive passengers and goods; thereafter the company was committed to paying fifty shillings for each day's delay in loading either passengers or freight. As soon as the ships were ready, their orders were 'to sett sayle from England with the first oppertunity of Wynd and weather' and head straight for Jamestown, taking 'their direct course accordinge to their best skill and knowledge'.[7] If pirates threatened – a genuine hazard, as the *Tiger* discovered – the master's orders were to do everything possible 'to hinder their proceedinges or doe them violence'. The *Warwick* finally departed around the middle of September on a journey that lasted a full three months, as we know that she arrived in Jamestown on 19 December 1621, a long and wearisome voyage, even by the standards of the day.[8]

The route taken by the original settlers who founded Jamestown in 1607 went to Virginia via the Caribbean. While taking advantage of prevailing winds and currents and allowing passengers and crew to refresh themselves in the West Indies, this route risked provoking the hostility of Spanish men-of-war guarding their possessions. As early as 1610, Captain Samuel Argall had pioneered a more direct crossing, steering south-south-west to latitude 30 degrees north and then, leaving the Canary Islands a hundred leagues to the east, 'hee found the windes large, and so tooke his course direct West, & did never turne nearer the South'. Although becalmed for fourteen days around Bermuda, he completed the voyage in nine weeks and publicly vowed to achieve it in seven.[9]

Within two years Argall made good his promise, departing from the English coast on 23 July 1612 and arriving at Virginia's Point Comfort on 17 September with his men in good health and stores in good condition. This time, instead of sailing down to the Canaries, he had turned west some fifty leagues north of the Azores.[10] On both these shorter journeys Argall had sailed in summer, before storms engulfed the Atlantic and fog and ice created further hazards. As he knew only too well, after September the cold westerly and north-westerly Atlantic winds would make for a long passage, and after September the weather was 'so unconstant that goods cant be landed or shipt without hazard or damage'.[11]

Argall recommended September as the best time for magazine ships to arrive in the colony, bringing much-needed clothes before the onset of winter and shipping out tobacco and corn produced by the harvest. The colony's secretary John Pory urged new settlers to arrive in Virginia a little later, at 'ye leafefall and ye winter', having found both spring and summer 'fatall and unproffitable to new Comers'. To support his advice, Pory pointed to the arrivals in spring 1620 of the *London Marchant*, the *Jonathan* and the *Duty*, whose passengers 'Came in sickly, and too late eyther by plantinge, settinge, howinge, clearinge ground, or buyldinge, to doe any worke of ymportance'.[12] Among those on the first two ships were many of the ninety-odd women who formed the earlier shipment of brides sent to the colony.

While the maids who sailed on the *Marmaduke*, the *Warwick* and the *Tiger* escaped the health hazards of arriving in Virginia's sultry summer heat, they faced a tempestuous Atlantic crossing and the notoriously rough seas around Bermuda,[13] putting their trust in sailors whose job it was 'to save Ship, goods, and lives… especially in foule weather, the labour, hazard, wet and cold is so incredible I cannot expresse it…'.[14] The sea at its worst reduced even the voluble John Smith to silence.

All this lies ahead of them. Imagine the women as they thread their way through the teeming quayside, keeping their emotions in check as best they can as they step into the small boats hired to take them to their ship anchored in the roads, followed by an awkward scramble up the ladder and on to the deck, where fear gives way to dread as they contemplate the flimsy bark that will be their kingdom for the coming months.

They are entering an alien world, and a very masculine one, where they must live among sailors clad 'in scanty rags of appalling filthiness', where drunkenness is the norm, at least in the popular imagination, and discipline brutally enforced. Women were thought to bring bad luck at sea,[15] although plenty had by now travelled to Virginia, and relations between sailors and all their passengers were notoriously poor.

As they climbed on deck and took account of their surroundings the maids must have baulked at the numbers of people crowding with them onto the ship, passengers and crewmen. Ships were measured according to the weight of cargo they could carry: the

Marmaduke's 100 tons compares with 160 tons for the *Warwick*, just 40 tons for the *Tiger*, and 120 tons for the *Susan Constant*, the largest of the three merchant ships that had carried the first group of permanent settlers to Jamestown.[16] Larger than all of these was the *Mayflower*, at an estimated 180 tons, which had taken the Plymouth settlers to New England the previous year. The Jamestown brides aboard the *Marmaduke* were crammed with a total of some eighty passengers and a crew of between fourteen and eighteen officers and men[17] into a ship that measured no more than 116 feet from prow to stern, and nearly 25 feet at its waist.[18] The larger *Warwick* carried one hundred passengers and as many as twenty-two officers and crew, plus a good share of the general magazine of supplies sent out to the colony as one of the self-financing trades designed to attract investment from individual adventurers.[19]

You can board a replica of the *Susan Constant* moored at the Jamestown Settlement in Virginia and pace the length of the open deck between the raised forecastle and quarterdeck at either end. It takes less than fifteen paces to walk from the door to the cook room in the forecastle to the accommodation for the ship's executive officers in the stern, with a great cabin for the master and other cabins for the mates and the carpenter. Other senior crew members slept in boarded cabins in the gun room and in the forecastle, where space would also be found for high-ranking passengers. The remaining seamen slept on straw mattresses or hammocks in the spaces in between.[20]

While the Jamestown brides were surely quartered together during the long voyage, their status did not merit special treatment and there were anyway too many of them. Assuming they boarded when the ship was ready to sail, they will have been ushered with the other passengers to a grated hatch in the upper deck and directed down a short ladder to the gun deck or lower hold below, a space known as the 'tween deck, which was situated above the cargo hold and between the bulkhead shutting off the gun room at the stern and the forepeak at the bows. On the larger *Mayflower* this space measured an estimated 78 feet from the bow of the ship to the bulkhead, and 19 feet across its widest point.[21] A woman of small to ordinary height could stand upright here, since the headroom was at least 5 feet 4 inches and more in the spaces between the beams, but only when the deck was unencumbered.[22]

Aside from any accommodated at either end of the lower hold, the women will have shared the central 'tween-deck space with the other passengers – and not just people, either. As well as the mounted guns along either side, which needed space around them in case of hostile encounters, lighter freight was stored here together with anything required during the voyage.[23] Just the year before, the crew of the 160-ton ship carrying Dr Bohune was forced to resort to delaying tactics after encountering hostile Spaniards in the Caribbean, 'being pestered with goods and fardels [bundles] betweene the deckes, and altogether unprovided for any fight'.[24] Despite the known dangers of encumbering the deck around the guns, Virginia's council nonetheless wrote to the company in London soon after the *Warwick*'s safe arrival in Jamestown, expressly requesting that perishable supplies such as silkworm seed and foodstuffs should 'nott bee stowde in the holde butt betweene the Decks, for yt the heate of the Holde will spoyle whatt Corne or seede soe ever you shall sende'.[25]

Here among the guns, casks and trusses of ship's stores and perishable cargo, and the jostle of humanity, the *Marmaduke* women slept two to a makeshift bed, lying on straw mattresses placed inside small wainscot boxes that could be stacked one on top of the other during the daytime, covered with rugs provided for their use by the Virginia Company. Those sailing on the *Warwick* enjoyed a little more privacy, as William Webb's accounts tell us that £1 11s. was spent on constructing cabins for them.[26] These were almost certainly hanging cabins made of canvas, either suspended from hooks or stretched over wooden frames that could be folded away to give the passengers more space during the day.

I can only speculate how the women chose their bedfellows. On the *Marmaduke* Yorkshire-born Margaret Bourdman was recommended by Catherine Finch's brother Erasmus, so the pair were likely companions. Age, birthplace and station in life will also have determined friendships between the women as they settled down for the voyage. Sailing on the *Warwick* were three widows aged twenty-five or twenty-six (Ann Richards, Marie Daucks and Elizabeth Grinley), two young women of roughly similar ages from Lothbury in London (cutler's daughter Frauncis Broadbottom and baker's daughter Sara Crosse) and four gentry daughters whose ages ranged from sixteen (Elizabeth Markham), nineteen (Elizabeth Nevill) and twenty-two (Lucy Remnant) up to twenty-five (Cicely Bray).

At least some light and ventilation penetrated the 'tween deck from the gun ports and the grated wooden hatch to the upper deck, which was closed in bad weather to stop seawater pouring into the hold. Down here the women lived, slept, ate, shat, sickened and recovered, penned like chickens in the gloom and allowed on deck only when their presence would not disturb the routine business of running a ship under sail.

Once all the passengers and goods are safely aboard, and the last tubs of beef, pork and salted fish secured by plates of iron bolted onto the side of the ship, the master commands the company to set sail. Even if the passengers down below can see very little, they can hear the master's shouted commands barked in the nautical language recorded by Captain John Smith in his dictionary for young seamen instructing them to:

> get the sailes to the yards, and about your geare, or, Worke on all hands, stretch forward your maine Halliards, hoise your Sailes halfe mast high. Predy!, or, Make ready to set saile. Crosse your yards, bring your Cable to the Capsterne. Boatswaine, fetch an Anchor aboord. Breake ground, or,

Weigh Anchor! Heave a head! Men into the Tops! Men upon the yards! Come, is the Anchor a' pike?… What, is the Anchor away? Yea, yea! Let fall your fore-saile. Tally!… Who is at the Helme there? Coile your Cables in small fakes! Hale the Cat! A Bitter,… belay,… loose fast your Anchor with your shank-painter! Stow the Boat![27]

Starting out from the Isle of Wight, the *Marmaduke*'s master could choose to sail east or west from Cowes depending on the winds and out into the English Channel, guided by a skilled pilot past the island's dangerous coastline, which presented 'a continuall ridge and range of craggy Cliffes, and Rockes, and Bankes very dangerous for Saylers, as the Needles, so called by reason of their sharpenes'.[28] Negotiating the Thames estuary from Gravesend and on round the coasts of southern England was scarcely any easier. The water poet John Taylor made the journey in 1623, rowing in a wherry to Portsmouth with four crew. Battered by strong winds and high seas, they were driven ashore at Dungeness on the Kent coast and again near Hastings, looking for all the world 'like five poore rats halfe drownd', and stumbling onto the beach near Goring, only to be mistaken for pirates by a suspicious constable.[29]

Bad weather and similar emergencies forced many a vessel to seek shelter in ports along the south coast. One famously delayed departure was that of the *Mayflower* carrying the pilgrims to New England in 1620, forced to return to Dartmouth and again to Plymouth when her sister ship the *Speedwell* supposedly sprang a leak.[30] Captain John Smith's last planned voyage to New England failed even more spectacularly when his three good ships were wind-bound for three whole months at Plymouth until they sailed instead for Newfoundland, 'which was to me and my friends no small losse'.[31]

But finally, all sight of England has vanished and the passengers settle into the monotonous rhythms of the sea. Although not as regimented as the sailors' hours, which are parcelled into four-hour watches, their lives on board are reduced to a routine of days, nights, sleeping and meals, the monotony broken by occasional forays into the fresh air on deck. The women have plenty of time to get to know each other and the other passengers, and to form friendships that will hold fast on the other side of the Atlantic.

On the *Marmaduke* Ann Jackson was a point of contact with the 'twelve lustie youths' bound for her brother's settlement of Martin's Hundred, although nothing suggests that romantic bonds were formed between the young men and any of her companions. The Virginia Company would anyway have disapproved, as it hoped to marry the women off to richer planters. Ursula Lawson was another link between the passengers, since she was travelling out with her kinsman, seasoned planter Richard Pace and his wife, Isabella. Sailing on the *Warwick*, nineteen-year-old Mary Ellyott accompanied her 'father-in-law' (more likely her stepfather) Maximillian Russell, who was also bound for Martin's Hundred; and the orphaned Alse Dollinges from Dorset clearly knew Goodwife Bennet 'that now coms along in the Warwicke', who had vouched for her 'honest Conversation'. Among their many fellow passengers on the *Warwick*, Tristram Conyam recorded the names of Christopher Stokes, his wife and children, and of Goodwife Unwon and her two children, identifying her as the wife of a tenant of Southampton Hundred who had previously travelled out with Captain Bluett, the probable father of Jamestown bride Elizabeth.[32]

Conditions for the passengers, barely tolerable at the start of the voyage, can only have worsened as the ships battled their way across the Atlantic against contrary winds and currents. Seasickness was their first hazard. If the maids were anything like the pilgrims aboard the *Mayflower*, a prosperous wind brought some encouragement 'yet, according to the usual manner, many were afflicted with seasickness'.[33] To the smell of vomit must be added the stink of primitive sanitary arrangements. The main toilet for the crew was in the ship's head, the area immediately behind the figurehead constructed of slatted or solid timber with holes cut through to allow human waste to drop straight into the sea.[34] The women are more likely to have used buckets attached to ropes and doused with seawater.

Coping with their monthly 'flowers' was an added trial. Most women used folded rags or clouts to absorb their menstrual flow, preferably old cloths made from linen, which was thought to draw moisture from the body;[35] this may have been the purpose of the linen contained in Jane Dier's small box loaded into the hold.[36] The clouts could be pinned or tucked into a girdle, since women did not yet wear briefs. But the cloths needed frequent washing and drying, a difficult operation on board ship, so you may have simply allowed your menstrual blood to seep into your shifts, worn next to the skin under a petticoat and an outer dress. Your soiled undergarments still needed washing since menstrual blood was considered physically and spiritually abhorrent, especially to men. 'For I am uncleane and filthie: and all my righteousnesse is like a foule bloudie clout,' wrote Thomas Bentley in a psalm he included in *The Monument of Matrones*, a compilation of prayers and meditations written largely by and for women.[37]

Keeping clean and free from lice, bed bugs and all the other infestations common on a crowded ship also required determined attention. Washing with water was not yet generally associated with personal cleanliness, and while higher-status women might resort to sweet waters, flower compounds and pomanders to mask the stink of daily life (a compound of roses was a French remedy for curing 'the goat-like stench of armpits'),[38] the Jamestown brides were more likely to have kept as clean as they could by rubbing their skin with linen cloths and brushing their hair with switches of pig's hair to dislodge the lice.[39] Although habits clearly differed between families, most people did not think it necessary to bathe or wash all over, preferring to keep just the visible parts clean, and the usual practice was condensed into the popular proverb: 'Wash thy hands often, thy feete seldome, but thy head never.'[40]

The thoughts of sixteen-year-old Elizabeth Markham, a passenger on the *Warwick*, might have turned to her father's handbook *The English House-wife* for ways of keeping clean. Among his many remedies are cures for stinking breath (distilled young oak buds), vermin-infested ears (ear drops of lovage), stinking nostrils (a powder of burned red nettles and pepper stuffed up the nose) and washes for tired eyes. In easier circumstances Elizabeth might have followed her father's advice to wash her face morning and night with distilled rosemary water to achieve 'a faire and cleere countenance', and – unusually for the times – to wash her head with the same to prevent hair loss and encourage more hair to grow. She may also have thought longingly of his detailed instructions for perfuming gloves and jerkins, distilling perfumes and damask water, and making washing balls, musk balls, sweet bags and pomanders. But while her father happily pontificated on the inward and outward virtues he thought desirable in an English housewife, he offered little practical advice on the daily business of keeping clean, reserving his endorsement of good hygiene habits for a housewife's duties in the dairy.[41]

Poor food was another complaint of those bound for Virginia. The cook was an important member of the crew, allotted his own cabin next to the cook room in the forecastle, reached by a door from the upper deck. His cooking apparatus was necessarily limited: a large round kettle hung from a metal beam suspended over a brick furnace, a grill and a spit for turning meat, copper fish kettles and assorted cans, platters, spoons and lanterns; forks and individual knives were not yet in general use. Tables for the passengers could be set up on the lower deck and stacked in odd corners at night.[42]

The Virginia Company's calculation of the rations needed to feed its mariners included a daily allowance of three quarters of a pound of hard ship's biscuit and three quarts of beer per man, plus additional meal and cider daily, and a varied diet throughout the week: salt pork and pease for dinner on Sundays, Mondays and Thursdays, and salt beef at supper; dried fish, oil and vinegar on Tuesdays and Wednesdays; and dried fish, butter and cheese on Fridays and Saturdays.[43] Dramatists poked fun at shipboard meat 'so salt, that one woulde thinke after dinner his tongue had been powdred [salted] ten daies', and dried ship's biscuit so hard 'that one must carrie a whetstone in his mouth to grinde his teeth'.[44] Poor John was the name given to salted and dried hake. Shakespeare throws it into *The Tempest* when the jester Trinculo stumbles across the monstrous Caliban. 'What have we here', he declares, 'a man or a fish? Dead or alive? A fish: he smells like a fish, a very ancient and fish-like smell, a kind of – not of the newest – poor-John.'[45]

No one perceived the limitations of shipboard food more clearly than Captain John Smith, who urged sea commanders to disregard the notion that 'any thing is good enough to serve men at sea' and castigated the usual diet served to naval seamen:

> a little poore John, or salt fish, with oyle and mustard, or bisket, butter, cheese or oatemeal pottage on fish dayes, salt beefe, pork and pease and sixe shillings beere, this is your ordinary ships allowance… and after a storme, when poore men are all wet, and some not so much a cloth to shift him, shaking with cold, few of those but will tell you, a little Sacke or Aquavitae, is much better to keepe them in health, [than] a little small beere or cold water…[46]

Smith's preferred diet, recommended especially for mariners who were sick or dying, included 'a dish of buttered Rice, with a little Cinamon and Sugar, a little minced meate, or roast beefe, a few stewed Prunes, a race of greene ginger, a flap-Jacke, a Can of fresh water brued with a little Cinamon, Ginger and Sugar' – hardly the rations fed to the Jamestown brides on board ship, although the

Warwick maids and the settlers bound for Martin's Hundred were each provided with three casks of prunes to supplement their diet at sea.[47] But however unpleasant their journey, all the passengers who travelled with the maids on the *Warwick* and the *Marmaduke* survived the experience, unlike many of those who endured the horrific shipboard conditions aboard the *Margaret & John* in 1623 and died from lack of food or infected beer.[48]

On such a lengthy crossing the women will have experienced the gamut of conditions, to which Captain John Smith devoted a chapter in *A Sea Grammar*, explaining to young seamen the names by which different seas were known: 'We say a calme sea or Becalmed, when it is so smooth the ship moves very little, and the men leap over boord to swim. A Rough Sea is when the waves grow high. An over-growne Sea when the surges and billowes goe highest. The Rut of the Sea, where it doth dash against any thing. And the Roaring of the Sea is most commonly observed a shore, a little before a storme, or after a storme.'[49]

Smith's crescendo of terms for different winds makes the same progression, from 'A calme, a brese, a fresh gaile; a pleasant gail, a stiffe gayle, it overblowes, a gust, a storme, a spoute, a loume gaile, an eddy winde, a flake of winde, a Turnado, a mounthsoune [monsoon], a Herycano [hurricane],'[50] explaining that a 'faire Loome Gale' was best for sailing 'because the Sea goeth not high and we beare out all our sailes', while the winds in a West Indian hurricane blew so violently that 'the Sea flies like raine, and the waves so high, they over flow the low grounds by the Sea'. He knew of ships driven many leagues inland over the tops of high trees, like the *Phoenix* commanded by Englishman Captain Francis Nelson, which finally arrived in Jamestown in April 1608 after being blown to the West Indies by a hurricane.[51]

Storms were the stock ingredient of any good traveller's tale, and given their late departure from England all the ships carrying the

Jamestown brides will have encountered North Atlantic storms of the kind experienced by the soon-to-be-shipwrecked passengers in the opening scene of Shakespeare's *The Tempest*, ordered to keep to their cabins by the boatswain, whose shouted orders might have come straight from Smith's nautical dictionary: 'Heigh, my hearts! Yare! Yare! Take in the topsail. Tend to the master's whistle! Blow, till thou burst they wind, if room enough.'[52]

Shakespeare may have drawn his inspiration for *The Tempest* from the Atlantic voyage of the Third Supply in 1609, when the flagship *Sea Venture* carrying Virginian governor Sir Thomas Gates, Admiral Sir George Somers, John Rolfe and his pregnant first wife and more than a hundred settlers was driven off course near the Bermudas. William Strachey's eyewitness account of the voyage drops you inside the 'hideous' storm, which had blown up from the north-east, swelling and roaring by fits and starts until it 'at length did beate all light from heaven; which like an helle of darkenesse turned blacke upon us, so much the more fuller of horror'. The storm raged for twenty-four hours, ever more constant, 'fury added to fury', one storm urging on another even more outrageous than the first, spreading fear 'amongst women, and passengers, not used to such hurly and discomforts', making them look 'one upon the other with troubled hearts, and panting bosomes: our clamours dround in the windes and the windes in thunder'.[53] The heavens remained black until the Thursday night, when Sir George Somers on watch duty 'had an apparition of a little round light, like a faint Starre, trembling, and streaming along with a sparkling blaze', a description of the weather phenomenon known as St Elmo's fire, which finds its echo in Shakespeare's Ariel.[54] If all else failed, the practice was to furl the sails, secure the helm to leeward and abandon the ship to the elements, a manoeuvre known as hulling.[55]

Huddled in the 'tween deck as storms raged, the women will have feared for their lives, wretched with seasickness and railing at their collective fate. Storms experienced at night were the worst, according

Sailing across the Atlantic in their small wooden ships, the Jamestown brides could expect terrifyingly stormy seas.

to Dr James Barton, who sailed across the Atlantic in 1985 in the replica ship *Godspeed*, retracing the historic voyage that had brought the first permanent English settlers to Jamestown. As they were tossed around in total darkness, Barton recalls how sounds would appear terrifyingly loud: barked orders, cursing, thuds, waves crashing against the wooden hull, the cabin shuddering, wind roaring in the rigging, footsteps clomping on deck above their heads. 'At those times', he told me, 'I actually preferred being on deck, where I could at least observe how the ship was faring. However, I must admit I was returning to family and friends at home in Virginia. Your future brides were leaving home, family and friends behind, and heading for a land that was totally new to them, hostile and foreign.'[56]

Of course not everybody who crossed the Atlantic experienced the dark hell of a Bermuda hurricane, and some travellers even relished the crossing, seeing in their deliverance a sure sign of God's mercy. One such account was written by a New England settler, Master Wells, to his people back home in Essex, who reported himself to be as cheerful as ever 'in spite of Divells and Stormes…

my wife all the voyage on ye sea better then at land, and sea sicke but one day in xi weekes, att sea my children never better in their lives. They went ill into ye ship but well there and came forth well as ever.' The ship's eighty passengers included women big with child, and a sixty-year-old consumptive woman with a strong cough of many years' standing, who not only survived but 'came forth of the shipe fully cured of the cough as fresh as [an] Egele that hath cast her bill and renewed her strength'.[57] In quieter times the maids on the *Marmaduke* may even have enjoyed readings from the two psalters and twelve copies of the catechism thoughtfully supplied by the company to Mr Andrews, the master's mate, for their use.[58]

Unusually, no passenger complaints were levied against conditions on board either the *Marmaduke* or the *Warwick*. The year after taking the maids to Virginia, the *Marmaduke's* master, John Dennis, petitioned to be granted the freedom of the company 'by his carefull transporting of Passengers to and from Virginia',[59] having already been granted his freedom by the council in Virginia. Somewhat grudgingly the London company granted his request, noting that Dennis had overcharged three passengers by a total of forty shillings for their homeward journey, and cautioning the Virginian governor to be more careful in future and bestow such freedom 'upon none in this kinde but such as shall deserve extraordinary well by their care and good usage of Passengers'.

But if the maids who travelled by the *Marmaduke* and the *Warwick* emerged relatively unscathed from their long crossing, those who sailed on the *Tiger* were not so fortunate. Commanded by Master Nicholas Ilford, the 40-ton *Tiger* was too small to merit a 'tween deck, so space for the passengers would have been found in the forecastle and aft cabins: twenty-six paid for by the Virginia Company and as many as forty in total.[60] Among the passengers went four Jamestown brides, only three of whom were of marriageable age: sixteen-year-old Londoner Elizabeth Browne, twenty-one-year-old Anne Gibbson and twenty-eight-year-old gentlewoman Allice Goughe, whose higher status is reflected in the title of Mistress accorded to her by Nicholas Ferrar in contrast to plain 'Ghibson & Browne' for the other two.[61] The fourth maid on the *Tiger* was Priscilla Palmer, who was only seven or eight years old and travelling with her parents.

The *Tiger* left England soon after the *Warwick* in mid-September and headed straight into storms and contrary winds. Blown hundreds of miles off course, she fell into the path of Turks, the usual name for pirates operating out of the Barbary ports of North Africa, 'who commonly lurke neere Ilands, and head-lands, and not in the maine Ocean'. While the Mediterranean was their primary hunting ground, from mid-August they could sometimes be found off the coast of Spain, lying in wait for ships coming in from the Indies.[62] Mistaking the pirates for 'Flemmings' bound for Holland or England, the *Tiger*'s master approached their boat to speak with them, only to fall prey to 'mercilesse Turkes', who robbed them of most of their victuals, all their serviceable sails, tackle and anchors, leaving them without so much as an hourglass or a compass to steer their course, 'thereby utterly disabling them from going from them, and proceeding on their voyage'.

For the women on board the *Tiger* this must have been a terrifying encounter. Captain John Smith portrayed pirates as 'riotous, quarrellous, treacherous, blasphemous, and villanous', presumably from personal experience, having been captured by French privateers on a journey to New England in 1615.[63] Yet against all the odds, the women came to no harm. They could so easily have been sold into slavery 'like beasts in a market-place', as Smith claimed happened to him after he was captured by Tartars and taken as a slave to Constantinople.[64] I can only assume that the pirates who attacked the *Tiger* were not returning to port immediately and lacked the resources to bring the women safely to market, since pirate ships rarely carried sufficient provisions to undertake long journeys.[65]

The full story of what happened to the *Tiger* – or at least the story the company wanted broadcast – appeared in a sermon preached before members of the Honourable Virginia Company assembled at Bow church in Cheapside, London, on 18 April 1622. The preacher was Patrick Copland, rector-elect of a college for native American children which the company wished to found at Henricus in Virginia, who took as his title 'Virginia's God be thanked, or A Sermon of Thanksgiving for the happie successe of the affayres in Virginia this last yeare'.[66] But while Copland used the *Tiger's* safe delivery to demonstrate God's 'loving kindnesse' towards the colony, events in Virginia had moved on, and kindness was the last word anyone could use, as we shall see.

In the course of his sermon Copland asked his audience to consider the hazards involved in the Virginian adventure: the dangers of the Atlantic crossing and of life in the colony, and also the perils experienced by those at home, by which he meant principally the economic risks born by members of his audience. But Virginia had at last begun to prosper, he said, quoting the words of John Martin, an Armenian colonist who intended to live out the rest of his days in Virginia: 'I have travailed (said he) by Land over eighteene severall kingdomes; and yet all of them in my minde, come farre short of Virginia, both for temperature of ayre, and fertilitie of the soyle.'

The fate of the *Tiger* fitted neatly into Copland's narrative of God's providence. After the Turks had left the ship rudderless and drifting, the *Tiger* was spied by another ship, which escorted it safely to Virginia with all passengers and crew except two English boys, young seamen most likely, whom the pirates had exchanged for two other youths, one French and one Irish. Aside from cloth dispatched to make clothes for some Frenchmen and other Europeans then living in the colony, the *Tiger's* cargo also came safely to Jamestown.[67] 'Was not there the presence of God printed as it were, in Folio on Royall Crowne Paper and Capitall Letters?' asked Copland of his audience. By this strange act of providence Elizabeth Browne, Anne Gibbson, gentlewoman

Allice Gough, the young Priscilla Palmer, her parents and the rest of the passengers were spared, and the *Tiger* maids were free to join those from the *Marmaduke* and the *Warwick* in their search for husbands on the other side of the ocean.

CHAPTER NINE

Land ho!

They say you can smell land before you can see it, especially after weeks at sea incarcerated in a reeking ship. On nearing the coast of Virginia around midnight, William Strachey described catching 'a marvellous sweet smell from the shoare, (as from the Coast of Spaine, short of the Straits) strong and pleasant, which did not a little glad us'.[1] The smell was all the sweeter as it came after a winter marooned on Bermuda with Sir Thomas Gates and his party and an epic journey that had lasted nearly a year since the *Sea Venture* quit the Devon coast.

Strachey recorded other signs of the land they were approaching: a change in the colour of the sea and 'much Rubbish' swimming by the side of the ship. And then, an hour after daybreak on 20 May 1610, 'so soone as one might well see from the fore-top', one of the sailors caught sight of land, doubtless crying out 'Land to!' in the time-honoured words recorded by Captain John Smith in his dictionary for young seamen.[2]

Although they were arriving at the onset of winter, when human noses lose their edge and smells travel more slowly, we can imagine that the Jamestown brides shared Strachey's relief that their journey was nearly over. And we can hope that Masters John Dennis, Nicholas Norburne and the others allowed their passengers on deck to witness their arrival off the land that was to become their home. Captain John Smith describes it well:

'There is but one entrance by Sea into this Countrey, and that is at the mouth of a verie goodly Bay, the widenesse whereof is neere eighteene or twentie miles. The Cape on the South side is called Cape Henrie, in honour of our most Noble Prince. The shew of the Land there is a white Hilly Sand like unto the Downes, and along the shoares great plentie of Pines and Firres.'[3]

The northern cape was named Cape Charles 'in honour of the worthy Duke of Yorke', Smith tells us, although by the time the women arrived in Virginia Prince Henry was dead and Prince Charles had replaced him as heir to the throne. After crossing the threshold of the two capes, the bay runs north for some 200

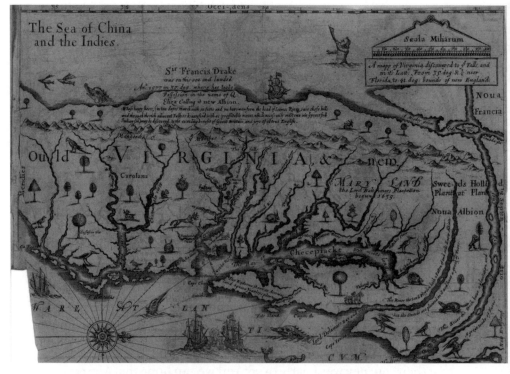

John Ferrar's map of Virginia – printed in 1651 – clearly located Martin's Hundred on the James River but placed the China Sea and its fabled route to the Indies just beyond the mountains. As in most early maps of Virginia, north is oriented to the right.

miles, with mountains to the far north-west and also 'Hils, Plaines, Vallies, Rivers and Brookes, all running most pleasantly into a faire Bay compassed but for the mouth with fruitful and delightsome Land. In the Bay and Rivers are many Iles both great and small, some woodie, some plaine, most of them low and not inhabited.'

To the women who had sailed from Gravesend, their first sight of the Chesapeake Bay carried reassuring echoes of the Thames estuary: wide open waters encompassed by a distant rim of land. For William Strachey too the points of reference were plainly drawn from the Thames; seven leagues separated the two capes at the mouth of the bay, he noted, 'as broad as betweene Queeneburrough [Kentish Queenborough] and Lee [Leigh-on-Sea in Essex]. Indeed, it is a goodly Bay and a fairer, not easily to be found.'[4]

Strachey records the delicate manoeuvre required to juggle the winds and tides and so pass safely between the two capes, where 'we purposed to lye at an Anchor untill the next flood, but the wind comming South-west a loome gale about eleven, we set sayle againe, and having got over the Barre, bore in for the Cape'. By the morning of the next day they had reached the mouth of the James River at Point Comfort, so named by the first group of permanent settlers because the channel here was deep enough to take their ships upriver and the river 'as broad as between Greenwich, and the Ile of Dogges'. Like Gravesend, Tilbury and Cowes on the Isle of Wight, Point Comfort was fortified, since it controlled access to the river, although the fort originally built there, Fort Algernon, had gone by the time the maids arrived.

It was the trees that most newcomers to Virginia noticed first, the 'goodly tall Trees' that so ravished early settler George Percy, together with fair meadows and fresh water running through the woods. Percy and the others had left their ship anchored off Cape Henry for a spot of exploring, which ended badly when they were ambushed by 'Savages' creeping on all fours, coming down from the hills 'like Beares, with their Bowes in their mouthes', leaving one sailor wounded in two places and Captain Gabriel Archer hurt on both hands.[5]

That was more than fourteen years ago. Relations with the native population were generally more settled, although subject to periodic outbreaks of violence on both sides, and the ships carrying the women had orders to proceed directly to Jamestown, doubtless stopping first at Kecoughtan to take on board a pilot to guide them up the tidal stretch of the river, which was 'Shelvie and dangerous'.[6] The bay here provided a natural harbour for fishing boats and other small craft, and 'so conveniently turneth it selfe into Bayes and Creekes that make that place very pleasant to inhabit', according to Captain John Smith, whose sharp descriptions of the landscape provided the lens through which later colonists viewed their new home.[7]

Writing in 1608, when Kecoughtan was still in Indian hands, Smith reported that the town consisted of some eighteen Indian houses 'pleasantly seated' on three acres of ground, bounded on one side by Kecoughtan Bay in the James River and on the other by a bay in a tributary river.[8] When the Indians were driven from their town and the English settled in their place, they requested a change in name from Kecoughtan to Elizabeth City, although both names remained in use. By March 1620, eighteen months before the maids' arrival, fifty-four English colonists were living at Kecoughtan and on both sides of the Hampton River: twenty-eight men, twelve women and fourteen children.[9] Assuming that the Jamestown brides stayed on deck, we can imagine the curiosity with which they regarded their first view of a Virginian settlement peopled by Englishmen.

Once the pilot was aboard and the winds and tides judged to be favourable, the *Marmaduke*, the *Warwick* and the other ships will have weighed anchor and made their slow progress up to Jamestown, a distance of less than fifty miles. It had taken William Strachey's party two days to complete the journey, helped only by the tides since no wind was stirring. From Kecoughtan the river continues on to Point Hope and a new settlement called Newportes News, where the first signs of forest clearance may just have been visible from the river. To the south and south-west of the James were lands inhabited largely by Algonquin-speaking Indians of the Nansemond tribe after Powhatan had eliminated the Chesapeakes to the south.[10] From their vantage point on deck, the women will have seen little evidence of the inhabitants: wisps of smoke from a few fires perhaps, but little else, as the Indian towns were located further down the Nansemond River. The best fields for growing Indian corn were anyway upriver, west of Jamestown, together with the freshwater marshes that supported Indian food crops such as tuckahoe (green arrow arum), spatterdock or cow lily and wild rice.[11]

So the women will have seen little to alarm them as they rounded the point at Newportes News, where a spring provided fresh water for ships and a new settlement was taking root. The river then turns to the north-west, some five miles across at its widest. More goodly tall trees on both sides of the river to be inspected whenever they sailed close enough to the shore and the swampy fringes of creeks and sandy bays.

And so they continued their journey as the tides permitted, tacking backwards and forwards across the river to catch the wind. The twists in the river mean that you can turn full circle on deck and see land all around you, an impression that is both comforting and final. Virginia is swallowing you up; there is no turning back. Somewhere along the way the ships will have dropped anchor for one last night. Visiting Jamestown in the 1630s, Dutchman David Peterson de Vries broke his journey about halfway up to Jamestown from the Chesapeake Bay. 'Here, the river is full three miles wide,' he noted, 'but shoally, so that it is only by sounding the passage that you can get along.'[12] By noon the next day de Vries had reached the house and magnificent garden of merchant George Menefie, a scant two hours' sail from Jamestown, but when the women entered the last leg of their journey virgin forest still lined the riverbanks.

Despite the impenetrable walls of green on both sides of the river, the women will nonetheless have witnessed occasional signs of settler activity. Like the Indians, the English preferred the more fertile soils of the Upper James, where the air and water were considered healthier, and they liked to save themselves labour by taking over land already cleared by the Indians.[13] But by 1621 English plantations had begun to appear on both sides of the Lower James, within easy reach of the river. Settlers on the north side included Edward Waters at Waters Creek, a couple of miles below Blunt Point, and another survivor from the Bermudan shipwreck, Jamestown resident Captain William Pierce, who had patented 650 acres on Mulberry Island and was beginning to develop his property.[14]

Across the other side of the river, the newcomers may also have spied the new plantation of Basses Choice up the Pagan River and the curving sands of Burwell's Bay, where London merchant Edward Bennett was poised to establish a plantation variously known as Bennett's Welcome and Warrascoyack, which eventually took in some of the maids, among them the widowed Marie Daucks. Was 'Goodwife Bennet', a fellow passenger on the *Warwick*, related to the Bennetts who founded the plantation? If so, she may have been travelling here with Alse Dollinges, the Dorset-born maid whose 'honest Conversation' she had vouchsafed. On a clear still day the white sands of the bay glisten in the sunlight, and the waters of the James lap gently onto the shore, belying the tragedy that would soon strike this quiet corner of the wilderness. A little further upstream was the site of Captain Christopher Lawne's plantation just east of Lawne's Creek. Lawne had died by the time the women sailed up the James and the surviving settlers relocated upriver to Charles City. Undeterred, his investors clung on to their claim and renamed their patented lands the Isle of Wight Plantation in November 1620.[15] The adventurers included Robert Newland, the merchant who had organized the departure of the *Marmaduke* maids from the Isle of Wight. Newland may even have told them about his stake in the colony to which they were bound. Another of Lawne's backers was Sir Richard Worsley, member of parliament for Newland's home town of Newport. Worsley died in 1621, the same year the women travelled, and his parliamentary seat was filled by Sir William Uvedale, a cousin once removed of Lettice King, who sailed on the *Marmaduke*. The maids' connections to their new home are multiplying fast.

Both the *Marmaduke* and the *Warwick* carried passengers with links to the next settlement on the north side of the river; forest clearance will have been evident along its ten miles of river frontage. This was Martin's Hundred, home to Ann Jackson's brother and his wife, also called Ann. It sits on a low bluff overlooking the river, dominated today by a stately brick mansion known as Carter's Grove. One of the colony's earliest and most substantial 'particular plantations' financed by private investment rather than company funds, Martin's Hundred was at last making progress after hesitant beginnings, planting its palisades and incipient township on flattish ground that may have been cleared by the Indians for growing corn in the not-too-distant past.[16] A new leader, William Harwood, had arrived in the summer of 1620, and the ships transporting the maids were also bringing in many new recruits for the plantation: the *Marmaduke*'s dozen lusty youths, twenty-eight more on the *Warwick* and a further dozen aboard the unfortunate *Tiger* delayed by pirates. A new patent issued soon after their arrival defined the plantation's extent as 20,000 acres centred on Wolstenholme Town and extending five miles upstream to Jamestown and five miles downstream to Newportes News, 'all along the great River called Kinge James River and Northward to the River called the Queenes River alias Pacomunky', now the York River.[17] The maids were not the only passengers who will have looked for signs of activity beyond the waterfront.

After the sweep of Martin's Hundred, the James narrows as it turns between the low-lying marshy peninsula of Hog Island on the south shore and Archer's Hope to the north. The site of an early blockhouse and long used to pasture swine, Hog Island had been patented by now, the land claimed among others by Mary Bayly, heir of ancient planter John Bayly and an ancient planter in her own right (a term applied to settlers who had arrived by 1616);[18] Captain Ralph Hamor, an old Virginia hand and author of one of the early treatises extolling life in the colony,[19] and Captain William Powell. On the river's north side the women would catch a good look at Archer's Hope, which some of the original colonists preferred to Jamestown Island as a place to settle despite its one main drawback, the lack of deep-water mooring for their ships. George Percy praised its good and fruitful soil and excellent timber, its abundance of turkey nests and eggs. 'There are also great store of Vines in bignesse of a mans thigh, running up to the tops of the Trees in great abundance. We also did see many Squirels, Conies [rabbits], Black Birds with crimson wings, and divers other Fowles and Birds of divers and sundrie collours of crimson, Watchet, Yellow, Greene, Murry, and of divers other hewes naturally without any art using.'[20]

You can sense Percy's wonder at the lushness of the land they were discovering for the first time. The maids may have been more subdued, their relief at nearing their journey's end tempered by natural anxiety for the future. The ship that they had inhabited for so long was both prison and refuge; however much you want to escape confinement, you sometimes dread to leave the safety of your cocoon.

Still tacking back and forth, the ship rounds the tip of Jamestown island, a stubby peninsula joined to the mainland by a narrow isthmus that will eventually disappear under exceptionally high tides, when gales sweep in from the south and east.[21] Approached from downriver, the reedy saltmarshes of Back River accentuate the island's detachment from the mainland. The vegetation is chiefly cordgrass, showing a dry winter brown.[22] Here the main channel of the James is further constricted to about one and a half miles across. All you can see are flatlands packed with trees broken by occasional clearings, evidence of the homesteads that are creeping into this part of the island, perhaps some small boats carrying workmen such as sawyers and people at work in their gardens, and Indian canoes.

The place you have heard so much about is not quite as you imagined. What you see as your ship approaches the landing at Jamestown is this: a triangular fort strategically placed close to the river but above the high-water mark, guarded by a wooden palisade with mounted guns pointing from the half-moon bulwarks at each corner. Along the waterfront are vestiges of a timber landing stage, while clustered within and around the fort are mud-clad cottages,[23] some timber-framed and of two storeys, a wooden church and a few larger buildings that look like granaries. A fair-sized patch of land has been cleared to the east of the fort, for crops or new building you cannot tell, beyond the few flimsy dwellings strung out along the waterfront.

A gaggle of curious onlookers is gathering on the shoreline, hardly a crowd and mostly Englishmen dressed in familiar fashion. You feel sticky and stained after months at sea, your petticoats grimy, the backs of your hands tasting of salt spray and sweat, your scalp itching under its coif.

So this is the place they call Jamestown, James Cittie even, a mockery of a name. You judge it no larger than an English village, from an age when even villages needed their fortifications. For this you have departed a city of 200,000 souls intent on transforming itself into one of the great capitals of the world and criss-crossed a stormy North Atlantic, covering thousands of miles more than the 3,750 miles that separate Europe from America.

A question I would ask of the widowed Ann Richards from the parish of St Sepulchre in the fair city of London: is this what you had in mind when you declared that you were 'mynded and purposed to dwell elswhere'?

PART TWO

Virginia

Who knowes not England once was like
a Wildernesse and savage place,
Till government and use of men,
that wildnesse did deface:
And so Virginia may in time,
be made like England now;
Where long-lovd peace and plenty both,
sits smiling on her brow.

*Anon, 'Londons Lotterie', sung to the tune of 'Lusty Gallant',
London, printed for Henry Robards and sold
at his shop near St Botolph without Aldgate, 1612.*

CHAPTER TEN

Arrival at Jamestown

O nce their ship had safely anchored, the women's first ordeal
was to face any welcome party assembled to greet them, under
the watchful stares of curious onlookers, some of whom may have
hoped to pick themselves a wife or at least to judge the kind of
women on offer. Governor Dale's wharf had long since decayed,
but Yeardley had ordered the building of a 'bridge', possibly a new
wharf, where the women might have landed, or they may have
transferred onto small boats to be rowed the short distance to
shore. Given the importance the Virginia Company had placed
on the maids' magazine, it is likely that they were met by the new
governor, Sir Francis Wyatt, and as many of his officials as he could
muster. A decade or more later, David Peterson de Vries arrived to
find Governor John Harvey waiting for him on the beach attended
by halberdiers and musketeers. While the Jamestown brides scarcely
merited such a display, their arrival in the winter of 1621 was
recorded among the benefits conferred on the colony that year.[1]

Just as their arrival in this most masculine of environments
turned the women into objects of curiosity, so they will have picked
out any 'strangers' among the people gathered to greet them: native
Indians visiting the settlement or the tiny few who worked for the
settlers, some of whom were beginning to 'affect English ffassions'.
They may also have spotted one or other of the thirty-two Africans
– fifteen men and seventeen women – recorded as living in the

colony in early 1620; they included the '20 and odd Negroes' which John Rolfe revealed had come from a Dutch man-of-war that had arrived in late August 1619 at Virginia's Point Comfort, where they were exchanged for supplies.[2]

A good many Virginians and some Africans had already passed through London of course, among them the Virginia Indian maids Mary and Elizabeth and the occasional 'blacke a moore servant', who left sad reminders of their passing in burial records.[3] Some of the older Jamestown brides may even have glimpsed Mistress Rebecca Rolfe when she passed through London in the winter of 1616 with her entourage, or heard tell of her brother-in-law Tomocomo, who remained 'blatantly and proudly Indian'[4] to judge from his hairstyle (one side of his head close shaven, the other sporting a 'Devill-lock' several feet long) and the 'diabolicall' dances he performed for scholars curious about his religion. From now on, such strangeness would be part of their daily lives, surely a sobering thought for the new arrivals, who will have looked to each other for support and to whatever welcome the colony's governor had provided to ease them into their new home.

Governor Wyatt had only recently taken over from Sir George Yeardley, having arrived a few weeks earlier on the *George* accompanied by a clutch of new officials for the colony: Sir Edwin Sandys' younger brother George in the new post of treasurer; Christopher Davison, who replaced John Pory as secretary; William Claiborne, charged with surveying all public tracts of land and private plantations such as Martin's Hundred; and the colony's new doctor, John Pott.[5] Wyatt's wife Margaret, a niece of Sir Edwin Sandys, came out later, but her place in any welcome party would usefully have gone to Yeardley's wife, the former Temperance Flowerdew, whose example showed that women who married well could thrive in the colony, although she undoubtedly had the advantage of birth and breeding over most of the Jamestown brides. By the winter of 1621 the Yeardleys already had a daughter, Elizabeth, aged between one and two, and Lady Yeardley was either carrying Argall, the first of her two sons, or caring for him as an infant.[6]

One man who was obliged to greet the maids was the Virginia Company's agent, John Pountis, a relatively recent recruit to the colony whose initial interest centred on fishing for sturgeon. Pountis had brought forty company tenants to Virginia in late 1619 or early 1620, and was rewarded with the title of vice admiral to the colony, supported by a stipend of 300 acres and twelve tenants.[7] His instructions about the maids came in a letter from the Virginia Company to Governor Wyatt and his council in Virginia, brought by the captain of the *Marmaduke*. The governor and council were to take the women into their care and Pountis was to see that they were housed, lodged and fed until they could be married. Those who could not be married immediately were to stay with householders who had wives living with them. How this should be accomplished was left to the governor's discretion, but the company hoped that an endeavour begun in London out of piety 'and tending so much

The arrival of brides for Virginia's early settlers has long captured the public imagination; this 'Shipload of Wives' dates from the early twentieth century.

to the benefitt of the Plantation shall not miscarry for any want of good will or care on yor partes'.[8]

The company's instructions also named the officials responsible for collecting the bride price from husbands, which had been calculated in best-leaf tobacco, then the colony's standard currency. John Pountis was charged with collecting the tobacco owed for the *Marmaduke* maids,[9] while Edward Blaney, who returned to Virginia aboard the *Warwick* as the colony's new cape merchant, was to collect tobacco from the husbands of maids who travelled on the *Warwick* and later ships, and to keep a separate account;[10] these responsibilities he would later deny, saying that he had nothing to do with any of the maids. Pountis was also to collect the 'little quantitie' of tobacco owed to *Marmaduke* passenger Richard Pace, an ancient planter who had paid for the passage and other charges of his kinswoman Ursula Lawson and was therefore personally benefiting from her marriage.[11]

For most travellers to Virginia, their first call was to repair to Jamestown's wooden church to offer up thanks for their safe delivery. When Governor Sir Thomas Gates arrived in Jamestown on 23 May 1610 after a winter shipwrecked on Bermuda, he headed straight to church, causing the bell to be rung to summon all who were able to attend a service, 'where our Minister Master Bucke made a zealous and sorrowfull Prayer, finding all things so contrary to our expectations, so full of misery and misgovernment'.[12] Eleven years on, the same Reverend Richard Buck was on hand to offer up thanks and also no doubt to proffer solemn words on the virtues of wifely subordination.

Like any newcomer walking the short distance from the waterfront to the church, the maids cannot fail to have noticed Jamestown's air of dilapidation. In contrast to the city they had left behind, here was no stone or brick. Everything was fashioned out of timber or muddy earth slapped on skimpy wooden frames and crudely patched in a make-do-and-mend spirit as each new governor sought to restore order and direction to an enterprise that endured cyclical decline, renewal and subsequent attrition.[13] It was also a place stripped of the amenities that English town and city dwellers took for granted: a bustling market place, shops, taverns, places of entertainment;[14] only the church, the whipping post and a guardhouse bore witness to the order the colonists had imposed on this unruly frontier. And the settlement was pitifully small: barely two dozen houses in all, less than half the 'fiftie or sixtie houses' plus 'five or sixe other severall Forts and Plantations' counted in 1609 by Captain John Smith.[15]

The earliest settlers had built their fort in the shape of a triangle on low-lying ground fronting directly onto the water, its southern edge extending some 140 yards along the river with two shorter sides of a hundred yards each to east and west. To keep out wild beasts and marauding Indians they had constructed a palisade fence fourteen or fifteen feet high from oak and walnut planks and posts sunk four feet deep into the ground, with bastions at each of the three corners.[16] Inside the fort three streets of houses ran parallel to the palisade, enclosing a market place, store house, guardhouse and 'likewise a pretty Chappell', which in 1610 was 'ruined and unfrequented' but undergoing extensive repairs.[17]

The renovations to Jamestown's urban fabric did not last long, however. When deputy governor Samuel Argall arrived in May 1617 – the voyage that should have brought Pocahontas back to Virginia – he found just five or six houses left standing, the church down, the palisade unable even to keep out hogs, Sir Thomas Dale's landing stage in pieces, the freshwater well spoiled, the storehouse used as a church, 'the market-place, and streets, and all other spare places planted with Tobacco, the Salvages as frequent in their houses as themselves.'[18] Argall attempted to restore order, building a new timber church 'wholly at the charge of the inhabitants' in the extended eastern area of the fort and claiming credit for improving conditions in the colony.[19] But like other leaders who came before and after him, he soon diverted his attention from public to private matters, placing the settlers bound for Martin's Hundred on land set aside for the governor's use, where he tried to establish a particular plantation of his own.[20]

Two years had passed since Argall's hasty departure to avert public disgrace, and two more men had presided over the colony: acting governor Nathaniel Powell, in post for just ten days, and Captain – now Sir – George Yeardley, an old Virginia hand who had sailed on the *Sea Venture* with Sir Thomas Gates and spent the winter shipwrecked on Bermuda. Commenting on Yeardley's appointment as governor, John Chamberlain called him a 'meane fellow by way of provision… and to grace him the more the King knighted him this weeke at Newmarket; which hath set him up so high that he flaunts yt up and downe the streets in extraordinarie braverie, with fowrteen or fifteen fayre liveries after him'. Yeardley took with him to Virginia as secretary his wife's first cousin John Pory, a man known for his drinking habits. In Virginia, said Chamberlain slyly, Pory would without question become 'a sufficient sober man seeing there is no wine in all that climat'.[21]

Aside from the newly built church, Yeardley – like his predecessors – found Jamestown in disrepair and virtually unfortified, its only houses the dozen or so built by Gates including the governor's house, which Argall had enlarged, while its 'fort' was reduced to just four demi-culverin guns mounted on rotten carriages.[22] Also like his predecessors, Yeardley set about repairing the damage, not always with the settlers' approval. Pory recounts the discontent over Yeardley's insistence that the men at Jamestown should contribute their labour to building or repairing a bridge and to constructing gun platforms for the town's better defence; indeed, the men 'repyned as much as yf all their goods had bene taken from them'.[23] Following instructions from London, Yeardley was also much preoccupied with land distribution, and he acted as midwife to North America's first representative assembly, which met in July and early August 1619 in Jamestown's church.

Now that Sir Francis Wyatt had taken charge, he will have moved straight into the governor's house inside the fort, which Yeardley vacated for a house he had built some way behind the fort across the Pitch and Tar Swamp on land abutting Back River, which he patented in 1624 'for his better conveniency and the more Comoditye of his houses & dwellings'.[24] Yeardley had other properties around the James River and beyond, including extensive landholdings at Weyanoke, a private plantation on the north side of the James River; at Flowerdew Hundred south of the James River; and a fine 'Mansion house' at Southampton Hundred a few miles west of Jamestown at Dancing Point, where the Chickahominy River meets the James; as well as land on Virginia's Eastern Shore. But Jamestown remained his principal residence for the rest of his life.

After giving thanks to God for the maids' safe deliverance into his hands, Pountis faced the unenviable task of finding chaperoned accommodation for them, a task made even more difficult by their lack of provisions to tide them over until they might be married. Yeardley had already warned the Virginia Company about the dangers of sending new settlers without proper stores, but London seemed neither to listen nor to care about their predicament.[25] Some of the maids could remain on board until the colonists were able to receive them, since captains and masters bringing servants to Virginia could be 'injoyed to keepe them aborde if need be a fortnight after there arrival att James Citty', allowing the scattered planters time to receive notice and come to Jamestown to see them.[26] But this was only a short-term solution as ships were expected to stay no more than thirteen days at Jamestown.[27]

The colony had long bemoaned the absence of a guesthouse to accommodate new arrivals, and although Jabez Whitaker had finally built one on company land in James City, it was promised to Captain Norton and his Italian glassworkers, who also arrived on the *Marmaduke*. Whitaker had even employed an old woman to wash their clothes and keep the place clean.[28] The glassworkers and the brides could clearly not be accommodated together in a space measuring just forty by twenty feet, so where could they go?

It was usual for the governor to put up any visitor requiring special treatment. A few of the better-born brides may have been accommodated by Sir Francis Wyatt in the governor's small house inside the fort, despite the absence of his wife, but first call on his hospitality doubtless went to the new officials who had arrived with him and his younger brother, the Reverend Haut (or Hawte) Wyatt, a 'sufficient preacher' sent to Virginia as minister for the governor's tenants.[29] The Yeardleys may have accommodated several of the women in their house near the Pitch and Tar Swamp, and others may have found temporary lodging with the Reverend Richard Buck, by all accounts 'a verie good Preacher'.[30] Buck lived with his family about a mile outside Jamestown on a twelve-acre plot close to Back River recently purchased from ancient planter William Fairfax, on which stood a house and another small dwelling. Although the minister had the benefit of glebe land and a further 750 acres which he had patented at Archer's Hope, he and his wife preferred living on Jamestown Island, where they brought up four young children.[31] Buck's wife died some time in the early 1620s, possibly before the maids' arrival, but as Jamestown's respected preacher the Reverend Buck would surely have been considered a fit person to receive young women until their marriage.

Other married settlers from Jamestown's elite may have given temporary lodging to the maids. Possible hosts included the influential and wealthy merchant, planter and military man William Pierce and his wife, and John Rolfe, who had taken the Pierces' daughter Joan as his third wife. When the Jamestown brides arrived, the Rolfes were most likely living with their young daughter Elizabeth on one of two plots of land in urban Jamestown owned by Joan's father.[32] Both properties were in the area known as New

Jamestown's fort and waterfront as it may have appeared in 1622, a few months after the maids' arrival, enlarged from the engraving shown on page 213.

Town, which surveyor William Claiborne was just starting to lay out to the east of the fort along both sides of Back Street down by the waterfront. Several of the colonists whose names are linked to the Jamestown brides would cluster here by the mid-1620s, among them Dr John Pott and his near-neighbour Edward Blaney, who both had maids living in their households in early 1624.

Some women may even have been billeted with the handful of ancient planters who had cleared land and established homesteads on twelve-acre plots on the eastern part of the island, following a precedent set by Sir Thomas Dale before he left the colony in 1616. One of the first planters to settle here was William Spence, described variously as a gentleman, a farmer and a labourer, who established himself on land extending east from Back River to the James.[33] Dale himself had patented a narrow ridge of land at Goose Hill on the south-eastern edge of the island. Though swampy and cramped – the whole island covered just 1,700 acres, much of it marshland cut by rivers and creeks – the soil was extremely fertile, producing fine crops of corn and wheat, good foraging for hogs and ample space for tobacco.[34]

But to fulfil his duties, Pountis will have wanted the women to see and be seen by prospective husbands, and hiding them away in a corner of Jamestown Island was hardly likely to achieve that aim. The land there was anyway considered the 'outback' and unhealthily low-lying. Far better to summon husbands to Jamestown and disperse clutches of maids to plantations that were actively seeking to expand. The women had thankfully arrived in the one short break in the toilsome business of growing tobacco and its relentless cycle of 'Sowing, plantinge, weedinge, wormminge, gatheringe, Cureinge, and making up'.[35]

For January and early February at least the marriage business would give the colony a welcome distraction from the hardships of settler life, but the lucky couples would have to hurry. Between the arrival of the ships in December and Easter the window to marry was relatively tight. Advent and Lent were traditionally forbidden for weddings in the Protestant Church of England, and while local clergy often ignored the Church's calendar, even Puritan preachers such as William Gouge at Blackfriars generally avoided marrying couples during 'unseasonable times' and conducted few marriages in March.[36] 'Marry in Lent, you'll surely repent' was a warning still heeded by country folk. Lent that year began with Ash Wednesday on 13 February, so women wishing to observe the Lenten ban had just a few short weeks in which to choose a husband, complete the formalities of marriage and settle into their new homes.

CHAPTER ELEVEN

The Choosing

Old ballads have plenty of advice for young men wishing to choose a bride. Let her not be a dirty foul slut, a rich gossip, a jealous widow, a cuckolding 'fair Venus', a babbling scold, a wench with an ash-coloured face or one with 'round Cherry-cheeks and red hair'. Rather,

> The bonny Wench with the black brow,
> oh she is a good one indeed;
> For she will be true to her vow,
> I would we had more of her breed.[1]

But what if it's the woman who does the choosing? What should she look for in a good mate?

On paper at least the Virginia Company insisted that the Jamestown brides were free to choose their marriage partners, notwithstanding the delicate matter of the bride price their husbands would be required to pay for them. We can imagine John Ferrar picking his words with care when he composed the company's letter to the governor and council in Virginia sent with the *Marmaduke* maids. The company admitted that

> though we are desireous that mariadge be free according
> to the law of nature, yett would we not have these maides
> deceived and married to servantes, but only to such

freemen or tenn[an]tes as have meanes to manteine them: wee pray you therefore to be fathers to them in this bussines, not enforecing them to Marrie against theire willes; neither send we them to be servantes, save in case of extremitie ['necessitie' crossed out], for we would have theire condicon so much bettered as multitudes may be allured thereby to come unto you.[2]

As an added inducement, husbands who bought themselves wives would be assigned servants from the next batch sent to Virginia, as it was company policy 'to preserve families, and to preferr married men before single p[er]sons'.

The promise of free choice for the women and future apprentices for their husbands was repeated in the company's instructions sent with the maids who sailed on the *Warwick* and the *Tiger*, a grand total of fifty-six women dispatched as part of the maids' magazine, or fifty-seven according to the official tally, which included Mistress Palmer's seven-year-old daughter Priscilla. All the brides came with 'good testimony of theire honest life and cariadge' enclosed like a bill of sale for the satisfaction of 'such as shall Marry them', and the company reiterated its hope that the women would all be married to 'honest and sufficient men, whose names will reach to p[re]sent re-payment: but if any of them shall unwarily or fondly bestow her self (for the libertie of Mariadge we dare not infrindg) uppon such as shall not be able to give p[re]sent sattisfaccon; we desire that at least as soon as abillity shalbe, they be compelled to pay the true quantitie of tobacco proporconed, and that this debt may have p[re]cedence of all others to be recovered'.[3]

Clearly if the women chose impecunious husbands the magazine was to become a preferred creditor, to be paid at the first opportunity. The company further expressed its hope that all the women would be received with 'the same Christian pietie and charitie as they are sent from hence', and that Virginia's planters would provide them with 'fitting services' until they married, with the expectation that they would be reimbursed by the women's husbands once a deal was struck. The lack of provisions continued to rankle, and the colonists would later beg the company that the 'next Supplie of m[aids]' might arrive with at least 'some smale pvisione' to tide them over 'untill they may bee convenientlie disposed of'.[4]

Wives did not come cheap, however. In the colony's prevailing tobacco currency the required bride price of 150 pounds in weight far exceeded the 100-pound limit on permitted annual production per head which the Virginia Company had set only that July in a desperate attempt to encourage planters to diversify their crops.[5] Expressed in English money, 150 pounds of best-leaf tobacco was worth as much as £22 10s., a considerable sum that would have taken a young woman working in service back home more than seven years to amass. In the colony, by contrast, where labour was desperately short, wages for independent male workers such as carpenters and bricklayers were astronomically high – as much as three to four times those established by county justices in England – which should have tipped the balance in the women's favour. A master carpenter in Virginia could earn himself a bride by working for just 115½ days, for instance, or 150 days if his employer supplied him with meat and drink.[6] A master joiner could pay for a bride even faster.

But in the colony's early days few artisans travelled independently to the colony; most workmen came as indentured servants or company tenants. In return for their transportation, clothing and food, servants typically committed themselves to work for between four and seven years. Only on completion of their indentures could they begin to amass capital for themselves. Tenants technically fared better: their contracts generally allowed them to keep one half of the product of their labour, passing on the rest to the company or to investors in their particular plantation; but both tenants and servants were liable to exploitation by acquisitive masters, and few recent arrivals will have been affluent enough to bid for one of the brides.[7]

Whatever arrangements Pountis and Governor Wyatt put in place to match planters to brides, they succeeded in keeping away poorer settlers such as Thomas Niccolls (or Nicholls), who wrote a bitter letter of complaint to Sir John Wolstenholme, one of the chief investors in Martin's Hundred. 'Women are necessary members for the Colonye,' declared Niccolls, 'but the poore men are nevr the nearer for them they are so well sould.' As a skilled surveyor, Niccolls had been released from the company's land the previous year and was employed at Martin's Hundred to help divide up the plots there. What he wanted was not a wife but a woman to undertake those domestic duties then considered women's business, such as laundry, which cost Niccolls three pounds sterling a year in labour charges and soap, and caring for the sick, without which the poor tenants of Wolstenholme Town 'dye miserablie through nastines & many dep[ar]te the World in their owne dung for want of help in their sickness'. The bitterness of his plight prompted Niccolls to call for women to be sent to Virginia under contract to serve the company 'for certayne yeares whether they marry or no. For all that I can find that the multitude of women doe is nothing but to devoure the food of the land without dooing any dayes deed.' By February of the following year, Niccolls himself was dead.[9]

Realistically, only elite settlers and established planters were likely to have sufficient capital to secure one of the brides, and the brides themselves will have wanted a mate who could provide for them materially in Virginia's crude but thrusting society. The group most likely to provide husbands for the Jamestown brides were the ancient planters who had come to Virginia before the departure of governor Sir Thomas Duke in 1616, many as labourers or company tenants. According to the instructions given to the incoming governor Sir George Yeardley in 1618, ancient planters – men and women – were entitled to 100 acres of land each and a few other privileges, so they should have been able to afford one of the maids.[10] Many also came from the same artisan class that provided the core of the Jamestown brides. Their survival proved that they had adapted to life in the New World and might be expected to marry and put down roots. As John Rolfe reported to Sir Edwin Sandys in January 1621, once they were freed many had chosen their own land, where 'they strive and are pr[e]pared to build houses & to cleere their groundes ready to plant'.[11] And it seems that many of these early settlers did indeed find themselves a wife. Of all the settlers still living in Virginia in January 1625, those who had arrived in the colony between 1607 and 1616 were more than twice as likely to be married than the average for all eligible adults – 70.3 per cent compared to 30.7.[12]

But the pool of eligible men was surprisingly small. Eighteen months or so before the women arrived in Virginia a census recorded just 670 able men and 119 women throughout the entire colony, a ratio of roughly six men to every woman in a total population of 928, which included Christians, non-Christians, serviceable boys and children.[13] Given this huge gender imbalance, the maids should have found it easy to secure a husband from the unattached men. Yet the same census counted just 222 habitable houses, excluding barns and storehouses, which puts a rough ceiling on the number of 'suitable' husbands for the Jamestown brides, and a fair proportion of these men were of course already married. Servants tended to live communally or in the households of their masters, while relatively few free men lived as joint heads of households with other men. Although many more people arrived in the colony in the months that followed, most came as tenants or indentured servants, and mortality rates remained high, so the numbers of eligible men did not increase by very much.

Those planters who could afford one of the brides will undoubtedly have weighed up the economics of the transaction. Land and labour provided the key to prosperity in Virginia: land to grow tobacco and servants to tend and harvest it. As a prospective husband considering your options, the bride price of 150 pounds of tobacco would also buy you two houses and six acres of land in Charles Hundred.[14] While you would expect a wife to contribute to your endeavours, these women came without land (an express condition laid down by the Virginia Company) and they were not to be treated as servants. Viewed purely as a commercial transaction, buying one of the brides was twice as expensive as buying an indentured maidservant, which would cost you £6 for the Atlantic crossing and £4 or so for clothing and provisions – and against this you could claim fifty acres of land for transporting her to Virginia. If you married a servant who had not completed her indentured term, you would expect to repay her master any outstanding costs of transportation but this was not always the case. The Jamestown court judged one Thomas Harvey not liable to pay for his wife's passage, a serving maid, on the grounds that she had been freely given to him by her master.[15]

Also to their disadvantage, the fifty-six Jamestown brides who arrived in 1621 followed in the wake of the ninety-odd young women dispatched to the colony the previous year on the *Jonathan*, the *London Merchant* and perhaps the *Bona Nova*. We have no record of who they were, but we do know that they came at a far cheaper price: independent planters had had to pay no more than the cost of their transportation, for which they were entitled to claim fifty acres of land, while company tenants had been able to marry them for free. And it seems that the earlier brides were more successful at securing husbands. Out of nearly a hundred male ancient planters still alive in 1625, at least ten married women who had arrived in 1620 on the *Jonathan*, the *London Merchant* and the *Bona Nova* compared with just three who definitely married women who came the following year on the *Marmaduke*, the *Warwick* and the *Tiger*. Altogether a little over a third (thirty-eight) of the surviving ancient planters may have been available to marry when the Jamestown brides arrived, but eleven of these were still servants or living in the households of others in 1625. Other ancient planters – and their

Virginia had its own laws regulating marriage, which required maids and maidservants to obtain permission from those who exercised authority over them, but marriage rites and customs reflected those of home.

wives – may have died in the intervening years, but the numbers indicate how small the pool of eligible men really was.[16]

So which of the Jamestown brides succeeded in securing that elusive husband for whom they had crossed the Atlantic? For some at least a marriage deal was quickly brokered. In its list of achievements for the year 1621 (which continued until 24 March 1622) the Virginia Company recorded the arrival of ships bringing new people to the colony, among them young maids 'sent to make wives for the Planters, divers of which were well married before the comming away of the Ships.[17] 'Divers' is a slippery word that expresses multiplicity without distinguishing between 'many' and 'few', but we know of at least seven maids who found themselves husbands, even if we cannot precisely determine when or where their marriages took place.

Virginia's first general assembly had ordered ministers to keep a record of christenings, marriages and deaths, and report annually to Virginia's secretary.[18] Since so few of the colony's early records have survived, tracing those maids who adopted their husbands' surnames then died within two or three years is virtually impossible, aside from fleeting appearances in court records. But crucially for this story, King James ordered a count of everyone living in Virginia in January 1625 grouped into musters or households, which also sought details of their relationships to each other and how well supplied they were in terms of food, livestock, buildings, arms and servants. Settlers were in addition asked to record the ship that had brought them to Virginia and the date of their arrival. While not everybody complied in full, we can make reasonable guesses about the identity of brides with less common Christian names who had arrived by any of the bridal ships in 1621 and were still living early in 1625.[19]

We should be cautious nonetheless about identifying wives by their first names and arrival ships alone, especially when arrival dates are not given. You may read that the Margaret who arrived on the *Warwick* – arrival date unknown – and went on to marry the Lincolnshire smith Ezekiah Raughton (or Wroughton)[20] was Margaret Dauson from Suffolk, one of the Jamestown brides, brought up in Southwark by Mistress Elizabeth Stevenson. In 1625 the Raughtons were recorded as living on the College Land at Henricus, but at least one other Margaret had arrived in the colony by the same ship, 'Mrgrett Riche', one of several servants imported by the Kentish gentleman Thomas Crispe, who might just as easily have become Raughton's wife.[21]

Of the thirteen maids who arrived on the *Marmaduke*, we can be reasonably confident that two married ancient planters: twenty-three-year-old Catherine Finch, originally from Herefordshire, and nineteen-year-old Audry Hoare, whose stories I pick up in later chapters. Both husbands had travelled to Virginia in 1611 in a fleet of ships under Sir Thomas Dale, Catherine's husband Robert Fisher arriving by the *Elizabeth*, and Audry Hoare's husband Thomas Harris on the *Prosperous*. Sailing via the Canaries and the West Indies, the ships had reached Point Comfort by 22 May 1611, bringing 300 people, supplies, horses, cattle, goats, rabbits, pigeons and poultry. The men were company servants for the most part, described as 'honest, sufficient artificers… carpenters, smiths, coopers, fishermen, tanners, shoemakers, shipwrights, brickmen, gardeners, husbandmen and laboring men of all sorts.'[22] Like other ancient planters, they gained their freedom when Sir George Yeardley returned to the colony as governor with instructions to free all company servants who had arrived before Dale's departure in 1616.

Harder to identify by their Christian names are the multitude of Anns and Elizabeths who came to Virginia on any of the bridal ships, so I cannot positively name the third Jamestown bride to net herself an ancient planter, one of several Elizabeths who arrived on the *Warwick* in 1621. Like the other two husbands, John Downeman had come to Virginia in 1611, travelling by the *John & Francis*. In January 1625 he gave his age as thirty-three, eleven years older than his wife. Of the seven Elizabeths aboard the *Warwick*, the best matches in age are the gentleman's daughter from Westminster, Elizabeth Nevill, and the plasterer's daughter Elizabeth Pearson from Oxford, both aged nineteen at the time of their embarkation, or twenty-year-old Elizabeth Bovill (or Borrill), presented to the company by her mother, Edith Smith. We can discount Elizabeth Dag, who married William Cobb (see Chapter 14) and the widowed Elizabeth Grinley, who was surely too old. Recorded as twenty-six in 1621, Grinley would have been twenty-nine or thirty by 1625, when John Downeman's wife was reputedly just twenty-two. The two other *Warwick* Elizabeths (Gervase Markham's sixteen-year-old daughter and Elizabeth Starkey) were surely too young.

The Downemans may have married soon after Elizabeth came to the colony. By February 1624 they were living in Elizabeth City, and shortly after that Elizabeth gave birth to a daughter, Mary, who did not survive long and was buried on 23 November 1624. The following January, childless again, the Downemans were living in some comfort in a fortified house with reasonable supplies of arms, six barrels of corn, one kid goat and a sixteen-year-old servant lad called Moyses Stones.[23] Fellow residents of Elizabeth City included John and Ann Laydon – formerly Ann Burras, one of the first two English women to come to Jamestown – and their four daughters, Virginia, Alice, Katherin and Margerett, all born in Virginia.

On paper, John Downeman was an ideal catch.[24] A modest landowner, he patented one hundred acres across from Elizabeth City on the south side of the James River,[25] which was still considered dangerous territory, as settlement had barely started there. All we know of his character is that, like many settlers, he had an explosive temper. For making 'oprobrius speeches' to a naturalized French Protestant settler called Nicholas Martiau he was fined ten pounds by the Jamestown court and ordered to make a public apology in church.[26] Such behaviour did not prevent his appointment as a burgess for Elizabeth City, however, or as one of eight commissioners to a new monthly court established there in spring 1629.[27]

The Virginia Company will have thought less highly of two settlers who each married one of several Anns sailing on the *Marmaduke*. Both men were relatively recent arrivals: Thomas Doughtie, who came by the *Marigold* in 1619; and Nicholas Baly, who arrived by the *Jonathan* in 1620. The Balys lived for a time at West and Shirley Hundred, but by January 1625 both couples, still childless, were living at Sir George Yeardley's old plantation of Flowerdew Hundred, which by then had been renamed Peirsey's Hundred after its new owner, Abraham Peirsey, Virginia's cape merchant and a hugely successful planter.[28] Although Doughtie and Baly each headed his own household, neither man owned a house and they had no servants of their own. Relatively well provided with arms (the Doughties had one gun, one coat of mail, a sword, four pounds of powder and twenty pounds of lead), they had only modest food supplies: the Baly household had four barrels of corn and one hundred dry fishes, while the Doughties had less corn and only fifty dry fishes, but they did possess one pig.

Nicholas Baly sounds a particularly poor catch. Having arrived as an indentured servant just one year before his future wife, he persuaded Abraham Peirsey to buy his freedom from Sir George Yeardley, along with that of another servant called Jonas Riley. Peirsey paid Yeardley 500 pounds of tobacco for the two men's freedom, clearly expecting the debt to be repaid, but the pair dragged their heels and in early 1625, by which time Nicholas and Ann were married, the Jamestown court ordered the two men to pay Peirsey 396 pounds of tobacco and twelve barrels of corn, or to saw 10,000 feet of boards for him.[29]

The *Marmaduke* brought at least four Anns who might have married either Doughtie or Baly. Since Ann Jackson never married (see Chapter 18) and the ages of the two wives are unknown, I cannot say for certain which of the other three married either of the two men. In her late twenties, husbandman's daughter Ann Tanner from Chelmsford in Essex was skilled at brewing, baking, making butter and cheese, sewing, spinning and general 'huswifery', all useful skills in a planter's wife.[30] Gentleman's daughter Ann Harmer from Baldock in Hertfordshire was younger, at twenty-one, and came from a family of eight children. Of a higher social status, she was raised by a seamstress and possessed rarefied though less immediately useful sewing skills, working with gold and silks. Of the third woman, Ann Buergen, we know only that she was taken on board at the Isle of Wight by Robert Newland, after the well born Mistress Joan Fletcher was 'turned back'.

The seven brides whose husbands can be traced were surely not the only Jamestown brides to marry; others clearly adopted their husband's surname and sank without trace. But as the women's stories unravel, we discover that not all the maids found husbands and the obvious question is why. Were they any less handsome than their married sisters, or less obviously endowed with the skills and mettle required in a planter's wife? Were they simply unlucky? Or were they rather more fastidious in their choice of mate and disappointed by the poor calibre of available husbands?

The brides who came from gentry families will have found it especially hard to secure husbands to match their previous station in life. Virginia's elite had other ways of finding a wife,[31] and the gentlemen adventurers who came over in large numbers in the colony's early years had for the most part proved unsuited to the hardships of frontier life. Captain John Smith castigated them as useless parasites, ignorant of toil and labour and much given to melancholy when conditions proved tougher than expected.[32] Most had either died or gone home, and by the early 1620s a new breed of gentlemen colonists either had wives back home, like Captain George Thorpe, or had brought their wives and children with them, like Captain John Woodlief, Thorpe's associate in the plantation of Berkeley Hundred.[33]

Aside from the company's instructions to the governor and council to be as fathers to the women in the matter of choosing a husband, we know little about the mechanics of how the matches were made. It is reasonable to suppose that eligible men – those without wives and with reasonable prospects of paying the tobacco price required – were called to Jamestown, much like the burgesses required to attend the colony's periodic general assemblies held in the church. This is how the Virginian novelist Mary Johnston imagined it would happen in her wildly popular novel *To Have and to Hold*, which borrowed the central idea of the Virginia Company's importation and sale of brides in the colony's early years. First serialized in the *Atlantic Monthly* and published in book form in 1900, Johnston's novel (her second) brought her fame and fortune and was turned into two silent films in 1916 and 1922, both now presumed lost.[34]

Johnston's atmospheric novel starts with the hero, Ralph Percy, sailing down a deserted James River in reluctant pursuit of a bride, having heard about the women's arrival from his friend Master John Rolfe. As he steps ashore at Jamestown, he hears the ringing of the newly installed church bells and sees the women emerging from their houses to gather in the market square, where the Reverend Bucke and Master Wickham of Henricus are waiting for them.

These were not the first women to come to Jamestown, as Johnston rightly implies. Once the native population was removed from the reckoning, this 'natural Eden' had boasted several thousand Adams and but some three score Eves, for the most part 'either portly and bustling or withered and shrewish housewives, of age and experience to defy the serpent'. These new arrivals were very different, however: 'Ninety slender figures decked in all the bravery they could assume; ninety comely faces, pink and white, or clear brown with the rich blood showing through; ninety pair of eyes, laughing and alluring, or downcast with long fringes sweeping rounded cheeks; ninety pair of ripe red lips.'[35]

Women and colonists crowd into Jamestown's small church to hear a long service of praise and thanksgiving. Towards the end Percy catches sight of the woman who will become his wife. She is clothed Puritan-style in a dark woollen dress, severe and unadorned, close ruff and prim white coif, beyond her 'a row of milkmaid beauties, red of cheek, free of eye, deep-bosomed, and beribboned like Maypoles'.

From the church the congregation disgorges to a 'fair green meadow' where four ministers have established pulpits of turf and set themselves up for business. Scorned by the women for his workaday dress, Percy stays aloof, a silent spectator to their courting, watching a 'shepherdess from Arcadia' as she waves back 'a dozen importunate gallants' then tosses her knot of blue ribbon into their midst before marching off with the wearer of her favour. Tall Jack Pride courts a milliner's apprentice, the pair endlessly bobbing and bowing to each other. A pastoral maid quizzes her beau about his wealth and material possessions. 'I'll take you,' she says promptly on discovering that he is the proud possessor of two cows, three acres of tobacco, a dozen hens, two cocks, three beds, one chest, one trunk, one leather carpet, six calfskin chairs and two or three of rush, five pairs of sheets, eighteen coarse linen napkins and six alchemy spoons.

Is that how it was? I imagine that most negotiations were more protracted than Johnston suggests, as each party weighed up the suitability of the other. Prospective husbands will have inspected the women's particulars listing their skills and provenance, although not all the men could read, as we shall see. The carefully annotated lists should have steered the men towards women who were skilled at sewing or the mysteries of housewifery, women who could bake and brew and supply the 'good drinke' for which the colony pined, 'wine beinge too deere' and Virginia's climate too hot to make malt from barley.[36] Virginian farmers might also be expected to favour the daughters of gardeners or husbandmen, who would be used to working the land, even if they came without any knowledge of growing tobacco.

The women for their part would want to assess the men's present and future prospects, measured not by English coin but by land acreage and tobacco yield and by the extent of their homestead: the precise number of houses, boats, pieces of armour, storehouses, tobacco houses, barrels of corn and other produce, dry fish, wet fish, biscuits and bacon flitches, cattle and swine and other livestock, poultry, and all the material possessions, many imported from the home country, that brought civility to the frontier. We may hope that the colony's leaders took their parental responsibilities seriously and helped to guide the women in their choices, as family and friends would have done at home.

Determined to protect property interests by regulating marriage, especially among the servant population, Virginia's first general assembly of 1619 had decreed that any maid or maidservant wishing to marry must obtain permission from those who exercised power over her: parents, masters and mistresses, or both the magistrate and minister of the place where she lived.[37] The Jamestown brides came expressly with their parents' or their relatives' blessing and were not to be treated as servants, but this requirement allowed the colony's political leaders to veto unsuitable husbands, if they chose. Once a marriage was approved, we can safely assume that one of Virginia's several ministers will have conducted a short ceremony before the congregation assembled at church in Jamestown or elsewhere, followed by a sermon or communion.

In seventeenth-century England the giving of rings was common, as a token of love and commitment and a mark of ownership of the woman by the man.[38] Fragments of braided and gold rings from the colony's early years have survived at Jordan's Journey, where the former Catherine Finch settled with her husband, and also at Flowerdew Hundred, home to two of the *Marmaduke* Anns. The Flowerdew collection at the Alderman Library in Charlottesville boasts a charming gold posy ring inscribed, 'Grace mee with acceptance'[39] but the brides shipped out by the Virginia Company were surely married off without the niceties of a betrothal ritual. They did, however, arrive with another traditional bridal gift: white lamb gloves supplied by London perfumer William Piddock, the one touch of luxury among the clothing provided by the Virginia Company.[40]

After the marriage ceremony in church came riotous feasting and drinking, in England at least, accompanied by music, dancing and much ribaldry until the newly weds were finally bedded and left to themselves. January and February were lean months in Virginia's agricultural cycle and the dearth of good liquor often lamented, so any marriages that took place immediately were unlikely to match the wedding feast for more than a hundred guests provided in Bermuda for one of Pocahontas's attendant Indian maids.[41] Marriage was nonetheless an occasion to be celebrated, and for the pranksters among Virginia's population English ballads provided plenty of ribald source material, none better than 'A Market for Young Men', which told of 'pretty young Women and Maids' – widows too – to be offered at reasonable rates by public sale:

> At Maidenhead-court, I well can report,
> There's one which no Gallant e're enter'd her Fort,
> Drest in a Nightrail, with a train to her tail,
> This Lady she will be exposed to sale
> For Clip'd Money.[42]

CHAPTER TWELVE

Dispersal

The maids who failed to find a husband immediately could not remain indefinitely in Jamestown; the place was simply too small to house so many single women. Since they had arrived without stores, company agent John Pountis needed to dispatch them to settlements that could feed them and where he could be sure of meeting the Virginia Company's demand that unmarried maids should be 'putt to severall houshoulders that have wives till they can be provided of husbandes'.[1] Pountis clearly took his responsibilities seriously, later receiving 'very hartie thanks' from the Virginia Company's council for his abundant 'care & charitie' in providing for the maids and a special 'remembrance of theire loves' from the adventurers in the maids' magazine, who doubtless hoped for a good return on their investment.[2]

It is nonetheless curious that Pountis picked two of the colony's newest settlements to receive some of the maids, where they will have experienced frontier life at its rawest. Perhaps he had no choice. Provisions that winter were as scarce as ever, prompting Frenchman Peter Arondelle to complain personally to Sir Edwin Sandys about his family's meagre rations, 'but a pinte and a halfe of musty meale for a man a day',[3] a far cry from the plentiful pigs, turkeys, geese, cocks, hens, ducks and good fat capons promised in the Virginia Company's promotional literature and in popular ballads such as 'The Maydens of Londons brave adventures'.[4]

And so the women parted company. The ones who had quickly netted a husband slipped quietly into their new lives as wives to the planters. Of the remaining maids, some may have stayed on at Jamestown while others dispersed in small groups to settlements up and down the James River. If Jamestown's shabby state had come as a shock, we may hope that their new homes opened their eyes to the glorious Eden promised to them by the Virginia Company, a land that was 'rich, spacious and well watered; temperate as for the Climate; very healthfull after men are a little accustomed to it; abounding with all Gods naturall blessings: The Land replenished with the goodliest Woods in the world, and those full of *Deere*, and other Beasts for sustenance.'[5]

Despite all the colony's earlier tribulations, the women had come to Virginia at a time of great optimism for the future. On first landing in the country, Governor Sir Francis Wyatt judged it 'setled in a peace (as all men there thought) sure and unviolable'. Swords were rarely worn and guns brought out even more rarely, except for hunting deer and fowl. Able at last to reap the benefit of their long years of toil, the ancient planters and investors in particular plantations had chosen the richest grounds for their settlements, placing them 'scatteringly and straglingly... and the further from neighbors held the better', keeping their houses open to 'the Savages, who were alwaies friendly entertained at the tables of the English, and commonly lodged in their bed-chambers'. Not only were planters 'placed with wonderfull content upon their private dividents', new settlements 'pursued with an hopefull alacrity' and all the colony's projects set to thrive, but relations with the natives appeared to open 'a faire gate' for their conversion to Christianity, one of the stated aims of the whole Virginian adventure.[6]

All was not as it seemed, however. Edward Waterhouse, the Virginia Company's secretary in London, would later use Wyatt's letter to condemn with hindsight the colony's fatal complacency in the months leading up to the catastrophic events of 22 March 1622, but at the time of the maids' arrival Virginia's future did indeed

Virginia's rivers, creeks and bays teemed with fish, which the Indians were far more skilled at catching than the early settlers.

look bright. Their coming to the colony was just one of the many good things that happened that year. The Earl of Southampton also lauded the sixteen or so people sent to make glass beads for the Indian trade, the magazine of essential supplies valued at £2,000, the dispatch of the *Discovery* to trade in furs with the Indians, twenty-five people brought to Virginia to build boats, ships and pinnaces, and seven more to plant one thousand acres as financial backing for a projected 'East Indie School' to raise native children in the ways of Christianity.[7]

Since Virginia possessed only primitive trails, and the swampy rivers and creeks impeded travel by land, it was surely by boat or canoe that Sir Edwin Sandys' kinswoman Cicely Bray and Barbara Burchens – both still without husbands – travelled to Powle-Brooke, one of the smaller private plantations then springing up around the James River. Located at the western mouth of Powell Creek, a tributary on the south side of the river some twenty-five miles upriver from Jamestown, it had begun as a plantation of six hundred acres laid out from around 1619 for Captain Nathaniel Powell and John Smith, not the legendary captain but an ancient planter who had come to Virginia in 1611 aboard the *Elizabeth* at the same time as Catherine Finch's husband, Robert Fisher.[8] The women's new home was less than ten miles by water from Flowerdew Hundred, Sir George Yeardley's thousand-acre plantation at Tobacco Point.

Aside from having travelled together on the *Warwick*, Cicely Bray and Barbara Burchens had little in common. Eight years apart in age, they hailed from very different social ranks. Seventeen-year-old Burchens was a cloth maker's daughter from Denby, either the Derbyshire village in the Peak District or the Welsh market town of Denbigh celebrated for glove making and weaving. She came to the Virginia Company highly commended as a 'Mayde of honest and Cyvill Conversation' by Mistress Brewer, the wife of John Brewer, a yeoman of His Majesty's guard. Cloth working was an honourable trade, ranked twelfth in order of precedence among the twelve great City livery companies, and living in service with a member of the king's personal bodyguard shows that young Barbara Burchens had good connections to London's elite workers. But she came undeniably from artisan stock.

Cicely Bray, by contrast, was gentry to the core. A century or more before her birth a Sandys of the Vyne branch of the family had married the daughter of John Bray, half-brother to the celebrated courtier, architect and Chancellor of the Duchy of Lancaster, Sir Reginald Bray. Two generations before that, a male Bray (Richard) had married a Sandys female (Margaret Sandys of Furness Fell), creating the first of the links that joined the two families and their several branches.

Cicely belonged to the line of descent that had settled ultimately in Gloucestershire, where her relatives included 'John Bray gent.' of Donnington and Captain Edmund Bray of nearby Great Barrington – possibly her grandfather – who died in 1620 and was buried in the church of St Mary the Virgin there. You can find the captain's stone effigy lying on a plinth in the south aisle squeezed between the organ and the wall. Although his face has quite worn away, his fine Jacobean ruff clings crisply to his neck and he wears his sword strapped to his right side, apparently in penance for having killed a man in the Low Countries. Captain Bray's second son Sylvester had married Cicely or Cecily Mayne, bringing her Christian name into the Gloucestershire Brays and implying a connection between the Cicely Bray who travelled to Jamestown in 1621 and the captain commemorated in stone in a Cotswold village.[9]

The man in charge of Powle-Brooke, where the two women were bound, was precisely the sort of colonist the company had hoped would take unmarried maids into their care. A gentleman from the same class as Cicely Bray, Captain Nathaniel Powell was one of the few survivors from the very first group of settlers still in the colony. Captain John Smith praised him as a 'valiant Souldier' (they had explored the Chesapeake together, and Powell had gone in search of the lost colonists), and Powell obligingly completed some of the gaps in Smith's *Generall Historie* of Virginia, published long after Smith had left the colony.[10] No stranger to public office, Powell had served as acting governor for ten days after deputy governor Samuel Argall abruptly left the colony and was appointed to Virginia's council of state in 1621. He was, in the words of the Virginia Company's council, 'a man of extraordinary merritt'.[11]

As an ancient planter and co-founder of his own plantation, Captain Powell would have made a splendid husband for Bray or any of the better-born maids, but sadly for them he was no longer free, having married Joyce Tracy just the year before. While of similar rank to Bray, Joyce Tracy had one advantage the other could not match: a stake in Virginian land through her father William Tracy, an active investor in the Virginia Company and in the new plantation of Berkeley Hundred on the north side of the James, settled in 1619 under the initial command of Captain John Woodlief. Joyce's father had set out for the colony the following September, taking his family with him: wife Mary, son Thomas, daughter Joyce and a young kinswoman, Francis Grevill. They left Bristol in the *Supply* on 18 September 1620 with a group of fifty or so men, women and two children, bound for Berkeley Hundred where William Tracy and George Thorpe were to take over as joint commanders.[12] Eight of the men were described as gentlemen, although two of these returned to England, one (Nicholas Came) by the ship that had carried him to Virginia.

By the time the group reached Berkeley Hundred on 29 January 1621, Captain Powell and Joyce Tracy were married; tradition has it that they wed at sea, or they may have married soon after the *Supply* arrived at Jamestown. Francis Grevill also quickly found a husband among Jamestown's elite, marrying Nathaniel West, a younger brother of Virginia's one-time governor Lord Delaware. But William Tracy did not survive long enough to reap his anticipated rewards. By April he was dead, seriously indebted,[13] and Powell had taken his new bride to the plantation named after him. Accompanying the new Mistress Powell was her maidservant, Isabell Gifford, who had travelled out to Virginia with the Tracys and married Adam Reymer (or Raynor) at sea.[14]

Today the site of Powle-Brooke forms part of the James River National Wildlife Refuge, which I visited one hot, still morning in early spring, before the trees turned green. Aside from the highway's distant drone and occasional hooting from a railroad, the silence was broken only by warbling birds and throatier bullfrogs, and the tramp of my feet through winter-crisp leaves.

The water is glassy still, reflecting upside-down trees that mingle with the saplings growing from the swamp. A bird darts in close, spots me sitting by the water's edge then flies off to squawk from a nearby tree. More sounds of wildlife disturbed: wings flapping and the plop of a waterfowl ducking underwater. I marvel at the freshly aromatic smell of wax myrtle rubbed between my fingers, a clean, sweet smell, mildly antiseptic. The blue water of the creek ripples in the wind. Only the margins are brown, clogged and oily.

What did they think of their new home, Cicely Bray and young Barbara Burchens? Did they feel trapped by the trees, the water, the harsh drudgery of frontier life? Were they fretful at the dangers they faced, living far from Jamestown in the midst of so-called savages, the streets of London and the rolling Gloucestershire countryside a distant memory? Or were they glad to be making a new life for themselves away from fathers, brothers, family members, masters and mistresses who sought to control their every action?

They were not alone of course. The settlement where they lived was home to a dozen people at least, and they had Mistress Joyce Powell and her maidservant Isabell for female company. Just the year before, nearby Flowerdew Hundred counted five women and four children among its total population of seventy-seven people.[15] Even closer to Powle-Brooke was a cluster of smallish settlements, all begun in 1618 or 1619: Captain John Ward's plantation, Captain Bargrave's plantation and Martin's Brandon, but these were clearly unsuitable for unchaperoned maids. In March 1620 they counted just one woman among their settler population of eighty-four.

Still on the south side of the James but some way downriver on the lower reaches of Burwell's Bay lay Edward Bennett's plantation, also known as Bennett's Welcome or Warraskoyack after the Indian tribe that lived in what is now Isle of Wight County. Fort Boykin marks the approximate spot today, close to the oyster beds and the dwindling ghost fleet of mothballed merchant ships held in reserve for national emergencies, fittingly painted a ghostly grey. At least three of the maids came here from Jamestown, all still unmarried: the widowed Marie Daucks, twenty-five years old and commended for her honesty and 'good Carriage' by her kinsman, Master Slocum of Mauden Lane in London; twenty-one-year-old Alse (Alice) Jones from Kidderminster in Worcestershire, lately come out of service with a Mr Binneons of Bishopsgate Street; and London-born Parnell Tenton, twenty years old, presented to the Virginia Company by her mother (her father was dead), and one of two maids recommended by Mr Hobson, an official of the Drapers' Company. ' She cann worke all kinds of ordinary workes' is all we know of her accomplishments.[16]

The Bennetts' plantation was even rawer than Powle-Brooke, settled only from late January or early February 1622, suggesting that the three maids will have spent the months of December and January at Jamestown before travelling downriver to their new home. Edward Bennett, the plantation's chief backer, was a London merchant, shipowner and member of the Virginia Company who obtained the patent to his land in the autumn of 1621 and immediately set about dispatching some two hundred settlers.[17] One of his associates was Richard Wiseman, who had invested in Captain Lawne's vacated property nearby, along with merchant Robert Newland from the Isle of Wight, who had organized the departure of the *Marmaduke* maids.[18] The main group of 120 settlers arrived at Bennett's Welcome in February 1622, led by seasoned settler Captain Ralph Hamor,[19] an ancient planter who had first come to the colony in 1609. Among them were two more Bennetts: Edward's brother Richard and the Reverend William Bennett, who became the plantation's minister.[20] It is possible that both were unmarried when the maids came to Bennett's Welcome: Richard would die intestate five years later, and the Reverend Bennett's wife did not come to Virginia until December 1622, on the *Abigail*, although they may have married before then in England and travelled to Virginia at different times.

A third plantation to which some of the maids dispersed was Martin's Hundred, one of the largest of the new breed of particular plantations and located some seven miles east of Jamestown: in 1620, its population of seventy-two people included fourteen women and thirteen children and young people.[21] Ann Jackson had come here to join her brother and sister-in-law, and since Martin's Hundred was settled by several married couples, other maids will almost certainly have accompanied her, among them nineteen-year-old Mary Elliott, brought up by her 'father-in-law' Maximillian Russell, whose 'good deserts' drew praise from Nicholas Ferrar.[22] Living with the Jacksons were two servants who had travelled out to Virginia with them: 'pottmaker' Thomas Ward, in his early to mid-forties, reputedly English North America's first craftsman potter,[23] and John Stevans (or Steephen), aged a little over thirty. Had life turned out differently for the young gardener's daughter from Wiltshire and Westminster, one or other might have made a bid for her hand, despite their lack of independent means and Ward's somewhat advanced age.

After a difficult birth, the plantation to which she had come was at last seated in the right place and 'do now againe go forward cherefully'.[24] What happened here was clearly of great concern to the Virginia Company back home, which looked on Martin's Hundred as a model for future plantations.[25] Formed in 1618, the settlement took its name from Richard Martin, the company's legal counsel who had defended the colony to parliament in 1614, when he declared in a witty if somewhat rambling speech that all Virginia required was 'but a few honest laborers burdened with children', by which he plainly meant hard-working family men with equally 'honest' wives.[26] Martin died in 1618, soon after his appointment as Recorder of London, and Sir John Wolstenholme took over as the society's chief investor, giving his name to Wolstenholme Town at the heart of the settlement. A patent of late January 1622 named several men connected with the maids' magazine among the society's many investors, including the Virginia Company's husband William Webb, organizer of the Virginia lotteries Gabriel Barbor, Christopher Martin and Nicholas Ferrar. The same patent directed the adventurers, tenants and servants of Martin's Hundred to diversify into products other than tobacco, among them corn, wine, iron, silk, silkgrass, hemp, flax and timber.[27]

Martin's Hundred was not in quite such good shape as many hoped, however. Only recently its leaders had declined a Virginia Company proposal to foster native children in order to instruct them in the 'true religion', claiming that the plantation was 'sorely weakened and as then in much confusion'. The arrival of maids without accompanying provisions would only add to their difficulties. The company worried that even the dozen lusty youths who arrived by the *Marmaduke* might need to be forcibly billeted among the existing settlers and was therefore heartily relieved to hear that the newcomers were received 'willinglie and lovinglie'.[28]

Ann herself will surely have received the warmest of welcomes from her brother and sister-in-law, her spirits lifted, one hopes, by the plantation's fine riverside location commanding views across a wide bend in the James River to Hog Island on the far side. Like all the maids who came with her, Jackson will have experienced the complex emotions of immigrants everywhere: relief at her safe arrival tempered by inevitable disappointment that her new life was not quite as she had imagined. And like all immigrants she will have struggled to cloak the wild and the strange with the mantle of old habits, her senses strained by the sights, sounds, smells of her new surroundings beside the majestic River James, where pinnaces and Indian canoes replaced the familiar wherries and lighters of the Thames, and where merchant ships like the *Marmaduke* and the *Warwick* – however incongruously framed by virgin forest – brought back memories of home.

Surveying her new domain, she cannot fail to have been struck by the precarious nature of her new existence, akin to England's Irish plantations but unlike anything she had experienced herself in Wiltshire or Westminster. As well as arming themselves against Indian attacks, Virginia's early settlers feared marauding Spanish

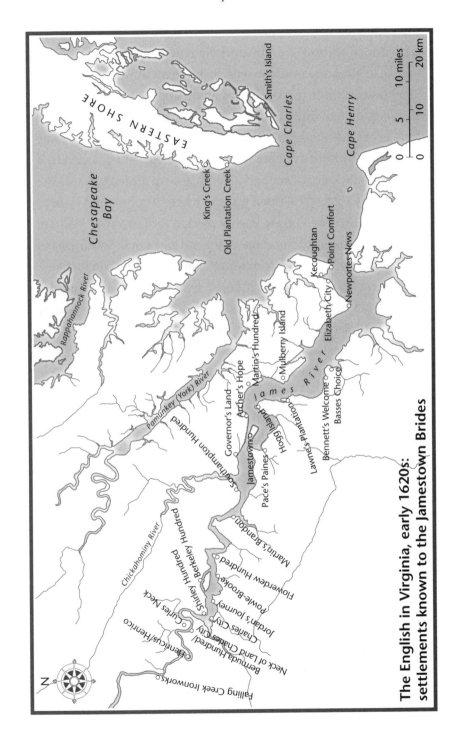

The English in Virginia, early 1620s: settlements known to the Jamestown Brides

ships and erected riverside forts, which Spanish spies dismissed as fashioned without craft by unskilled men and built of wooden boards 'so weak that a kick would break them down'.[29]

Yet however flimsy its defences might appear to their enemies, Ann Jackson had undeniably entered a fortified environment. At the heart of Wolstenholme Town stood a palisaded fort a little way back from the bluff, roughly trapezoid in shape and guarded by a watchtower at one corner and a gun platform aimed towards the river across a stretch of open ground where troops could muster. Inside the fort was a house hastily erected for Governor William Harwood, a couple of storehouses, a pond and a well. South-east of the fort lay the company compound, fenced rather than fortified, containing a three-room farmhouse with an open enclosure for animals tacked on to one end and three smaller structures, where potter Thomas Ward may have begun to make his pots.[30] Even closer to the river stood the homestead of warden John Boyse, John Jackson's fellow burgess at the general assembly of 1619, his house tightly palisaded and flanked with gun emplacements, one facing downriver towards the ravine known as Grice's Run, the other pointing squarely towards the river to cover any direct approach.[31]

Pushed right to the edge of the 'civilized' world, Ann Jackson, Cicely Bray and all the other maids who dispersed to distant settlements will have experienced the full shock of frontier life as they participated in the daily struggle to carve new homes from the wilderness. For anyone used to city life, the work involved was back-breaking. To clear space for growing crops, the English settlers had adopted native methods – 'spoiling the woods', as Captain John Smith called it, cutting broad notches in the bark of trees to kill them then burning or cutting the stumps, and planting their corn between the blackened remains.[32]

Once the land was properly cleared, most farmers turned to growing tobacco, the colony's one successful cash crop and its economic foundation. Back in England, labouring outdoors was men's work, while women took charge of the house and its surrounding yard, plus all the parallel tasks of 'huswifery'. Although the same division of labour theoretically applied in Virginia, the reality for many settler women was very different. In a land where labour was scarce and tobacco a greedy master, even wives might be called from their domestic tasks to help hoe the fields or perform sickening tasks like killing the worms that destroyed the tobacco crop.[33]

The plight of indentured serving women and the small number of recently arrived African captives was infinitely worse, of course. 'Give ear unto a Maid,/ That lately was betray'd,/ And sent into Virginny O', sings the heroine of a late seventeenth-century ballad, 'The Trapann'd Maiden: OR, The Distressed Damsel', which paints a miserable picture of life in Virginia. Transported against her will and forced to serve a five-year term, the 'damsel' recounts her litany of woes: underfed, dressed in rags and sleeping on straw, she works at her mistress's beck and call from daybreak, carrying water from the well on her head, pounding grain with her mortar, tending her mistress's child and 'a thousand Woes beside'.

> I have play'd my part,
> Both at Plow and at Cart,
> In the Land of Virginny, O:
> Billats from the Wood,
> Upon my back they load,
> When that I was weary,
> weary, weary, weary, O.

> Instead of drinking Beer,
> I drink the Water clear,
> In the Land of Virginny, O;
> Which makes me pale and wan
> Do all that e'r I can,
> When that I was weary,
> weary, weary, weary, O.[34]

Regardless of whether you worked alongside the men in the fields and whether or not you found a husband, all the Jamestown brides will have toiled long and hard at the essential domestic tasks that made life tolerable for everyone. Idleness was not an option; the company's insistence that 'no man be suffred to lyve Idlie, the example whereof might prove p[er]nitious unto the rest' applied just as firmly to women, prompting Virginia's first general assembly to insist that women should qualify for land shares as ancient planters alongside their menfolk, because 'in a newe plantaton it is not knowen whether man or woman be the most necessary'.[35]

Women typically looked after the animals, tended gardens, fetched water from nearby creeks and wells, washed clothes, raised young children, kept the household decently and cleanly clothed prepared food for the table. It was women's work to butcher, preserve and boil the homestead's precious hogs and goats, and to tend the domestic cattle that had arrived in the colony as early as 1611.[36] Although Virginia's summers were too hot to make hard cheeses, the women's industry can be linked to the milk pans that start appearing from about this time, patiently sifted from excavated sites in and around Jamestown. Used to separate milk from cream in the process of making butter and cheese, they helped to supply 'white meat' for the settlers' diet.[37]

Maids who could spin or weave, such as Essex-born Martha Baker, will have found their skills redundant, since all cloth was imported, and those with rarefied needle skills would have been thwarted by the Virginia Company's ban on wearing gold and silver thread by all but the colony's elite.[38] But ordinary sewing skills were much in demand for making and mending clothes for the entire plantation: 'we m[u]st here all perishe for want of clothinge and other necessaries' was a habitual complaint.[39] As for tasks like laundry, Thomas Niccolls was not the only male settler who yearned for female help. Some plantation sponsors stipulated that the wives of new tenants should be paid for helping with 'Cookinge washing mendinge of Clothes and other huswiferie.'[40]

For most aspects of daily life, the settlers relied on imports from home as the colony had as yet virtually no productive industries. The lack of pack thread for drying tobacco was a constant source of complaint; and ships' holds were crammed with basic necessities for frontier life such as needles, thread, leather points, kettles, axes, fishing nets, frying pans and nails.[41] You had to be nimble to adapt and survive. To overcome a shortage of sieves, settlers sifted their meal through pieces of leather 'burned full of holes with a hote Iron w[hi]ch is soe wide that the bran and all of the males [meal] goes through w[hi]ch I am p[er]swaded makes theire bread verie unhoulsome and is a great cause of theire fluxes.'[42]

Houses were similarly crude, surely a source of further disillusionment for the better-born maids and those who had worked in service for London's professional elite or master craftsmen. Virginian houses were put together quickly using light wooden frames and earthen walls, an 'earthfast' type of construction borrowed from Captain John Smith's native Lincolnshire and commonly used in medieval peasant homes.[43] They looked shoddy and deteriorated rapidly. 'Ther Howses are generally the worst yt ever I sawe ye meanest Cottages in England beinge every way equall (if not superior) with ye moste of the beste,' declared the visiting Captain Butler in 1623, an opinion that the daintier maids may well have shared.[44]

Yet in Virginia building houses as quickly as you could made perfect sense, reserving what capital you had to buy land and labour to grow the tobacco on which your fortune depended. Timber was in any case plentiful, stone virtually absent and bricks not yet in regular manufacture. Defending themselves against Butler's politically motivated criticism (discussed in Chapter 14), the planters argued that their homes were built 'for use and not for ornament and are soe farr from beinge soe meane as they are reported yt throughout his Mats: Dominions here, all labouringe mens houses (w[hi]ch wee cheifly p[ro]fesse our selvs to be) are in no wise generally for goodnes to be compared unto them.'[45]

But as a woman fresh from England, your spirits will inevitably have sunk as you crossed the threshold of your new home. Most contained just one room, measuring perhaps twenty-five feet by sixteen, which served as 'ther Kitchen, their Chamber, their all'.[46] A wooden ladder led up to the loft space, where children and servants slept. Aside from an enormous fireplace, furnishings were typically sparse: a bedstead if you were lucky, a chest for storage, wooden platters, a cooking pot, a mortar and pestle for pounding corn, a few knives and spoons, a bench or storage barrels for seating. A single glance was all it took to survey your new surroundings, which naturally lacked any additional rooms set aside for those 'home industries' that were your particular domain: baking, brewing, dairying, salting and curing.

Less obviously but no less painfully, you were entering a society and a social order in flux. Back home in England, servants, apprentices and their masters or mistresses commonly lived together in a cohesive household. Had you lived in service yourself, it was probably with neighbours, kinsmen or family connections as you passed through the young adult stage of your life before marrying and forming a household of your own. Here in Virginia the ties of kinship and community were broken, creating a more restless, fractured society and households that little resembled the family-centred social groups of blood relations and seasonal help you will have known back home. Even discounting the rascals and ruffians swept off the streets to rid the mother country of undesirables, most indentured servants were young, male and rootless, 'on the loose and on the make', which required a different sort of domestic arrangement that separated masters from servants. So as well as transplanting yourself geographically, you were entering a new kind of social space where the rules were not yet written. Adapting to your new environment would prove especially difficult for the women among you that failed to find husbands, who were neither servants nor mistresses but caught somewhere in between.

House construction in a few settlements was beginning to reflect this new order. Sir Thomas Dale had attempted to lure colonists to his settlements on the Upper James with the promise of 'a hansome howse of some foure roomes, or more if he have a family, to repose himselfe in rent free, and twelve English Acres of ground',[47] but he was doubtless bragging and by 1619 other places were taking the lead in matters of building. Within visiting distance of Cicely Bray and Barbara Burchens at Powle-Brooke, Sir George Yeardley's plantation at Flowerdew Hundred boasted a four-bayed house in which a lobby entrance and an internal chimney stack separated a parlour on one side from a hall and kitchen plus one or more service rooms on the other. Householders could withdraw to the parlour, away from the domestic activities taking place on the other side of the wall.[48] The planters were rightly proud of such developments, insisting that 'the houses of men of better Ranke and quallety they are soe much better and convenyent yt noe man of quallety wthout blushinge can make excepcon against them'.[49]

Food and drink could also cause problems for new arrivals accustomed to bread made with English grains, which required well tilled soiled and a more forgiving climate. Corn or maize was now your staple diet, as it was for the Indians, fruity and slightly musty in taste. For the middle rank of settlers cattle and pigs provided the primary source of meat, supplemented by Virginia's abundant wildlife, which included exotic birds like the great blue heron, the common loon and the trumpeter swan, as well as opossum, grey squirrel, sturgeon, Canada geese, ducks, turtles and passenger pigeons.[50]

Despite such apparent abundance, complaints about meagre rations and poor food recur throughout Virginia's formative years. In May 1621 newcomer Captain Thomas Nuce observed that the men under his command lived 'very barely for the most part: haueing no other foode but bread & water and such mann[er] of meate as they make of the Mayze: w[hi]ch I would to God I could say they had in any reasonable plenty.'[51] Nuce's wife had nonetheless just added a 'jolly boy' to the colony and remained in good health. Another recent settler, the perspicacious and generally sympathetic George Thorpe, blamed the Virginia Company's propaganda for exciting false expectations, insisting that 'more doe die here of the disease of theire minde then of theire body by haueing this countrey victualles over-praised unto them in England & by not knowinge they shall drinke water here.'[52]

Water was indeed a problem for early immigrants, who sickened and died in their hundreds from a lethal mix of contaminated wells and saltwater poisoning. Jamestown's water was especially deadly in summer, as the discharge from freshwater rivers fell and saltwater penetrated further up the James estuary.[53] Settlements upriver from Jamestown, such as Powle-Brook, escaped the brackish water, although Martin's Hundred and Bennett's Welcome lay in the saltwater zone. Europeans anyway preferred drinking beer to water. In England most adults drank at least one gallon of ale a day; men, women and even children drank alcohol at every meal, breakfast included.[54] Virginia's inability to produce ale or wine remained a source of vexation until well into the century, despite a beer made from Indian corn which George Thorpe claimed to prefer over 'good stronge Englishe beare'. The 'Dutchmen' recruited for the sawmills were so disgusted by the colony's lack of ale and entertainment that they threatened to return home, but noted tippler Secretary John Pory remained optimistic that Virginia could produce good wines, requesting slips of the large vine of 'Corynth grapes', which he had seen at the London house of merchant Nicholas Leate. In Virginia you could scarcely walk three steps 'in any place unmanured' without tangling your foot in some vine or other, he told Sir Edwin Sandys back in London, commenting, 'I drinke water here w[i]th as much (yf not more) pleasure and contente as I dranke wine in those partes'. 'Bravely spoken' added John Ferrar in the margin of Pory's letter, but Governor Wyatt was less forgiving. 'To plant a Colony by water drinkers was an inexcusable errour in those, who layd the first foundacion, and have made it a recieved custome, which until it be laide downe againe, there is small hope of health'.[55]

So what do you make of your new environment now that you have recovered from the shock of arrival and begun the slow process of acclimatization? February is habitually Virginia's coldest month, but you have known extreme cold back home. The older maids among you might remember the bitter winter of 1608 when the Thames froze over completely, just as it will freeze again in the winter of the year you left.

Writing mid-century, George Gardyner of Peckham attributed Virginia's unwholesome air to its changeable climate, 'which is mighty extream in heat and cold', and to Virginia's many 'Swamps, standing-waters and Marishes, and mighty store of Rivers'. Two other 'pernicious companions' haunting the English settlers he identified as 'Country Duties', his coy euphemism for venereal disease, and rattlesnakes, so called 'for the rattle in her taile, whose bitings are present death'. Gardyner was presumably referring to the canebreak rattlesnake, which inhabits the forests and swampy glades of south-eastern Virginia, over-wintering in hollow trees and tree stumps.[56] By arriving in winter, you are at least spared an encounter with such creatures until the onset of Virginia's steaming-hot summers, when 'this vermine… is so stirring that they are in the fields, woods, and commonly in their houses, to their great anoyance'.[57]

But there is one strange presence you cannot ignore: that of the Indians who lurk unseen in the encircling forests and come daily into your settlements, sitting at your tables and even sleeping in your beds, if Governor Wyatt is to be believed. A decade before you came to the colony William Strachey painted their different dispositions for a European audience, considering some Indians

For maids who survived into the summer, rattlesnakes will surely have become a fact of life, drawn here by Mark Catesby for The Natural History of Carolina, Florida and the Bahamas.

too fearful to trust the settlers, others bold and audacious enough to enter the English forts to 'truck and trade with us and looke us in the face, crying all freindes, when they have but new done us a mishchief'. For all his prejudices, William Strachey has left us one of the most closely observed accounts of how the native population appeared to European eyes. As a woman, you would surely have been more circumspect in your observations, less blatant in your curiosity and perhaps a little fearful of coming too close to the 'other'.

Skin colour was the first difference to which Strachey drew attention, describing Virginia's indigenous people as 'generally of a Coulour browne, or rather tawnye', a sort of sodden quince colour, which he attributed to a paste made from red-tempered earth and the juices of certain roots with which mothers smeared their newborn infants, who remained 'so smudged and besmeered' throughout their lives, partly from custom and partly to protect against Virginia's swarms of stinging mosquitoes 'which heere breed aboundantly, amonst the marish whorts [plants], and fenburies'.[58] Turning to hair, physiognomy and anatomy, Strachey noted that 'Their hayre is black, grosse, longe and thick, the men have no beardes, their noses are broad flatt and full at the end, great bigge Lippes, and wyde mouthes, (yet nothing so unsightly as the Moores,) they are generally tall of stature, and streight, of comely proportion.'

To clothe themselves, Indian men wore animal skins in winter and the 'better sort' donned large mantles of several skins decorated with white beads, copper or painted, 'but the Comon sort have scarse wherewithall to cover their nakednes, but stick long blades [of] grasse, the leaves of Trees or such like under broad Baudricks [belts] of Leather which covers them behind and before'. The better sort of women also wore mantles of animal skins, 'fynely drest, shagged and frindged at the skirt, carved and coulored' and prettily decorated with beasts, fowl, tortoises or more fanciful images. Young girls went naked until they were eleven or twelve, when they would don a leather apron 'as doe our artificers or handicrafts men'.

English fear of the Indians was enshrined in the very first law laid down by Virginia's general assembly of 1619, which implicitly recognized that the way the settlers behaved could affect their relations with the local population: 'be it enacted that noe injury or oppression be wrought by the English ag[ain]st the Indians whereby the present peace might be disturbed, & antient quarrels might be revived.[59]

As for drawing closer to some of the 'better disposed' of the Indians, the general assembly counselled against either rejecting or accepting their advances, but where Indians came voluntarily to the larger settlements, the settlers should admit no more than five or six into any one place and keep them under a 'good guard'. On no account should Indians be entertained by lone inhabitants, 'for generally (though some amongst many may proove good) they are a most trecherous people, & quickly gone when they have done a villainy'.

By 1621, despite the uneasy peace that prevailed, most English settlers bestowed upon the Indians nothing but 'maledictions and bitter execrations'.[60] A notable exception was Captain George Thorpe, who had taken sole charge of the plantation of Berkeley Hundred after William Tracy's death. John Pory likened his coming to that of 'an Angell from heaven', while Sir George Yardley called him 'a most sufficient gentleman, virtuous and wise'.[61]

As Thorpe explained to Sir Edwin Sandys, his 'poore understandinge' led him to believe that 'if there bee wronge on any side it is on o[u]rs who are not soe charitable to them as Christians ought to bee'. The Indians – especially the better sort – were of 'a peaceable & vertuous disposition', their only fault being that they were 'a litle cravinge and that in a niggardly fassion for they will comonly p[ar]te w[i]th nothinge they have whatsoever is given them'. To cement relations between the two nations, he urged Sandys to send English clothes and other household stuff for trading purposes, and to make a public declaration of the company's desire to convert the people to Christianity.[62]

So determined was Captain Thorpe to improve relations between the two peoples that he went to see Opechancanough, Powhatan's brother and effective successor as paramount leader of the Indians. Their conversation went well, he reported, declaring that the Indian leader 'had more motiones of religione in him, then Coulde be ymmagined in soe greate blindnes, for hee willinglye Acknolwedged that theirs was nott the right waye, desiringe to bee instructed in ours and confessed that god loved us better then them'.[63] They talked also of the stars and of the constellations, and Thorpe learned to his delight that the Great Bear was called the same in both languages. The Indians were then in the midst of their hunting, said Opechancanough; Thorpe should visit him again when their hunting was done. Poor unsuspecting George Thorpe failed to realize that Opechancanough was playing him like a pawn in his bid to sweep away the English usurpers.

Others have documented the many atrocities committed on both sides of the conflict and viewed events through Indian eyes.[64] *The Jamestown Brides* offers a different perspective: that of young women fresh from England caught up in a clash of cultures sparked by the Europeans' rapacious hunger for land. Like the just and gentle George Thorpe, they had no idea what the Indians were planning next.

CHAPTER THIRTEEN

Catastrophe

*The Lord hath sayd to the destroying angel,
It is sufficient, hold now thy hand; the mortality of your
people is ceased abroad: and the hope of your good
returns is increased at home.*[1]

News travelled slowly then. By the time Patrick Copland preached his sermon of thanksgiving for the happy success of Virginian affairs on Thursday 18 April 1622, a month had elapsed since the so-called Good Friday Massacre had devastated the colony in Virginia. The tag is wrong on two counts: fairness demands that you call it an Indian attack, not a massacre; and Easter that year fell on 17 March by the Julian calendar then in use across English North America.[2] Language aside, neither Copland nor his congregation of Virginia Company worthies gathered at Bow church in Cheapside had any inkling of how sickeningly inappropriate was his chosen theme.

Taking his text from Psalm 107, Verses 23 to 32, about God calming a storm at sea, Copland spoke of the 'happie league of Peace and Amitie soundly concluded, and faithfully kept, betweene the English and the Natives, that the feare of killing each other is now vanished away'. Among his many wonderful works, God had stayed the hungry lions and mollified the savages, said Copland, setting out his vision of Virginia as a place to take England's excess population, especially the starving poor who cluttered up the streets of its capital, a kind of bloodletting, said Copland, 'For, even as bloud, though it be the best humour in the body, yet if it abound in greater quantitie, then the vessell and state of the body will contayne and beare, doeth indanger the body, and oftentimes destroyes it.' But as Copland and his audience would learn to their horror nearly three months later, the bloodletting in Virginia was all too real and in no way metaphorical.

For the colonists in Virginia, Friday 22 March 1622 had begun as an ordinary day devoted to the usual tasks of plantation life. Assuming that they followed routines developed in rural England, the settlers will have risen an hour or two before sunrise, around six in the morning at this time of year, the men going off to work in the yard or the fields for a couple of hours before returning for a communal breakfast prepared by the women, who will meanwhile have set the house in good order, milked the cows and tended to any young children.[3] The women fresh from England may have been a little alarmed by the appearance of more Indians than usual, but according to the Virginia Company's later account they came without bows and arrows or other weapons, apparently to trade the many deer, turkeys, fish, furs and other provisions they brought with them.[4]

Although the colonists could not know this, small bands of unarmed Indians were appearing at the same appointed hour at settlements up and down the James River, in some places even sitting down to breakfast with the colonists, 'whom immediately with their owne tooles and weapons, eyther laid downe, or standing in their houses, they basely and barbarously murthered, not sparing eyther age or sexe, man, woman or childe'. The same fate befell those colonists working about their homesteads or out in the fields planting corn and tobacco, gardening, making bricks, building, sawing; the Indians slaughtered anyone caught unawares, being perfectly familiar with the settlers' daily routines 'for the desire we had of effecting that great master-peece of workes, their conversion.'

During that one fatal morning, 347 men, women and children were reportedly killed by 'that perfidous and inhumane people' – between a quarter and a third of the entire colony, most of them slain with their own weapons. As choreographed by Opechancanough, the events of 22 March demonstrated the lethal efficacy of the Indians' strategy: taking their enemy by surprise, instilling sudden terror by erupting into a fearsome din, 'leaping and singing after their accustomed tune, which they use onely in Warres' and giving 'such horrible shouts and screeches, as so many infernall hell hounds could not have made them more terrible'.[5] Not content with mere murder, the Indians 'fell after againe upon the dead, making as well as they could, a fresh murder, defacing, dragging, and mangling the dead carkasses into many pieces, and carrying some parts away in derision, with base and bruitish triumph'. Wherever possible, they set fire to plantation houses and outhouses, killing cattle and stealing guns, returning afterwards to burn settlements abandoned in the pandemonium.[6]

From both an English and an Indian point of view, what was truly shocking about the day's events was the slaughter of so many women and children. Had they reflected on their own conduct, the English should have recognized the extraordinary brutality they had themselves shown towards women and children they viewed as savages and therefore without claim to 'Christian' treatment. George Percy relates the story of an Indian queen who was captured with her children. As the English sailed back to Jamestown, the children were killed by 'Throweinge them overboard and shoteinge owtt their Braynes in the water'. Censured by Lord Delaware for sparing the queen, Percy drew the line at burning her as requested but had her taken into the woods and put to the sword.[7] Killing women and children ran counter to the Indians' own code of conduct, however, which dictated that they should be taken captive rather than killed and put to work by the victors – a fate shared by a few

The savagery depicted in this classic image of the Indian attack, published in 1634 in Frankfurt, mirrors Edward Waterhouse's account for the Virginia Company. The settlements attacked did not include Jamestown, shown here in the distance.

handfuls of settler women reported killed that day, as we shall see.[8] The ferocity of Opechancanough's carefully planned attack signified that he sought not just to avenge the many killings and atrocities committed by the settlers on the native population but to drive the rapacious settlers from their lands for ever.

While they experienced many acts of terror that day, it is to be hoped that none of the maids saw what happened to gentle George Thorpe, deputy to the College Land and leader of the new plantation of Berkeley Hundred. Forewarned by a servant that Indian 'hellhounds' threatened mischief, Thorpe was so 'void of all suspicion' towards the Indians he had befriended that instead of saving his skin, like the servant who ran away, he met a dreadful death at the hands of this 'Viperous brood, as the sequell shewed: for they not only wilfully murdered him, but cruelly and felly, out of devillish malice, did so many barbarous despights and foule scornes after to his dead corpes, as are unbefitting to be heard by any civill eare'.

Similar atrocities were taking place all along the James River. Among the settlements that suffered the highest casualties were the ironworks at Falling Creek, an enterprise begun by Elizabeth Bluett's father, Captain Benjamin Bluett, and now led by Captain John Berkeley. Berkeley was one of twenty-seven settlers killed there, the most westerly of the colony's plantations. Others slain at the ironworks included two married couples with one child each and Dr Pott's apothecary, Joseph Fitch. Thirteen more settlers were slain at Master Thomas Sheffield's plantation some three miles away, among them Thomas Sheffield and his wife Rachel, although their mute two-year-old son Samuel was spared, saved perhaps by his silence.[9]

Moving further east along the river, more settlers (all men or boys) were slain at Henricus, at the College Land, at Master Abraham Peirsey's plantation on the Appomattox River and at Charles City. Eight more settlers lost their lives at nearby plantations, including Henry Milward, his wife, his child, his sister and Goodwife Redhead. Among the ten dead at William Farrar's plantation on the Appomattox River were Henricke Peterson, his wife Alice, William her son, four men (two of them clearly servants) and two maidservants, Mary and Elizabeth. Among further casualties at George Thorpe's Berkeley Hundred were Richard Rowles, his wife and child. Six died at Richard Owen's plantation near Westover, including an old maid called Blind Margaret. Elizabeth Bennett was one of three women slaughtered at Flowerdew Hundred and the lands immediately across the James. And so the killings continued:

at Mr Swinhowe's and at Mr William Bikar's house on Chappell Creek; at Sir George Yeardley's 2,200-acre Weyanoke plantation; at Southampton Hundred and Martin's Brandon; at Captain Spilman's house and Ensigne Spence's; at Mr Thomas Peirce's house near Mulberry Island; and at Edward Waters' house in Elizabeth City.[10]

Especially badly hit were three plantations sheltering some of the Jamestown brides: Powle-Brooke, Bennett's Welcome and Martin's Hundred. Among the dozen settlers killed at Powle-Brooke were Captain Nathaniel Powell and his wife, the former Joyce Tracy, then 'great with childe'. Their deaths were gruesome in the extreme. The Indians not only slew the valiant captain and his family but 'butcher-like hagled their bodies, and cut off his head, to express their uttermost height of cruelty'.[11] Killed alongside the Powells were Joyce's maidservant Isabell Gifford and the two Jamestown brides who lodged with them. 'Mistris Bray' is surely Sir Edwin Sandys' kinswoman Cicely Bray, whose grandfather clasps his hands in prayer above his Cotswold tomb. Listed among the dead immediately after Bray was 'Barbara Burges', who can only be cloth maker's daughter Barbara Burchens.

Even more people were slaughtered at Edward Bennett's plantation downriver at Warraskoyack: fifty-three by the Virginia Company's reckoning. Nine of the dead were women (ten if Francis Winder was female) and of these at least three can be identified as Jamestown brides: Mary Dawks (the widowed Marie Daucks), Alice (Alse) Jones and 'Parnel a maid', surely Parnel Tenton from London. The other dead women were named as 'Mistris Harrison' (presumed wife of Ensign Harrison, slain alongside her); 'Mistris Chamberlen'; Rebecca ——; Anne English; Thomas Brewood's wife; and 'Mathew a maid'.

Captain John Smith described the confusion that engulfed the homesteads in and around Edward Bennett's plantation, where Mary Daucks and the others were slain.[12] Settlers who had their wits or their guns to hand were able to ward off their more numerous attackers: two against sixty at Master Baldwin's house, where Baldwin saved his grievously wounded wife, himself, his house and many others by repeatedly firing his gun. Just half a mile away, at Master Harrison's house, Thomas Hamor was busy writing a letter in the company of six men and as many as eighteen or nineteen women and children. So many women clustered together was exceedingly rare in the colony; might these have included more of the Jamestown brides, other than the three known to have died there, along with Master Harrison and his wife?

Disguising their intentions with 'many presents and faire perswasions', the 'salvages' claimed they had come to fetch Thomas's brother, Captain Ralph Hamor, to go hunting with their king. When the captain failed to materialize, the Indians set fire to a tobacco house, prompting settlers to emerge from a nearby house to help fight the blaze. As the settlers rushed out, the Indians shot them full of arrows then beat out their brains, all except Thomas Hamor, who was still labouring over his letter.

When he stepped outside to investigate the commotion, Hamor was shot in the back by an Indian bowman. Able to stagger inside, he barricaded the doors, so the Indians set fire to the house. Hamor and the others were saved by Harrison's quick-witted boy. Finding his master's gun ready loaded, he discharged it at random, 'at which bare report the Salvages all fled', allowing the wounded Hamor to escape with twenty-two people to the other property, where Baldwin was still firing his gun.

Meanwhile, the unsuspecting Captain Ralph Hamor had returned to his brother's house, having received an invitation to go hunting with the Indian king. Meeting hostile Indians along the way, he quickly withdrew to a house he was building nearby and, armed only with spades, axes and brickbats, successfully defended himself and his company until the Indians departed. With the aid of half a dozen musketeers sent by the master of a ship out on the James, Hamor then reached the family's storehouse, where he armed more men, and together with thirty unarmed workmen he and his party joined his brother and the others sheltering at Baldwin's house. Seeing all their possessions burned and consumed, the Hamors retreated with the survivors to Jamestown. 'Yet not far from Martins hundred,' wrote Captain John Smith, 'where seventy three were slaine, was a little house and a small family, that heard not any of this till two daies after.'

Despite the heavy casualties apparently sustained at Martin's Hundred, neither Captain John Smith nor company secretary Edward Waterhouse described in detail what happened there. Among the dead, Waterhouse included 'Master John Boise his Wife', although Sara Boyse was not in fact killed in the attack but taken prisoner and held captive by Pamunkey Indians, along with fourteen other women and five men.[13] How many of the captives came from Martin's Hundred is not known, but they certainly included Ralph Dickenson's wife Jane, listed among the settlement's dead, and gardener's daughter Ann Jackson, whose story appears in Chapter 18.

The attack at Martin's Hundred was as sudden and as brutal as everywhere else. Whole households were reportedly wiped out, including that of another Boise called Master Thomas, killed along with his wife, a sucking child, four of Boise's men, a maid and two children, all unnamed. With the master's death went the memory of exactly who lived in his household but that unnamed maid is surely significant. At William Farrar's house near Charles City, Elizabeth and Mary were plainly identified as maidservants, not maids pure and simple, and were dignified with names. Unmarried maids had as yet no economic status, being neither wife nor tradeable servant. At Martin's Hundred, where casualties appear grouped into households, a total of four maids featured among the dead, two listed immediately after Richard Staples, his wife and child; one after John Boyse's wife; and the unnamed maid from Thomas Boise's household. Were all four actually Jamestown brides, grouped with the married couples who had given them a home while they looked for a husband?[14] And was the 'maid' in John Boyse's household in fact Ann Jackson, taken by the Indians along with his wife Sara? We know Ann's brother and his wife survived the attack, and the only Jackson recorded as slain was a 'child of John Jacksons' sandwiched between Edward How, his wife and child and four male servants.

Although no written records survive to tell us how the attack unfolded at Martin's Hundred, archaeological excavations suggest what might have happened there.[15] When the Indians struck, those settlers inside the palisaded fort probably survived, since the Indians retreated in the face of armed resistance. Governor Harwood, who lived through the attack, had his home inside the fort, and no graves were uncovered here, although evidence suggests that the interior of the fort was burned either during or after the assault.

Those who found themselves in the company compound closer to the river were not so lucky. Here the archaeologists found a man's skeleton buried in a deep grave behind the longhouse. All signs point to a violent injury sustained during the attack and a hurried burial at some point after the settlement was set alight by the Indians. Ivor Noël Hume, then director of archaeology at Colonial Williamsburg, describes in cold detail the condition of the 350-year-old skeleton unearthed in 1978.

> The body had been dumped unceremoniously into the hole, its arms swinging loose and its left buttock jacked up against the wall of the grave. Underneath the body were scraps of charcoal blown or knocked into the open hole. But most revealing of all was the condition of the skull. Physical anthropologist Larry Angel tentatively attributed the cause of death to a frontal blow from a cutting tool like a cleaver, followed by blows to the side or back of the skull while the man lay on the ground.[16]

The archaeologists concluded that the short deep gash to the victim's forehead corresponded to a blow from an iron-shod spade, one of the settlers' own tools, rather than a sword blade or an Indian axe. While lying face down on the ground, the victim then had his brains beaten out with a club, shattering the skull into little pieces the size of poker chips or cornflakes. Noël Hume was also in no doubt that a shallow groove from the left ear up to the crown indicated that the man's attacker had first held a lock of the victim's hair in his left hand and cut himself a scalp before beating out his brains. The body had then lain undisturbed for several hours, long enough for the blood to congeal and glue the bone fragments in place. He was buried deeply and alone in the company compound some hours later, apparently tossed there by the gravediggers in their hurry to bury so many dead.[17]

Some thirteen more graves were clustered around a small domestic unit closer to the river but still within the company compound, all contemporary with the attack, some containing little more than teeth or fragments of bone. At least two of the graves may have contained women, one aged around eighteen and the other twenty-five. Another grave contained no human remains at all, just a piece of wood with nails hammered into it.

The palisaded homestead of John Boyse delivered up the human remains of four more men and three women, all of them tentatively linked to the attack. The men, possibly Boyse's four menservants killed in the attack, were buried head-to-toe sardine fashion in a single, sharply cut grave just outside the palisade, while the skeleton of a young woman aged eighteen to twenty-one lay buried in a shallow grave to the west of the compound, again outside the fence and with no trace of a coffin. A second woman, clearly buried in a hurry, survived only as an incomplete pair of legs, the rest destroyed by subsequent ploughing or scavenging animals. She had gone to her grave fully clothed, with a key hanging from her girdle and a copper-alloy thimble in a purse-like bag, both items indicating her status as the mistress of a household. Given where they found her, the gravediggers may have mistaken her for the abducted Sara Boyse.

Of all the attack victims at Martin's Hundred, the third woman buried near the Boyse compound attracted the most attention when she featured in *National Geographic* in January 1982.[18] She was lying on her side in a large hollow outside the palisade's south-western gate, buried under accumulated trash. Nicholas Luccketti, then a young archaeologist, nicknamed her Granny on account of her missing teeth, but her actual age was later estimated at between thirty-five and forty-five years.[19] The twisted metal ear iron she wore to keep her cap in place was damaged, perhaps by scalping during the attack, and she may have crawled into a hollow left where a tree had blown over, slipped into unconsciousness and died from loss of blood.

The official casualty list at Martin's Hundred ends with the names of thirteen men, which suggests they were slaughtered en masse out in the fields rather than within the homesteads of Wolstenholme Town. They include Maximillian Russell, presumed stepfather of nineteen-year-old Mary Elliott, who might have been one of the maids either slain that day or taken prisoner by the Indians.

Such was the ferocity of the attack at Martin's Hundred it seems remarkable that anyone survived, but perhaps sixty or more settlers escaped with their lives in addition to those taken captive.[20] The settlers who sought refuge in the fort will have heard the Indians' devilish cries as they carried out their murderous rampage, but the attack was probably short-lived, especially if the English were able to man the guns. It may still have been several hours before the shell-shocked survivors emerged from the safety of the palisade to survey their familiar plantation turned into a battlefield: homes set alight, crops destroyed, the ground stained with slaughtered cattle and littered with the bodies of dead and dying men, women and children.

Jamestown itself was spared that day, so any brides remaining there survived. They owed their salvation to an Indian convert who worked for William Perry, an ancient planter with estates on the south side of the James. Known as Perry's Indian, the man lived directly across the river from Jamestown in the house of another ancient planter, Richard Pace, who treated him like a son.[21] On the night of 21 March Perry's Indian was joined by a second Indian, who relayed Opechancanough's order to kill Pace the following day; he himself would kill Perry. He further revealed that 'by such an houre in the morning a number would come from divers places to finish the Execution.' After some heart-searching, Perry's Indian revealed the plot to Richard Pace, who promptly secured his house then rowed across the river before daybreak to warn the governor at Jamestown, thereby saving Jamestown and any settlements they were able to alert in time.

Captain John Smith, that great mythologizer, grasps Opechancanough by the hair and takes him captive. However exaggerated, the incident doubtless sparked seething resentment in the Indian chief, which erupted in the Indian attack of 1622.

C. Smith taketh the King of Pamavnkee prisoner. –1608.

In fact more than one friendly Indian warned the settlers of impending disaster, their identities later merged into a single composite figure called Chanco or Chauco, about whom it was said that he 'had lived much amongst the English, and by revealing that plot to divers on the day had saved their lives'.[22] Perry's Indian has particular resonance for the story of the Jamestown bride, since the colonist he warned about the impending slaughter, Richard Pace, had returned to Virginia aboard the *Marmaduke* with the first group of maids, accompanied by his wife and a young kinswoman, Ursula Lawson, whose passage he had paid with the express intention of receiving the bride price of 150 pounds of tobacco owed on her marriage.[23] The young woman may even have been living with the Paces at the time of the Indian attack, unless she had already found a husband.

For those who crowded into Jamestown, the place will quickly have felt like a town under siege. Ex-governor Yeardley took ship that afternoon for his plantation at Flowerdew Hundred and had reached Captain Sanders' plantation near Martin's Brandon, about halfway upriver, when the tide turned. He went ashore to see if he could rescue any wounded Englishmen but there was no one to be seen and nothing much to save: some poultry, a sow, a small chest of 'very ill condiconed Tobacco'. The Indians had carried away everything of value, strewing old chests and barrels about the fields. The next day Yeardley received word that the houses there and everything within had been burned.[24]

Responsibility for the immediate relief of Martin's Hundred went to ancient planter Captain William Pierce, a close friend of Governor Francis Wyatt and commander of Jamestown Island so a good choice of officer to bring the battle-scarred survivors back to the relative safety of Jamestown.[25] He was also able to rescue between ten and thirty barrels of corn from the houses of Richard Staples and Walter Davies, both recorded as killed in the Indian attack, which suggests that Pierce reached Martin's Hundred before the Indians returned to burn the plantation to the ground.[26]

For three weeks Jamestown was frozen in shock, then the governor and his council recovered sufficiently to order the evacuation of endangered plantations and the forcible removal of survivors either to Jamestown or the handful of fortified settlements judged strong enough to withstand further Indian attacks: Paspehay on the mainland close to Jamestown, Kecoughtan, Newportes News, Southampton Hundred, and two plantations that became home to Jamestown brides: Flowerdew Hundred and, a little further west, Samuel Jordan's plantation on Jordan's Point. Jamestown was back on a war footing and Governor Wyatt issued a series of commissions to senior officers setting out their duties. Captain Roger Smith was given absolute power and command over the people of Charles City, Henricus Island and Coxendale, and ordered to 'use all care and vigilancie, for the safe bringeing away of all the said people, and cattell, and goodes'. Captain Ralph Hamor was given similar powers over the people of Martin's Hundred and ordered to bring survivors and goods from Warraskoyack to James City.[27]

After the last of these commissions was issued on 20 April 1622, Governor Wyatt sat down to compose the difficult letter to the Virginia Company in London, recounting what had happened on that dreadful day in March and outlining the measures his council had taken to restore order to 'this unhappie State'.[28] Their first task was to find a defensible seat 'that neyther the Indyans may infest us... nor forraine enemy subvert us'. Faith in Jamestown's ability to withstand either Spanish aggression or infiltration by Indians was clearly dwindling, and Virginia's Eastern Shore was one of the places under consideration.[29] Their next major concern was how to feed so many people, 'two third p[ar]tes wherof are women Children & unservisable people'. The need to mount a constant armed guard represented another drain on their limited manpower, and fear of Indians lying in wait among the trees meant that they could not plant corn in many places. The Indians would anyway destroy any crops that grew, so Wyatt begged the company to send sufficient corn to last the colony a full year. Finally, he spelled out their most pressing needs, which he hoped the company would supply: for weapons, skilful engineers to help construct fortifications, plus a 'great store' of spades, shovels, mattocks, pickaxes and other tools, promising to give the company 'full satisfaction' by paying with good tobacco.

England's response – when news of the attack finally filtered through in the first two weeks of July – betrayed little sympathy for the colonists' plight. The immediate reaction was to blame the settlers for their own carelessness and for falling victim to so base an enemy. As John Chamberlain confided to Sir Dudley Carleton, 'Yt was by their owne supine negligence that lives as careles and securely there as yf they had ben in England, in scattered and stragling houses far asunder, whereby they were so easilie subject to the surprise of those naked people, who besides other spoyle and bootie have possessed themselves of armes and weapons, but the best is they have no skill to use them.'[30] Reporting the deaths of Captain John Berkeley at the ironworks and of Captain George Thorpe, whom Chamberlain knew well, he said the shame and disgrace was as bad as the loss, 'for no other nation wold have ben so grossely overtaken.'

The Virginia Company was similarly hard on the colonists, calling the manner of their defeat 'by the handes of men so contemptible' more miserable than the slaughter, and blaming the settlers for their own misfortunes. God Almighty was punishing them for their transgressions, wrote the company in its official response to Wyatt's letter begging for help, urging on the colony 'the speedie redresse of those two enormous excesses of apparell and drinkeing; the crie whereof cannot but have gon up to heaven.'[31] And the company repeated its frequent injunction to diversify into staple commodities other than tobacco.

As for the colonists' request for a year's supply of corn, the Virginia Company could only declare itself much perplexed, 'the publique stock being utterly as you know exhausted', and the colony's failure to pay for the magazines dispatched the previous year (of which the maids' magazine was one) precluded the raising of a new magazine by private subscription. 'Other waies and meanes are so uncertaine, as wee cannot wish you to rely uppon any thing, but yorselves'. Indeed, the only help the company could offer to its beleaguered colony was a promise from King James, urged on by the Privy Council, to supply arms 'unfitt for any moderne service' stockpiled at the Tower of London and the imminent dispatch by the *Abigail* of four hundred young men furnished at twenty pounds per head to make up the numbers that were lost. The company wanted these new people settled in compact and orderly villages rather than the straggling plantations that had occasioned the attack. And London expressed its extreme displeasure at the abandonment of Charles City, Henricus, the ironworks, the College Land and Martin's Hundred, declaring that 'the replanting of them is of absolute necessitie; lest the best fire that maintaines the accon here alive be putt out'.

For the English colonists in Virginia and the Virginia Company back home in London, the Indian attack of 22 March 1622 marked a turning point in relations between the settlers and Virginia's native population. Blind to their own rapaciousness for land, which had provoked the Indians' fury, they could see only the Indians' 'treachery' in repaying their 'gentleness and fair usage' with murder most foul. From now on, the company urged the settlers to root out 'so cursed a nation, ungreatefull to all benefittes, and uncapable of all goodnesse'.[32] As Edward Waterhouse explained in his official report of the 'barbarous Massacre', colonization could proceed much more quickly and effectively since the English no longer had to bother themselves with the painful business of civilizing the natives or effecting their conversion. Now they were perfectly justified in destroying those who had sought to destroy them and seizing their cultivated lands, 'turning the laborious Mattocke into the victorious Sword (wherein there is more both ease, benefit, and glory)'. Victory could be gained in many ways:

> by force, by surprize, by famine in burning their Corne, by destroying and burning their Boats, Canoes, and Houses, by breaking their fishing Weares, by assailing them in their huntings, whereby they get the greatest part of their sustenance in Winter, by pursuing and chasing them with our horses, and blood-Hounds to draw after them, and Mastives to teare them, which take this naked, tanned, deformed Savages, for no other then wild beasts.

As their actions would show, the English could be at least as bloodthirsty and cruel as the Indians, especially when intoxicated by a righteous indignation that lacked the restraining influence of Captain George Thorpe and the handful of other colonizers who believed in conversion rather than conquest. Naturally for the times, no one questioned the Englishman's right to venture to Virginia in the first place. But while the Indian attack breathed murderous fire into English hearts, it also marked the beginning of the end for the Virginia Company, which stumbled on for two more difficult years before it collapsed into dust.

CHAPTER FOURTEEN

The End of the Affair

For anyone who survived the Indian attack of 22 March 1622, life in Virginia was desperately hard – homes destroyed, tobacco crops and food stores plundered, livestock killed, years of hard labour undone in a single day. Fear of the Indians prevented farmers from venturing out of their stockades to replant, and London had burdened the colony with hundreds more hungry, sick and ill-provisioned settlers and a stock of rusting, obsolete weapons and armour from the Tower of London that might nonetheless prove useful in skirmishes with the Indians.[1] Ordered to abandon the straggling plantations that made them vulnerable to attack, the jittery colonists crowded into Jamestown and the few settlements considered defensible.

What happened to the survivors among the Jamestown brides reflects the fortunes of the colony as a whole. Not everyone prospered, naturally. While the months after the attack were miserable for everybody, they will have been especially hard for any maids who had failed to find a husband. Uprooted only recently from England, lacking kith, kin or natural protectors in the colony, they were ripe for exploitation by those who wielded power, elite company officials especially and those who 'knew how to turn private distress to private profit'.[2]

Shockingly, nearly two years after the attack two maids were still living in the households of company officials, unmarried and apparently working as servants despite the Virginia Company's insistence that the maids were not to be treated as such 'save in case of extremitie'.[3] According to a census compiled in mid-February 1624, London tailor's daughter Elizabeth Starkey (only sixteen at the time of her embarkation) was living in the Jamestown household of company agent Edward Blaney, nominally in charge of collecting money for the *Warwick* women, while Fortune Taylor, a couple of years older, lodged with Dr John Pott.[4] Both women had sailed with Blaney on the *Warwick*. Before she came to Virginia, Taylor had served another Virginia Company master, Gabriel Barbor of East Smithfield, one of the organizers of the now defunct lottery.

Pott and Blaney lived next door to each other in Jamestown's New Town, which had spread eastwards from the fort towards

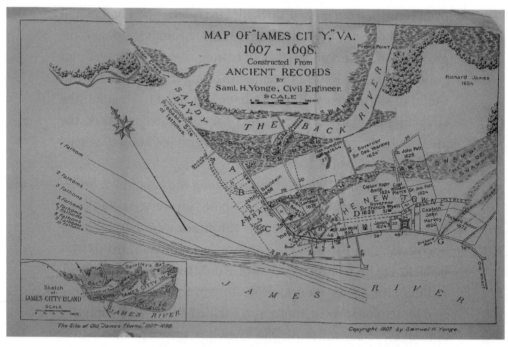

By 1624 two unmarried 'maids for Virginia' (Fortune Taylor and Elizabeth Starkey) were living next door to each other on Back Street in the Jamestown households of Dr John Pott and Edward Blaney.

Orchard Run, its irregularly shaped lots laid out with the help of William Claiborne, the colony's official surveyor.[5] In the mid-1620s this was the colony's political, social and commercial heart. Almost all the property owners here were successful merchants, public officials or both. Close neighbours were Joan and William Pierce, whose Jamestown garden covered three or four acres, yielding nearly 'an hundred bushels of excellent figges' in a single year, where they kept tame geese, ducks and turkeys. Joan Pierce boasted to Captain John Smith that she could keep a better house in Virginia drawing on her own provisions 'than here in London for 3[00] or 400 pounds a yeare, yet went thither with little or nothing'.[6]

Both Pott and Blaney performed well in Virginia's 'servant sweepstakes', one of the main pathways to wealth in the colony, since the more servants you possessed, the more tobacco you could grow.[7] At the 1624 census, Blaney had eighteen people living in his household, including himself. Although he was married by then, his wife had returned to England to make a claim on her late husband's estate[8] and we can assume that the other seventeen people were servants. Only three were female: the wife of Edward Hudson, who appears near the top of his list, and two women at the bottom of the heap: Elizabeth Starkey and 'Elinor', who may have been one of the colony's few Africans.[9] Although the 1624 census did not identify relationships within households, it reflected their hierarchy, placing family members first and servants and Africans at the bottom.

As the colony's physician, Dr Pott commanded three acres on the adjacent plot along Jamestown's Back Street, which he would later extend by twelve acres.[10] In 1624 he was living here with his wife Elizabeth, who had travelled out to Virginia with him in 1621; among their six servants were two women, Jane Dickenson and Fortune Taylor. At the time of the Indian attack, Jane Dickenson and her husband Ralph were living at Martin's Hundred as indentured servants employed by Nicholas Hyde, one of the settlement's principal investors. Both Dickensons were reported killed in the attack[11] but Jane actually survived, 'Caried away with the Cruell salvages, amongst them Enduring much misery for teen monthes'. She was later redeemed for glass beads supplied by 'friends of the Prissoners'.[12] As one of these friends, Dr Pott had insisted that she worked for him as a servant to repay a double debt: the remaining years of her slain husband's seven-year term of indenture and her own ransom of beads.

One year on, Pott was still refusing to release her and threatened to make her serve 'the uttermost day, unles shee p[ro]cure him 150 li waight of Tobacco' – the price of a woman's freedom, it seems, as well as that of a bride. So in March 1624, while Dickenson and Taylor were both living in the Pott household, Jane submitted a 'humble petition' to the governor, asking to be released from her debt as she had already served Pott for ten months, which was surely too much for two pounds of beads, and her servitude in his household 'much differeth not from her slavery with the Indians'.

Might Edward Blaney have been another friend of the prisoners? And might Fortune Taylor and Elizabeth Starkey have been taken captive at the same time as Jane Dickenson and like her been forced to redeem ransom beads with their own labour? We cannot know for certain, and their servant status can be explained in other ways. Having failed to find husbands, they may have been coerced into repaying the cost of their transportation and clothes, or they may have been working voluntarily to fund their passage home. Whatever the explanation, their desire to better themselves by marrying a Virginian planter had not borne fruit, and after 1624 both disappear from the records.

The failure of these two young women to attract the right sort of husband – one who could afford to pay for and maintain them – underlines how flawed the scheme was from the outset. As a young single man with good prospects in the colony, Edward Blaney could have taken his pick of the Jamestown brides.[13] But rather than pay for a wife with hard-earned tobacco, he chose instead to marry a widow who could bring him the lands he needed to build his fortune. 'Mr Blanie is now married in Virginia, and when he hath discharged your trust in the magazine wilbe a Planter amongst us,' wrote George Sandys to John Ferrar in London in April 1623, calling Blaney a man 'of a good understandinge.'[14]

Blaney's wife Margaret was the widow of Captain William Powell, a resident of New Town on whose land the Blaneys were now living with their many servants. By 1625, the Blaneys' storehouses on Jamestown Island bulged with thirty barrels of corn and two thousand dry fishes plus copious stores of oatmeal and peas, and their many cattle and wandering swine were causing friction with their neighbours.[15] Most of their servants (but not Elizabeth Starkey, whereabouts unknown) had been transferred to another plantation on the lower side of the James River, which the Powells had fraudulently appropriated after the Indian attack of 1622.[16] This was Powle-Brook, where Cecily Bray and Barbara Burchens had died alongside the plantation's true owner Captain Nathaniel Powell and many others. Although not related in any way, William Powell had successfully claimed the estate through their fortuitously shared surname, and the lands passed to Edward Blaney when he married William's widow. Nathaniel's brother Thomas was trying to recover the estate on behalf of himself and 'his poor brothers and sisters'[17] when Edward Blaney died himself, still indebted to the investors in the Virginia Company's general magazine, his affairs in disarray.[18] No one asked for any of the tobacco Blaney may have collected for the maids who travelled by the *Warwick* or the *Tiger*, nor had he offered to reimburse the adventurers of the maids' magazine for transporting Elizabeth Starkey to the colony.

In the matrimonial game of musical chairs played by Virginia's wealthy elite, after Blaney's death his widow Margaret swiftly married

Captain Francis West, a younger brother of Thomas West, the third Lord Delaware, whose arrival on the James River had halted the abandonment of Jamestown after the Starving Time over the deadly winter of 1609–10. In final settlement of Edward Blaney's debts to the general magazine dispatched by the *Warwick* and the *Abigail*, Francis West agreed – as the husband of Blaney's widow – to pay 5,000 lbs of good tobacco in November 1626 and a further 3,000 lbs of tobacco from the following year's crop.[19] Then Margaret West died and Captain Francis West immediately married again, this time Temperance Flowerdew Yeardley, just four months after the death in Virginia of Sir George Yeardley. When Temperance died intestate, West tried but ultimately failed to divert to himself the inheritance of the Yeardley children. Marriage could bring riches to both men and women, providing you had the status, power, connections or lack of scruples to advance your cause. And providing you stayed alive.

After the Indian attack of 1622 the Virginia Company limped on for another two years. The factionalism that had riven the company since Sandys assumed control erupted into open warfare, pitting former treasurer Sir Thomas Smythe and his son-in-law Alderman Robert Johnson against the Earl of Southampton, Sir Edwin Sandys, fellow parliamentarian Sir Edward Sackville and 'divers others of meaner qualitie'.[20] Both sides hurled allegations of mismanagement and corruption at the other, and now Robert Rich, second Earl of Warwick, and his cousin Sir Nathaniel Rich threw themselves into the Smythe camp, incensed by the efforts of the Sandys and Southampton clique to curb their use of Virginian plantations as a base for privateering – piracy in all but name – in the Caribbean.[21]

The king was drawn into the controversy, impelled by his equal loathing for Sir Edwin Sandys, who had blocked his parliamentary manoeuvres at every turn, and for the 'vile custome' of smoking tobacco, on which Virginia depended, a habit that was, in his own words, 'lothsome to the eye, hatefull to the Nose, harmeful to the braine, daungerous to the Lungs, and in the blacke stinking fume thereof, neerest resembling the horrible Stigian smoke of the pit that is bottomelesse'.[22] The king's response to the ruckus was to set up a royal commission to investigate company affairs headed by Sir William Jones, justice of the Court of Common Pleas. Hearsay evidence and personal resentments were not to be aired: adventurers and colonists submitting evidence were to focus exclusively on their own private business. While neither faction had a monopoly of right, each manipulated the evidence to its own ends.

King James was not alone in condemning Virginia's staple, tobacco: doctors linked it to coffee drinking as a cause of scurvy.

For the Smythe faction, Sir Nathaniel Rich took charge of collecting testimonies from Virginia that painted a dismal picture of life in the colony and drew attention to the Sandys administration's reckless expenditure on 'vast and wild projects'. Much of Rich's evidence about conditions in Virginia was culled from letters dispatched to England from Virginia aboard the *Abigail*, whose outbound cargo of stinking beer was thought to have caused a plague of sickness in the colony in that first dreadful winter after the Indian attack. The letters were confiscated and sent on to the Privy Council after Rich had summarized their most damning contents.[23] Among the letters was one written by Lady Wyatt, a niece of Sir Edwin Sandys, who had travelled out on the *Abigail* in late 1622 to join her husband the governor. Their ship was so full of infection, wrote Lady Wyatt to her 'Sister Sandys', 'that after a while we saw little but throwing folkes over boord'. Much troubled, their captain had laid the blame squarely on the two Ferrar brothers, and 'to make the people amendes dyed himselfe'. After their arrival in Virginia life hardly improved, she said, 'for as well our people as our Cattle have dyed, that we are all undone'. She begged her mother and sisters for butter and cheese, and for malt carefully packed in very good casks, clearly intending to remedy the colony's lack of English beer.[24]

Two more letters – written by Richard Frethorne, a young servant indentured to the governor of Martin's Hundred – played directly into the hands of Warwick and the Smythe faction and may have been engineered by them.[25] By March 1623, when Frethorne wrote his first letter, a ragged band of settlers had returned to Martin's Hundred, its population of 140 reduced to 'butt 22 lefte alive, and of all theyr houses there is butt 2 lefte and a peece of a Church'. Their leader William Harwood, who had survived the attack, said it would take £3,000 to make good the plantation.[26] In a letter calculated to tug the heartstrings of any parent, Frethorne described his meagre rations to his mother and father: 'for since I came out of the ship, I never at[e] anie thing but pease, and loblollie (that is water gruell) as for deare or venison I never saw anie since I came into this land, ther is indeed some foule, but Wee are not allowed to goe, and get yt, but must Worke hard both earelie, and late for a messe of water gruell, and a mouthfull of bread, and beife.'

His one coat was stolen off his back by a fellow servant, and he now wore only rags, possessed of nothing more than one poor suit, a pair of shoes, a pair of stockings, one cap and two cap bands. Indian attacks were continuing, wrote Frethorne, recounting the gruesome capture of Mr Pountis's pinnace, when the Indians killed the captain, stuck his head on a pole and then rowed home.[27] By February 1624 Frethorne too was probably dead.[28]

Even before the royal commission began gathering evidence, a privateering ally of the Earl of Warwick had come to the aid of the Smythe faction with a blistering report on conditions in the colony during its first winter following the Indian attack. On his way back to England from a controversial spell as colonial governor of Bermuda, Captain Nathaniel Butler had spent a few months at Jamestown, distilling his findings for the Privy Council in *The Unmasked face of our Colony in Virginia, as it was in the Winter of the yeare 1622.*

Butler portrayed a colony on the verge of collapse, its plantations seated on 'meere Salt marshes full of infectious Boggs and muddy Creekes and Lakes'; settlements unfortified and abandoned to the Indians; just four fixed guns for the whole colony, all unserviceable; fledgling industries like the ironworks 'utterly wasted and the men dead'. Food was so short that meal was selling at thirty shillings a bushel and Indian corn at ten to fifteen shillings a bushel, and the lack of guesthouses meant that new arrivals in winter were 'dyinge under hedges and in the woods but being dead ly some of them for many days Unregarded and Unburied'.[29]

While Butler's view of conditions in Virginia was undoubtedly partisan, the planters' rebuttal of his accusations resorted to lame excuses, self-justifications and evasions – 'As for dyinge under hedges there is no hedge in all Virginia.' But no beating about the bush could mask the cardinal error of the Sandys administration in dispatching hundreds more poorly provisioned settlers to a colony already reeling from the Indian attack.[30] After scrutinizing the company's affairs through the spring and early summer of 1623, the Jones commission concluded that the colony's state was most 'weak and miserable'. Although exact numbers were hard to obtain, Jones calculated that the Sandys administration had sent over 4,270 settlers to join the thousand or so people living in Virginia when Smythe left office in 1619. Only a few of these remained, all living in great want.[31]

It took a year for legal process to shut the company down. The Privy Council set up another commission to enquire into the condition and needs of the colony, headed by Captain (later Sir) John Harvey; its members included former secretary John Pory, cape merchant Abraham Piersey and wealthy planter Samuel Matthews.[32] This commission took the view that most settlers wanted to be under the immediate protection of the king, apart from a few Virginia Company employees who 'feare by the Change of government theire losse of imployment and so desire to bee still under the Company'. Among its recommendations was the construction of a palisade fence across the York peninsula, from Martin's Hundred on the James up to Cheskiak on the Pamunkey River, a tributary of the York, to keep the Indians out and the settlers with their livestock safe within. The government also went to law to revoke the Virginia Company's charter, claiming that the Sandys faction had usurped authority for which it held no warrant. On 24 May 1624 the chief justice handed down his decision: Nicholas Ferrar and the other defendants had indeed failed to show sufficient proof of their privileges, which were now assumed by the king. The Virginia Company effectively went into receivership, holding its last court on 7 June 1624, and Virginia became a royal colony.

Sir Edwin Sandys survived for another five years, easing the passage through parliament of a major bill promoting free trade, for which he had been arguing for years, and assisting in the impeachment and downfall of his one-time friend Lord Cranfield, who had triggered the Virginia Company's demise in parliament.[33] He died in October 1629 and lies buried in St Augustine's church, Northbourne, near Deal on the Kentish coast. In a free-standing memorial carved from black marble and alabaster, he and his wife lie stiffly at different levels in their four poster bed, hands clasped in prayer, overlooked by cherubs and two awkward angels added at a later date.[34]

After Nicholas Ferrar saved his brother John from financial ruin by buying the manor of Little Gidding in Huntingdonshire from John's bankrupt business partner, using money from their mother's dower, the extended Ferrar family settled there in 1626, leading lives devoted to daily contemplation and readings of the scriptures, rigorous education and bookbinding.[35] The church survives on the edge of farmland, its odour of piety reinforced by the many memorials to the Ferrars in stained glass and tablets. Outside, the plain table tombstone of Nicholas Ferrar (who died first) left space for a pavement slab for John by the west door. The American-born poet T. S. Eliot, visiting in 1936, left the rough road to the manor and, passing behind the pigsty to face the church's dull facade and the tombstone, experienced a moment of timelessness when time past, present and future intersect. Little Gidding gave its name to the last of his *Four Quartets.*

So did the individual shareholders who subscribed to the maids' magazine ever receive the rich rewards they were expecting? The likely answer is no, or not much. Timing did not favour any of the magazines. When the *Warwick* arrived at Jamestown in December 1621 most of the tobacco crop had already been carried away by other ships, so potential husbands for the brides had little to spare.[36] Certainly the promised Maydes Towne never materialized, and the two men responsible for collecting tobacco from prospective husbands both failed to meet their obligations.

Three months after the maids left England, the company wrote a gently nagging letter to the governor and council in Virginia, reminding them that the adventurers were seeking a good return for their investment and enclosing copies of the company's earlier letters 'to revive thinges in yor memorie'.[37] When that elicited no response, the company wrote again, in June 1622 (a month before London caught wind of the Indian attack), urging the Virginian authorities to give their 'best favor and assistance' to the four magazines – the glassworks, the fur trade, the maids and the shipment of general supplies. While the adventurers had not yet received the returns they were expecting, the company hoped that 'the good proceed of theire Adventures' might enable such ventures to continue'.[38] The company had heard privately that Pountis wanted to return to England but earnestly entreated him to stay, 'both in regard of his skill and office'.

Six months on, Virginia's governor had more pressing matters on his hands than securing payment from recalcitrant husbands, but Sir Francis Wyatt nonetheless tried to reassure the adventurers in London that Virginia's treasurer, Sir Edwin's brother George Sandys, would let them know what was being done about returning profits from the glassworks, and Mr Pountis would do the same for the maids.[39]

By August 1623, some two years after the dispatch of the maids, the Virginia Company was losing patience. For the magazine of general supplies sent by the *Warwick* and valued at nearly £2,000, Edward Blaney had returned less than 2,000 lbs of tobacco, a fraction of its value.[40] Although the investment had been made by private men, the consequence of non-payment was 'of publique good, or evill, to the Colony', warned the company, suggesting that while the adventurers were not doubting the 'integritie of mr Blany', they were nonetheless 'offended' that he had not even bothered to submit accounts.[41] Likewise the adventurers who had invested in the maids wanted to hear from Mr Pountis, 'from whom they hope the full return this yeare, wch we earnestly desire, that it may in the same, or some other profitable maner be readventured'. At no point did the company ask whether any of the maids it sent over had died in the attack, nor did it address the issue of payment for brides who had been slaughtered or who remained unmarried.

His health clearly suffering, Pountis could take the strain no longer. Having had his request to return to England rejected, he left the colony abruptly without settling his account for the brides. Virginia's governor and council could only express themselves 'such strangers' to his proceedings that they could give the Virginia Company no account thereof, although before Pountis went abroad they had reminded him about his duties and shown him the company's letters, 'therfore he cannot be unmindfull to give you Satisfactione'.[42]

Pountis died before he could give any satisfaction to the Virginia Company or to the adventurers in the maids' magazine,[43] and then the company died too, leaving Virginia's governor and council to sort out the mess as best they could. In mid-June 1625 they wrote to the Commissioners for the Affairs of Virginia, declaring that 'mr Blany never medled with the disposinge of the maides', thereby absolving him of any part in their finances, despite the Virginia Company's clear instruction that he should collect tobacco for the *Warwick* women, and keep a 'pticular accompt'.[44] Pountis's death had inevitably left his accounts 'much intangled & perplexed', said the council. Many of the husbands had made payments, 'and most of ye rest pretend the like', but the council had not yet had time to examine their proofs.[45] Treasurer George Sandys was able to send accounts for the shipwright business, and for the glassworks, which made sorry reading: 'the death of one of ye princypall woorkmen, an other beinge subject to the falinnge sicknes, and many defects wch render the woorke unservable'. The council had therefore conceded to the glass workers' request to return to England, having achieved precisely nothing.

The council in Virginia had already started to investigate who owed what for the maids, ordering that those indebted to the maids' magazine should pay the tobacco they owed or appear at Jamestown before the governor and council to explain themselves.[46] Just one man came forward in response, William Moch (or Mutch) of James City, who testified on behalf of another planter called William Cobb who had married one of the maids: nineteen-year-old Elizabeth Dag from the mariners' district of Limehouse on the Thames. Before setting off on a trading voyage, Cobb had made a will and asked Moch to convey it to John Pountis together with three bills of money owed to him, offering them in 'Satisfactione for the Passage of the said Elizabeth Dagg'. Another witness swore that Moch had delivered the papers as requested into the hands of Pountis, where they presumably disappeared into his tangled accounts.[47] William Cobb was clearly dead by this time, or he would have appeared in court himself, and no one enquired after the fate of his wife, the former Elizabeth Dag. No evidence survives to prove whether any of the other planters ever paid for their wives either.

After the Virginia Company's demise and the financial collapse of the maids' magazine, no more official bridal shipments came to Virginia, although individual women continued to travel out in hope. A deed from the Isle of Wight is said to record that on 1 October 1624 John Kent of Newport, innkeeper, had responded to the 'earnest request' of his widowed sister-in-law to ship her daughter to Newportes News in Virginia by the *Ann*, 'uppon his owne adventure and charge'. Both mother and daughter were called Elizabeth Baker, and the younger woman was travelling to Virginia with her mother's consent. Apparently named in the deed were two gentlemen from Newportes News, William Blackwell and Thomas Cheeseman, who were to look after the girl in Virginia and pay to John Kent 'six score pound wayte of good marchauntable Virginia Tobacho' on her marriage. My search at the Isle of Wight Records Office failed to produce the original deed, but I was able to confirm that John Kent's wife Mary and the widowed Elizabeth Baker were sisters, as claimed.[48]

More generally, the idea prevailed that Virginia could provide good husbands for women without dowries. In his practical guide to making a fortune in Virginia, published in 1649, Englishman William Bullock advised male servants to buy a heifer in their first year and to begin trading with England. Bullock calculated that after four years they will have accumulated at least sixty pounds and a stock of cattle, sufficient 'to wooe a good mans Daughter'.[49] He would like to advise maidservants too, he said, but 'they are impatient and will not take advice but from a Husband, for if they come of an honest stock and have good repute, they may pick and chuse their Husbands out of the better sort of people'. Never having travelled to Virginia himself, Bullock told his readers that all the women servants he sent out to his Virginian plantation were married within three months of their arrival, aside from one 'poore silly Wench', and even she found a suitor who was willing to work for a full twelve months to reimburse Bullock for clothing and transporting her. 'To conclude this, whereas in England many Daughters makes the Fathers purse leane, the Sonnes here make the leane purses, wherefore to avoid this danger, I shall advise that man that's full of Children to keepe his Sonnes in England, and send his Daughters to Virginia, by which meanes he shall not give but receive portions for all his Children.'

The maids whose married lives I trace in the next three chapters bear out Bullock's optimism. Two of these women, Catherine Finch and Audry Hoare, settled upriver from Jamestown, at Jordan's Journey and Neck of Land Charles City, while Bridgett Crofte went with her husband to Virginia's Eastern Shore. Given the difficulties of finding a husband in England, in London especially, their varied fortunes supply ample proof that with luck and good health women of spirit could prosper on North American soil, providing they learned to adapt to the much rawer circumstances of a new world in the making.

CHAPTER FIFTEEN

The Crossbow Maker's Sister

For young Catherine Finch from a small rural parish close to the Welsh borders, her new life in Virginia had more in common with her childhood than with the teeming tenements of St Martin-in-the-Fields, where she had once lived in service with her brother. Yet Erasmus Finch holds the key to his sister's departure, I feel certain, on account of his links to the gentry of this Westminster parish, which was home to a number of Virginia Company investors and adventurers. In the area's many taverns he will surely have picked up gossip about the company's plan to send brides to Virginia and perhaps even secured for his sister an introduction to George Thorpe Esquire, another Strand resident, who had gone to Virginia to take charge of the settlement of Berkeley Hundred.[1]

The man Catherine married was Robert Fisher, an ancient planter who had arrived in Virginia in 1611 aboard the *Elizabeth* with Sir Thomas Dale's fleet of ships. Although we know little about him, he was clearly skilled with his hands and probably a trained carpenter, for it was Fisher whom George Thorpe chose to build a house for Opechancanough. The coincidence is striking: like his future brother-in-law, Fisher made goods for royalty, Indian royalty in his case, compared with Erasmus Finch's crossbows for the English kings.[2] Fisher did well, it seems, and quite delighted the Indian chief with his 'faire house' built 'after the English fashion', especially with its lock and key, 'which he so admired, as locking and unlocking his doore a

242

hundred times a day, he thought no device in the world comparable to it'.[3] The work took five weeks, for which Fisher charged ninety pounds of tobacco, more than half the cost of his new bride, which may explain why he felt able to buy himself a wife.

Thorpe did not survive to settle the bill, however, dying at the hands of the Indians in the great attack of 1622. It was still unpaid more than two years later, when Fisher appears among a dozen creditors of George Thorpe, late of Berkeley Hundred, deceased. I wonder if he ever received his money; when the creditors reapply to the court less than two months later, Fisher's name has disappeared from the list.[4] That unpaid bill may nonetheless hold a clue as to where Fisher and perhaps his new bride were living at the time of the attack: at the new plantation of Berkeley Hundred on the northern bank of the James, next to the company land at Charles City. Thorpe would surely have commissioned a carpenter from among his own settlers, a man whose work he knew and trusted. The first group of settlers had arrived at the settlement on 4 December 1619 and celebrated North America's first official thanksgiving, adhering to their instructions to keep the date of their arrival holy 'yearly and perpetually... as a day of thanksgiving',[5] a full year before the Plymouth settlers arrived in New England.

If Catherine had come to Berkeley Hundred soon after she arrived at Jamestown, she will have experienced the full horror of the attack of March 1622. Altogether eleven settlers from the plantation were reported slain: Thorpe himself, described as 'one of his Majesties Pentioners', seven men listed individually, and a family consisting of Richard Rowles, his wife and child.[6] Many of the survivors found refuge at Samuel Jordan's fortified settlement across the James River, known as Jordan's Journey or Beggar's Bush, one of only a handful of settlements considered safe from Indian attack. 'Master Samuel Jorden gathered together but a few of the straglers about him at Beggers-bush', wrote Captain John Smith in *The Generall Historie of Virginia*, 'where he fortified and lived in despight of the enemy'.[7]

Berkeley Hundred survivors were still living at Jordan's Journey in 1625, when the muster recorded the presence of Robert Fisher, his wife Katherine, who had arrived on the *Marmaduke* in October 1621, and their one-year-old daughter Sisly. I cannot be certain that the Fishers were living here before then, since the census of February 1624 records a Henry Fisher, his wife and infant, rather than a Robert Fisher, but mistakes were common and the Henry Fishers are otherwise absent from official records, so it is reasonable to assume that Catherine's daughter Sisly Fisher was born here in late 1623 or early 1624.[8]

Founded by ancient planter Samuel Jordan, the settlement of Jordan's Journey sits on a triangular spit of land jutting into the James River from its southern bank, several bends upriver from Jamestown and close to where the James and the Appomattox Rivers converge.[9] A Virginia Company investor, Jordan had come to Virginia in 1610, the same year as his future wife Sisley, who arrived as a young girl aged nine or ten aboard the *Swan*. He lived for a time at Bermuda Hundred, where Audry Hoare would later settle, representing the plantation at Virginia's first general assembly held in the sweltering summer of 1619, when his particular task was to review the four books of law sent out from England. Like others who rose to prominence in Virginia, Samuel Jordan began to acquire land, originally on the north side of the James, and by 1621 had established his 450-acre settlement at Jordan's Point.[10] Two hundred of these acres came to Samuel and Sisley Jordan through their entitlement as ancient planters. According to a notorious gossip, Joan Vincent from Neck of Land Charles City, the Jordan marriage was not especially happy because of the 'great love' harboured by Samuel for a married woman, Alice Boyse, who attracted suitors like flies, as we shall see.[11]

When the first colonists ventured this far in 1607, the promontory was the site of a native village inhabited by Weyanoke Indians who

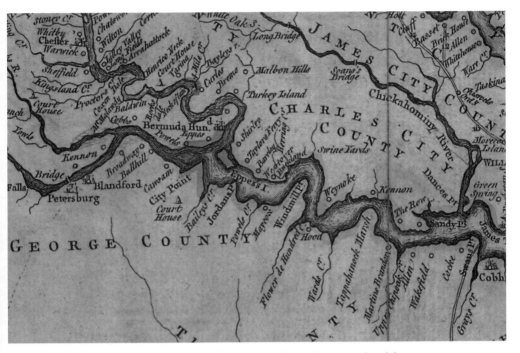

Catherine Fisher's home at Jordan's Point is shown here in a detail from a mid-eighteenth-century map of Virginia and Maryland by Joshua Fry and Peter Jefferson.

had long cultivated the land, clearing the fields for corn and erecting dwellings on the promontory's eastern side, orientated to deflect the gusty winds that sweep up the James in winter but able to take advantage of cooling summer breezes. The forested uplands made good foraging territory and the water margins supplied plentiful tuckahoe to supplement their diet.[12] What made the site attractive for the Indians appealed equally to the land-hungry English, and so the Weyanokes gradually lost their villages and corn-growing lands to the settlers, who stripped them of all but their traditional foraging territory.[13]

Catherine's world had shrunk dramatically since she had uprooted herself from her brother's home in the parish of St Martin-in-the-Fields, which in 1621 contained an estimated 1,916 households.[14]

Compare this with Jordan's Journey, which in January 1625 could muster a total population of fifty-six men, women and children living in just fifteen households.[15] Most of the adults were still in their twenties and, remarkably for early Virginia, nine of the fifteen households were families with a husband and wife (or wife-to-be) and in many cases (five out of nine) one or more children. Here you would find precisely the sort of settlers the Virginia Company had hoped to encourage: men rooted to the land with ties of family and children. Thanks to many more girl children than boys, the gender ratio of all ages was a respectable two males to every female. More than one third were servants, ranging in age from a boy of eleven to John Pead at thirty-five, the settlement's oldest resident. All were English or had English names; there were as yet neither Indians nor Africans.

Like any community in the Old or New Worlds, Jordan's Journey had evolved a pecking order based on breeding, social status and wealth. The Fishers were ranked around number four, making Robert Fisher a respectable catch for a woman who had arrived in the colony with nothing. At the time of the 1625 muster the community's leading household was headed jointly by Samuel Jordan's widow Sisley and the man who would become her next husband, William Farrar, an unusual – even scandalous – living arrangement. When the couple eventually married, Sisley Jordan would slip back to being a subordinate member of the household.

In 1625 the Jordan-Farrar household owned five of the settlement's twenty-two houses and employed almost half its servants (ten out of twenty-one). The extent of their other joint possessions bore witness to their wealth and status: two boats, twelve coats of mail, fourteen pounds of powder and 300 pounds of shot, eleven fixed guns, plus copious food stocks that included 200 bushels of corn, 200 dry fish, sixteen neat cattle 'yong and old', four swine and twenty hens. William Farrar had chosen the well trodden route to riches in Virginia by forging an alliance with a wealthy widow and securing his place as commander and premier resident of a settlement.

Next in the social hierarchy came the households of Nathaniel Causey, Thomas Palmer and Robert Fisher, who all owned two houses each and employed servants: five for the Causeys and one each for the Palmers and the Fishers. The Causeys also had a boat. A gentleman and clearly the settlement's second-in-command, Nathaniel Causey and his wife Thomasine were both ancient planters who by 1620 had settled at their plantation of Causey's Care on the north bank of the James, close to West and Shirley Hundred.[16] They survived the Indian attack of 1622, when Nathaniel, 'being cruelly wounded, and the Salvages about him, with an axe did cleave one of their heads, whereby the rest fled and he escaped'.[17] The Palmers, the next family of note, had sailed on the *Tiger* along with a handful of Jamestown brides, and shared their lucky escape from pirates. Catherine will surely have encountered them at Jamestown, if not before: husband Thomas Palmer, his wife Joan and her daughter Priscilla, whom Nicholas Ferrar had wrongly included among the Jamestown brides. She was still only eleven in 1625, the same age as the Palmers' servant Richard English.

Other offspring then living in the settlement included the Chapmans' two small children, Thomas aged two and six-week-old Ann; and Margaret Fludd's son William, just three weeks old, and her daughter from a previous marriage to William Finch, a tenant from Berkeley Hundred not known to be related to Catherine Finch. Extended families embracing children from several marriages were even more common in Virginia than in England.

As well as owning two houses, the Fisher household was moderately well provisioned, recording forty bushels of corn, fifty dry fish, a hog, sixteen chickens, three guns, one coat of chain mail, three pounds of powder and twenty pounds of lead. Their servant Idye Halliers, aged thirty, had arrived on the *Jonathan*, which had brought the earlier shipment of brides to Virginia. If Halliers had been one of the brides, this will have caused friction with her younger mistress, but she gave her arrival date as 1619 and is more likely to have come to Virginia as an indentured servant. Employing a servant will have relieved Catherine of the worst of the drudgery in the house and out in the fields, affording her time to devote to the couple's young daughter Sisly, doubtless named in honour of Sisley Jordan, who may have stood as godmother to the child.

Assuming the Fishers arrived at Jordan's Journey soon after the Indian attack, they will have witnessed the commotion that followed Samuel Jordan's death some time before the summer of 1623. As a wealthy widow with lands and provisions aplenty, Sisley Jordan immediately attracted suitors. The first to pounce was the Reverend Grivil Pooley, who lived at Flowerdew Hundred but also ministered to Chaplin's Choice, Jordan's Journey and Shirley Hundred. Pooley waited just three or four days after Samuel's death before declaring an interest in marrying his widow. Witnesses would later swear that the couple drank a toast to their engagement, but Sisley was also reported to have said that while 'she would as willingly have him as any other', she could not contemplate marrying anyone until she was delivered of the child she was carrying.[18]

Relations between Pooley and Sisley Jordan became increasingly strained by the presence of William Farrar, a kinsman of Nicholas Ferrar in London, who had taken refuge in Jordan's Journey after his own plantation on the nearby Appomattox River suffered heavy casualties in the Indian attack. Appointed to administer Samuel Jordan's estate, Farrar and Sisley openly lived together under the same roof with her two small daughters by Samuel – Mary and the infant Margaret, born posthumously – and young Temperance Bayley, who may have been a Jordan relative. Such an unorthodox arrangement prompted Pooley to complain to Virginia's general court in the hope of enforcing his prior claim to Sisley Jordan's hand. Called as a witness, Nathanial Causey said he had never observed any 'unfitting or Suspicyous familiarite' between the couple, although he had seen 'Mr ferrer kisse her'. Unconvinced,

Pooley maintained that it was 'Skandelous for Mr ferrer to breake the order in Courte, wch he hath done by beinge in ordynary dyett in Mrs Jurdens howse and to frequent her Company alone wthowt some body else to be in place accordinge to the order of the Court'.

Joan Palmer appeared fleetingly in the case, affording a glimpse into the highly charged atmosphere of this tight-knit community. According to Nathaniel Causey's sworn testimony, Mistress Palmer came into his house in some consternation, saying that she had witnessed a 'farefuyll thing' that had happened to Sisley Jordan. 'Shee saide yt Mrs Jrden being uppon her bed, she saw two hands, the one hande uppon her head the other hand uppon her Childs head and harde a voyce wch Cried, Judgment, Judgment'. When Causey suggested to Mrs Palmer that Sisley Jordan was simply dreaming, 'noe sayeth Mrs Palmer she was as broad Awake as I am now'.

Uncertain how to proceed in the delicate breach-of-promise suit between Pooley and Mistress Jordan, the court interrogated the witnesses then threw up its hands and sought advice from England, in the meantime insisting that Mr Farrar should behave himself 'wthowt Skandall'. But faced with Sisley Jordan's continued opposition, Pooley withdrew his suit, declaring,

> I Grevell Pooly Preacher of the woorde doe for my P[ar]te ffreely and absolutely acquitt and discharge Mrs Cycelie Jurden from all former Contracts p[ro]mises or Conditiones made by her to me in the waye of maryage and doe binde my selfe in five hundred pownde ster[ling] never to have any Claime Right or title to her that way In witnes wherof I have heerunto sett my hand & seal the thurde dye of January. Grevell Pooly Cler.[19]

Sisley Jordan and William Farrar were married soon afterwards, and as far as I can tell the Reverend Pooley failed to secure for himself a wealthy bride. He sounds an unpleasant fellow. One year on he was again hauled before the court after falling out with a Mr Paulett, who accused Pooley of being a 'blockheded parson', speaking false Latin and teaching false doctrines, and committing simony and bribery. Pooley responded by calling Paulett a 'base baudie ffellow' who went up and down the country singing bawdy songs. After lengthy discussions and some disagreement regarding penalties, the court ordered both parties to confess their faults to the congregation, and for the graver offence of charging Pooley with false doctrine, simony and perjury, Paulett was further ordered to pay him 300 pounds in tobacco.[20]

The Reverend Pooley's quarrelsome behaviour brings to mind Catherine's brother Erasmus Finch. Perhaps her life was not so very different from the one she had left behind.

Today Jordan's Journey lies directly south across the Benjamin Harrison Memorial Bridge, its footings marked by the Jordan Point Yacht Haven and a waterfront development of executive-style houses known as Jordan on the James, where meandering roads with names like Jordan Parkway and Farrar Landing carry echoes of Virginia's colonial past. I came here in 2016 while staying at a large house on the north side of the James, its fair lawns sloping down to the river, still wide at this point and very still, with views across the water to the belching smokestacks of Hopewell's paper mill on the far bank. Aside from the street names and Virginia Historical Markers to Samuel Jordan and Jordan's Point, I found little to remind me of Catherine Fisher née Finch.

But back in the 1980s, rumoured development of the Hopewell Airport site at Jordan's Point had prompted a series of archaeological and historical studies which brought to light the landscape and artefacts that the married Catherine Fisher, fresh from England, will have known.[21] At the community's social and geographical heart lay the compound of the Jordan-Farrar household, covering about an acre and a half on the western side of the promontory and affording its occupants a clear view up the James River, from where any attacking Indians might be expected to arrive.[22] Within the compound archaeologists uncovered eleven early colonial buildings, including a three-bay longhouse almost certainly occupied by the Jordan-Farrar household, another longhouse for their servants, further houses, a stable or barn, sheds and agricultural storehouses. Enclosing the compound was a wooden palisade of posts, pales and rails, culminating at the northern tip in a raised bastion for their many fixed guns.

Outside the fortified compound was a burial ground running parallel to the palisade's western and northern boundaries. Only a few of the dead had been buried in coffins and most showed signs of hasty interment. A surprising number were women. More than half the dead had perished between the ages of ten and nineteen, and almost another third were in their twenties. Two of the women were buried in coffins, one aged between twenty and twenty-four and the other between twenty-five and thirty-five. This last woman had a groove in her teeth, suggesting that she often gripped sewing pins in her mouth. The most elaborate burial was of a white male aged between thirty-five and thirty-nine, presumably either Samuel Jordan, the settlement's founder, or his successor William Farrar, who had been placed in a flat-lidded coffin almost six and a half feet long, which was then lowered into a deep and carefully dug grave.

Archaeologists explored three further housing complexes at Jordan's Journey. The first, which curators tentatively attributed to Nathaniel Causey, had two large houses and several outhouses, all encompassed by a simple palisade. Lying on the promontory's north-eastern side, it would have given Causey a clear view of his property across the James. Although both this and the Jordan-Farrar property produced household and personal items of a refined character, the people who lived in this second complex had lesser means. Sisley Jordan had tucked a beautifully chiselled silver bodkin into her hair, for instance, while Thomasine Causey

Women settlers at Jordan's Journey left behind bodkins they had tucked into their hair like this young woman etched by Wenceslaus Hollar, a small thread dangling from her bodkin's eye.

(if indeed she lived in the smaller property) had made do with a bodkin of brass.

Of the other two buildings revealed during excavations, the archaeologists concluded that one had probably been occupied by a single man, and the other by a relatively large group of people living communally, probably refugees from Berkeley Hundred to judge from the high-status items recovered, such as Roemer glass, porcelain and a silver ear scoop that could be attached to a chatelaine worn at the waist.

Domestic waste from trash pits yielded more clues about the daily lives of Catherine and her fellow colonists, and what they ate. The higher your status, the more domestic livestock you consumed. Nearly half the meat eaten by the Jordan-Farrar household came from their many cattle and less than 10 per cent from locally caught deer. They also ate substantial amounts of Atlantic cod and imported haddock, undoubtedly salted or pickled in brine and brought to Virginia in barrels. The so-called Causey household, by contrast, ate four times as much venison as the Jordan-Farrars, suggesting that they either traded with the Indians or hired them to hunt deer on their behalf. Wild fowl, local mammals and fish were on everyone's menu, although perhaps less than you might expect. Among the stranger foods Catherine may have tasted were opossum, muskrat, bear, raccoon, pelican, horned grebe, loon and egret, while imported stores such as oatmeal, cheese, butter, prunes, vinegar and brandy will have stirred memories of home, growing fainter all the time. As we saw in Chapter 14, the governor's wife, Lady Margaret Wyatt, had implored her sister to send butter and cheese soon after arrival, 'for since th' Indyans & we fell out we dare not send a hunting'. [23] But Lady Wyatt did not stay long in the colony, and Catherine was here for good, slowly adapting as all immigrants must to the realities of her new life.

The archaeologists have long since departed from Jordan's Point, their excavations back-filled or buried under the executive homes and shared lawns of Jordan on the James. But you can still sift through the detritus of the people who lived here four hundred years ago, all suitably bagged and labelled in boxes and drawers at the Virginia Department of Historic Resources in nearby Richmond, which I visited in spring 2017.

Fed on tales of colonial privation, I am overwhelmed by the sheer colour and variety of household goods enjoyed by Virginia's better-off settlers, especially the ceramics, which came to Jordan's Journey from England, France, Germany, the Low Countries, Portugal, Spain and far-flung China: south-Somerset slipware, fragments of Dutch and English delftware, Westerwald and Frechen stoneware jugs, a caudle cup of Portuguese majolica, a porcelain wine cup that must have come from China, slipware and earthenware costrels from Italy. From closer to home I am shown a coarseware porringer made in the Jamestown area in the 1630s by the potter Thomas Ward, who lived with John Jackson, the brother of Jamestown bride Ann Jackson.[24]

I am struck too by the incongruity of European arms and armour worn in the Virginian wilderness to ward off nimble and near-naked attackers: a peascod breastplate, sword hilts and backplates, remnants of a protective brigandine. But what I am seeking most of all is evidence of women's lives, like the bodkins they tucked into their hair and the tiny black earring dangle decorated with even tinier projections of white glass which came to light in the Jordan-Farrar household. Since their servants were all men, did Sisley Jordan and young Temperance Bayley once use the mass of sewing pins, needles and brass thimbles found here? And did Sisley own the finely decorated gold ring, which survives as a fragment, and the remnant of gold braid that may once have graced an elegant pair of gloves? The smaller Causey household similarly yielded a length of silver embroidery, which Thomasine Causey could lawfully have worn as the wife of a plantation owner with an estate across the water.

As for their moments of leisure, compare the whistle or flute made of bone and the brass book clasps found at the Jordan-Farrar household with the heavy lead gaming dice unearthed in the communal house, probably made from melted-down lead shot. Virginia may have lacked the playhouses and taverns of London, but people found their own ways of keeping themselves amused.

I find nothing that I can link absolutely to Erasmus Finch's sister but feel I am getting closer. Catherine Fisher née Finch had done well for herself. Against all the odds she had secured a capable husband, survived the Indian attack, given birth to a daughter and settled into a small but relatively stable community of like-minded ancient planters and more recent arrivals on the healthier freshwater reaches of the James River. Here were other young wives and mothers for company, busy growing their families, and she had a servant to carry out the heavier tasks around the home and perhaps in the fields, unless her husband sold his skills as a carpenter instead of trying to get rich by growing tobacco. Like all uprooted people, she will have experienced the steps along the route to assimilation, from shattered expectations, through coping as best she could with unimagined hardships, then mimicking the actions of the more successful settlers around her, anticipating the day when she could fully accept and adapt to the challenges thrown at her by her newly adopted home.[25]

And then the Fishers simply disappear from the record. No land patent survives to document the hundred acres which Robert Fisher could have claimed by right as an ancient planter, nor is there any record of land passed on to Catherine or the young Sisly. They may have moved elsewhere, but they have left no trace on Virginia's Eastern Shore, which attracted many settlers who survived the Indian attack, and travel further afield was unlikely. Migration to Maryland had not yet started and New England had only recently been colonized. You anyway needed the governor's permission to travel more than twenty miles from your home plantation or to embark on a voyage lasting more than a week.[26]

The most probable explanation is that the family succumbed to one of Virginia's deadly diseases and that all three lie buried at Jordan's Journey, perhaps in the burial ground beside the Jordan-Farrar compound, which became for them the end of the road.

CHAPTER SIXTEEN

The Planter's Wife

Bridgett Crofte came late to the Virginia Company's notice. Hers was the penultimate name added to the list of *Warwick* women by the Ferrars' clerk Tristram Conyam: 'Bridgett Crofte Aged 18 years borne att Burford [now Britford] in Wiltsheire her fathers name was John Crofte hee is deceased. She is commended by Robert the porter.'[1]

Tracing what happened to her is all the more rewarding because we know so little about her, but at least her birth record survives, which proves that she was a little older than the age she gave to the Virginia Company, turning twenty as she sailed across the Atlantic.[2] Once she arrived in Virginia, she may have spent Christmas in Jamestown looking for a husband then travelled on to Edward Bennett's new plantation on Burwell's Bay in January or February, experiencing the full horrors of the Indian attack in March 1622. Her presence at Bennett's Welcome can only be supposed, but the man she married was living there at the time of the attack and erroneously recorded among the dead. His name was John Wilkins. A year or two older than Bridgett, possibly more, he had come to Virginia in 1618 aboard the *Mary Gould*, having apparently paid his own passage; at least no record survives that would identify him as a servant or a tenant.[3] Nothing is known of his early life in England: who his parents were, where he lived or whether he acquired a trade before venturing himself to Virginia. Like many settlers, he was vague about his age and may have been born any time between 1596 and 1599.[4] While he could apparently afford to buy himself a wife, he was unable to read or write and had to work hard to earn the respectful title of Mister.

In the chaotic aftermath of the attack Wilkins and perhaps Bridgett would have been among the survivors from the straggling plantations of Warraskoyack rounded up and shipped back to Jamestown under the command of Captain Ralph Hamor, together with any livestock, stores and possessions they could salvage.[5] But Wilkins did not stay long in Jamestown. Like others who had witnessed the harsh realities of life – and death – on the James River, he was drawn to the relative safety of Virginia's Eastern Shore across the Chesapeake Bay, where the Accomac Indians were less hostile towards the English. Their *weroance* or chief, Esmy Shichans (also known as Debedeavon and the Laughing King of Accomack), had broken with Opechancanough the previous year after refusing to participate in the latter's plans to poison English dignitaries with spotted cowbane, a plant that grows freely on the Eastern Shore, or to launch a concerted attack that would drive the foreigners from their lands. Esmy Shichans had even warned the English about the impending attack, although not apparently about the poisoning, forcing Opechancanough to postpone his planned assault for another year.[6]

Wilkins probably went over to the Eastern Shore in 1622. He may even have accompanied Sir George Yeardley's mission to scout for a suitable place to seat some three to four hundred men, ordered by Governor Wyatt in late June, when the English considered moving survivors away from Jamestown.[7] Yeardley's instructions were to leave any colonists willing to 'make a begining there for a Plantation, giving to every one of them fouer acres of land for his p[ar]ticular employment'. Wilkins was not the sort of man to be satisfied with just four acres, but he was sufficiently enterprising to grasp any opportunity that came his way.

By February 1624 he was definitely married and living on the Eastern Shore with 'Goodwife Wilkins', named the following year as 'Briggett Wilkines', aged twenty, who had arrived by the *Warwick* in 1621.[8] The couple had no children as yet, and no servants. Land patents would later confirm her identity as 'Bridgett Craft', when 'John Wilkines' claimed fifty acres for paying her passage to the colony.[9] Whether or not Wilkins ever paid the Virginia Company the required 150 pounds of tobacco for his bride, he was certainly not entitled to claim any land on her behalf, since the company had explicitly granted the maids' headrights to investors in the maids' magazine. This may explain why Wilkins used his wife's maiden name and included her among a list of servants he had reputedly imported to the colony when seeking the local court's endorsement of his headrights claim, but he had at least the grace to put her name first.[10] He was sitting as a commissioner at the time, and none of his fellow commissioners disputed his claim.

The English had long turned their eyes to Virginia's Eastern Shore, a thin, flattish peninsula on the far side of the Chesapeake Bay. Then half a day's journey across its narrowest part, the Eastern Shore has a coastline that is scooped and indented on both ocean and bay side with innumerable coves, rivers and forking creeks. Surveyors had a hard job identifying boundaries. Land lying 'on the northern side of the northern branch of the forked branches of the middle branch of the creek' was how one seventeenth-century land sale attempted to locate a settler's property.[11] Rich in natural resources and visited by mighty flocks of geese, it has a gentler climate than inland Virginia, its proximity to the sea taking the edge off winters and tempering the summer heat with welcome sea breezes.

Captain John Smith came exploring here in 1608, crossing the Chesapeake Bay in an open barge of two or three tons with a mixed company of gentlemen, soldiers and sundry craftsmen: a blacksmith, a fishmonger, a fisherman and a doctor of physick.

The first people they saw were two 'grimme and stout Salvages upon Cape-Charles' armed with bone-headed poles like javelins, who boldly demanded to know who the foreigners were and what they wanted. Apparently satisfied with the strangers' responses, the Indians became 'very kinde' and took them to see their king, who struck the colonists as 'the comliest proper civill Salvage wee incountred' and his country 'a pleasant fertill clay-soile'. The English nonetheless had trouble finding fresh water, and they experienced the bay's fiercely unpredictable weather, when 'an extreame gust of wind, raine, thunder, and lightning happened, that with great daunger we escaped the unmercifull raging of that ocean-like water'.[12]

Captain John Smith's original map of Virginia, printed in 1612, recorded his explorations of Virginia's Eastern Shore across the Chesapeake Bay, where Bridgett Crofte settled with her husband John Wilkins.

Next to visit the Eastern Shore was the kidnapper of Pocahontas, Captain Samuel Argall, who brought with him deputy governor Sir Thomas Dale in November 1612 and returned the following May to explore further.[13] Argall praised the Eastern Shore's many small rivers and good harbours for small boats and barges, and its 'multitude of Ilands bearing good Medow ground'. It offered excellent commercial opportunities for salt manufacture and fishing, he felt, enjoying plentiful stocks of both fish and shellfish, and the native people 'seemed very desirous of our love'.[14]

One of the peninsula's greatest enthusiasts was secretary John Pory, who had heard such good reports that he believed the Eastern Shore offered 'as good ground as any in Virginia' and 'such a place to live in by ye reporte of those that have bene there… ye like is skarce to be found againe in ye whole country'. Its only drawback was the mosquitoes, which Pory – ever the optimist – believed would vanish once the land was cleared, declaring himself 'never so enamoured of any place wch I have not seene, nor shalbe satisfyed till I have seene it'.[15]

The English had begun to settle the Eastern Shore from around 1615, when Dale sent a small contingent of men under Lieutenant William Cradock to catch fish and to establish a salt works on Smith Island, making salt by boiling seawater. Fed and maintained by the colony, the men lived at Dale's Gift at the bottom of the peninsula. Dale's widow, Lady Elizabeth Dale, would later claim title to a vast estate at Old Plantation Creek on the bay side covering several thousand acres.[16] In 1616 Dale's Gift was one of only six settlements in the whole of Virginia named in a letter to King James by John Rolfe when he was visiting London with Pocahontas,[17] but by 1619 the salt works had failed from lack of funds and expertise, like so many of Virginia's early industries, its workers either dead or departed, and by March 1620 most if not all of the English had left the peninsula.[18]

Undeterred, other Englishmen began laying claims to land on the Eastern Shore, concentrating their plantations on two creeks a little to the north of Old Plantation Creek: King's Creek and Cherrystone Creek. One of the first independent planters was the interpreter Thomas Savage, who had come to Virginia as a boy in 1608 and spent three years with Powhatan in exchange for an Indian boy. He became particularly close to Accomack's Laughing King, who gave him a large tract of land above Cherrystone Creek, known to this day as Savage's Neck. About this time the Virginia Company earmarked 500 acres south of Cherrystone Creek as company land and granted another 500 acres to support the post of secretary in Virginia. Having opted for the Eastern Shore on Governor Yeardley's advice, John Pory settled his tenants on the neck of land between the mouths of Cherrystone and King's Creeks. In time the Secretary's Land developed into a thriving village community known as the Towne or Town Fields, clustered around the seat of local government. By 1634 there was even a ferry across King's Creek, bringing people to court and to church.[19]

It was on King's Creek that Wilkins established his home with Bridgett, on a highly desirable property right next door to the Secretary's Land, which suggests that he must have staked his claim very early. With the demise of the Virginia Company, uncertainty clouded the colony's land policy and Wilkins did not trouble to patent the 500 acres of his home place until 10 March 1638,[20] although he was 'possest of it' by 1635 and undoubtedly very much earlier.[21] The list of headrights is missing from the patent records, if it ever existed, but he sought approval for his land transactions from his fellow commissioners sitting at the Accomack court.

The man Bridgett Crofte had chosen to marry was very different from Catherine Finch's husband, Robert Fisher. A recent arrival rather than an ancient planter, Wilkins and Bridgett started out with very little, recording just one house, one gun and seven barrels of corn in the muster of 1625 – no livestock, no wet or dry fishes, no peas, beans, English wheat, oatmeal, bacon flitches, no ammunition or shot, nothing to suggest that the couple enjoyed anything but a very basic standard of living.[22] Wilkins nonetheless proved himself a man of vigour and substance, adept at manipulating the system so that his public life supported his private advancement. A busy and successful planter, he built up extensive landholdings on both sides of the bay and attained high office in the county, first as a burgess elected to represent Accomack at Virginia's general assembly in February 1633, when he petitioned the Accomack court to pay him fourteen days' work for attending on the burgesses at James City.[23] Shortly afterwards he was named one of four new commissioners or justices appointed to the court to replace others who had died, serving almost continuously until his death.[24]

Membership of the court undoubtedly furthered his private ambitions by securing endorsement for his land claims despite absent or flimsy evidence, yet Wilkins remained illiterate. While other commissioners routinely signed their names to documents, he could only made his mark, signing a capital I for 'Iohn' with a cross hatch through the middle. And when Sir George Yeardley's son Argoll sent him an unsealed letter about a court matter, he had to summon a servant to read it for him.[25]

The decade or so that Bridgett spent on the Eastern Shore marked its gradual transition from an English community that was predominantly young, single and male to one where families with small children were becoming the norm. But numbers were still very low. In 1624 just seven of its seventy-six inhabitants were women, all married and described as 'Mistress' or 'Goodwife' (or Gody), depending on their status.[26] Of the two or three English children, one was apparently motherless. One year on, overall numbers had dropped to fifty-one, of whom six were wives. Gone were two married couples, and while Thomas Powell had lost his spouse, two had gained wives: the father of the motherless Margaret, Nicholas Hodgskines, now married to Temperance; and Thomas Savage, whose wife Hannah Elkington had unusually paid her own passage to Virginia, arriving on the *Seaflower* in 1621.[27] Two of the wives (Temperance Hodgskines and Ffrancis Blore) may have come to Virginia as part of the 1620 bridal shipment, as they had sailed on the *Jonathan* and the *London Merchant* respectively. Although the English settlement now had two young children born in Virginia, it was still composed largely of single men either living alone (nine), in two-man households (four), or in all-male households of several men of undefined status, some of whom may have been servants.

Until Accomack gained its own court presided over by commissioners,[28] the man charged with keeping order on the Eastern Shore was Captain William Eppes from Ashford in Kent, described by one contemporary as a 'mad, ranting fellow'[29] and arraigned for the manslaughter of a fellow settler in 1619 but soon restored to his command.[30] Eppes lived with his wife Margaret and thirteen servants on the Secretary's Land in a lavish muster that included two houses, three storehouses, sixty-five barrels of corn and two hogs. As befitted a settlement commander, his compound was properly fortified and he was particularly well provided with arms for himself and his men, possessing five guns, 120 pounds of powder and 200 pounds of lead, six suits of armour, four coats of mail and six coats of steel. He also commanded one of the colony's two shallops (the other belonged to the governor at Jamestown), the only vessel on the Eastern Shore capable of crossing the Chesapeake Bay.[31]

As commander of the Eastern Shore, Eppes was given 'full power & Authority' to administer oaths to anyone living there 'for ye better decidinge of any small cause (that may there arise) by way of Compremise', to save the trouble and expense of sending witnesses to Jamestown.[32] Since a number of planters were moving here from the James River, he was also ordered to review each household's store of corn and to trade with the Indians for more corn if necessary to prevent price inflation and disorderly trading. But his own conduct on occasion brought him before the Jamestown court, notably over his relations with Alice Boyse, the same woman rumoured to have caused friction between Samuel and Sisley Jordan.

A few months after Boyse was widowed but Eppes remained very much married, the pair were accused of scandalous behaviour at Martin's Brandon, a plantation south of the James, after a night of heavy drinking in the company of others. Several witnesses attested to Alice Boyse lying down fully clothed on the bed beside Captain Eppes, then removing her gown and upper petticoat and climbing between the sheets. All the witnesses repeated the same story: that after a time they heard 'a great bussleing and juggling of the bed', followed by whispering between Mrs Boyse and Captain Eppes, at which point Captain John Huddlestone rose and said 'for shame doe not doe such thinges before soe many people', to which Captain Eppes replied, 'fye brother thats too plaine'.

One of the witnesses said he heard the 'bussleing' two or three times during the night, and after it had stopped a final time he saw Mrs Boyse rise from the bed, shake her petticoats down then go outside without putting on her gown. When she came back 'this deponent covered himselfe over head and eares, but when he rose he saw Mrs Boise to have her gowne on'.[33] More witnesses came forward at a subsequent hearing, when Sergeant John Harris told the court, 'he is not able to say that Capt Epes was uppon the sayd Mrs Boise, but sayth that the cloathes were raised to a great hight'.

The court delivered its verdict more than a month later. Despite all the evidence to the contrary, its members concluded that 'it is noe way proved or manifest by those depositions that Capt Epes and Mrs Boise have offended the Law but that they are cleare and guiltlesse'.[34] In Virginia as elsewhere one law existed for the powerful and another for lesser mortals. Just a month before, the same court had sentenced a man found guilty of having 'lewdly behaved himself' to forty lashes of the whip at James City and another forty lashes at Shirley Hundred, where the offending behaviour had taken place. The woman involved was ordered to stand in a white sheet at divine service before the congregations of the two parishes, a far gentler punishment and one that was positively benign compared with the execution of men convicted of sodomy or buggering animals.[35]

Captain Eppes remained on the Eastern Shore with his wife Margaret throughout much of the 1620s, patenting 450 acres of his own and producing a son, William, and a daughter, Frances.[36] Bridgett Wilkins also gave birth to a daughter, Mary, while her close neighbour Hannah Savage had a son called John in the early months of 1625.[37] So of the six married women present on the Eastern Shore in 1625, who had all come to Virginia since 1618, five were now living in households with children, while the sixth family, the Blores, may have lost their son John between 1624 and 1625.

Was Bridgett content with her new life and the man she had chosen to marry? John Wilkins had surely provided well for her and her daughter. She lived to see his election as a burgess and will have enjoyed the status that came from his appointment as a commissioner. During all the time they lived together he was busy trading cattle and extending his landholdings as a tobacco planter, although these would not be patented until after her death. They included the 500 acres on King's Creek where they lived, 1,300 acres across the bay in New Norfolk (now Surry) and a further 500 acres on the Eastern Shore's sea side, later enlarged to 600, which Wilkins claimed in 1640.[38] Among his claimed headrights in 1636 was 'his Negroe', perhaps one of the first Africans brought to the Eastern Shore, although Wilkins may have put him to work on his lands across the bay. And with his neighbour Obedience Robins he operated the first known windmill on the Eastern Shore, so he was clearly enterprising.[39]

But his many appearances in county court records – as commissioner, suitor and defendant – reveal him as a hot-tempered, outspoken fellow, fined for swearing in court on one occasion, along with several other commissioners.[40] He was not above manipulating evidence (witness his claim for Bridgett's headright) or hearing cases in which he had an interest. When a neighbour accused him of rebranding one of his hogs, the court delicately judged Wilkins's actions a 'mistake', ordering him nonetheless to give the man a year-old heifer in compensation and pay his costs.[41] He appeared many times as both creditor and debtor, and was prone to falling out with business associates and servants. But the servant who declared he wanted to 'knock his Maister John Wilkins on the head' and give him a 'Kinge Henry knocke' later became a partner and close friend, acting as a witness to his will in 1649 despite having been ordered by the court to receive thirty lashes on his bare shoulders for his 'enormous offences' in speaking against Commissioner Wilkins.[42] Another festering business dispute was finally settled in Wilkins's favour when four fellow commissioners attested to his good character, declaring that throughout their long acquaintance with him 'they never see nor heare by him of any ill Carriage towards any person whatsoever', while his opponents 'lived very basely and suspiciously in the County'.[43]

Bridgett Wilkins's one foray into Accomack's court records tells a different story, however, and calls into question their relations as man and wife. As with so many neighbourly disputes that surfaced in the Virginian courts, the 'evidence' was little more than hearsay and tittle-tattle, catching Bridgett in the crossfire. The case, which came before the court on 8 September 1634, concerned a dispute between two married couples, the Drews and the Butlers. The five commissioners sitting in judgment included Wilkins's neighbour Obedience Robins but not Wilkins himself.[44]

First Edward Drew petitioned the court against Joan Butler for having called his wife Marie a 'common Carted hoare', referring to the punishment meted out to scolds and whores – to be tied to the back of a horse and cart and whipped through the streets. The court agreed with Drew and for her slanderous statement ordered Joan Butler to be dragged across King's Creek at the stern of a boat or canoe from one cow pen to the other (the Virginian equivalent of carting), or else to present herself before the minister at divine

Virginia's equivalent of the ducking stool for punishing scolds and disorderly women was to tie them to a boat and drag them across a bay.

service on the following sabbath, between the first and second lesson, and to repeat these words: 'I Joane Butler doe acknowledge to have called Marie Drew hoare and thereby I confesse I have done her manefest wronge, wherfor I desire befor this congregation, that ye syd Marie Drew will forgive me, and alsoe that this congregtion, will joyne, and praye with me, that God may forgive me.'

Joan Butler's husband Thomas then issued a counterblast, accusing Marie Drew of spreading rumours that he had committed adultery with 'Bridgett the wife of mr. John Wilkins'. Confusingly, the slander seems to have originated with Joan Butler, since the witness called to give evidence (Joane Muns, aged about thirty) swore that while they were going down to the Old Plantation together Joan Butler had told her 'that her husbound shewed her wher he layed the Head and heeles of Bridgett Wilkins, and that the syd Bridgett would have given him as much Cloth as would make him a shert'. How Marie Drew spread these rumours is not made clear, but the implication is that Bridgett Wilkins was offering favours in return for sex.

One week later, with John Wilkins sitting in judgment alongside Obedience Robins and several other commissioners, the court ordered Marie Drew to be punished for calling Joan Butler a carted whore and declaring to witnesses that she had seen her 'carted in England'. Bridgett Wilkins has disappeared from the story and no mention is made of an adulterous liaison between Bridgett and Thomas Butler. Marie Drew's punishment mirrored that meted out to Joan Butler, to beg her forgiveness in church, a clear case of tit for tat.

This is the last we see of Bridgett Wilkins, who dies soon afterwards. By early 1636 John Wilkins had married again and settled into what looks like a happy second marriage. Ann Wilkins had a temper to match her husband's and was a ferocious beater of servants. She called a neighbour a whore and a 'pissa bedd Jade' for accusing her servant Walter of stealing a pot of butter, giving her a 'slapp in the Chopps' for good measure.[45] In one particularly nasty incident she insisted on exchanging maidservants with a neighbour then 'most unconscyonably and dangerousely Beate her', treatment that was amply confirmed by her former servant, who complained of 'the unchristian like and violent oppression of her Mistresse and by her continuall strikeing Beateing and abusinge her with her careless resolute Blowes'.[46] But Ann Wilkins bore her husband six children (John, Argoll, Nathaniel, Lydia, Anne and Frances)[47] as opposed to Bridgett's only daughter. And he trusted her well enough to appoint her as his attorney during his second long absence from Virginia between 1643 and 1645, when he returned on business to England or perhaps continental Europe.[48]

A full year before his death John Wilkins wrote his final will, having resolved to take a voyage for England and 'consideringe with myselfe that all men are mortall not knowing how things maye interveene or whether it shall please god I shall return againe or not'. He bequeathed his whole estate, real and personal, 'unto my loveinge wife Ann Wilkins And my children (which god hath blessed me with by her)'.[49] He was away for some eleven months and returned close to death. In December 1650, just before he died, he recorded a deed of gift to his son-in-law John Baldwin and Baldwin's wife Mary, his daughter by the former Bridgett Crofte. Originally party to the gift, his wife Ann has been crossed out of the final deed, suggesting a falling-out between the young couple and Mary's stepmother.

Wilkins gave Mary and her husband four cows, one heifer, one bull, three barrels of corn, one horse, two shoes, 150 acres of land, one bed and bolster, one rug and blanket, three pairs of sheets, one pillow-board, one tablecloth, six napkins, three towels, three pewter dishes, six spoons, one candlestick, one salt and a dramcup, one iron pot, one iron kettle and one brass kettle – a substantial gift from a man who had arrived in Virginia with nothing to his name some thirty years previously.[50]

Less than three months after John Wilkins's death, Ann Wilkins married again. Her third and final husband died in 1662 and she then remained a widow until her own death in 1690, almost seventy years after Wilkins's first wife had sailed to Virginia as a hopeful bride.

I returned twice to Virginia's Eastern Shore, looking for traces of Bridgett and her husband, the first time with cultural anthropologist Helen Rountree.

The waters of the bay were grey and choppy as we crossed the twenty-three-mile Chesapeake Bay Bridge Tunnel, the wind as fierce and gusty as Captain John Smith had warned. The Eastern Shore feels immediately different to the James River plantations: the land flatter, the light brighter, the air distinctly breezy. You sense the sea even when you cannot see it. At Old Plantation Creek signs commemorate Esmy Shichans, the Laughing King, whose village of Accawmack (Accomack) lay scattered about the head of the creek. Even on grey days the white sands of the inlets and coves glisten sharply and the air is noticeably salty.

After Arlington we head north to Cheriton and Eastville then west towards the Atlantic coast along Indiantown Road, past the patched fields and woodlands of the former Gingaskins reservation, as the Accomac Indians were later known.

At the Virginia National Wildlife Refuge on the peninsula's southern tip, our last stop of the day, I tell the ranger about my quest for the Jamestown brides. It has been a long day and I muddle the names, saying that I am looking for the descendants of John Downeman, who married one of the *Warwick* Elizabeths. The ranger shakes his head: there are no Downemans on the Eastern Shore, it seems, but he brightens immediately when I correct the name to Wilkins. Ah yes, there are still plenty of Wilkinses on the Eastern Shore. Origins matter here. For anyone born and bred in this part of Virginia, who you are is closely linked to who you once were and when your ancestors first arrived.

The winds of the Chesapeake Bay are fiercer than ever on my next visit. Halfway across the bridge part of the crossing, a tornado warning advises taking immediate shelter, allowing me just enough time to pull into the Chesapeake Grill in the middle of the bay and run for cover. No one inside the cafe-bar pays the slightest attention to the bucketing storm, which is quickly gone.

My host this time is Nancy Harwood Garrett, an authenticated descendant of Thomas Savage and of John Wilkins through his second wife Ann, who also counts Obedience Robins among her ancestors.[51] A wise and generous host like Helen Rountree, she shows me a meticulously referenced monograph on John Wilkins written by her relative Elliott Wilkins, on which I have drawn heavily. We talk about whether Wilkins was a Puritan, but the evidence is slight: one reference to him affirming rather than swearing an oath, a sign of nonconformity usually associated with the later Quakers, which anyway sits uneasily with his fine for blasphemy in open court.[52]

After a night eating shrimp caesar and onion rings by the foot in a local bar, the next morning we take a map of early land patents and go hunting for the 500-acre plot on King's Creek that was once home to John and Bridgett Wilkins. We find it surprisingly close to where Nancy lives now. The landscape is unremarkable: flat fields of winter grass, boundary trees in straight lines, pines mixed with broadwoods that are barely showing green. Only the street names hint at the history of these fields as we drive sedately towards King's Creek along Townfield Drive, past Obedience Lane and on to Wilkins Drive, which today marks the boundary of his land patent.

At the Eastville Court House clerk of the court Traci L. Johnson produces for me the original record detailing the sorry tale of Bridgett Wilkins's presumed adultery with Thomas Butler, who reputedly showed his wife where he had laid the head and heels of Bridgett, and she promised him a shirt. Aside from her name in John Wilkins's land patents, fraudulently used to claim land to which he was not entitled, I hold in my hands the one surviving record of who she might have been, a scrap of malicious gossip dutifully recorded for posterity, nothing more.

CHAPTER SEVENTEEN

The Cordwainer's Daughter

⁂

You need perseverance today to find Neck of Land in Charles City, Virginia, more commonly known as Bermuda Hundred, where Audry Hoare settled after her marriage to ancient planter Thomas Harris. Take Highway 10 heading north from Hopewell, come off at North Enon Church Road then turn east along Bermuda Hundred Road, past the rather desolate Bermuda Memorial Park and several sprawling industrial complexes interspersed with trees and occasional swamps. When you feel you have lost your way, continue along the narrow 'no-issue' road that dog-legs past the First Baptist church (DEFEAT IS NOT AN OPTION) down to the James River and a view across to Shirley Plantation on the other side, which is closer than you might expect.

Here a rough-hewn stone tablet erected by the Daughters of the American Revolution tells you that Sir Thomas Dale established Bermuda Hundred in 1613, the year before it became Virginia's first incorporated town. Pocahontas's husband John Rolfe lived here for a time, and the Reverend Alexander Whitaker ministered here, but the Daughters then leapfrog three centuries to 1938 and the construction of Richmond's early port. So you learn nothing about the mid-1620s when this particular Neck of Land was home to a thriving, jostling, bickering but relatively rooted community of English settlers, much like villages back home.[1]

As we saw in Chapter 1, Audry Hoare was two years younger than the age she gave to the Virginia Company, travelling out to Virginia when she had barely turned seventeen. Both still alive, her parents lived in Aylesbury, Buckinghamshire, although Audry herself may have lodged in Blackfriars, London, with a married sister. We know from his will that Audry's father Thomas was a cordwainer, a maker of new shoes from fine leather rather than a cobbler who repaired old ones.[2] While

Originally from the lace-making town of Aylesbury in Buckinghamshire, Audry Hoare brought refined needlework skills to Virginia, like many of the Jamestown brides.

Captain John Smith is sometimes wrongly labelled a cordwainer, he nevertheless recognized the value to colonists of stout footwear, telling the Company of Cordwainers that 'for want of Shooes among the Oyster Bankes wee tore our hatts and Clothes and those being worne, wee tied Barkes of trees about our Feete to keepe them from being Cutt by the shelles amongst which wee must goe or starve'.[3]

Like Catherine Finch, Audry Hoare married an ancient planter, in her case Thomas Harris, who had come to Virginia in 1611. Although Harris would later earn the title of Captain, he appears in early Virginian records without the courtesy Mister before his name, which implies that his origins were relatively humble, like those of Catherine's husband, Robert Fisher.[4] While we cannot know for certain where Audry and Thomas Harris spent the first months of their married life, the couple had settled in Neck of Land Charles City by February 1624,[5] probably arriving early in 1623 after the Indian attack.[6] In the 1625 muster Harris's wife is identified as Adria – a variant of Audry and the name by which she was commonly known in Virginia – who had arrived by the *Marmaduke* in 1621. Living with them was a seven-year-old kinswoman, Ann Woodlase, possibly John Woodlief's daughter from Berkeley Hundred,[7] and a fifteen-year-old servant, Elizabeth (surname not recorded), who had come to the colony as a girl of ten or eleven in 1620. As a family, they were relatively well provisioned, owning two houses, a boat and a quantity of foodstuffs, including seven and a half bushels of corn and one of peas. Their livestock was particularly plentiful: eleven cattle 'yong and old' and thirty hens, which would have been Adria's responsibility. Thomas Harris possessed the military equipment one would expect of an aspiring captain, including three fixed guns, a quantity of powder and lead, one sword, a complete suit of armour and a coat of mail. Although the couple had as yet no children of their own, their daughter Mary must have been born shortly afterwards, and they also had a son called William, born around 1629. Both children survived into adulthood.[8]

To create an English settlement on the promontory where the James and the Appomattox Rivers meet, deputy governor Sir Thomas Dale had first expelled the Appamattuck Indians from their scattered village and the cornfields they had so conveniently cleared. To safeguard livestock and deter Indian attacks, Dale constructed a two-mile palisade between the two rivers, securing some eight miles of land, 'the most part champion, and exceeding good Corne ground'.[9] John Rolfe noted how the river wound around a good circuit of land and how the fence running across the neck of land turned it into an island. 'The houses and dwellings of the people are sett round about by the ryver, and all along the pale [fence] so farr distant one from the other, that upon anie All-arme they can second and succor one the other.'

Although many of Dale's plantations were abandoned soon after he left the colony in May 1616, Bermuda Hundred endured and prospered, identified variously as Charles and Nether Hundred and Neck of Land Charles City, its population fluctuating from around 119 settlers on Dale's departure to as many as 184 in 1620, when numbers were swollen by refugees from Captain Christopher Lawne's ailing plantation close to Bennett's Welcome.[10] Its defences proved effective in the Indian attack of March 1622 since no settlers at Bermuda Hundred were reported killed, although several died at neighbouring settlements. It seems likely, however, that the plantation was abandoned in the general mayhem and the colonists either brought back to Jamestown under the command of Captain Roger Smith or dispersed to nearby strongholds such as Jordan's Journey.[11]

By February 1624 a still childless Adria and her husband Thomas Harris were among the forty or so settlers who had returned to live at Neck of Land Charles City, which may have extended beyond Dale's original palisade. The ratio of men to women in this small community was far more balanced than in Virginia as a whole. Altogether, twelve married couples lived here in 1624, three of them with infant children. Thanks to the 'good and wholesome' air of the upper reaches of the James River,[12] all twelve couples and their children were still alive the following year, and six more children had been born. The Sharps had produced two children during the year, while the Bradwayes had christened their daughter Adria, perhaps after Adria Harris, who may then have been pregnant with her first child. Three of the wives had arrived on either the *Jonathan* or the *London Merchant* in 1620 – Susan Greenleafe, Ann Coltman and Sisley Bradway – suggesting that they may have travelled with the earlier bridal shipment to Virginia. Two other wives had arrived the same year, Elizabeth Sharp and Ann Price, both by the *(Francis) Bonaventure*.[13] Of the eleven married women who declared their ages in 1625, eight were in their twenties, one in her thirties and two in their forties, giving Adria a good choice of companions. At forty-two, the oldest was Joan Vincent, whose sharp tongue has already been noted.

As well as enjoying a better gender balance, the small community was also remarkably stable. Between 1624 and 1625 no families left and no new families arrived, although ancient planter Joshua Chard found himself a wife called Ann, who had arrived on the *Bony Besse* in 1623. Four individuals were no longer there: William Clements (probably dead), the boatswain Nathaniel Reeve (presumably just passing through the year before), Robert Turner (who may have gone as a servant to Jordan's Journey) and Margaret Berman, who may have lived with Thomas and Adria Harris in 1624 but who then simply disappears.

Others have speculated that Margaret Berman was in fact Margaret Bourdman, another of the Jamestown brides who sailed on the *Marmaduke* with Catherine Finch and Audry Hoare.[14] Had she lived with the Harrises at Neck of Land, this would have given Adria companionship and help in the household, although their differences in age and social rank would have created tensions between them. Born in Yorkshire and orphaned by the time she left England, Bourdman was four years older than Adria and higher in social status,[15] claiming as her maternal uncle Sir John Gibson, knighted by King James in 1607 and later appointed sheriff of Yorkshire.[16] Bourdman's guarantors were equally impressive and tell us much about how the Virginia Company's network of contacts succeeded in attracting women of her class: they included a seasoned Virginia hand, Captain Wood, one of Captain John Smith's 'ould Soldiers'; the coachman to a City dignitary, the Recorder of London (then Sir Edwin Sandys' fellow parliamentarian Heneage Finch); and Erasmus Finch, brother of fellow Jamestown bride Catherine Fisher now living at Jordan's Journey.[17] Bourdman had lived in service with Captain Wood and the recorder's coachman, and possibly with all three since both Master and Mistress Finch had 'long known her'. But whether Bourdman and Berman are one and the same, and what happened to her, I cannot say. At the muster of 1625 all but two Margarets living in the colony had either been born there or had arrived by ships other than the *Marmaduke*.[18]

Virginia's surviving records nonetheless provide tantalizing glimpses of Thomas Harris and his household, enabling us to plot his progress through life and gauge his character: assertive, calculating, determined to succeed, a leader of men apparently undamaged by his reputation as a womanizer. Like Catherine Finch's husband, Harris was owed money from the estate of Captain George Thorpe, murdered and mutilated at the plantation of Berkeley Hundred during the Indian attack of 1622. Harris originally claimed he was owed 'twenty five pownd lawfull money of England', a substantial sum compared with Robert Fisher's ninety pounds in weight of tobacco for building a house for Opechancanough.[19] Altogether a dozen creditors were recorded, among them some of the colony's political or commercial leaders such as Sir George Yeardley, merchant Abraham Peirsey, Captain Francis West, treasurer George Sandys (for two 'Duty Boys'), Virginia Company factor

Edward Blaney, and the Reverend Richard Buck from Jamestown. When Thorpe's debts were later translated into tobacco, Harris emerged as the largest creditor, owed 333 pounds of tobacco, with 40 pounds rebated.[20]

However humble his origins, Harris was transforming himself into one of the community's leading members, which may have rankled with some of the other ancient planters who had settled at Neck of Land before him. In 1624 he was one of two burgesses elected to represent Neck of Land at the general assembly in Jamestown.[21] The other was Luke Boyse, whose wife Alice had reputedly sown discord between Samuel Jordan and his wife Sisley, and who would later scandalize her drinking partners at Martin's Brandon over her 'hustling and bustling' in bed with Captain William Eppes. Although Harris remained a Neck of Land burgess for just one year – and was still plain Thomas Harris – other public offices soon followed: commissioner on the monthly court for the Upper Partes, to be held at either Jordan's Journey or Shirley Hundred across the river,[22] and second-in-command under Lieutenant Thomas Osborne of a military posse from Neck of Land and the College Land, instructed to 'goe upon the Indians & cutt downe their corne' in a co-ordinated attack planned for 1 August 1627, their particular target being the Tanx Powhatans.[23]

By 1640 he had transformed himself into Captain Thomas Harris,[24] a burgess for Henricus, which he represented in the general assemblies of 1639/40 and 1647/8, and commander of the Henrico militia. And as such he is remembered on a historical marker I chanced upon while meandering along State Route 5 on the north bank of the James River. The board stands by the entrance to Curles Neck Farm and usefully documents Harris's growing landholdings, starting with a patent issued in 1635 for a 750-acre property originally called Longfield and later Curles. By the time he died, Captain Harris's lands exceeded 2,500 acres. The sign makes no reference to a wife or to any blot on his steady progress through the ranks of Virginian society.

The source for the gossip about Thomas Harris's supposed sexual improprieties was again Joan Vincent, who lived at Neck of Land with her husband William Vincent and had already appeared in court accused of spreading malicious rumours about Alice Boyse and Samuel Jordan. In March 1626 Harris's reputed womanizing surfaced in the court at Jamestown. One of their neighbours, fifty-year-old ancient planter Richard Taylor, was called to give evidence before the governor concerning Harris's behaviour. In his sworn evidence Taylor repeated Joan Vincent's claim that 'there was ffowerteene women in the Church, And that seven of them were Thomas Harris his whoores' – a claim that suggests Adria's husband had sexual relations with half the women at Neck of Land. According to Joan's hearsay evidence, 'Thomas Harris made faste the doore and would have layne with a woman in the Plantacione against her will'.[25]

One week later, Joan's husband William Vincent procured a warrant against Thomas Harris and his wife, calling John Chambers as a witness. The Harrises and John Chambers duly turned up at court, but Vincent failed to appear so the court ordered him to pay Thomas Harris and his wife thirty pounds of tobacco 'in lew of theire Charges and loss of tyme' and the same amount to John Chambers.

The following year, it was Richard Taylor's turn to take Thomas Harris to court in a land dispute that also involved William Vincent.[26] When he came to Neck of Land Harris had signed an agreement with Richard Taylor, William Vincent and George Grimes that land cleared by the three men should be divided between Thomas Harris '& such others as were then to plant on ye said land'. Jealous of Harris's steady rise in esteem, perhaps, Taylor complained to the Jamestown court that Harris had planted on his dividend, but Harris was able to produce in court the signed deed which upheld his claim to the land. Having failed in his suit, Taylor was ordered to pay twenty pounds of tobacco in damages to Harris. The court also backed Thomas Harris's right to a further five acres of land granted by Governor Wyatt in January 1623 to 'Tho: Harris & others that then intended to goe & plant uppon ye said necke of land', supporting the view that Thomas and Adria Harris came there after the Indian attack of 1622.

Had seething resentment about land provoked Joan Vincent's tongue and Richard Taylor's belated attempt to claim back land he felt was rightly his? Or was sexual jealousy the root cause of bad relations in the community? As ever, we need to read between the lines of Thomas Harris's land grants to disentangle the facts of his life.

Still to this day a working farm of several thousand acres, the main Harris lands are situated on the north bank of the James, across the river and a little to the west of Neck of Land Charles City. In Harris's time the land was known as Longfield, a reference perhaps to the long fields of Indian corn running parallel to the river. Between 1635 and February 1639 Harris obtained four land patents of 750, 700, 700 and 820 acres.[27] The last three of these clearly relate to the same piece of land in Henrico County, varying slightly in extent but called 'Long Feild' in all three patents, beginning at a little creek over against the land of Captain Martin, bounded to the north by the back side of the swamp, to the west by the main river, and to the south-east by another planter's dividend. Confusingly, all three use different bases for Harris's claim. And while the land in the first patent is placed a little to the east in Digges' Hundred, it names the same people as one of the Longfield patents to claim the fifty-acre headrights granted to Harris for each person brought to the colony at his expense. Like other planters, Thomas Harris was clearly adept at manipulating the system to his own advantage.

Equally telling are the patents' hidden clues to the women in his life. The second of the Longfield patents, dated 12 July 1637, reveals that 400 acres of the land was granted by the Virginia Company to another ancient planter, Edward Gurganey, and bequeathed to Harris by his widow Ann Gurganey in her will dated 11 February

1620.[28] No obvious kinship exists between Thomas Harris and Ann Gurganey, so was she a friend or one of his amorous conquests? And if the latter, why did he not simply marry her, since marrying widows for their land was perfectly normal behaviour for the time? The remaining acres of this patent came to him as headrights for importing eight people whose names are not disclosed.

Two patents claim a fifty-acre headright for having imported the same thirteen named people: ten English men, one English women and two negroes, a man and a woman, who are not dignified with names.[29] In each case Harris correctly claimed a further hundred acres for himself as an ancient planter but in the second of these patents, dated 25 February 1639, he claimed an additional hundred acres for the personal adventure of his first wife, 'Adry Harris, as being Ancient Planter'. This was fraudulent on two counts. Adria Harris was not an ancient planter, and by the terms of the maids' magazine he was not entitled to claim *any* land for the bride he had married. Like John Wilkins, Thomas Harris chose to ignore this stipulation, and even doubled the amount he claimed in his late wife's name.

Perhaps the greatest surprise of all lurks in Harris's earliest land patent for 750 acres in Digges Hundred, Henrico County, granted on 11 November 1635.[30] The patent describes the land as extending southwards to the land of Edward Virgany (Gurganey), then extending northwards up to the land of Joan Harris, his wife. So Adria was dead by now – possibly quite recently – and Harris had married a woman who owned land in her own right. The only Joan known to own land in the area was Joan Vincent, by now presumably a widow and the inheritor of William Vincent's lands at Curles, named after the curling river in its upper reaches.[31] However unlikely it seems, Virginia genealogists now generally accept that Thomas Harris married the woman who had spread rumours about his sexual conquests, a woman four years his senior and more than twenty years older than his first wife, which means that she cannot have been the mother of either of the two Harris children.[32]

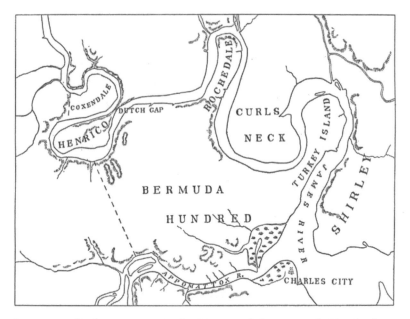

Some time after her marriage Audry Hoare settled at Bermuda Hundred (Neck of Land Charles City) with her husband Thomas Harris, who later patented land across the James River on Curls Neck.

You can follow the family down six successive generations in the latest edition of *Adventurers of Purse and Person*, the accepted sourcebook for tracing your ancestry back to Virginia's early settlers.[33] Mary Harris, the oldest child of Adria and Thomas Harris, was born around 1625 and her brother William some four years later. Both belonged to Virginia's plantation elite. Mary's eventual husband, Thomas Ligon or Lyggon, was a burgess for Henricus like his father-in-law,[34] lieutenant colonel of the militia and surveyor of Henrico County until his death. Adria's son William also served as a justice and burgess of Henricus, and was elevated from captain to major of the Charles City and Henrico militia by the Jamestown assembly of 1656.[35]

Adria Harris's direct descendants are scattered across North America's eastern seaboard and beyond. I contacted a handful with help from the Jamestowne Society, which restricts its membership to people who can prove descent from Virginia Company stockholders or settlers living in Virginia by the time of the 1625 muster, plus a few others. Among those who wrote to me was Elizabeth Ellen Jones, descended from Adria and Thomas Harris through their daughter Mary, who said she sometimes feels related to most families that settled in Virginia early in the seventeenth century.[36] Her family line includes coal company managers and shipbuilders, and she now lives in Staunton, Virginia, where the American Shakespeare Center has reconstructed the Blackfriars Playhouse, neatly echoing Adria Hoare's early life in London.

Virginia Ann Catalano, another direct descendant of Adria through her son William, told me about the Kentucky statesman Henry Clay, also descended from Thomas and Adria Harris.[37] On the day of Clay's funeral stores were closed in Springfield, Illinois, and Abraham Lincoln (not yet president) delivered the eulogy in Springfield's Hall of Representatives. I soon get lost in multiple branching family trees – 'Henry Clay's grandfather was the brother of my ancestor Charles Hudson,' Catalano tells me. 'Their father was John Hudson, who married Elizabeth Harris, great-granddaughter of Thomas and Adria Harris' – but I am struck by the consequences of Adria Hoare's decision to uproot herself and start afresh in the New World. When Catalano and I finally get to meet, over coffee at the British Library in London, I ask her if she feels proud to be descended from one of America's earliest settlers. 'I don't look at it that way,' she replies. 'Rather, I feel connected to the beginning of my country, and to the whole adventure of coming across the ocean. I feel connected to England too. I first came here at twenty, and I keep returning.'

My search for the reasons behind Adria's decision to sail on the *Marmaduke* ends where it should have begun, with her father's will lodged in Aylesbury's Centre for Buckinghamshire Studies. Written on 31 January 1627, when Thomas Hoare, cordwainer, was 'sicke of body but of perfect remembrance thankes bee to the Lord', the will is brutally short and implies a family in sorry need.[38]

After delivering his soul into the hands of Almighty God and his body to the ground whence it came, he named just four legatees: his daughter Agnes, his daughter Audry, Audry's unnamed daughter and his wife. To Agnes he gave just twelve pence (one shilling), which she was to receive within a month of his death. As for his youngest child, 'I give to my daughter Awadrye [Audry] xijd [12d.] to be payde her when she doth demande it after my desease and allso to her daughter xijd [12d.]'. We can assume that his other three children had died. The rest of his 'goods chattels lands and tenements unbequeathed' he left to his wife, whom he named as his executrix, but these are stock phrases and in truth he probably had little to give her. He also named two trusty, well beloved friends as overseers of his will, John Fforriste and Jonas Orton, to whom he gave sixpence each for their pains.

The will was probated on 5 April 1627. Eight years later Audry was dead too, aged thirty or thirty-one at most. Whether she ever asked for the shilling her father had left her is not known.

CHAPTER EIGHTEEN

Captured by Indians

Of all the maids who travelled to Jamestown, the one who experienced the most extreme reversals in her fortune was Ann Jackson. Originally from Salisbury in Wiltshire, she sailed to Virginia with the blessing of her gardener father, intending to join her brother John Jackson and his wife (another Ann) at Martin's Hundred.[1] While having family in Virginia meant that she was taking less of a leap into the unknown than most of the maids, even her wildest imaginings could not have braced her for what the future might hold.

Like the other Jamestown brides, Jackson had three scant months to settle into her new life before the Indians attacked on the morning of 22 March 1622, causing more devastation at Martin's Hundred than at any other English settlement. Presumed killed during the attack, Ann was in fact taken prisoner and survived in captivity, resurfacing in court records only in January 1629, when her brother was ordered to keep her safe until she could be shipped back to England.[2] Some Jamestown historians maintain that Jackson was released from captivity along with other English women after a year or so, I believe she remained with the Indians far longer and perhaps for six long years or more.[3]

Anyone who lived through the horrors of that dreadful day will have witnessed acts of random brutality as the Indians attacked, burned and destroyed their homes, much like those recorded later in the century by Mary Rowlandson, a minister's wife from Lancaster, Massachusetts, whose graphic account of her captivity by Indians and subsequent restoration set the mould for a whole genre of captivity narratives.[4] Rowlandson had watched from her house as the 'murderous wretches' burned and destroyed all before them, until her own house was set on fire and she was forced outside,

> the fire increasing, and coming along behind us roaring, and the Indians gaping before us with their guns, spears, and hatchets to devour us. A wounded man begged for his life, promising money, but the Indians bashed out his brains, stripped him naked and split open his bowels. Another was chopped on the head with a hatchet, stripped naked and yet was crawling up and down.
>
> It was a solemn sight to see so many christians lying in their blood, some here, and some there, like a company of sheep torn by wolves. All of them stript naked by a company of hell-hounds, roaring, singing, ranting and insulting, as if they would have torn our hearts out.

Her brother-in-law, wounded in the throat, fell down dead and the Indians stripped him of his clothes. Rowlandson was hit in the side, and the child in her arms through the bowels and hand. One of her sister's children broke his leg, then the Indians knocked him on the head. 'Thus were we butchered by those merciless heathens, standing amazed, with the blood running down to our heels.' After their attack on Rowlandson's community the Indians carried away alive twenty-four captives, who were marched for about a mile, wounded and bleeding, before they rested for the night. 'Oh the roaring, and singing and dancing, and yelling of those black creatures in the night, which made the place a lively resemblance of hell.'

The Indians who seized fifteen women and a handful of men from Martin's Hundred and perhaps from other Virginian plantations will have travelled further that first day, spurred on by fear of reprisals. Their destination was Opechancanough's capital well up the Pamunkey River, across the neck of land separating the James River from the river basin to the north.[5] While the usual fate of male captives was to be slowly tortured to death by Indian townsfolk of both sexes, women and children became the property of the victor, valued for their labour and for the ransom they could command.[6] Such was the eventual fate of the English men and women taken captive that day: the men put to death and the women enslaved until the English could be persuaded to buy them back.[7]

For several months the colonists remained unaware that some of their number had been spirited away by their attackers. The first news to filter into the public record was a letter written in May 1622 by Mistress Sara Boyse to John Smith's old associate Captain Raleigh Crawshawe, asking him to intercede with Governor Wyatt to help secure her release along with nineteen more prisoners held at Pamunkey. Crawshawe concocted a complicated plan involving the Patawomeck Indians from the Potomac River as intermediaries between Opechancanough and the English, but the commanders at Jamestown seemingly did not care for his plan, so the attempt fizzled out.[8]

The governor nonetheless made overtures to Opechancanough for 'restoringe of the captive English', receiving an 'insolent answer' that confirmed the colonists in their desire to make war on their enemy, 'hoping by Godes helpe this winter to cleare the Country of him and setlinge the Colony in a farr better estate, then it was before'.[9] Yeardley was particularly active in leading punitive raids against the Powhatan Indians, burning their houses, killing where they could and bringing home corn for the beleaguered colonists at Jamestown, 'but as he adventured for himselfe, he accordingly enjoyed the benefit', remarked Captain John Smith caustically.[10]

The rest of the summer remained relatively quiet as the English regrouped and licked their wounds. They sought no real revenge until after the Indian corn was ripe, determined to 'lull them the better in securitie', then they called together three hundred of their best soldiers to 'leave their private businesse, and adventure themselves amongst the Salvages to surprize their Corne'. Commanded again by Yeardley, they went first to Nansamund, from which the Indians had already fled, then sailed to Pamunkey, 'the chiefe seat of Opechankanough, the contriver of the massacre: the Salvages seemed exceeding fearefull, promising to bring them Sara [Boyse], and the rest of the English yet living'.

In fact the Indians stalled for ten or twelve days, until they had harvested their cornfields upriver, then fled with their captives, making life even harder for the English women among them. Mary Rowlandson described the hardships of being constantly on the move, tracked by English soldiers. 'And then like Jehu they marched on furiously, with their old and their young,' she wrote of her captors, 'some carried their old decriped mothers, some carried one, and some another.'[11] Although the records do not say what happened to the Virginia captives at this time, it is logical to think they were moved, or the English would surely have found them.

When the English realized that the Indians' promises were 'but delusions', they seized what corn they could, set fire to their houses and chased after them. 'Some few of those naked Devils had that spirit, they lay in ambuscado, and as our men marched discharged some shot out of English peeces, and hurt some of them flying at their pleasures.' In the fight that pitted European firepower against Indian fleetness of foot, the natives simply melted away, being 'so light and swift, though wee see them (being so loaded with armour) they have much advantage of us though they be cowards'.[12]

Nothing more was heard of the captives over the winter, which was especially bitter. An Englishman whose ship ran aground near Kecoughtan wrote of 'the ground so cold, their bodies became so benumbed, they were not able to strike fire with a steele and a stone he had in his pocket'. So great was the frost, 'the clothes did freeze upon their backs', but neither the English nor presumably

Jackson's Indian captors could risk betraying their position by smoking fires.[13]

Cold was not the only hardship endured by Ann Jackson and the other captives. Until ransomed, women were treated as slave labour and given the hardest tasks. In Indian societies it was anyway the women who gathered firewood and hauled water; made and repaired houses; produced household equipment such as pots, baskets and mortars; prepared food and processed the deer carcasses hunted by the men; bore all kinds of burdens and took charge of the children.[14] The women's lives in England will have prepared them for many of these tasks, but here they were kept under constant watch for fear they might run away, and they were unfamiliar with one of the women's chief winter tasks: foraging for wild plants, berries and nuts in the forests and for tuckahoe by the river margins.[15] Rowlandson writes of being forced to gather groundnuts in the mornings. 'I went with a great load at my back; (for they when they went, tho' but a little way, would carry all their trumpery with them;) I told them the skin was off my back, but I had no other comforting answer from them than this, that it would be no matter if my head were off too.'[16]

Famine threatened both the Indians and the English that winter as they skirmished over what little corn was available. For the captives, unfamiliar food, exacerbated by constant hunger, will have made their lives a misery. To begin with, says Rowlandson, she would grow faint from hunger, unable to 'get down their filthy trash', but by her third week as a prisoner food that had previously sickened her was 'sweet and savory to my taste': a bit of bear given to her by one of the native women which she kept all night, stinking in her pocket, unable to broil it for fear of discovery; a pancake made of parched wheat beaten and fried in bear's grease; a spoonful of corn porridge mixed with broth from boiling horses' feet; and bits of 'ruffe or ridding' from the small guts, which she broiled on coals. Most of the time they lived off groundnuts supplemented by acorns, artichokes, lily roots and 'several other weeds and roots that I know not'.

They would pick up old bones, and cut them in pieces at the joints, and if they were full of worms and maggots, they would scald them over the fire, to make the vermin come out, and then boil them, and drink up the liquor, and then beat the great ends of them in a mortar, and so eat them. They would eat horses' guts, and ears, and all sorts of wild birds which they could catch. Also bear, venison, beavers, tortoise, frogs, squirrels, dogs, skunks, rattle-snakes. Yea, the very bark of trees.[17]

The food Rowlandson recalls most clearly came to her through acts of kindness from her captors as random as their cruelties. When some of the liver she was roasting on coals was snatched away from her she gobbled the rest half-cooked, her mouth slavered with blood. 'I cannot but think what a wolvish appetite persons have in a starving condition,' she wrote, 'for many times, when they gave me that which was hot, I was so greedy, that I should burn my mouth that it would trouble me many hours after.'[18]

As well as adapting to unfamiliar food, Jackson and the other Virginia captives had to get used to very different living conditions. The Algonquian-speaking Powhatans built their houses of saplings bent and tied together, much like English arbours in John Smith's view, closely covered with mats or the bark of trees, 'very handsomely, that notwithstanding either winde, raine or weather, they are as warme as stooves, but very smoaky'.[19] A hole directly above the fire allowed some smoke to escape, and the Indians slept on reed frames ranged about the fire, 'some covered with mats, some with skins, and some starke naked lie on the ground, from 6 to 20 in a house'. Here the women lived with their captors, in houses gathered haphazardly into small towns, except when fear of English raiders drove them deeper into the forest.

Having spent barely three months in Virginia before the Indian attack, Jackson will have picked up little more than a smattering of

Algonquian. The words William Strachey collected for his dictionary of the Powhatan language would have helped her to negotiate her new life, giving names to the objects that surrounded her and the beasts and berries of the forest, and allowing her to make rudimentary conversation.[20] As the weeks of her captivity passed into months, the strangeness of her new surroundings – already uprooted from the clattering streets of Westminster – will have become strangely normal: the quietness of an Indian town, lacking the sound of London's horse-drawn carts or the crowing cocks and farmyard noises of Martin's Hundred; and the scanty clothing of

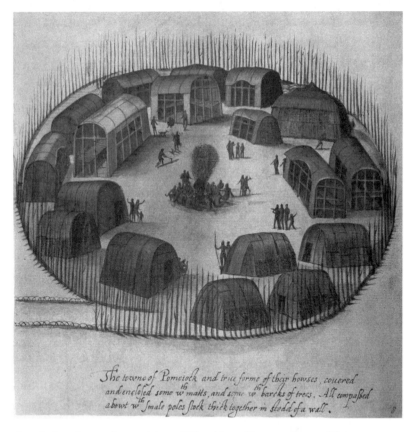

Ann Jackson's years in captivity will have forced her to adapt to life in an Indian village such as Pomeiooc, shown here in a watercolour by John White.

her hosts, especially the men, in contrast to her own many-layered modesty in dress.[21] Only the constant plague of fleas and lice will have been as familiar in the Indian villages up the Pamunkey as in Martin's Hundred and Westminster.

And she remained a prisoner, subject to the whims of her captors. Although life in the settlements (and in England) will have inured the women to the cruelties of English justice, the fate of some of their fellows at the hands of their captors was harrowing in the extreme. We know that the handful of English men taken prisoner in the Indian attack of 1622 were put to death, as reported in a letter sent from Virginia in April 1623,[22] and it is possible that Jackson and the other women may have been forced to witness their killing. Captain John Smith reported the gruesome execution of settler George Cassen, who was tied to a tree by his Indian captors, his extremities cut off with mussel shells or reeds, 'then doth [his executioner] proceed with shels and reeds to case the skinne from his head and face; then doe they rip his belly and so burne him with the tree and all'.[23]

After the long hard winter the Indians were the first to crack in the spring of 1623, always a hungry time before they could reap their native corn. Having spurned English overtures the previous autumn, Opechancanough now sent two messengers to Martin's Hundred offering a peace deal. The settlers recognized one of the messengers as Chauco, who had warned the English of the impending attack but clearly retained the Indian leader's trust. The other was an Indian called Comahum, who had taken part in the attack on Martin's Hundred. Chauco they sent on to Governor Wyatt at Jamestown but Comahum they put in chains.

Opechancanough's message to the English was that 'blud inough had already been shedd [on] both sides'. Many of his people were starving because the English had taken away their corn and burned their houses. They wanted to be allowed to plant their corn in peace at Pamunkey and at their former seats, 'wch yf they might

Peaceablely do they would send home our People (beinge aboute twenty) whom they saved alive since the massacre, and would suffer us to plant quietly alsoe in all places'.[24] No mention was made of any captives put to death.

The English sent Chauco back to Opechancanough, agreeing that if the Indians 'sent back the prisoners they should quietly set their corne'. Within a week the Indians released just one of their prisoners, Mistress Sara Boyse, 'sent home appareled like one of theire Queens, wch they desired we should take notice of'. The Indians blamed the absence of the other captives on threatening speeches delivered by the mischievous interpreter Robert Poole, who had accompanied Chauco back to Opechancanough, and they asked for another Englishman to reassure them that if they returned all the prisoners, they could plant their corn in peace.

Instead of complying with the Indians' request, the English hatched another plan: to lull the Indians' suspicions by offering to buy back the captives with 'Certen beads from the ffreends of the Prissoners, wch by our experience of their Covetousness (we doupt not) will hasten theire retourne'. As the governor explained to the Virginia Company back in London, if the Indians 'send home our people & grow secure uppon the treatie, we shall have the better Advantage both to surprise them, & to cutt downe theire Corne'. As would become abundantly clear, the English in Virginia were more concerned with exacting revenge and driving the Indians off their lands than with the impact of their actions on a dozen or more of their own women caught on the wrong side.

Apparently complying with an offer from Opechancanough's brother Opitchapam to deliver up the rest of the captives if the colonists would send a dozen men to the Potomac River to fetch them, the English sent Captain William Tucker with twelve men to conclude a peace treaty with the 'great Kinge'.[25] Since the methods employed by the English were plainly unethical even for the times, the only clear account of what happened is contained in a private letter from Robert Bennett, master of the *Samuel*, to his merchant brother Edward Bennett in London.[26] 'After manye fayned speches the pease was to be concluded in a helthe or t[w]o in sacke [fortified wine] whch was sente of porpose in the butte with Capten Tucker to poysen them.'

Captain Tucker and the interpreter drank first, but from a different source, and the poisoned wine was then offered to Opechancanough and the other men assembled for the peace treaty, perhaps as many as two hundred in all. When the wine began to take effect, the English hastily retreated, pausing only to shoot some fifty Indians and collect a trophy bag of scalps. While glossing over the details, Governor Wyatt and his councillors – among them Dr Pott, who had helped to concoct the poison – informed the Virginia Company by a letter written in June 1623 that by their successful stratagem they had 'not only regayned our People, but cutt off some kings, and divers of the greatest Comanders of the Enimy, amongst whom wee are assured, yt Apochancono is one, it beinge ympossable, that he should escape.'[27]

They were wrong about Opechancanough, who may have been weakened but was not killed, since he would reappear to lead another assault in 1644. And while some of the captives were redeemed with the glass beads sent to buy their freedom, the records are silent about precisely who was returned and when. As we have already seen, one whose freedom was clearly bought was Jane Dickenson, an indentured servant at Martin's Hundred whose husband Ralph was killed in the attack. Jane remained with the Indians for ten months until she was redeemed with glass beads supplied by Dr John Pott,[28] who forced her to work for him to pay off her own debt and the remaining years of her husband's indenture, servitude she considered little different from her slavery with the Indians.

You will find a memorial tablet to Dr Pott in the small church at Jamestown, erected by the Medical Society of Virginia. Despite the Virginia Company's praise of him as a man 'well practised in Chirurgerie and Phisique, and expert allso in Distillinge of waters',[29] his moral sense was crude. Virginia's treasurer George Sandys described him as a 'pitiful counselor' and a 'cipher'[30] who enjoyed the company of his inferiors 'while his good liquor lasted'. For supplying the poisoned sack that Captain Tucker took to the Indians he was temporarily suspended from his post, but in March 1629 his fellow councillors elected him deputy governor 'after full and serious Consideration'.[31] His time in charge of the colony was short and not distinguished: Sir John Harvey would later write of the 'Divers foule Complaints, against the said Doctor for manie disorders in the tyme of his government by him done'.[32]

Recorded as living in Dr Pott's household in Jamestown in the census of 1624, Jane Dickenson has disappeared by the following year, so she either died, succeeded in escaping her master or remarried. But you will not find either of the other two women known to have been captured in the 1622 Indian attack, Sara Boyse and Ann Jackson. After her terrifying ordeal, Sara Boyse must have returned to England with her husband, who went to plead with King James on behalf of some 'poore Planters in Virginia'. Their petition asking to be relieved of tobacco taxes came before the Virginia Company in April 1624, with the comment that the planters had 'lately com from Virginia'.[33]

So what happened to Ann Jackson? Missing from the census of 1624, she was still not back among the English colonists by early 1625, when her brother John Jackson was living at Martin's Hundred as the head of a household containing his wife Ann, a child of twenty weeks and the two servants who had travelled with them on the *Warwick*: forty-seven-year-old Thomas Ward and thirty-five-year-old John Steephens. The Jackson daughter recorded as living in 1624 had died during the year.[34] Although the rest of the household had survived the attack and its aftermath, life was clearly a struggle, not least because the governor of Martin's Hundred, William Harwood, took half their produce, including tobacco. So

Jackson was a tenant, not a freeholder, and he signed his name to a bitter letter of complaint written jointly with his servant Thomas Ward to Nicholas Ferrar in London just as the Virginia Company was unravelling. Identifying Ward as a 'pottmaker' and Jackson as a bricklayer, the letter speaks out for the 'poor tenants of martins hundreth', who had reached the point where they could no longer endure this kind of life.[35] A pair of shoes cost five pounds of tobacco, they wrote, their clothes and shirts were all worn out 'and we are not able to buy any more'.

Ann Jackson will have known nothing of her brother's hardship. Although some names were mistakenly omitted from the censuses, especially that of 1624,[36] one plausible explanation for her absence from both censuses is that she remained with the Indians, either by choice or circumstance, and may have been with them still in April 1626, when her brother John and a settler named Robert Linsey 'went from Martins Hundred wth certaine Indians into Pamunky', a journey that would have required permission from Governor Harwood. Why they should have gone with the Indians is unclear. If it was to bring John's sister back, there is no hint that this happened. Jackson returned home safely but his companion was detained by the Indians, who refused to allow Linsey even to give Jackson the key to his chest of belongings back at Martin's Hundred.[37]

Two years later, in April 1628, the council under Governor Francis West received a message 'from some English men at Pamunky' written on a piece of bark and delivered by four Indians from Pasbehay near Jamestown.[38] After some discussion, they decided to try and procure the freedom of 'those English that are amongst them & to lerne in what places they plant their corne'. Again the intention was to lull the Indians into a sense of false security 'that we may live ye quietlier & have the better oportunity to be revenged on them for their treachery'. Ann Jackson may have been discovered living among the Pamunkey Indians as part of this operation, or she may have already come back to the English. All we know for certain is that at the Jamestown quarter court of 20 January 1629, after 'good Consideracon', the court ordered that 'Anne Jackson wch Came from the Indians shall bee sent for England with the first opportunity of Shipping and that her brother John Jackson shall give security for her passage and keepe her safe till shee bee shipped aboard'.[39] The wording implies an urgency to Ann Jackson's situation, which suggests to me that her return was relatively recent. More than five years had elapsed since Sara Boyse was released, dressed like an Indian queen. Penny-pinching as ever, the court ordered John Jackson to fund his sister's passage home and noted that the commander of Martin's Hundred, William Harwood, had undertaken to see its wishes performed.

Whether she stayed with the Indians for four years (until 1626, when her brother went to Pamunkey) or for the full six and a half years up to late 1628, Ann Jackson will have experienced culture shock twice over: first becoming accustomed to Indian ways and her own status as a captive, and second when she returned to the English.

Although they were very different in age and experience, Mary Rowlandson's example shows that it was possible to adapt to a harsh new life in captivity. As a minister's wife, Rowlandson was fortified by her Christian faith and given a bible by a friendly Indian. Like most of her compatriots, she saw the Indian always as 'other', contrasting the 'foul looks of those heathen' with the 'lovely faces of Christians', yet she was still able to perceive and record the kindnesses she received. And she was never raped or sexually assaulted. 'I have been in the midst of those roaring lions', she wrote, 'and savage bears, that feared neither God, nor man, nor the devil, by night and day, alone and in company; sleeping all sorts together, and yet not one of them ever offered the least abuse of unchastity to me, in word or action.'[40]

We can assume that Ann Jackson received similar treatment: forced to work very hard at unfamiliar tasks, often on the move, wading through swamps and creeks, subjected to the whims of an Indian master and mistress. But Rowlandson's captivity lasted only eleven weeks and five days; Jackson stayed with the Indians far longer. Gradually the houses and towns in which she lived would begin to seem less flimsy and messy, better adapted to the surrounding landscape than the straight lines and hard edges of an English village deposited in the midst of a wilderness, which was how this 'virgin land' appeared to Europeans.

Cultural historian Helen C. Rountree has written of how the 'lost colonists' – women and young boys especially – might have survived as they gradually assimilated into the Indian world.[41] As her company-issued petticoat, smock, stockings, apron, coif and shoes wore out, Ann Jackson would have had no option but to adopt Indian dress: a buckskin apron for summer and a buckskin mantle for extra warmth in winter, plus leggings and moccasins for the forest.[42] As well as shedding her English sense of modesty, she must also get used to different notions of hygiene, washing herself daily in cold Virginian rivers instead of rubbing her skin with a linen cloth. The longer she stayed, the more likely it is that she formed an attachment with one of her captors, perhaps even had a child with him, and it is in the arena of human relations that she would have experienced most keenly the gulf that separated the English from the Indians.

Like society as a whole, the English family was hierarchical in structure and repressive in nature, especially in its treatment of women. Although loving relations could and did exist between some husbands and wives, the woman and everything she owned became the property of her husband on marriage; as we saw in Chapter 3, he could beat her as long as he did not kill her, and his word held sway. The doctrine of original sin meant that children too were viewed as inherently sinful, to be chastised into behaving correctly. In coming to the New World, it is unlikely that Ann or any of the other Jamestown brides expected anything different: aggression

As her English clothes wore out, Ann Jackson will necessarily have adopted Indian dress and its very different standard of modesty.

was an accepted character trait of the English, and only the most serious acts of wife-beating reached the Jamestown court, such as the 'Tumulte' between Joseph Johnson and his wife when they fell onto a bed fighting and had to be forcibly restrained, clearly a frequent event, which Johnson's master blamed on having tried to separate 'Newgate birds and Bridewell whores'.[43] English women could also be quarrelsome, witness the 'unquiett life wch they the people of Archers Hope had through the scoldings railings & fallings out with Amy the wife of Christopher Hall & other abominable contentions lyeing betweene them'.[44] Amy Hall's punishment was to be towed after the *Margaret & John* and ducked three times.

Relations between Indian wives and their husbands were more autonomous and easy-going, and parent–child relations were very warm indeed.[45] William Strachey describes how Indian men courted their prospective brides by presenting them with 'the fruictes of their Labours, as by Fowle, Fish, or Wild Beasts' which they had caught by their prowess in hunting and fishing, 'as also of such Sommer fruictes and berryes, which their travell abroad hath made them knowe readily where to gather'.[46] Such gifts from an Indian suitor would surely have gladdened the heart of a captured English woman far from home, just as Mary Rowlandson was comforted by two spoonfuls of meal given to her by one Indian and half a pint of peas by another, 'which was worth more than many bushels at another time'. In Indian marriages the husband was expected to provide his wife with a house, some platters, mortars and mats, and to keep her supplied with provisions and deerskins. Chiefs could take as many wives as they wished; other males could marry second and subsequent wives for a set time, according to Strachey, but if they kept them any longer they must take responsibility for them for ever. Women were free to take lovers with their husbands' consent, and they loved their children 'very dearely'.

Whatever her mental and physical state on release from the Indians – and whatever occasioned her release – Ann Jackson will surely have been traumatized all over again by her return to the loud, volatile and hierarchical English society at Martin's Hundred, which rewarded the aggressive pursuit of self-interest and demanded that its womenfolk did as they were bid or suffer the consequences. Given the choice, many English men who fled to the Indians preferred staying with them than returning to the society of their birth.[47] As a woman, Jackson will have been worked extremely hard by her captors but once she returned to the English, she lost all say over what happened to her. Forced back into European dress, separated from any family at Pamunkey, Ann found herself once again the property of men who controlled her fate – her brother first of all, but also the governor and his councillors sitting in judgment at Jamestown, and William Harwood, commander of Martin's Hundred, charged with seeing that the court's ruling was carried out.

Like so many of the other maids, after her silent appearance in court Ann Jackson slips quietly from view. Assuming that a ship was found to take her home, she may have returned to St Margaret's parish in Westminster, nearly a decade after she had left. The Virginia Company was disbanded by now; the Ferrar brothers had moved to Little Gidding, and Sir Edwin Sandys died that year. The records show that several Ann Jacksons were buried at St Margaret's – in 1632, 1636, 1637 and 1641 – but hers was a common name and she may anyway have gone elsewhere.[48]

Return to Jamestown

I have returned twice to Virginia in the course of writing this book and expect to come back many times more. Jamestown Island counts as one of my favourite places on earth, in ways that are hard to explain.

Once you leave behind the razzmatazz of Jamestown Settlement on the far side of the isthmus, you find yourself enveloped in a kind of contemplative calm, despite milling school parties and family groups for whom Jamestown is one more stop on the tourist trail, interspersed with quaintly costumed eighteenth-century Williamsburg and the many battle sites of the Civil War. Reading over the diaries I kept of my many visits to the island, I see that the same calm descends each time, starting from the moment I drop down to the Colonial Parkway that loops round from Yorktown to Jamestown, tunnelling under Williamsburg and avoiding all the paraphernalia of modern roads. In some sections the speed limit drops to an unhurried 35 mph, encouraging you to stop and reflect on the many historical signboards marking the route and sometimes just to sit and stare, shaded by loblolly pines, looking across Back River to the narrow wooded peninsula that is Jamestown Island – flat and quite insignificant, really – where Europe first put down permanent roots in North America and changed the course of both continents.

The island has moved on since I came here for *Strange Blooms* in 2004, without losing its timeless spirit. Now a footbridge whisks

Jamestown's melancholic air – evident in this engraving from an earlier century – persists to this day.

you from the Visitor Center across the Pitch and Tar Swamp, where turtles teem in the oily water below, little cooters and long-necked snapping turtles, which daily fed the early colonists. Drawn at first to the Jamestown of Captain John Smith and Pocahontas, centred on the church and the palisaded fort area, I now mostly turn left after the footbridge and walk the grassy stretch of Back Street to the plots of Dr John Pott and Edward Blaney, where Fortune Taylor and Elizabeth Starkey pitched up as servants rather than wives. My Jamestown is increasingly peopled with history's minor characters, who speak to me all the more loudly for having been silent so long.

The first time I came to Virginia expressly for this book, I concentrated on finding and walking the places where the women went. My friend the historian Martha McCartney jump-started my researches by marking the sites on a map, which I kept with me at all times, its paper folds now barely holding together. Some of these former settlements I visited on my own: Jordan's Journey, Neck of Land Charles City, the College Land near Henricus, and

Powle-Brook, now part of the James River National Wildlife Refuge, where Cicely Bray and Barbara Burchens met their grisly end. You need a permit to visit the refuge and if you are lucky, as I was, you may have it all to yourself. Helen Rountree kindly drove me to other sites further east: Edward Bennett's plantation close to Fort Boykin; Elizabeth City on Hampton Roads, across from the US naval station in Norfolk; and over to the Eastern Shore by way of the dune forests and cypress swamps of First Landing State Park and the Great Dismal Swamp on the borders with North Carolina, which we had visited together many years previously. With Helen I walked again the sights on Jamestown Island and Jamestown Settlement's re-created Indian village, where her keen anthropologist's eye found fault with a cone-shaped device for catching fish, which might work in rapids, she said fiercely, but not in the tidal reaches of the James. I love the company of experts. They care that we get things right.

My visit to Martin's Hundred with archaeologist Nicholas Luccketti was one of the high points of my next research trip, having failed to arrange access the first time, when I got no further than its stout perimeter fence liberally posted with PRIVATE PROPERTY notices warning that hunting, finishing, trapping or trespassing FOR ANY PURPOSE are strictly forbidden. In the sharp sunshine of early April, Luccketti walked me through the site, reliving the different stages of their excavations and pointing out the underground museum, now closed, although the current owner Samuel M. Mencoff has poured more money into the site than Colonial Williamsburg ever did during the plantation's four decades as a rural adjunct to its main attraction.

The wind is bitterly keen. Under the pines by Grice's Run, the lime-green leaves of jack-in-the-pulpit (*Arisaema triphyllum*) are just poking through.

At the end of our visit Luccketti directs me to the flat-topped site on the far side of a ravine which was occupied some time after the

Indian attack by the Jackson family and their two servants, including the potter Thomas Ward. Ann Jackson will have lodged here after she came back from the Indians but before a ship could be found to take her back to England. Leaving my guide for a few minutes, I scramble down the ravine and up the other side, wondering why Jackson should have situated his homestead here rather than more conveniently among the houses of Wolstenholme Town.

More pines and some spindly trees throw long shadows across the wide clearing of bare earth buried under a light covering of crisp brown leaves. Back on a level with the main site, you feel connected but nicely separate. I am acutely aware that I am treading the same ground as one of the brides, who (in my imagination, at least) came here in a distressed state after her long sojourn with the Indians. Having remembered to take with me a black-and-white photograph of the excavated site after the top layer of earth had been peeled back to reveal the post holes and hearth of the Jacksons' home, I pace the ground carefully, looking for an infant's grave which I believe to be that of Ann Jackson's niece who died during Ann's captivity. Forty years have elapsed since the site was excavated, so I cannot be certain that I have identified the precise spot.[1]

During this second visit to Virginia I spent much of my time tracking the bits and bodkins of material culture stored in various research collections at Richmond, Williamsburg, Jamestown and Charlottesville, guided throughout by the many contacts of Beverly 'Bly' Straube, senior curator at the Jamestown Rediscovery archaeological project when I first met her and now much in demand as an independent archaeological curator and material culture specialist. It was to Bly I would return with my questions, which she answered patiently and expertly in a way that explains why 'things' have increasingly come to elucidate our histories. My notebooks are full of references to random artefacts dug out of the ground. Inevitably those of higher status catch my eye first, like the silver ear scoop and nail scraper unearthed at the communal house at Jordan's

Journey and the diminutive Chinese porcelain wine cup decorated with a frieze of stylized flames that may once have belonged to Catherine Fisher's neighbours Nathaniel and Thomasine Causey.[2]

At all the collections I ask to see objects that relate particularly to women and their domestic lives, marvelling at the wealth of sewing items that have survived the intervening centuries: scissors, thimbles (some large enough for male thumbs, admittedly), pins, needles, metal aiglets, buttons, hooks and eyes; also earrings, gold and copper-alloy finger rings, and hair ornaments. Chamber pots are puzzlingly rare, whether locally made or imported from England (they lacked privies too). Among many privileged moments, I feel the thrill of holding in my hand fragments of earthenware dishes and a milk pan, glazed on the inside, attributed to Thomas Ward, the Martin's Hundred potter, who lived with Ann Jackson's brother. His pots have a finer shape and texture than those made by other local potters, and he gave even functional items a decorative twist using wavy lines and pie-crust edges.

Also on display at several collections are the laddish items of European armour reminiscent of medieval warfare which protected the English invaders as they clanked around the Virginian swamps. No wonder the Indians of the Eastern Shore demanded to know 'what we were, and what we would' on first encountering such outlandish apparitions.[3]

Now I must try to answer the question I posed at the outset: were the Virginia Company's 'maids for Virginia' the victims of a patriarchal society, or were they true adventurers, willing to risk their own 'carkases' (in John Pory's memorable phrase) in so dangerous a business? Or were they both victims and adventurers, as I have come increasingly to believe, only some of whom triumphed in the end?

However carefully the Virginia Company picked its words to describe the transaction at the heart of the maids' magazine, the company's money troubles meant that it needed to satisfy its investors by making a profit on each marriage transacted. Was this so very different from the way the colony's market economy profited from the labour of indentured servants, who had to purchase their freedom if they wanted to opt out of the contract before their time was done? Or the way that established planters bought and sold the first Africans to arrive in Virginia, without the dignity of proper names, allowing only a handful of blacks to establish independent lives?[4] I suspect not, or rather that many indentured servants and imported Africans suffered a far worse fate.

The Virginia Company could claim that as far as the women were concerned it acted for the greater good – the continued survival and comfort of the entire colony – and it took pains to stress that in theory at least the women were free to choose a husband from the planters allowed to approach them. Modern sensibilities nonetheless baulk at the notion of a near-monopolistic trading company deriving profits from women imported as brides, an enterprise that may have pricked a few consciences even then. Supplying dowries that allowed indigent young women to marry was a respectable form of charitable giving, although in this case the intended beneficiaries were not the brides or their prospective husbands, required to put their tobacco on the table, but individual investors who hoped to reap their rewards in cash and in the promised settlement of Maydes Towne. For those of us who find this distasteful, the scheme's financial failure excites a certain *Schadenfreude*, so it is worth remembering that it was fatally flawed from the outset. The company had failed to calculate how many planters might actually want to spend good money on brides, especially since gentlemen and wealthier planters had other ways of finding themselves a wife.

Determined to attract the best calibre of women through its wide network of contacts, the Virginia Company was undoubtedly cavalier with the truth, concealing from the women the true condition of the colony and its shocking mortality – a complaint levelled against the company throughout its seventeen-year history. At times London seemed wilfully ignorant of what conditions in Virginia were really like. Others have argued that the colony survived only because the company collapsed along with its pig-headed insistence on retaining disease-ridden Jamestown as its chief 'city', dispatching ever more shiploads of settlers without proper provisions.[5] 'I often wish little Mr Farrar here, that to his zeale he would add knowledge of this Countrey', wrote a weary Governor Sir Francis Wyatt to his father after the Indian attack of 1622, faced with London's wildly optimistic instruction to raise an army of five hundred men.[6]

Whatever gloss you put on the company's actions in setting up a trade in brides, I remain shocked that I found not a single expression of regret from the leaders of the Virginia Company – Sir Edwin Sandys, the Ferrar brothers, the Earl of Southampton or any of the others – about sending so many of these women to their deaths. They naturally had no prior warning of the Indian attack, but simply regarded the women as commercial commodities and tried to exact a financial return even after the attack, without stopping to enquire if the 'merchandise' was still alive. Profit came before Christian charity, clearly. More than three and a half years after the attack, the court in Jamestown cancelled a planter's debt of 150 pounds of tobacco advanced to buy six acres of ground and two houses at Charles City, which the Indians had burned in the 1622 attack before the purchaser was able to occupy them. In its judgment the court did not 'conceave in equitie yt ffrancis Michell should be compeld to paye the said Debt'.[7] But while the Jamestown court could apparently forgive money owed for houses and land, the investors back in England expected payment for a dead wife. *Caveat emptor.* Let the buyer assume the risk in any transaction.

Whether the company had inveigled the women into travelling to Virginia under false pretences, or whether the fifty-six women travelled willingly and knowingly, once they arrived at Jamestown they did what women have always done: they got on with their lives as best they could, even if Bridgett Wilkins had to offer a shirt to persuade a man to lie with her and Adria Harris had to deal with a philandering husband. Without being privy to their inner thoughts, it is impossible to say whether they were happy in the lives they had chosen. A letter from a male settler in Jamestown suggests that after the Indian attack wives found the settler's life especially hard. 'As you know this land hath felt the afflication of Warr, sense of sicknes and death of a great nomber of men', wrote William Rowlsley to his brother in England, begging him to send a hogshead of beef and some neats' tongues, 'for here is not a bitt of flesh to be had at any Rate'. Rowlsley and his wife were as well as any people in the land, he wrote reassuringly, 'but my wife doth nothing but talke of gooing home'.[8] The maids who came to Virginia will undoubtedly have regretted their decision at times, but I like to think that some may have looked back with satisfaction at the lives they had made for themselves. All the settler women who endured Jamestown's privations in those early years deserve a church memorial, not just the Dr Potts of this world.

On my last visit to Jamestown Island I slipped once more into Historic Jamestowne's small museum, the Archaearium, where I came across a display of clipped money whose significance had previously eluded me. The words of the old English ballad came instantly to mind, sung to a jaunty air:

> The brown, or the black, or the mackarel-back.
> Or if a buxome, brisk Damsel you lack,
> As plump as a Doe, both above and below,
> You may have what you can desire I know
> For Clip'd Money.[9]

Of course. Until that moment I had carelessly assumed that clipping a coin was a guarantee of authenticity, proving that it had been properly minted. In fact the opposite is true. 'Clip'd Money' might result from the practice of shaving off the edges of silver or gold coins to make counterfeit coins or to sell on to goldsmiths.

Or it might indicate coins that had been clipped into bits to make small change, each piece valued by weight. Examples on display in the Archaearium included a silver English three halfpence and a half groat, both from the time of Queen Elizabeth I.

Unlike the cut-price women offered for sale in the ballad, the Jamestown brides were in truth quite expensive, but their real worth lay in their courage and in the steadfast way they made this brave New World their own.

The Maids

The names of the maids sent in the *Marmaduke* bound for Virginia Anno 1621, August

1. **Lettice King** Aged 23 years, born at Newbury in Berkshire, her father and mother are dead. She has a brother that is an attorney in the law dwelling at Newbury. Her father was an husbandman. Sir William Udall is her cousin removed. She hath an uncle dwelling in the Charterhouse named Edward Colton.

2. **Allice Burges** Aged 28, born at Linton in Cambridgeshire, her father and mother are dead. He was a husbandman. She hath two brothers, one a husbandman dwelling at Linton the other a soldier. She served about three years sithence [since] one Mr Collins, a silkweaver right over against Whitechapel church, after she served Mr Demer, a goldsmith in Trinity Lane. She is skilful in many country works. She can brew, bake and make malt &c.

3. **Catherine Finche** Aged 23, born at Mardens parish in Herefordshire. Her father and mother are dead. She was brought by her brother Mr Erasmus Finch dwelling in the Strand, who is the king's crossbow maker, with whom she was and is in service. She hath likewise two other brothers, Edward Finch, locksmith, dwelling in St Clement's parish without Temple Bar and John Finch, crossbow maker, dwelling in St Martin's Lane in the Strand.

4. **Margaret Bordman** Aged 20 years, born at Bilton in Yorkshire, her father and mother dead. Sir John Gypson of Yorkshire is her uncle by the mother side. She hath been in service with Captain Wood who giveth a good testimony of her and so doth Mr Fynch having long known her, her mistress Mrs Kilbancke, Mr Recorder's coachman's wife, giveth a good testimony of her.

5. **Ann Tanner** Aged 27, born at Chelmsford in Essex, her father Clement Tanner dwelling in Chelmsford, by profession a husbandman. She can spin and sew in blackwork. She can brew, and bake, make butter and cheese, and do housewifery. She hath a cousin named Thomas Tanner, saddler, dwelling within Aldgate.

6. **Mary Ghibbs** Aged 20. A maid born in Cambridge town, her father was a smith. Her mother is alive & dwelleth at Deptford. Mr Lott Peere is her uncle by her mother side, with whom she dwelleth. She can make bone lace. Mr Barbor likewise knows her.

7. **Jane Dier** Aged 15, born in St Katharine's, her father was a waterman, her mother is alive, her name Ellen Dyer and dwells in St Katharine's. She was commended by her mother and goes with her consent.

8. **Ann Harmer** Aged 21, born at Baldock in Hertfordshire, her father is a gentleman. She hath five brothers and two sisters. Mr Underell the grocer is her cousin and Mr Fartlow a grocer, both dwelling in Bucklersbury. She hath an uncle by her mother side named Mr George [Kympton] now dwelling at Weston. She

hath been brought up with Mrs Morgan, a seamstress, and can do all manner of works gold and silk.

9. **Susan Binx** Maid aged 20, born in St Sepulchre's parish in Seacoal Lane, her father and mother is alive. Her father is a wire drawer, She hath three sisters. One Mistress Gardiner, a gentlewoman and widow in the Strand, is her aunt by her mother side. She was in service with one Mr Edward Batten a [durner?] that dwells at the lower end of Bartholomew Lane and before in other good services. She can work white and black work and knit.

10. **Audry Hoare** Maid aged 19, born at Aylesbury in Buckinghamshire. Her father and mother are alive, her father a shoemaker. She hath two sisters, one whereof brought her, whose name is Joane Childe, dwelling in the Blackfriars down in the Lane near the Catherine Wheel. She had a brother called Richard, apprentice to a fustian dresser. She can do plain work and black works and can make all manner of buttons. One Mr Thomas Biling a merchant is her first cousin and one Mr George Blunden an upholsterer in Cornwall.

11. **Ann Jackson** Born in Salisbury, her father's name is William Jackson. He is a gardener and dwelleth in Tuttle [street] in Westminster near to the Red Lion. Her father brought her, and her brother John Jackson goeth for Martin's Hundred in Virginia.

12. **Ann Buergen** She was shipped at the Isle of Wight by Mr Robert Newland in the room of Mrs Joane Flecher, who was turned back from thence.

13. **Ursula Lawson** A maid aged [blank]. Kinswoman to Richard Pace an old planter in Virginia who hath given his bond to pay for her passage and other charges. She went in the company of the said Richard Pace and his wife.

The names of the maids and young women sent in the *Warwick*, September 1621

1. **Cicely Bray** Aged 25 years, born in Gloucestershire, her parents gentlefolk of good esteem. She is of kin to Sir Edwin Sandys, recommended by Mr Hall.

2. **Elizabeth Markham** Aged 16 years, daughter to Mr ~~James~~ Jervis Markham. She is by her father and mother presented.

3. **Parnell Tenton** Aged 20 years, born in London, presented by her mother (her father being dead) and her honest carriage testified by Mr Hobson, one of the officers of the Drapers' Company. She can work all kinds of ordinary works.

4. **Ellen Borne** Aged 19 years, born at Eye in Suffolk. Her parents are dead. She is recommended by Mr Hobson and his wife for a sober and industrious maid skilful in many works.

5. **Lucy Remnant** Aged 22 years, born at Guildford in Surrey. Her father and mother are dead. Sir William Russell is her uncle by her mother side.

6. **Alse Dollinges** Aged 22 years, of Mounton in Dorsetshire. Goodwife Bennet that now comes along in the *Warwick* testified her to be a maid of honest conversation and to have lived in good services, her parents being dead.

7. **Ann Richards** Widow, aged 25 years, born in St Sepulchre's Parish, her life in all the states thereof is assured to have been very honest and industrious by the minister and chiefs of that parish.

8. **Jennet Rimer** Aged 20 years. Born at North Mills in Lancashire. She had an uncle dwelling near Moorgate named Allen Morrice by whom and by Mr Spark clerk of Blackfriars she comes recommended.

9. **Cristian Smyth** Aged 18 years. Born at Newbury in Berkshire, her parents are dead. She came out of the service of Mr Newton at Mile End and is by divers of those parts very well commended.

10. **Ellen Davy** Aged 22 years. Born in Northampton, brought by her dame Goodwife Smith, with whom she was in service, and by her and other neighbours assured to be of honest and good carriage.

11. **Elizabeth Bovill** (or **Borrill**) Aged 20 years. Her father is dead, her mother's name Edith Finch presented her and brought other good testimonies of her good life.

12. **Ann Parker** Aged 20 years. Born at Chayton in Hampshire, dwelling at the time of her entertainment for Virginia with Mr Emmons, a scrivener near the Exchange, whence being enquired of, she had report of an honest and faithful servant.

13. **Ann Holmes** Aged 20 years. Born at Newcastle being fellow servant with the former in Mr Emmons house and having the like good reports.

14. **Martha Baker** Aged 20 years. Born at Ilford, skilful in weaving and making of silk points, being in service with one Randall, Stationer, by whom and the clerk of the Minories' wife she was recommended.

15. **Ann Westcote** Aged 20 years, her father is a victualler in St Martin's Lane, by whom she was presented, and Mr Collingwood secretary of the company knows and affirms her to be an honest and a sober maid.

16. **Mary Thomas** Aged 18 years, brought up and born in London by her grandfather Roger Tudor, clothworker, known for a very honest man by divers of the company.

17. **Frauncis Broadbottom** Aged 19 years, daughter to Robert Broadbottom of London, cutler, dwelling in Lothbury. She was brought up by her father and mother who were very honest people.

18. **Mary Morrice** Aged 20 years. Born at Derby, recommended by Mr Webb the husband to the company for an honest and sober maid.

19. **Alse Jones** Aged 21 years. Born at Kidderminster in Worcestershire. Lately come out of service of one Mr Binneons dwelling in Bishopsgate Street.

20. **Alse Dauson** Aged 18 years. Born in London and brought up by her mother, whom Mrs Farrar reputed to be a very honest woman.

21. **Anste Hawkings** Aged 18 years, brought by her mother, her father was a draper at [Shaftesbury?].

22. **Sara Crosse** Aged 21 years, she is daughter to Peter Crosse, a baker in Lothbury.

23. **Mary Ellyott** Aged 19 years, daughter-in-law to Maximillian Russell, who now goeth over in Martin's Hundred, by whom she was brought up and likewise recommended by many good testimonies from Mile End.

24. **Elizabeth Starkey** Aged 16 years, daughter to Frauncis Starkey Taylor, dwelling at the Three Cranes in the Vintry, by whom and her mother she was brought.

25. **Margaret Dauson** Aged 25 years. Born at Woodham [Wickham?] Market in Suffolk, brought up by Mrs Elizabeth Stevenson, leather seller's wife in Southwark, who gives report to have long known her to be a good and faithful servant.

26. **Elizabeth Dag** Aged 19 years. Born in Limehouse, recommended by Mr Christopher Marten and Sir Nicholas Couch.

27. **Elizabeth Nevill** Aged 19 years. Born at Westminster. Her father was a gentleman of worth, her mother's name is Frauncis Travis. This and her good carriage is testified by divers of the company of their own knowledge.

28. **Fortune Taylor** Aged 18 years. Mr Barbor in East Smithfield is her uncle by whom she is recommended.

29. **Marie Daucks** Widow aged 25 years. Mr Slocum in Maiden Lane is her near kinsman, by whom and other good testimonies her honesty and good carriage is testified.

30. **Jeane Wildman** Aged 18 years. Brought by Mr Eaton and much commended by him out of his knowledge for her good behaviour and carriage.

31. **Jean Grundye** Aged 21 years, daughter of William Grundie's brother in Newgate Market. Her mother is living. She is commended by Mr Joseph Stone, one of the yeomen of His Majesty's Guard, and Mrs Stone his wife, to be a maid of honest and civil conversation.

32. **Barbara Burchens** Aged 17 years. Born in [Denby or Denbigh], daughter of John Burchens, cloth worker. Her mother's name was Margaret Burchens. She is commended by Mrs Jeane Brewer, her mistress (wife to one John Brewer, yeoman of His Majesty's Guard) to be a maid of honest and civil conversation.

33. **Jeane Joanes** Aged 17 years. Born in [blank], daughter of Evenes Jones, hat maker. Her mother's name was Elizabeth. She was commended by Mistress Gilbert in Holborn, Mrs Gilbert known by Mrs Cuffe.

34. **Elizabeth Pearson** Aged 19 years. Born in Oxford, daughter of William Pearson, plasterer, deceased. Her mother is dead. She is commended to the company by Mr Ryder.

35. **Bridgett Crofte** Aged 18 years. Born at Burford [Britford] in Wiltshire. Her father's name was John Crofte. He is deceased. She is commended by Robert the porter.

36. **Elizabeth Grinley** Widow aged 26 years. She was taken in the stead of Allice Lillowe.

The names of the maids sent in the *Tiger* September Anno 1621

1. **Allice Goughe** Maid aged 28, her parents were gentlefolk.
2. **Anne Gibbson** Maid aged 21, brought and recommended by [Master or Mistress] Switzer dwelling in the Blackfriars.

3. **Elizabeth Browne** Maid aged 16 years, born in London, her father and mother alive dwelling in the Blackfriars.
4. [Blank] aged [blank]. Daughter to Mrs Palmer who with her husband went along in the *Tiger*.

The names of the maids sent in the *Bona Nova*

1. **Elizabeth Bluett** Daughter to Captain Benjamin Bluett.
2. **Allice Grove** Aged 26.
3. **Priscilla Flint**
   Joane Haynes went in the *Charles* before any of the rest. She is sister to Minturne the joiner.

The list of maids sent to Virginia in August and September 1621 is taken from the Ferrar Papers, Magdalene College Cambridge Old Library, FP 309. Compiled by Nicholas Ferrar and Tristram Conyam, it has been transcribed and reproduced with modernized spelling and punctuation by permission of the Master and Fellows of Magdalene College Cambridge. FP 306 contains an earlier listing of the *Marmaduke* maids, including the widowed Joan Fletcher who never in fact sailed.

ACKNOWLEDGEMENTS

This book has been a long time in the making. To Chris Potter I owe an incalculable debt of thanks for his encouragement and support from the outset and dedicate the results to his memory: he was the very best of brothers. During the book's gestation I benefited from the wise counsel of Anne Laurence, professor of history (now emeritus professor) at the Open University, and Qona Wright of British Library's Rare Books and Music Reference Team. An early visit to view the Ferrar Papers at the Pepys Library, Magdalene College, Cambridge, was followed by several more; my thanks go especially to the librarian, Dr Jane Hughes; the deputy librarian, Catherine Sutherland; and to the master and fellows who generously gave their permission to quote from the papers.

In England the British Library became my second home. I wish to thank the staff of the Rare Books and Music, Maps, and Manuscripts reading rooms for their patience and good humour. Staff at the London Library were always helpful, and I am infinitely grateful for the library's support in offering me Carlyle membership. In London these archival collections provided much useful information: City of Westminster Archives Centre (special thanks to archivist Alison Kenney), London Metropolitan Archives, Guildhall Library and the National Archives at Kew. I am grateful to the many specialists who shared their knowledge and their contacts: Dr Stephen Porter, archivist at the Charterhouse, who helped me trace an uncle of Lettice King; Lynne Berry OBE, who took me to a riotous Christmas lunch at the Company of Watermen and Lightermen in search of waterman's daughter Jane Dier; Robert Crouch, former queen's bargemaster, who introduced me to the working lives of Thames watermen; Justin Hopper, who ran an inspirational course on 'Writing the Landscape' at Tate Britain; and landscape historian Chris Sumner, who walked me from Tothill Street in Westminster to Billingsgate in the City, deftly revealing what remains of 1620s London. Outside London I record my thanks to Richard Smout and archival staff at the Isle of Wight Record Office & Archive, Newport; Peter White and colleagues at East Cowes Heritage Centre; archivist Mrs June Wailling at the Centre for Buckinghamshire Studies in Aylesbury; Steven Hobbs at Wiltshire and Swindon Archives; Lorna Standen at Herefordshire Archive and Records; Liz Jack, who helped me trace the Gloucestershire Brays; and Myles Sandys, who showed me the portrait of Sir Edwin Sandys at Graythwaite Hall and sent me off to view the tombs of Sir Edwin's grandparents at Hawkshead parish church nearby.

My researches in and around Gravesend in Kent benefited from many events commemorating the 400th anniversary of the death of Pocahontas and her burial at St George's church. My thanks go to the Reverend Chris Stone, rector of St George's, and to speakers at a programme of commemorative talks, especially Malcolm Gaskill, professor of early modern history at the University of East Anglia, and Hazel Forsyth, senior curator of post-medieval history at the Museum of London. A high point for me was a gathering at Syon House attended by three chiefs representing the Powhatan tribes of Virginia for the unveiling of a plaque by HRH the Duke of Gloucester to commemorate Pocahontas's stay in Brentford.

In September 2016 a conference on the Ferrars at Magdalene College, orchestrated by Dr Jane Hughes, provided many insights into the Ferrar family's role in the early colonization of Virginia and their subsequent community at Little Gidding, which we memorably visited. Among many encounters at the conference I benefited in particular from conversations with David Ransome, Joyce Ransome and Emily Rose.

A generous Authors' Foundation grant from the Society of Authors allowed me to undertake two research trips to Virginia, guided by contacts I had made a decade earlier. Historian Martha W. McCartney plotted for me the Virginian trajectories of those Jamestown brides I was able to trace and remained a constant source of help and advice throughout my researches, commenting perceptively on early drafts of the Virginian chapters. Ethno-historian and cultural anthropologist Helen C. Rountree similarly shared a lifetime's experience working with North America's indigenous people. Together we visited Jamestown's historic sites and early settlements on the Lower James River and across the Chesapeake Bay on Virginia's Eastern Shore. Aside from our many conversations, I draw heavily on her insights into the clash of cultures experienced by English settlers in the early seventeenth century. Archaeologist Beverly A. Straube introduced me to the fascination of material culture and the way discarded objects speak for the people who made and used them, helpfully directing me to institutions holding early seventeenth-century artefacts from the James River settlements.

Among the collections I visited, special thanks go to these curators and staff: Dee DeRoche, Katherine Ridgway, Andrew Foster and Ywone Edwards-Ingram at the Virginia Department of Historic Resources; Karen Shriver, curator of the Flowerdew Hundred Collection at the University of Virginia Library; Merry Outlaw, curator of collections, Jamestown Rediscovery; and Kelly Ladd-Kostro, associate curator of archaeological collections, Colonial Williamsburg Foundation. And I found much of interest in these research libraries: the Library of Virginia, Richmond; the Virginia Historical Society's collection at the Virginia Museum of History and Culture; and my favourite of all, Colonial Williamsburg's John D. Rockefeller Jr. Library, where Susan Shames, decorative arts librarian, and Marianne Martin, visual resources librarian, were especially helpful.

Visiting places where the Jamestown brides lived or died was crucial to my research. Samuel M. Mencoff, the owner of Carter's Grove plantation, generously granted access to Martin's Hundred, a visit facilitated by estate manager Chris Price and illuminated by archaeologist Nicholas M. Luccketti, who walked me through the site and shed light on other early settlements. Chapter 16 records my gratitude to Nancy Harwood Garrett, an authenticated descendant of husband John Wilkins; and I was fortunate in my two guides to the James River: Captain Mike Ostrander of Discover the James, who introduced me to the Upper James; and Jamie Brunkow, riverkeeper for the Lower James, who took me out on the water with the blessing of Bill Street, chief executive officer of the James River Association.

My thanks go also to historian Nancy D. Egloff and education manager Anne Price-Hardister at the Jamestown-Yorktown Foundation, who shared their vision of early women settlers; Captain Eric Speth, who paced the deck of the *Susan Constant*; Lyle Browning, who took me to the Falling Creek Ironworks; Cyrus Brame of the James River National Wildlife Refuge; Ellen LeComte in Richmond; John D. Pagano and Nicole Pisaniello at Henricus Historical Park; Traci L. Johnson, clerk of Northampton County Circuit Court, who gave generously of her time and resources; and Dr James Barton, whose personal experience of crossing the Atlantic under sail breathed life into the perilous conditions endured by early travellers.

Aided by Bonnie Hofmeyer, executive director of the Jamestowne Society, several descendants of Audry Hoare told me their stories, among them Virginia Ann Catalano, Elizabeth Minnich Kaminer, Elizabeth Ellen Jones and Fran McVeigh. And I enjoyed the hospitality of family and friends throughout Virginia, among them Bill Ritchie and Andrea Bartello; Gill, Mark, Katie and Billy Ruffa; Helen Rountree; and Nancy Harwood Garrett.

I record my debt to the Royal Literary Fund, which has supported my writing with fellowships at universities in London and as a consultant fellow, and to all my family, friends and fellow writers who have sustained me with their company and provoked my curiosity with their questions, especially Chris Potter, Lynn Ritchie, Rob Petit, Catherine King, Stephen Powell, Ros Franey, Louie Burghes, Philippa Campbell, Jude Harris, Sue and John Lloyd, Marina Benjamin, Esther Selsdon, Jana Teteris, Mary Griffin, Judith Wilcox and fellow members of the Gardeners Club, and Rita Cruise O'Brien, with whom I shared the joys and frustrations of writing about the early settlement of North America.

Finally I warmly thank Caroline Dawnay and Sophie Scard at United Agents for their help in getting this book off the ground; Margaret Stead, who commissioned the book and took such an early interest in it; and my publishers, Atlantic Books, especially Will Atkinson, managing director, and my editor, James Nightingale.

Endnotes

Preface: Witness

1. Ferrar Papers, Magdalene College Cambridge Old Library, FP 309 lists a total of fifty-seven women travelling by the various ships. As Mistress Palmer's daughter was only seven or eight years old I have omitted her from the reckoning, except where indicated.

2. David R. Ransome, 'Wives for Virginia, 1621', *William and Mary Quarterly*, Third Series, issue 48, January 1991, pp. 3–18.

3. See Douglas Bradburn and John C. Coombs (eds), *Early Modern Virginia: Reconsidering the Old Dominion* (Charlottesville, University of Virginia Press, 2011), p. 309.

Part One: England and its Virginian Colony

Chapter 1: The *Marmaduke* Maids

1. The original dozen *Marmaduke* maids are named in the Ferrar Papers, Magdalene College Cambridge Old Library, FP 306, and the thirteen who actually travelled in FP 309. Except where stated, all references to the maids' Virginia Company listing are taken from these two papers.

2. See FP 299.

3. FP 280.

4. See John Duncumb, *Collections Towards the History and Antiquities of the County of Herefordshire* (Cardiff, Merton Priory Press, 1996), vol. 2, pp. 138–9.

5. See 'The Charter of the Company of Gunmakers, London' in *Journal of the Society of Army Historical Research*, vol. 6 no. 23, January–March 1927, pp. 79–94; and Richard W. Stewart, 'The London Gunmakers and the Ordnance Office, 1590–1637' in *American Society of Arms Collectors Bulletin* no.55, fall 1986.

6. Except where stated, all birth details are from Ancestry.co.uk.

7. J. F. Merritt, *The Social World of Early Modern Westminster: Abbey, Court and Community, 1525–1640* (Manchester, Manchester University Press, 2005), p. 259.

8. See Walter Thornbury, 'Blackfriars', in *Old and New London: Volume 1* (London, 1878), pp. 200–19; Tiffany Stern, '"A ruinous monastery": the Second Blackfriars Playhouse as a place of nostalgia' in Andrew Gurr and Farah Karim-Cooper (eds), *Moving Shakespeare Indoors: Performance and Repertoire in the Jacobean Playhouse* (Cambridge University Press, 2014), pp. 96–114.

9. See Charles Lethbridge Kingsford (ed.), *John Stow, A Survey of London*, reprinted from the text of 1603 (2 vols, Oxford, Clarendon Press, 1971), vol. 2, p. 123; and Merritt, *The Social World*, pp. 259–60 and *passim.*

10. See http://www.british-history.ac.uk/old-new-london/vol4/pp14-26.

11. Percy W. L. Adams, *Betley Parish Register, 1538–1812* (Staffordshire Parish Registers Society, 1916), pp. 25–6, and Appendix I.

12. FP 308.

13. FP 309. A search of the alphabetical index of all people recorded in local

parish registers at the Isle of Wight County Record Office revealed no Bergens, Buergens or anything similar.

14. Susan Myra Kingsbury (ed.), *The Records of the Virginia Company of London* (4 vols, Washington, Library of Congress, 1906–35), vol. 3, pp. 492–8.

15. FP 309. Lawson is often transcribed as Clawson.

16. See John Nichols, *The Progresses, Processions and Magnificent Festivities of King James the First* (4 vols, London, Society of Antiquaries, 1828), vol. 2, p. 126; and the Victoria History of the Counties of England, *A History of Yorkshire* (London, Institute of Historical Research, 1974), vol. 2, p. 386.

17. Personal correspondence from Stephen Porter, honorary archivist to the Charterhouse, 12 December 2015. Charterhouse Muniments, G/2/1, Governors' Assembly Orders, Book A, June 1613–July 1637.

18. See: http://www.historyofparliamentonline.org/volume/1604-1629/member/uvedale-sir-william-1581-1652.

19. The watermen appeared in the sixth impression of Overbury's *Characters* (1615). See W. J. Paylor (ed), *The Overburian Characters to which is added A Wife by Sir Thomas Overbury* (Oxford, Basil Blackwell, 1936), p. 68.

20. Jonathan Barry and Christopher Brooks (eds), *The Middling Sort of People: Culture, Society and Politics in England, 1550–1800* (Basingstoke, Macmillan, 1994), p. 2.

21. See Jane Zimmerman, 'The Art of English Blackwork', www.janezimmerman.com/Site/Needlework_History/Blackwork.pdf.

22. See David W. Lloyd and Nikolaus Pevsner, *The Isle of Wight* (London, Yale University Press, 2006), pp. 119–23 and 25–6; East Cowes Heritage Centre, F/77/3B (but mostly unreferenced); and *Sir John Oglander's*

Commonplace Book, transcribed by the Isle of Wight County Record Office (see for instance OG 90/1 p. 127).

23. Kingsbury (ed.), *Records*, vol. 3, pp. 190–1.

24. http://www.iwhistory.org.uk/RM/iwcounty/iwplant.htm; Kingsbury (ed.), *Records*, vol. 3, p. 190; and Martha W. McCartney, *Virginia Immigrants and Adventurers 1607–1635, A Biographical Dictionary* (Baltimore, Genealogical Publishing Company, 2007), pp. 513 and 455–6.

25. Kingsbury (ed.), *Records*, vol. 1, p. 410.

26. Ibid. vol. 1, pp. 469–70 and vol. 3, p. 63.

27. *Sir John Oglander's Commonplace Book*, OG 90/2 f. 66 and OG 90/2 f. 102 bis.

28. Kingsbury (ed.), *Records*, vol. 2, p. 116.

29. Isle of Wight County Record Office, NBC 45/16a, Newport Convocation Book, entry for September 1621.

30. Kingbsury (ed.), *Records*, vol. 3, pp. 660–1.

31. FP 308.

32. FP 306.

33. Kingsbury (ed.), *Records*, vol. 3, p. 495.

34. For definitions of 'frieze' and 'falling bands', see Jill Condra, *The Greenwood Encyclopedia of Clothing Through World History* (Westport, Conn., Greenwood, 2008), p. 169; FP 308.

35. FP 315.

36. FP 328.

37. Isle of Wight County Record Office, OG/BB/174.

38. A John Jacson married Ann Gardner at St Margaret's Westminster on 26 April 1618, Ancestry.co.uk.

39. Isle of Wight County Record Office, Newport parish registers, NPT/REG/Com 2 (includes marriages 1545–1623). And see R. J. Eldridge, *Newport Isle of Wight in Bygone Days* (Newport, Isle of Wight County Press, 1952).

40. See http://www.virtualjamestown.org/Muster/muster24.html. Edward Marshall and Walter Beare survived as servants.

41. See 'Wight Island. Described by William White, Gent.' in John Speed, *The Theatre of the Empire of Great Britaine* (London, 1611), fols 15–17.

Chapter 2: The *Warwick* Women

1. Susan Myra Kingsbury (ed.), *The Records of the Virginia Company of London* (4 vols, Washington, Library of Congress, 1906–35), vol. 3, pp. 498–9.
2. For all listings of the *Warwick* and other maids in this chapter, see Ferrar Papers, Magdalene College Cambridge Old Library, FP 309.
3. See Robert Peirce Cruden, *The History of the Town of Gravesend in the County of Kent and of the Port of London* (London, William Pickering, 1843); James Benson, *A History of Gravesend*, revised and edited by Robert Heath Hiscock (Chichester, Phillimore & Co., 1976), p 2; and Robert Pocock, *The History of the Incorporated Town and Parishes of Gravesend and Milton in the County of Kent* (Gravesend, 1797).
4. *The Journals of Two Travellers in Elizabethan and Early Stuart England, Thomas Platter and Horatio Busino* (London, Caliban Books, 1995), pp. 9–10.
5. Ibid. pp. 109–10.
6. Cruden, *The History of the Town of Gravesend*, pp. 205–6.
7. See Platter in *The Journals of Two Travellers*, pp. 14 and 134.
8. See Kingsbury (ed.), *Records*, vol. 3, p. 389.
9. Gervase Markham, *Honour in his Perfection* (London, 1624), p. 21.
10. F. N. L. Poynter, *A Bibliography of Gervase Markham, 1568?–1637* (Oxford, Oxford Bibliographical Society, 1962), pp. 8–31.
11. Baptismal and marriage details from Ancestry.co.uk; and see http://www.british-history.ac.uk/vch/surrey/vol3/pp390-395.
12. Email from Steven Hobbs FSA, archivist at the Wiltshire and Swindon archives, 20 October 2015, confirming that Bridgett, daughter of John Croft, was baptized on 12 November 1601 in the church of St Peter at Britford, Wiltshire.
13. Fynes Moryson, *An Itinerary: London 1617* (Amsterdam, Da Capo Press/Theatrum Orbis Terrarum, 1971), Part III Chapter 3, p. 137.
14. 'Townships: North Meols', in *A History of the County of Lancaster: Volume 3*, ed. William Farrer and J. Brownbill (London, 1907), pp. 230–6.
15. *The Parish Registers of North Meols, 1594–1731* (Preston, Lancashire Parish Register Society, 1929), p. 3.
16. Baptized on 7 May 1600 at St Andrew Holborn on the western fringes of the City, Ancestry.co.uk.
17. T. C. Dale, *The Inhabitants of London in 1638* (London, Society of Genealogists, 1931) p. 97.
18. London Metropolitan Archives, *Church of England Parish Registers, 1538–1812*, reference no. *P93/DUN/255*.
19. FP 197.
20. Joseph Swetnam, *The Araignment of Lewd, Idle, Froward, and Unconstant Women* (London, 1615), p. 52.
21. Peter Wilson Coldham, *English Adventurers and Emigrants, 1609–1660* (Baltimore, Genealogical Publishing Co., 1984), p. 7.
22. Kingsbury (ed.), *Records*, vol. 1, pp. 632–3.
23. The recorder was also a Virginia Company adventurer: see Kingsbury (ed.), *Records*, vol. 1, p. 562.
24. Charles Lethbridge Kingsford (ed.), *John Stow, A Survey of London*, reprinted from the text of 1603 (2 vols, Oxford, Clarendon Press, 1971), vol. 1, p. 206.
25. Lawrence Price, 'The Maydens of Londons brave adventures', 1623–1661, English Broadside Ballad Archive, http://ebba.english.ucsb.edu/ballad/30869/image.
26. Anon, 'A Market for young Men', 1695–1703?, English Broadside Ballad

Archive, http://ebba.english.ucsb.edu/ballad/21894/image.

27. 'Anon, A Catalogue of young Wenches', 1675–96?, English Broadside Ballad Archive, http://ebba.english.ucsb.edu/ballad/22340/image.

28. Kingsford (ed.), *John Stow*, vol. 1, pp. 135–6 and p. 44. You can track this journey with the help of Adrian Prockter and Robert Taylor, *The A to Z of Elizabethan London* (London, London Topographical Society, 1979).

29. Kingsford (ed.), *John Stow*, vol. 1, p. 49.

30. Ibid. vol. 2, pp. 70–1.

31. Robert Simper, *Thames Tideway*, Vol. 6 English Estuaries Series (Lavenham, Suffolk, Creekside Publishing, 1997), pp. 54–5.

32. Platter in *The Journals of Two Travellers*, p. 99.

33. Quoted in Liza Picard, *Elizabeth's London: Everyday Life in Elizabethan London* (London, Weidenfeld & Nicolson, 2003), pp. 6–8.

34. 'A New Discovery by Sea', London to Salisbury (1623) in John Chandler (ed.), *Travels Through Stuart Britain, The Adventures of John Taylor, the Water Poet* (Stroud, Glos., Sutton Publishing, 1999), p. 102.

35. Kingsbury (ed) *Records*, vol. 3, pp. 639–40.

36. Ibid. vol. 3, p. 639 says August, but the *Tiger* left after the *Warwick* so September is more likely.

37. See biographies for the Palmers in Martha W. McCartney, *Virginia Immigrants and Adventurers 1607–1635: A Biographical Dictionary* (Baltimore, Genealogical Publishing Company, 2007), pp. 531–2.

38. Kingsbury (ed.), *Records*, vol.1, pp. 586–7.

39. Ibid. vol. 3, p. 298; vol.1, p. 379; and vol. 1, p. 588.

40. Ibid. vol. 1, p. 475.

41. Ancestry.co.uk; and see Caroline Gordon and Wilfrid Dewhirst, *The Ward of Cripplegate in the City of London* (London, Cripplegate Ward Club, 1985), p. 45.

Chapter 3: A Woman's Place

1. Gwendolyn B. Needham, 'New Light on Maids "Leading Apes in Hell"', *Journal of American Folklore*, vol. 75, no. 296 (April–June 1962), pp. 106–119; and William Corkine, Canto 14 of his *Second Booke of Ayres* (London, 1612).

2. Amy M. Froide, *Never Married: Singlewomen in Early Modern England* (Oxford University Press, 2005), p.17.

3. *The Lawes Resolutions of Womens Rights*, London, 1632 (reprinted Amsterdam, Walter J. Johnson Inc./Theatrum Orbis Terrarum, 1979), p. 6.

4. William Gouge, *Of Domesticall Duties, Eight Treatises* (London, 1622), pp. 272–3.

5. See https://www.bl.uk/collection-items/of-domesticall-duties-by-william-gouge-1622.

6. Quoted in Sara Mendelson and Patricia Crawford, *Women in Early Modern England, 1550–1720* (Oxford, Clarendon Press, 1998), p. 96.

7. See Joanna Innes, 'Prisons for the poor: English bridewells, 1555–1800', in Francis Snyder and Douglas Hay (eds) *Labour, Law, and Crime: An Historical Perspective* (London, Tavistock Publications, 1987), pp. 42–122, especially pp. 57–8.

8. H. F. Lippincott (ed.), '*Merry Passages and Jeasts': A Manuscript Jestbook of Sir Nicholas Le Strange (1603–1655)*, (Salzburg, Institut für Englische Sprache und Literatur, Universität Salzburg, 1974), p. 101, no. 347.

9. Joseph Swetnam, *The Araignment of Lewd, Idle, Froward [Contrary], and Unconstant Women* (London, 1615), pp. 1, 28, 52, 59.

10. Catherine Armstrong, *Writing North America in the Seventeenth Century: English Representations in Print and Manuscript* (Aldershot, Ashgate, 2007), pp. 38–9.

11. Society of Antiquaries, *Broadsides James I, 1603–1622*, no. 175. And see Mark Thornton Burnett, '"Fill Gut and Pinch Belly": Writing Famine in the English Renaissance' in *Explorations in Renaissance Culture*, vol. 21, 1995, pp. 21–44.

12. Norman Egbert McClure (ed.), *The Letters of John Chamberlain* (2 vols, Philadelphia, American Philosophical Society, 1939), vol. 2, p. 286.

13. *Three Pamphlets on the Jacobean Antifeminist Controversy* (Delmar, New York, Scholars' Facsimiles & Reprints, 1978).

14. McClure (ed.), *The Letters of John Chamberlain*, vol. 2, p. 289.

15. Amy Louise Erickson, *Women and Property in Early Modern England* (London, Routledge, 1993), pp. 5–6.

16. *The Lawes*, pp. 129–30, 128, 6.

17. Dier's age is given as fifteen in Ferrar Paper 309 and sixteen in FP 306. David R. Ransome, 'Wives for Virginia, 1621', *William and Mary Quarterly*, third series, no. 48, January 1991, p. 11.

18. Mendelson and Crawford, *Women in Early Modern England*, pp. 128–9; Vivien Brodsky Elliott, 'Single Women in the London Marriage Market: age, status and mobility 1598–1619' in R.B. Outhwaite (ed.), *Marriage and Society: Studies in the Social History of Marriage* (London, Europa publications, 1981), pp. 81–100.

19. Ferrar Papers, Magdalene College Cambridge Old Library, FP 306, and parish records from Ancestry.co.uk.

20. See E. A. Wrigley and R. S. Schofield, *The Population History of England, 1541–1871: A Reconstruction* (London, Edward Arnold, 1981), p. 263.

21. David Underdown, *Revel, Riot, and Rebellion: Popular Politics and Culture in England 1603–1660* (Oxford, Oxford University Press, 1987), p. 18.

22. David B. Quinn, 'Why they came' in David B. Quinn (ed.), *Early Maryland in a Wider World* (Detroit, Wayne State University Press, 1982), p. 135.

23. Christopher Brooks, 'Apprenticeship, Social Mobility and the Middling Sort, 1550–1800' in Jonathan Barry and Christopher Brooks (eds), *The Middling Sort of People: Culture, Society and Politics in England, 1550–1800* (Basingstoke, Macmillan, 1994), p. 70.

24. McClure (ed.), *The Letters of John Chamberlain*, vol. 2, p. 342.

25. See Erickson, *Women and Property*, pp. 85, and 88–9; Diana O'Hara, *Courtship and Constraint: Rethinking the Making of Marriage in Tudor England* (Manchester, Manchester University Press, 2000), p. 204; Catherine Frances, 'Making marriages in early modern England: rethinking the role of family and friends', in Maria Ågren and Amy Louise Erickson (eds), *The Marital Economy in Scandinavia and Britain, 1400–1900* (Aldershot, Ashgate, 2005), p. 45.

26. For decline in wages, see James Horn, 'Servant Emigration to the Chesapeake in the Seventeenth Century' in Thad W. Tate and David L. Ammerman (eds), *The Chesapeake in the Seventeenth Century* (Chapel Hill, University of North Carolina Press, 1979), p. 75. For dowry inflation, see O'Hara, *Courtship*, especially pp. 190–235; and Frances, 'Making Marriages', p. 45.

27. Erickson, *Women and Property*, p. 93.

28. FP 306 and 309.

29. Erickson, *Women and Property*, p. 5.

30. Ibid. p. 94.

31. Jane Whittle, 'Servants in rural England *c.*1450–1650: hired work as a means of accumulating wealth and skills before marriage' in Ågren and Erickson (eds), *The Marital Economy*, pp. 89–107.

32. Erickson, *Woman and Property*, p. 85.

33. McClure (ed.), *The Letters of John Chamberlain*, vol. 2, p. 198.

34. Anon, 'A Dialogue Between A/ Master and his Maid', 1684–1700?, English Broadside Ballad Archive, https://ebba.english.ucsb.edu/ballad/22059/image.

35. The first case appears among the general sessions held at Westminster on 11 and 12 April 1616, Sessions Roll 550/114, 115, Sessions Reg. 2/294, http://www.british-history.ac.uk/middx-sessions/vol3/pp194-239; the second on Sessions, 1616: 3 and 4 October, Sessions Roll 554/122, Sessions Reg. 2/356, http://www.british-history.ac.uk/middx-sessions/vol4/pp1-41.

36. *A History of the County of Gloucester: Volume 10, Westbury and Whitstone Hundreds*, originally published by Victoria County History, London, 1972, consulted online 18 January 2018 at: http://www.british-history.ac.uk/vch/glos/vol10/pp162-165.

37. Elliott, 'Single Women in the London Marriage Market', pp. 83–4.

38. Anon, 'A Maydens Lamentation for a Bedfellow', *c.*1615, English Broadside Ballad Archive, https://ebba.english.ucsb.edu/ ballad/20113/image.

39. Martin Parker, 'The wiving age. Or A great Complaint of the Maidens of London', 1627?, English Broadside Ballad Archive, https://ebba.english.ucsb.edu/ballad/20178/image.

40. See Anon, 'This Maide would give tenne Shillings for a Kisse', 1620?, English Broadside Ballad Archive, https://ebba.english.ucsb.edu/ ballad/20150/image; and 'Nobody his Consaile to chuse a Wife: OR, the diffference betweene Widdowes and Maydes', 1622, https://ebba.english.ucsb.edu/ballad/20177/image.

41. Susan Myra Kingsbury (ed.), *The Records of the Virginia Company of London* (4 vols, Washington, Library of Congress, 1906–35), vol. 3, pp. 275–80.

42. William S. Powell, *Letters and Other Writings*, microfiche supplement to *John Pory, 1572–1636, The Life and Letters of a Man of Many Parts* (Chapel Hill, University of North Carolina Press, 1977), pp. 50–1.

43. Armstrong, *Writing North America*, p. 182.

44. Louis B. Wright, *Religion and Empire: The Alliance Between Piety and Commerce in English Expansion, 1558–1625* (Chapel Hill, University of North Carolina Press, 1943), p. 88.

45. McClure (ed.), *The Letters of John Chamberlain*, vol. 2, p. 408.

46. FP 197; and Ransome, 'Wives for Virginia', p. 10.

Chapter 4: Point of Departure

1. Stephen Inwood, *A History of London* (London, Macmillan, 1998), pp. 157–9, 201; and A. L. Beier and Roger Finlay (eds), *London 1500–1700: The Making of the Metropolis* (London, Longman, 1986), p. 3.

2. Ibid. pp. 50–1; and see Roger Finlay, *Population and Metropolis: The Demography of London 1580–1650* (Cambridge, Cambridge University Press, 1981).

3. Ferrar Papers, Magdalene College Cambridge Old Library, FP 306 and 309.

4. Charles Lethbridge Kingsford (ed.), *John Stow, A Survey of London*, reprinted from the text of 1603 (2 vols, Oxford, Clarendon Press, 1971), vol. 2, p. 72.

5. Ibid. vol. 1, p. 179.

6. See Jennifer Potter, *Strange Blooms: The Curious Lives and Adventures of the John Tradescants* (London, Atlantic Books, 2006), pp. 28–9.

7. *The Journals of Two Travellers in Elizabethan and Early Stuart England, Thomas Platter and Horatio Busino* (London, Caliban Books, 1995), pp. xxii–xxiii.

8. Edward Arber (ed.), *Thomas Decker* [sic], *The Seven Deadly Sins of London*,

1606 (London, English Scholar's Library, 1880), p.31.

9. See Bruce R. Smith, *The Acoustic World of Early Modern England* (Chicago, University of Chicago Press, 1999), especially pp. 52–71; and http://quod.lib.umich. edu/e/eebo/A20054.0001.001/ 1:3?rgn=div1;view=fulltext.

10. *The Journals of Two Travellers*, p. xxv.

11. Kingsford (ed.), *John Stow*, vol. 1, p. 277.

12. Ibid. vol. 2, p. 21.

13. Ibid. vol. 1, p. 239.

14. See http://www.pepysdiary.com/ encyclopedia/2979/.

15. Liza Picard, *Elizabeth's London: Everyday Life in Elizabethan London* (London, Weidenfeld & Nicolson, 2003), pp. 14–15.

16. *The Journals of Two Travellers*, p. 134.

17. Smith, *The Acoustic World*, p. 57.

18. See http://www.british-history.ac.uk/ middx-sessions/vol1/pp452-462.

19. Sir Thomas Gresham's Royal Exchange in the City, built in the late 1560s, seems more likely than the New Exchange on the Strand, built in 1609.

20. See Vivian Thomas and Nicki Faircloth, *Shakespeare's Plants and Gardens* (London, Bloomsbury, 2014), p. 6.

21. Andrew Gurr and Farah Karim-Cooper (eds), *Moving Shakespeare Indoors: Performance and Repertoire in the Jacobean Playhouse* (Cambridge, Cambridge University Press, 2014), pp. 254–6.

22. Quoted in Irwin Smith, *Shakespeare's Blackfriars Playhouse* (New York, New York University Press, 1964), pp. 256–7 and 489–6.

23. City of Westminster Archives, St Martin-in-the-Fields parish records, Overseers' Accounts for the Poor for 1622, F348.

24. http://www.historyofparliamentonline .org/volume/1604-1629/member/

thorpe-george-1575-1622. For a brief biography, see Martha W. McCartney, 'George Thorpe's Inventory: Virginia's Earliest Known Appraisal' in Robert Hunter (ed.), *Ceramics in America*, 2016, pp. 2–32: http://www.chipstone. org/issue.php/40/Ceramics-in-America-2016.

25. City of Westminster Archives, St Martin-in-the-Fields parish records, Overseers' Accounts for the Poor for 1622, F345.

26. https://mapoflondon.uvic.ca/STRA9. htm.

27. https://mapoflondon.uvic.ca/BEAR1. htm?name=SOUT2.

28. Caroline Barron et al. (eds), 'The London Journal of Alessandro Magno 1562' in *The London Journal*, vol. 9, no. 2, winter 1983, pp. 143–4; and Smith, *The Acoustic World*, pp. 62–3.

29. Kingsford (ed.), *John Stow*, vol. 2, pp. 54.

30. Barron et al. (eds), 'The London Journal', p. 144.

31. *The Journals of Two Travellers*, p. 32.

32. Laura Gowing, '"The freedom of the streets": women and social space, 1560–1640', in Paul Griffiths and Mark S. R. Jenner, *Londinopolis: Essays in the Cultural and Social History of Early Modern London* (Manchester, Manchester University Press, 2000), p. 139.

33. http://www.british-history.ac.uk/old-new-london/vol4/pp14–26.

34. FP 306 gives her age as '20 or ther abouts'.

35. See Edward Walford, 'Westminster: Tothill Fields and neighbourhood', in *Old and New London: Volume 4* (London, 1878), pp. 14–26.

36. Martin Parker, 'Newes from the Tower-hill', 1631, English Broadside Ballad Archive, https:// ebba.english.ucsb.edu/search_ combined/?ss=20123.

Chapter 5: Of Hogs and Women

1. Kim Sloan, *A New World: England's First View of America* (London, British Museum Press, 2007), pp. 40–1.

2. See David Beers Quinn (ed.), *The Roanoke Voyages 1584–1590* (2 vols, London, Hakluyt Society, 1955), vol. 2, pp. 515–43; James Horn, *A Kingdom Strange: The Brief and Tragic History of the Lost Colony of Roanoke* (New York, Basic Books, 2010); and David Beers Quinn, *Set Fair For Roanoke, Voyages and Colonies 1584–1606* (Chapel Hill, University of North Carolina Press, 1985).

3. Horn, *A Kingdom Strange*, pp. 245–8.

4. Quinn, *The Roanoke Voyages*, vol. 2, p. 524.

5. Ibid. pp. 531–2.

6. Ibid. pp. 613–15.

7. George Percy, *Observations gathered out of a Discourse of the Plantation of the Southerne Colonie in Virginia by the English*, taken from http://www.virtualjamestown.org/exist/cocoon/jamestown/fha/J1002.

8. George Chapman, Ben Johnson, John Marston, *Eastward Hoe As it was playd in the Black-friers* (London, 1605), act 3, scene 2.

9. Louis B. Wright and Virginia Freund (eds), *The Historie of Travell into Virginia Britania (1612) By William Strachey, gent.* (London, Hakluyt Society, 1953), p. 34.

10. Wesley Frank Craven, *The Virginia Company of London, 1606–1624*, historical booklet no. 5 (Williamsburg, Va., Virginia 350th Anniversary Celebration Corporation, 1957), pp. 1–2.

11. http://www.historyofparliamentonline.org/volume/1604-1629/member/smythe-sir-thomas-1558-1625#footnote48_4xaxtl3.

12. Louis B. Wright, *Religion and Empire: The Alliance Between Piety and Commerce in English Expansion 1558–1625* (Chapel Hill, University of North Carolina Press, 1943), pp. 88–9.

13. Craven, *The Virginia Company*, p. 39. For a biography of Sandys, see Theodore K. Rabb, *Jacobean Gentleman: Sir Edwin Sandys, 1561–1629* (Princeton, Princeton University Press, 1998).

14. Lyon Gardiner Tyler, *The Cradle of the Republic: Jamestown and James River* (Richmond, Va., Whittet & Shepperson, 1900), pp. 15–16, 25.

15. 'Observations by Master George Percy, 1607', pp. 5–23 in Lyon Gardiner Tyler, *Narratives of Early Virginia 1606–1625* (New York, Charles Scribner's Sons, 1907), p. 15.

16. Ibid. pp. 21–2.

17. Robert Johnson, *The New Life of Virginea… Being the Second part of Nova Britannia* (London, 1612), taken from http://www.virtualjamestown.org/exist/cocoon/jamestown/fha/J1052.

18. William Strachey, 'A true reportory of the wracke, and redemption of Sir Thomas Gates Knight' in Samuel Purchas, *Hakluytus Posthumus or Purchas His Pilgrimes*, vol. 19 (Glasgow, James MacLehose, 1906), Chapter VI, p. 58.

19. http://historicjamestowne.org/history/history-of-jamestown/the-first-supply/. For survival rates, see Edmund S. Morgan, *American Slavery, American Freedom*, 115 n. and Appendix, 396 n.

20. Philip L. Barbour (ed.), *The Complete Works of Captain John Smith (1580–1631)* (3 vols, Chapel Hill, University of North Carolina Press, 1986), vol. 2, pp. 191–2.

21. Ibid. vol. 2, pp. 140–2.

22. See 'Musters of the Inhabitants in Virginia 1624/1625' in Annie Lash Jester, *Adventurers of Purse and Person, Virginia 1607–1625*, second edition (Sponsored by Order of the First Families of Virginia, 1964), p. 49.

23. George Gardyner of Peckham quoted this proverb in *A Description of the New World. OR, America Islands and Continent* (London 1651), pp. 98–102.

24. Letter from Sir Francis Wyatt in *William and Mary Quarterly*, third series, vol. vi, no. 2, April 1926, pp. 114–21.

25. Catherine Armstrong, *Writing North America in the Seventeenth Century: English Representations in Print and Manuscript* (Aldershot, Ashgate, 2007), pp. 38–9.

26. http://quod.lib.umich.edu/e/eebo/A14513.0001.001?rgn=main;view=fulltext.

27. Alexander Brown, *The Genesis of the United States* (2 vols, New York, Russell & Russell, 1964), vol. 1, p. 320; and Barbour (ed.), *Complete Works* vol. 2, p. 219.

28. Brown, *Genesis*, vol. 1, p. 244.

29. See *Oxford Dictionary of National Biography* entry on Yeardley by R. C. D. Baldwin, https://doi.org/10.1093/ref:odnb/30204, consulted online 24 January 2018; and William S. Powell, *John Pory/ 1572–1636: The Life and Letters of a Man of Many Parts* (Chapel Hill, University of North Carolina Press, 1977), p. 5.

30. See Strachey, 'A true repertory', p. 38, and Hobson Woodward, *A Brave Vessel: The True Tale of the Castaways Who Rescued Jamestown* (London, Penguin Books, 2009), p. 23.

31. See Annie Lash Jester, *Domestic Life in Virginia in the Seventeenth Century*, historical booklet no. 17 (Williamsburg, Va., Virginia 350th Anniversary Celebration Corporation, 1957), p. 6.

32. Barbour (ed.), *Complete Works*, vol. 2, p. 223–5.

33. Mark Nicholls on George Percy, *Oxford Dictionary of National Biography*, consulted online 24 January 2018, https://doi.org/10.1093/ref:odnb/21926.

34. Barbour (ed.), *Complete Works*, vol. 2, p. 232; and Woodward, *A Brave Vessel*, pp. 90 and 97.

35. Strachey, 'A true repertory', pp. 44–5, 54.

36. Charles E. Hatch Jr, *The First Seventeen Years, Virginia 1607–1624* (Charlottesville, Va., University of Virginia Press, 1957), p. 11.

37. Barbour (ed.), *Complete Works*, vol. 2, pp. 232–3.

38. This version comes from Strachey, 'A true repertory', pp. 69–70.

39. Jane's story is taken from James Horn, William Kelso, Douglas Owsley and Beverly Straube, *Jane: Starvation, Cannibalism, and Endurance at Jamestown* (Williamsburg, Colonial Williamsburg Foundation/Preservation Virginia, 2013).

40. Ferrar Papers, Magdalene College Cambridge Old Library, FP 309.

41. See Nicholas Canny, 'The permissive frontier: the problem of social control in English settlements in Ireland and Virginia 1550–1650' in K. R. Andrews et al. (eds), *The Westward Enterprise: English Activities in Ireland, the Atlantic, and America 1480–1650* (Liverpool, Liverpool University Press, 1978), pp. 17–44.

42. *For The Colony in Virginea Britannia. Lawes Divine, Morall and Martiall*, (London, 1612) from http://www.virtualjamestown.org/exist/cocoon/jamestown/laws/J1056.

43. Martha W. McCartney, *Virginia Immigrants and Adventurers 1607–1635: A Biographical Dictionary* (Baltimore, Genealogical Publishing Company, 2007), p. 767.

44. H. R. McIlwaine (ed.), *Minutes of the Council and General Court of Colonial Virginia, 1622–1632, 1670–1676* (Richmond, Va., Virginia State Library, 1924), p. 62.

45. Warren M. Billing, 'The transfer of English Law to Virginia, 1606–50'

in Andrews et al. (eds), *The Westward Enterprise*, p. 218.

46. https://www.encyclopediavirginia.org/ Tobacco_in_Colonial_Virginia.

47. Norman Egbert McClure, *The Letters of John Chamberlain* (2 vols, Philadelphia, American Philosophical Society, 1939), vol. 1, p. 471.

48. Ibid. vol. 2, p. 12.

49. Craven, *The Virginia Company*, pp. 31–2.

50. McClure (ed.), *The Letters of John Chamberlain*, vol. 1, p. 334.

51. *Three Proclamations Concerning the Lottery for Virginia 1613–1621* (Providence, R.I., John Carter Brown Library, 1907), p. 2.

52. See Robert C. Johnson, 'The "Running Lotteries" of the Virginia Company', *Virginia Magazine of History and Biography*, vol. 68, no. 2 (April 1960), pp. 156–65.

53. Anon, 'Londons Lotterie', 1612, English Broadside Ballad Archive, http://ebba.english.ucsb.edu/ ballad/20085/image.

54. Emily Rose, 'The End of the Gamble: The Termination of the Virginia Lotteries in March 1621', *Parliamentary History*, vol. 27, part 2 (2008), pp. 175–97.

55. See Susan Myra Kingsbury (ed.), *The Records of the Virginia Company of London* (4 vols, Washington, Library of Congress, 1906–35), vol.1, pp. 355 and 556.

56. Sir Francis Bacon's 'Of Plantations' appears in Brown, *Genesis*, vol. 2, pp. 799–802.

57. See Kathleen M. Brown, *Good Wives, Nasty Wenches, and Anxious Patriarchs: Gender, Race, and Power in Colonial Virginia* (Chapel Hill, University of North Carolina Press, 1996), pp. 24–7.

58. Peter Wilson Coldham, *Emigrants in Chains: A Social History of Forced Emigration to the Americas, 1607–1776* (Stroud, Glos., Alan Sutton, 1992), p. 41.

59. See http://www.virtualjamestown. org/exist/cocoon/jamestown/fha/ J1051, Robert Johnson, *Nova Britannia* (London, 1609).

60. *Analytical Index to the Series of Records Known as the Remembrancia Preserved Among the Archives of the City of London, A.D. 1579–1664* (London, E. J. Francis, 1878), pp. 361–2.

61. Robert C. Johnson, 'The Transportation of Vagrant Children from London to Virginia, 1618–1622' in Howard S. Reinmuth Jr (ed.), *Early Stuart Studies: Essays in Honor of David Harris Willson* (Minneapolis, University of Minnesota Press, 1970), pp. 138–43.

62. McClure (ed.), *The Letters of John Chamberlain*, vol. 2, p. 170.

63. The numbers are taken from Robert Hume, *Early Child Immigrants to Virginia, 1618–1642* (Baltimore, Md., Magna Carter Book Company, 1986), pp. 8–13.

64. Kingsbury (ed.), *Records*, vol. 1, p. 289.

65. Ibid. vol. I, p. 270–1.

66. Coldham, *Emigrants in Chains*, p. 46.

67. Hume, *Early Child Immigrants*, pp. 18 and 20.

68. *Calendar of State Papers, Domestic Series, of the Reign of James I, 1611–1618* (London, Longman, Brown, Green, Longmans, & Roberts, 1858), pp. 586, 594.

69. McClure (ed.), *The Letters of John Chamberlain*, vol. 2, p. 183.

70. Anon, 'The Trappan'd Maiden', 1689–1703?, English Broadside Ballad Archive, https://ebba.english.ucsb. edu/ballad/21947/image.

71. Anon, 'The Woman Outwitted' , 1705–1709?, English Broadside Ballad Archive, https://ebba.english.ucsb. edu/ballad/32021/image.

72. Kingsbury (ed.), *Records*, vol. 4, p. 82.

73. Quoted by David R. Ransome in 'Wives for Virginia, 1621' in *William and Mary Quarterly*, third series, no. 48, January 1991, p. 5.

74. Kingsbury (ed.), *Records*, vol. 4, p. 82.
75. Kingsbury (ed.), *Records*, vol. 1, pp. 256–7.
76. Ibid. vol. 1, 269.
77. Ransome, 'Wives for Virginia', p. 5. Ransome mentions just the *Jonathan* and the *Merchant of London*. Another ship often mentioned is the *Bona Nova*. See Kingsbury, *Records*, vol. 3, p. 239.
78. *A Declaration of the State of the Colonie and Affaires in Virginia With the Names of Adventurors, and Summes adventured in that Action*, 22 June 1620, taken from http://www.virtualjamestown.org/exist/cocoon/jamestown/fha/J1050.

Chapter 6: La Belle Sauvage

1. For much of the background to this chapter I am indebted to Helen C. Rountree, *Pocahontas, Powhatan, Opechancanough: Three Indian Lives Changed by Jamestown* (Charlottesville, Va., University of Virginia Press, 2005).
2. The text of Rolfe's letter is taken from http://www.virtualjamestown.org/rolfe_letter.html.
3. Thomas Harriot, *A Briefe and True Report of the New found land of Virginia* (New York, Dover Publications, 1972), p. 29.
4. Karen Ordahl Kupperman, *Indians and English: Facing Off in Early America* (Ithaca, Cornell University Press, 2000), pp. 41–76.
5. See Kim Sloan, *A New World: England's First View of America* (London, British Museum Press, 2007), especially pp. 122–3, 126–7, 130–1, 140–5.
6. Louis B. Wright and Virginia Freund (eds), *The Historie of Travell into Virginia Britania (1612) By William Strachey, gent.* (London, Hakluyt Society, 1953), pp. 71, 85, 112–13, 174–207.
7. Philip L. Barbour (ed.), *The Complete Works of Captain John Smith (1580–1631)* (3 vols, Chapel Hill, University of

North Carolina Press, 1986), vol. 1, pp. 263–5.
8. Alexander Brown, *The Genesis of the United States* (2 vols, New York, Russell & Russell, 1964), vol. 2, pp. 572–3.
9. Louis B. Wright (ed.), *The History and Present State of Virginia by Robert Beverley* (Chapel Hill, University of North Carolina Press, 1947), pp. 38–9.
10. Quoted in Leonidas Dodson, *Alexander Spotswood, Governor of Colonial Virginia, 1710–1722* (Philadelphia, University of Pennsylvania Press, 1932), p. 91.
11. *Virginea Britannia: A Sermon Preached at White Chappel, in the Presence of Many, Honourable and Worshipfull, the Adventurers, and Planters for Virginia*, 25 April 1609 by William Symonds, p. 35.
12. See Helen C. Rountree's entry on 'Marriage in Early Virginian Indian Society' for *Encyclopedia Virginia*, http://www.encyclopediavirginia.org/Marriage_in_Early_Virginia_Indian_Society.
13. Wright and Freund (eds), *The Historie of Travell*, pp. 72, 113.
14. Barbour (ed.), *Complete Works*, vol. 2, p. 198.
15. Wright and Freund (eds), *The Historie of Travell*, p. 62.
16. Brown, *Genesis*, vol. 2, pp. 640–4; Barbour (ed.), *Complete Works*, vol. 2, pp. 243–4; and Ralph Hamor, *A True Discourse Of The Present Estate Of Virginia, 1614* (London, 1615).
17. Norman Egbert McClure (ed.), *The Letters of John Chamberlain* (2 vols, Philadelphia, American Philosophical Society, 1939), vol. 1, pp. 470–1.
18. Taken from: http://www.virtualjamestown.org/rolfe_letter.html.
19. Rountree, *Pocahontas*, pp. 166–7.
20. Barbour (ed.), *Complete Works*, vol. 2, pp. 245–6.
21. For the biblical story of Isaac and Rebekah, see Genesis Chapter 24.
22. Hamor, *A True Discourse*; and see Rountree, *Pocahontas*, pp. 168–75.

23. Barbour (ed.), *Complete Works*, vol. 2, p. 258.

24. McClure (ed.), *The Letters of John Chamberlain*, vol. 2, p. 12.

25. Ibid. vol. 2, pp. 56–7.

26. Quoted in Rountree, *Pocahontas*, p. 177.

27. Ibid. p. 178.

28. Barbour (ed.), *Complete Works*, vol. 2, pp. 260–2; and see Rountree, *Pocahontas*, pp. 180–2.

29. http://www.npg.org.uk/collections/ search/person/mp08122/simon-de-passe. The British Museum calls him Simon van de Passe.

30. McClure (ed.), *The Letters of John Chamberlain*, vol. 2, pp. 56–7.

31. Tony Horwitz, 'How much do we really know about Pocahontas', *Smithsonian Magazine*, November 2013, consulted online 21 April 2016.

32. Rountree, *Pocahontas*, p. 182.

33. Parish records for St George's church, Gravesend.

34. McClure (ed.), *The Letters of John Chamberlain*, vol. 2, p. 66.

35. Philip L. Barbour (ed.), *The Complete Works of Captain John Smith (1580–1631)* (3 vols, Chapel Hill, University of North Carolina Press, 1986), vol. 2, p. 262.

36. Susan Myra Kingsbury, *The Records of the Virginia Company of London* (4 vols, Washington, Library of Congress, 1906–35), vol. 3, pp. 70–3.

37. Alden T. Vaughan, 'Powhatans Abroad: Virginia Indians in England' in Robert Appelbaum and John Wood Sweet, *Envisioning an English Empire: Jamestown and the Making of the North Atlantic World* (Philadelphia, University of Pennsylvania Press, 2005), pp. 59–60.

38. Kingsbury (ed.), *Records*, vol. 1, pp. 338–9. And see Rev. Edward D. Neill, *Pocahontas and Her Companions: A Chapter from the History of the Virginia Company of London* (Albany, NY, Joel Munsell, 1869), p. 29; and Camilla

Townsend, *Pocahontas and the Powhatan Dilemma* (New York, Hill and Wang, 2004), p. 166.

39. Kingsbury (ed.), *Records*, vol. 1, pp. 427–8.

40. Ferrar Papers, Magdalene College Cambridge Old Library, FP 282.

41. Kingsbury (ed.), *Records*, vol. 1, p. 496.

42. FP 292.

43. Barbour (ed.), *Complete Works*, vol. 2, pp. 384 and 386.

Chapter 7: Maids to the Rescue

1. *Oxford Dictionary of National Biography* and J. F. Wadmore, 'Sir Thomas Smythe Knt (AD 1558–1625)', *Archaeologia Cantiana*, vol. 20, 1893, pp. 82–103.

2. Wesley Frank Craven, *Dissolution of the Virginia Company* (Gloucester, Mass., Peter Smith, 1964), p. 27.

3. Susan Myra Kingsbury, *The Records of the Virginia Company of London* (4 vols, Washington, Library of Congress, 1906–35), vol. 3, p. 217.

4. See http://www.npg.org.uk/ collections/search/portraitLarge/ mw129154/Sir-Thomas-Smythe-Smith.

5. See Charles Lethbridge Kingsford (ed.), *John Stow, A Survey of London*, reprinted from the text of 1603 (2 vols, Oxford, Clarendon Press, 1971), vol. 1, p. 174.

6. Theodore K. Rabb, *Jacobean Gentleman: Sir Edwin Sandys, 1561–1629* (Princeton, Princeton University Press, 1998), frontispiece and see p. 393.

7. Kingsbury (ed.), *Records*, vol. 1, pp. 212–13 and 385. For Wolstenholme's family connections, see http://www. historyofparliamentonline.org/ volume/1604-1629/member/ wolstenholme-sir-john-1562-1639.

8. Stanley Spurling, *Sir Thomas Smythe knt 1558–1625* (New York, The Newcomers Society in North

America, 1955); and http://www.
historyofparliamentonline.org/
volume/1604-1629/member/smythe-
sir-thomas-1558-1625.

9. 'Nicholas Ferrar' in Rev. Christopher
Wordsworth, *Ecclesiastical Biography;
or Lives of Eminent Men Connected with
the History of Religion in England* (6 vols,
London, 1818), vol. 5, p. 76.

10. Rev. T. T. Carter, *Nicholas Ferrar, His
Household and His Friends* (London,
Longmans, Green, & Co., 1892), p. 6.

11. Joyce Ransome, *The Web of Friendship:
Nicholas Ferrar and Little Gidding*
(Cambridge, James Clarke & Co.,
2011), pp. 41–2.

12. Kingsbury (ed.), *Records*, vol. 1,
pp. 298, 301, and 334–7.

13. Ibid. vol. 1, p. 335.

14. Ibid. vol. 3, pp. 216–19.

15. Ibid. vol. 1, pp. 345–58.

16. Ibid. vol. 1, pp. 265–9.

17. Ibid. vol. 1, p. 220.

18. Ibid. vol. 1, p. 348.

19. Rabb, *Jacobean Gentleman*, pp. 75–86.

20. Kingsbury (ed.), *Records*, pp. 357–8.

21. Ibid. vol. 1, pp. 384–5.

22. Arthur Woodnoth, *A Short Collection
of the Most Remarkable Passages from the
Originall to the Dissolution of the Virginia
Company*, London, 1651, pp. 7–8.

23. Kingsbury (ed.), *Records*, vol. 1, p. 390.

24. Ibid. vol. 1, p. 412.

25. Ibid. vol. 1, p. 397.

26. See Robert C. Johnson, 'The Lotteries
of the Virginia Company 1612–1621'
in *Virginia Magazine of History and
Biography*, vol. 74, no. 3, July 1966,
pp. 259–92, especially pp. 288–92;
Emily Rose, 'The End of the Gamble:
The Termination of the Virginia
Lotteries in March 1621', *Parliamentary
History*, vol. 27, pt 2, 2008, pp. 175–
97; and Robert C. Johnson, 'The
"Running Lotteries" of the Virginia
Company', *Virginia Magazine of History
and Biography*, vol. 68, no. 2, April
1960, pp. 156–65.

27. Rose, 'The End of the Gamble', p. 182.

28. Kingsbury (ed.), *Records*, vol. 1,
pp. 469–70.

29. Ibid. vol. 1, p. 477.

30. Ibid. vol. 1, p. 485.

31. Ibid. vol. 1, pp. 510–11, 493.

32. Ibid. vol. 1, pp. 512–20.

33. See Martha W. McCartney, *Virginia
Immigrants and Adventurers 1607–1638:
A Biographical Dictionary* (Baltimore,
Genealogical Publishing Company,
2007), pp. 142–3.

34. Kingsbury (ed.), *Records*, vol. 1, p. 517.

35. Ibid. vol. 1, p. 596.

36. Ferrar Papers, Magdalene College
Cambridge Old Library, FP 280.

37. FP 280, and Kingsbury (ed.), *Records*,
vol. 3, p. 505.

38. Kingsbury (ed.), *Records*, vol. 3,
pp. 492–8, and 502–8.

39. Ibid. vol. 1, p. 520.

40. See FP 280.

41. Kingsbury (ed.), *Records*, vol, 2, pp. 15
and 26.

42. FP 280; and see David R. Ransome,
'Wives for Virginia, 1621', *William and
Mary Quarterly*, third series, no. 48,
January 1991, pp. 8–9.

43. Kingsbury (ed.), *Records*, vol. 1,
pp. 565–7.

44. Ibid. vol. 1, pp. 522–3.

45. Ibid. vol. 3, pp. 493–4.

46. Ibid. vol. 1, p. 391.

47. Ibid. vol. 3, pp. 312–17.

48. Ibid. vol. 3, p. 494.

49. Ibid. vol. 3, p. 502.

50. FP 305.

51. FP 306.

52. FP 302; and see Ransome, 'Wives for
Virginia' p. 16, and Holly Duggan,
'Osmologies of Luxury and Labor:
Entertaining Perfumers in Early
English Drama' for Michelle M. Dowd
and Natasha Korda (eds), *Working
Subjects in Early Modern English Drama*
(Farnham, Ashgate, 2011), p. 75.

53. FP 304.

54. FP 292, 306 and 322.

55. FP 315.

56. FP 308.

Intermezzo: Maidens' Voyage

Chapter 8: When Stormie Winds do Blow

1. Anon, 'A Voyage to Virginia', English Broadside Ballad Archive, https://ebba.english.ucsb.edu/ballad/33489/image.
2. C. H. Herford and Percy Simpson (eds), *Ben Jonson* (11 vols, Oxford, Clarendon Press, 1986), vol. 4, p. 544.
3. Robert D. Hicks, *Voyage to Jamestown: Practical Navigation in the Age of Discovery* (Annapolis, Maryland, Naval Institute Press, 2011), p. 42.
4. Ferrar Papers, Magdalene College Cambridge Old Library, FP 299.
5. Philip L. Barbour (ed.), *The Complete Works of Captain John Smith (1580–1631)* (3 vols, Chapel Hill University of North Carolina Press, 1986), vol. 3, p. 82.
6. Susan Myra Kingsbury, *The Records of the Virginia Company of London* (4 vols, Washington, Library of Congress, 1906–35), vol. 3, p. 465.
7. Ibid. vol. 3, pp. 498–501.
8. Ibid. vol. 3, p. 526.
9. *A True and Sincere declaration of the purpose and ends of the Plantation begun in Virginia* (London, 1610), pp. 8–9, authorized by the 'Governors and Councellors' of the Virginia Company.
10. Samuel Purchas, *Hakluytus Posthumus: or, Purchas his Pilgrimes* (20 vols, Glasgow, James Maclehose and Sons, 1905–7), vol. 19, pp. 90–4.
11. Kingsbury (ed.), *Records*, vol. 3, p. 78. For prevailing winds and currents in the North Atlantic see James Clarke, *Atlantic Pilot Atlas* second edition (London, Adlard Coles Nautical, 1996), pp. 8–33.
12. Kingsbury (ed.), *Records*, vol. 3, p. 301.
13. See 'A Voyage to Virginia by Colonel Norwood' in *A Collection of Voyage and Travels* (6 vols, London, Messrs Churchill, 1744–6), vol. 6, p. 163.
14. Barbour (ed.), *Complete Works*, vol. 3, p. 28.
15. Robert Ralston Cawley, *Unpathed Waters, Studies in the Influence of the Voyagers on Elizabethan Literature* (Princeton, Princeton University Press, 1940), p. 204.
16. Kingsbury (ed.), *Records*, vol. 3, pp. 639–40.
17. FP 210 implies a crew of some 22 officers and men for a ship the size of the *Warwick* (160 tons). But see Brian Lavery, *The Colonial Merchantman: Susan Constant 1605* (London, Conway Maritime Press, 1998), p. 24.
18. I am using the dimensions from the *Susan Constant* at Jamestown Settlement.
19. See Kingsbury (ed.), vol. 3, p. 526.
20. See Lavery, *The Colonial Merchantman*, pp. 24–8.
21. W. Sears Nickerson, *Land Ho! – 1620: A Seaman's Story of the* Mayflower*, Her Construction, Her Navigation, and Her First Landfall* (Boston, Houghton Mifflin, 1931), pp. 22–32.
22. Lavery, *The Colonial Merchantman*, p. 11.
23. Nickerson, *Land Ho!*, p. 34.
24. Purchas, *Hakluytus Posthumus*, vol. 19, p. 135.
25. Kingsbury (ed.), *Records*, vol. 3, p. 582.
26. FP 299.
27. Kermit Goell (ed.), *A Sea Grammar with the Plaine Exposition of Smiths Accidence for Young Sea-men, Enlarged* (London, Michael Joseph, 1970), p. 48.
28. See 'Wight Island' in John Speed, *The Theatre of the Empire of Great Britaine* (London, 1611), f. 15.
29. John Chandler (ed.), *Travels Through Stuart Britain: The Adventures of John Taylor, the Water Poet* (Stroud, Sutton Publishing, 1999), pp. 95–128.
30. Samuel Eliot Morison (ed.), *Of Plymouth Plantation 1620–1647* by William Bradford (New York, Alfred A. Knopf, 1952), pp. 52–3.

31. From *New Englands Trials* taken from James Horn (ed.), *Captain John Smith: Writings with Other Narratives of Roanoke, Jamestown, and the First Settlement of America* (New York, Library of America, 2007), p. 183.
32. FP 321.
33. Morison (ed.), *Of Plymouth Plantation*, p. 58.
34. Lavery, *The Colonial Merchantman*, pp. 18 and 27.
35. See Sara Read, *Menstruation and the Female Body in Early Modern England* (Basingstoke, Palgrave Macmillan, 2013), pp. 105–21.
36. FP 308. Private correspondence with Beverly Straube, 3 May 2017.
37. Read, *Menstruation*, p. 117.
38. See Jennifer Potter, *The Rose: A True History* (London, Atlantic Books, 2010), p. 349 and pp. 496–7.
39. Emily Cockayne, *Hubbub: Filth, Noise & Stench in England 1600–1770* (New Haven, Yale University Press, 2007), pp. 59–60.
40. Quoted in Keith Thomas, 'Cleanliness and godliness in early modern England', Anthony Fletcher and Peter Roberts (eds), *Religion, Culture and Society in Early Modern Britain* (Cambridge University Press, 1994), p. 58.
41. Gervase Markham, *The English House-Wife. Containing the inward and outward Vertues which ought to be in a compleate Woman* (London, 1631), pp. 2–4, 14, 19, 20, 148, 150–1, and 196.
42. Lavery, *The Colonial Merchantman*, pp. 26–7, 58–9, 83, 86–7; Goell (ed.), *A Sea Grammar*, p. 45.
43. FP 210.
44. Quoted in Cawley, *Unpathed Waters*, pp. 189–191.
45. William Shakespeare, *The Tempest*, edited by Virginia Mason Vaughan and Alden T. Vaughan (London, Arden Shakespeare, 2011), act 2 scene 2, p. 230.
46. Barbour (ed.), *Complete Works*, vol. 3, p. 29.
47. FP 322.
48. Martha W. McCartney, *Virginia Immigrants and Adventurers, 1607–1635: A Biographical Dictionary* (Baltimore, Genealogical Publishing Company, 2007), entry for Paul Jones, p. 430. And see Kingsbury (ed.), *Records*, vol. 4, pp. 232–3.
49. Goell (ed.), *A Sea Grammar*, p. 60.
50. Barbour (ed.), *Complete Works*, p. 21.
51. Goell (ed.), *A Sea Grammar*, p. 60.
52. Shakespeare, *The Tempest*, act 1 scene 1, p. 166.
53. Purchas, *Hakluytus Posthumus*, vol. 19, pp. 5–13.
54. See http://shakespeareoxfordfellow ship.org/bermuda-shipwreck-of-1609/.
55. Goell (ed.), *A Sea Grammar*, p. 51.
56. Personal communication with the author, 31 January 2018.
57. BL Sloane Ms 922, Nehemiah Wallington's Letterbook, f. 901.
58. FP 308.
59. Kingsbury (ed.), *Records*, vol. 1, p. 620.
60. See FP 314, and Kingsbury (ed.), *Records*, vol. 3, p. 639.
61. FP 315.
62. Sir Henry Mainwaring, 'Discourse on Pirates' in *The Council of the Navy Records Society*, 1921–22, vol. 56, The Life and Works of Sir Henry Mainwaring, vol. 2 (Navy Records Society, 1922), pp. 3–49. And see Jennifer Potter, *Strange Blooms: The Curious Lives and Adventures of the John Tradescants* (London, Atlantic Books, 2006), pp. 133–46.
63. See Gwenda Morgan's entry on Captain John Smith in the *Oxford Dictionary of National Biography*, consulted online 5 February 2018.
64. Barbour (ed.), *Complete Works*, vol. 3, p. 186.
65. Mainwaring, 'Discourse on Pirates', p. 34.

66. Patrick Copland, *Virginia's God be thanked, or A Sermon of Thanksgiving for the happie successe of the affayres in Virginia this last yeare* (London, 1622), especially pp. 19–20.

67. Kingsbury (ed.), *Records*, vol. 3, p. 582.

Chapter 9: Land ho!

1. William Strachey, 'A true reportory of the wracke, and redemption of Sir Thomas Gates Knight' in Samuel Purchas, *Hakluytus Posthumus or Purchas His Pilgrimes* (20 vols, Glasgow, James MacLehose, 1906), vol. 19, p. 42.

2. Kermit Goell (ed.), *A Sea Grammar with the Plaine Exposition of Smiths Accidence for Young Sea-men, Enlarged* (London, Michael Joseph, 1970), p. 55.

3. Purchas, *Hakluytus Posthumus*, vol. 18, p. 421.

4. Strachey, 'A true reportory', especially pp. 42–6.

5. 'Observations by Master George Percy, 1607', pp. 5–23 in Lyon Gardiner Tyler, *Narratives of Early Virginia 1606–1625* (New York, Charles Scribner's Sons, 1907), pp. 10–11.

6. David Peterson de Vries, *Voyages from Holland to America AD 1632 to 1644*, trans. Henry C. Murphy (New York, 1853), pp. 48–9; and George Gardyner of Peckham, *A Description of the New World. OR, America Islands and Continent* (London, 1651), p. 97.

7. Purchas, *Hakluytus Posthumus*, vol. 18, p. 423.

8. James Horn, *Captain John Smith, Writings With Other Narratives of Roanoke, Jamestown, and the First English Settlement of America* (New York, Library of America, 2007), p. 9.

9. See Martha W. McCartney, *Virginia Immigrants and Adventurers 1607–1635: A Biographical Dictionary* (Baltimore, Genealogical Publishing Company, 2007), pp. 44–5.

10. Helen C. Rountree, Wayne E. Clark and Kent Mountford, *John Smith's Chesapeake Voyages, 1607–1609* (Charlottesville, Va., University of Virginia Press, 2007), p. 144.

11. Ibid. pp. 154–5.

12. De Vries, *Voyages from Holland*, pp. 48–9.

13. Rountree et al., *John Smith's Chesapeake Voyages*, pp. 159–61.

14. McCartney, *Virginia Immigrants*, pp. 47–8.

15. Susan Myra Kingsbury (ed.), *The Records of the Virginia Company of London* (4 vols, Washington, Library of Congress, 1906–35), vol. 1, p. 414. And see Martha W. McCartney, 'An Early Virginia Census Reprised' in the *Quarterly Bulletin of the Archaeological Society of Virginia*, vol. 54, no. 4, December 1999, pp. 178–96.

16. Conversation with the author at Carter's Grove on 2 April 2017; and see Ivor Noël Hume and Audrey Noël Hume, *The Archaeology of Martin's Hundred* (2 vols, Philadelphia, University of Pennsylvania Museum of Archaeology and Anthropology, 2001), vol. 1, p. 26.

17. Kingsbury (ed.), *Records*, vol. 3, p. 594.

18. McCartney, *Virginia Immigrants*, p. 100.

19. Ralph Hamor, *A True Discourse of Virginia, and the successe of the affaires there till the 18 of June 1614* (London, 1615); online copy: http://www.virtualjamestown.org/exist/cocoon/jamestown/fha/J1004.

20. 'Observations by Master George Percy, 1607', p. 15.

21. Samuel H. Yonge, *The Site of Old "James Towne" 1607–1698* (Richmond, Va., The Hermitage Press, 1907), p. 24.

22. Alice Jane Lippson, Robert L. Lippson, *Life in the Chesapeake Bay* (Baltimore, Johns Hopkins University Press, 1984), pp. 160–1 and *passim*.

23. See Cary Carson et al., 'New World, Real World: Improvising English

Culture in Seventeenth-Century Virginia', *The Journal of Southern History*, vol. 74, no. 1 (February 2008), especially pp. 50–4; and for the 'bridge', see Yonge, *The Site of Old "James Towne"*, p. 31.

Part Two: Virginia

Chapter 10: Arrival at Jamestown

1. Susan Myra Kingsbury (ed.), *The Records of the Virginia Company of London* (4 vols, Washington, Library of Congress, 1906–35), vol. 4, p.178; and vol. 3, p. 302; David Peterson de Vries, *Voyages from Holland to America AD 1632 to 1644*, trans. Henry C. Murphy (New York, 1853), p. 50; and Samuel Purchas, *Hakluytus Posthumus or Purchas His Pilgrimes* (20 vols, Glasgow, James MacLehose, 1906), vol. 19, p. 144.

2. Kingsbury (ed.), *Records*, vol. 4, p. 446; Martha W. McCartney, 'An Early Virginia Census Reprised' in the *Quarterly Bulletin of the Archaeological Society of Virginia*, vol. 54, no. 4, December 1999, pp. 178–96; and Kingsbury (ed), *Records*, vol. 3, p. 243.

3. See http://www.history.ac.uk/gh/baentries.htm.

4. Alden T. Vaughan, 'Powhatans Abroad: Virginia Indians in England' in Robert Appelbaum and John Wood Sweet, *Envisioning an English Empire: Jamestown and the Making of the North Atlantic World* (Philadelphia, University of Pennsylvania Press, 2005), pp. 49–67.

5. Kingsbury (ed.), *Records*, vol. 1. pp. 477 and 489; and vol. 3, pp. 485–9; Philip L. Barbour (ed.), *The Complete Works of Captain John Smith (1580–1631)* (3 vols, Chapel Hill, University of North Carolina Press, 1986), vol. 2, p. 286; and Martha W. McCartney, *A Documentary History of Jamestown Island* (Williamsburg, Colonial

Williamsburg Foundation, 2000), vol. 1, p. 57.

6. See http://www.virtualjamestown.org/Muster.

7. See McCartney, 'An Early Virginia Census', pp. 182–3; and Kingsbury (ed.), *Records*, vol. 1, pp. 506, 546, 549.

8. Ibid. vol. 3, pp. 505–6.

9. Ibid. vol. 3, p. 494.

10. Ibid. vol. 3, p. 505. And see entry on Blaney in Sara B. Bearss et al. (eds), *Dictionary of Virginia Biography* (Richmond, Va., Library of Virginia, 2001), vol. 2.

11. Ferrar Papers, Magdalene College Cambridge Old Library, FP 309; and Kingsbury (ed.), *Records*, vol. 3, p. 494.

12. William Strachey, 'A true reportory of the wracke, and redemption of Sir Thomas Gates Knight' in Purchas, *Hakluytus Posthumus*, vol. 19, p. 44.

13. See Cary Carson et al., 'New World, Real World: Improvising English Culture in Seventeen-Century Virginia', *The Journal of Southern History*, vol. 74, no. 1 (February 2008), pp. 31–88; Cary Carson et al., 'Impermanent Architecture in the Southern American Colonies', *Winterthur Portfolio*, vol. 16 no. 2/3, summer/autumn 1981, pp. 135–96; and Cary Carson, 'Plantation Housing, seventeenth century' in Cary Carson and Carl R. Lounsbury (eds), *The Chesapeake House* (Chapel Hill, University of North Carolina Press, 2013), pp. 85–114.

14. See 'Jamestown Redivivus: An Interview with James Horn' in Donald A. Yerxa, *Recent Themes in Early American History: Historians in Conversation* (Columbia, University of South Carolina Press, 2008), p. 57.

15. Samuel H. Yonge, *The Site of Old "James Towne" 1607–1698* (Richmond, Va., Hermitage Press, 1907), p. 39; and Barbour (ed.), *Complete Works*, vol. 2, p. 225. He later dropped the number to 'about fortie or fiftie severall houses

to keepe us warme and dry', ibid. vol. 2, p. 324.

16. Ibid. vol. 2, p. 325.

17. Strachey, 'A true reportory of the wracke', pp. 5–72.

18. Barbour (ed.), *Complete Works*, vol. 2, p. 262.

19. Alexander Brown, *The Genesis of the United States* (2 vols, New York, Russell & Russell, 1964), vol. 2, p. 835.

20. See Jennifer Potter, *Strange Blooms: The Curious Lives and Adventures of the John Tradescants* (London, Atlantic Books, 2006), pp.104–11.

21. Norman Egbert McClure (ed.), *The Letters of John Chamberlain* (2 vols, Philadelphia, American Philosophical Society, 1939), vol. 2, pp. 188 and 190.

22. McCartney, *A Documentary History*, vol. 1, pp. 46–7; and see William S. Powell, *John Pory/1572–1636, The Life and Letters of a Man of Many Parts* (Chapel Hill, University of North Carolina Press, 1977), p. 83.

23. Kingsbury (ed.), *Records*, vol. 3, p. 302; and see Barbour (ed.), *Complete Works*, vol. 2, p. 262 n.3.

24. McCartney, *A Documentary History*, vol. 2, p. 28.

25. Kingsbury (ed.), *Records*, vol. 3, pp. 298–300; p. 583.

26. FP 336.

27. FP 285.

28. Kingsbury (ed.), *Records*, vol. 1, pp. 513–14; and vol. 3, pp. 441–3.

29. Ibid. vol. 3, p. 485.

30. John Rolfe, *A True Relation of the state of Virginia lefte by Sir Thomas Dale Knight in May last 1616* (New Haven, Yale University Press, 1951, p. 39.

31. Martha W. McCartney, *Virginia Immigrants & Adventurers, 1607–1635: A Biographical Dictionary* (Baltimore, Genealogical Publishing Company, 2007), pp. 167–9.

32. McCartney, *Virginia Immigrants*, pp. 545–7; 606–7. And see McCartney, *A Documentary History*, vol. 2, Study Unit 1 Tract D, pp. 41–52.

33. McCartney, *Virginia Immigrants*, pp. 661–2.

34. Lyon Gardiner Tyler, *The Cradle of the Republic: Jamestown and James River* (Richmond, Va., Whittet & Shepperson, 1900), pp. 15–16; and Carson et al., 'New World, Real World', p. 42.

35. Quoted in Carson et al., *The Chesapeake House*, p. 87.

36. David Cressy, *Birth, Marriage, and Death: Ritual, Religion, and the Life-Cycle in Tudor and Stuart England* (Oxford University Press, 1997), pp. 298–305.

Chapter 11: The Choosing

1. Anon, 'The English Fortune-teller… A brief instruction how to chuse a wife' 1660–1700?, English Broadside Ballad Archive, https://ebba.english.ucsb.edu/ballad/31806/image.

2. Susan Myra Kingsbury (ed.), *The Records of the Virginia Company of London* (4 vols, Washington, Library of Congress, 1906–35), vol. 3, p. 494.

3. Ibid. vol. 3, pp. 505–6.

4. Ibid. vol. 3, p. 583.

5. Ibid. vol. 3, p. 473.

6. Edmund S. Morgan, *American Slavery, American Freedom: The Ordeal of Colonial America* (New York, W. W. Norton & Company, 1975), p. 106.

7. Morgan, *American Slavery*, pp. 115–16.

8. Kingsbury (ed.), *Records*, vol. 2, pp. 102–3; and vol. 4, pp. 231–2.

9. John Camden Hotten, *The Original Lists of Persons of Quality, 1600–1700* (London, Chatto & Windus, 1874), p. 193.

10. See Nell Marion Nugent, *Cavaliers and Pioneers: Abstracts of Virginia Land Patents and Grants 1623–1800* (5 vols, Baltimore, Genealogical Publishing Inc., 1969), vol. 1, pp. xxvi–xxvii.

11. Kingsbury (ed.), *Records*, vol. 3, p. 245.

12. Irene W. D. Hecht, 'The Virginia Muster of 1624/5 as a Source for Demographic History', *William and Mary Quarterly*, third series, vol. 30, no. 1, January 1973, pp. 82–3.

13. Martha W. McCartney, 'An Early Virginia Census Reprised', *Quarterly Bulletin of the Archeological Society of Virginia*, vol. 54, no. 4, December 1999, p. 179.

14. H. R. McIlwaine (ed.), *Minutes of the Council and General Court of Colonial Virginia, 1622–1632, 1670–1676* (Richmond, Va., Virginia State Library, 1624), pp. 79–80.

15. Ibid. p. 115.

16. For a list of ancient planters still alive at the January 1625 muster, see Nugent, *Cavaliers*, vol. 1, pp. xxviii–xxxiv.

17. Kingsbury (ed.), *Records*, vol. 3, pp. 639–40.

18. See http://www.virtualjamestown.org/exist/cocoon/jamestown/fha/J1036.

19. You can consult the census or muster online at: http://www.virtualjamestown.org/Muster/introduction.html.

20. See Ferrar Papers, Magdalene College Cambridge Old Library, FP 295 and Martha W. McCartney, *Virginia Immigrants & Adventurers, 1607–1635: A Biographical Dictionary* (Baltimore, Genealogical Publishing Company, 2007), pp. 768 and 591–2.

21. McIlwaine (ed.), *Minutes*, p. 50.

22. Alexander Brown, *The First Republic in America* (Boston, Houghton, Mifflin and Company, 1898), p. 149.

23. John Camden Hotten, *The Original Lists of Persons of Quality, 1600–1700* (London, Chatto & Windus, 1874), pp. 185, 244, 257.

24. See his biography in McCartney, *Virginia Immigrants*, pp. 264–5.

25. Kingsbury (ed.), *Records*, vol. 4, p. 558. There are no patents for Downeman in Nugent, *Cavaliers*.

26. McIlwaine (ed.), *Minutes*, p. 43, 17, January 1624/5, so contemporary with the 1624/5 muster.

27. Ibid. p. 193.

28. Hotten, *Original Lists*, pp. 170, 172, 216; and see McCartney, *Virginia Immigrants*, pp. 548–9.

29. McIlwaine (ed.), *Minutes*, p. 39. See Chapter 15.

30. FP 309.

31. See for instance Annie Lash Jester, *Domestic Life in Virginia in the Seventeenth Century* (Williamsburg, Va., Virginia 350th Anniversary Celebration Corporation, 1957).

32. J. A. Leo Lemay, *The American Dream of Captain John Smith* (Charlottesville, Va., University Press of Virginia, 1991), pp. 170–1; see Barbour (ed.), *Complete Works*, vol. 2, p. 263.

33. McCartney, *Virginia Immigrants*, pp. 761–2.

34. See http://www.EncyclopediaVirginia.org/Johnston_Mary_1870-1936.

35. Mary Johnston, *To Have and To Hold* (Toronto, George N. Morang & Company, 1900, pp. 13–21.

36. Kingsbury (ed.), vol. 3, pp. 365–7.

37. See http://www.virtualjamestown.org/exist/cocoon/jamestown/fha/J1036.

38. David Cressy, *Birth, Marriage, and Death: Ritual, Religion, and the Life-Cycle in Tudor and Stuart England* (Oxford University Press, 1997), pp. 342–7.

39. University of Virginia, Alderman Library, Charlottesville, Va., Flowerdew Hundred Collection, 44PG77.

40. FP 302.

41. Philip L. Barbour (ed.), *The Complete Works of Captain John Smith (1580–1631)* (3 vols, Chapel Hill, University of North Carolina Press, 1986), vol. 2, p. 386.

42. Anon, 'A Market for young Men', 1695–1703?, English Broadside Ballad Archive, http://ebba.english.ucsb.edu/ballad/21894/image. For wedding celebrations, see Cressy, *Birth, Marriage, and Death*, pp. 350–76.

Chapter 12: Dispersal

1. Susan Myra Kingsbury (ed.), *The Records of the Virginia Company of London* (4 vols, Washington, Library of Congress, 1906–35), vol. 3, p. 493.
2. Ibid. vol. 3, pp. 648–9.
3. Ibid. vol. 3, pp. 534–5. And see Edward S. Morgan, *American Slavery, American Freedom: The Ordeal of Colonial Virginia* (New York, W. W. Norton, 1975), pp. 102–5.
4. Lawrence Price, 'The Maydens of Londons brave adventures' 1623–1661?, English Broadside Ballad Archive, https://ebba.english.ucsb.edu/ballad/30869/image.
5. Kingsbury (ed.), *Records*, vol. 3, p. 308.
6. Wyatt's letters are quoted in retrospect by Edward Waterhouse in his declaration of the state of the colony in 1622, Kingsbury (ed.), *Records*, vol. 3, pp. 549–50.
7. Samuel Purchas, *Hakluytus Posthumus or Purchas His Pilgrimes* (20 vols, Glasgow, James MacLehose, 1906), vol. 19, pp. 144–5.
8. E. Randolph Turner III and Antony F. Opperman, *Searching for Virginia Company Period Sites: An Assessment of Surviving Archaeological Manifestations of Powhatan–English Interactions, A.D. 1607–1624*, draft prepared for the Virginia Department of Historic Resources' Survey and Planning Report Series, 10/1/95 version, 4.13–15; and see Martha W. McCartney, *Virginia Immigrants and Adventurers, 1607–1635: A Biographical Dictionary* (Baltimore, Genealogical Publishing Company, 2007), p. 645.
9. See Rev. A. L. Browne, 'The Bray Family in Gloucestershire', *Transactions of the Bristol and Gloucestershire Archaeological Society*, 1933, vol. 55, pp. 293–315. I am indebted to Liz Jack of www.hidden-heritage.co.uk for directing me to this work. And see John Smith, *Men & Armour for Gloucestershire in 1608* (Gloucester,

Alan Sutton, 1980), especially pp. 135, 144 and 141. Further details from the *Oxford Dictionary of National Biography*, https://doi.org/10.1093/ref:odnb/3295.
10. Philip L. Barbour (ed.), *The Complete Works of Captain John Smith (1580–1631)* (3 vols, Chapel Hill, University of North Carolina Press, 1986), vol. 2, p. 295.
11. McCartney, *Virginia Immigrants*, p. 574; and Kingsbury (ed.), *Records*, vol. 2, p. 107.
12. See Kingsbury (ed.), *Records*, vol. 3, pp. 396–7; and Mrs Henry Lowell Cook, 'Maids for Wives', *Virginia Magazine of History and Biography*, vol. 50, no. 4, October 1942, p. 304.
13. Kingsbury (ed.), *Records*, vol. 1, p. 535.
14. Peter Wilson Coldham, *The Complete Book of Emigrants, 1607–1660* (Baltimore, Genealogical Publishing Co., 1987), pp. 20–21.
15. Martha W. McCartney, 'An Early Virginia Census Reprised' in *Quarterly Bulletin of the Archeological Society of Virginia*, vol. 54, no. 4, December 1999, p. 182.
16. Ferrar Papers, Magdalene College Cambridge Old Library, FP 309.
17. See John Bennett Boddie, 'Edward Bennett of London and Virginia', *William and Mary Quarterly*, vol. 13, no. 2, April 1933, pp. 117–30; and Kingsbury (ed.), *Records*, vol. 1, pp. 534 and 562.
18. Kingsbury (ed.), *Records*, vol. 1, p. 414.
19. See 'Isle of Wight County Records' in *William and Mary Quarterly*, vol. 7, no. 4, April 1899, pp. 205–315.
20. For brief biographies, see McCartney, *Virginia Immigrants*, pp. 125–9. Edward Bennett had two brothers called Richard and Robert and also two nephews of the same name, source of possible confusion between the generations.
21. McCartney, 'An Early Virginia Census', pp. 182 and 186.

22. FP 339.
23. See Martha W. McCartney, 'The Martin's Hundred Potter: English North America's Earliest Known Master of his Trade' in *The Journal of Early Southern Decorative Arts*, winter 1995, vol. 21, no. 2, pp. 139–150; and Beverly A. Straube, 'The Colonial Potters of Tidewater Virginia' in the same issue, pp. 1–40.
24. Kingsbury (ed.), *Records*, vol. 3, p. 506.
25. Charles E. Hatch Jr, *The First Seventeen Years: Virginia, 1607–1624* (Charlottesville, Va., University of Virginia Press, 1957), pp. 104–7; and McCartney, *Virginia Immigrants*, pp. 39–40.
26. Maija Jansson, *Proceedings in Parliament, 1614 (House of Commons)*, (Philadelphia American Philosophical Society, 1988), vol. 172, pp. 269–74.
27. Kingsbury (ed.), *Records*, vol. 3, pp. 592–8.
28. Ibid. vol. 3, pp. 506 and 583.
29. Lyon Gardiner Tyler (ed.), *Narratives of Early Virginia, 1606–1625* (New York, Charles Scribner's Sons, 1907), p. 221.
30. For the early structures at Martin's Hundred see Ivor Noël Hume and Audrey Noël Hume, *The Archaeology of Martin's Hundred* (2 vols, Philadelphia, University of Pennsylvania Museum of Archaeology and Anthropology, 2001), vol. 1, pp. 85–138, and Cary Carson and Carl R. Lounsbury (eds), *The Chesapeake House* (Chapel Hill, University of Carolina Press, 2013), pp. 93–4.
31. Hume and Hume, *The Archaeology of Martin's Hundred*, Site H, the Boyse Homestead *c.* 1619–1622, pp. 100–3.
32. Barbour (ed.), *Complete Works*, vol. 2, p. 291.
33. See Kathleen M. Brown, *Good Wives, Nasty Wenches, and Anxious Patriarchs: Gender, Race and Power in Colonial Virginia* (Chapel Hill, University of North Carolina Press, 1996);

Suzanne Lebsock, *Virginia Women 1600–1945* (Richmond, Va., Virginia State Library, 1987); Sylvia R. Frey and Marian J. Morton, *New World, New Roles: A Documentary History of Women in Pre-Industrial America* (New York, Greenwood Press, 1986); and Kathleen M. Brown, 'Women in Early Jamestown', http://www.virtualjamestown.org/essays/brown_essay.html.
34. Anon, 'The Trappan'd Maiden', 1689–1703?, English Broadside Ballad Archive, http://ebba.english.ucsb.edu/ballad/21947/image.
35. FP 285; and H. R. McIlwaine (ed.), *Journals of the House of Burgesses of Virginia 1619–1658/9* (Richmond, Va., 1915), p. 7.
36. For goats, see Martha W. McCartney, 'An Early Virginia Census Reprised', *Quarterly Bulletin of the Archeological Society of Virginia*, vol. 54, no. 4, December 1999, p. 179; and for cattle: http://www.virtualjamestown.org/exist/cocoon/jamestown/fha/J1034.
37. Joanne Bowen, 'Foodways in the 18th-Century Chesapeake' in Theodore R. Reinhart (ed.), *The Archaeology of 18th-Century Virginia* (Courtland, Va., Archaeological Society of Virginia, 1996), pp. 94–100, brought to my attention by Ywone Edwards-Ingram. And see https://anthropology.si.edu/writteninbone/comic/activity/pdf/Milk_pan.pdf.
38. FP 285.
39. FP 221.
40. FP 378.
41. See, for instance, FP 84, 199, 246 and 348.
42. FP 246.
43. Cary Carson et al., 'Impermanent Architecture in the Southern American Colonies', *Winterthur Portfolio*, vol. 16, no. 2/3, summer/autumn 1981, pp. 135–96; and Carson and Lounsbury (eds), *Chesapeake House*, pp. 67–9, 71, 85, 93–4.

44. http://www.virtualjamestown.org/
exist/cocoon/jamestown/fha/J1042,
and see Chapter 14.

45. Kingsbury (ed.), *Records*, vol. 2, p. 383.

46. Quoted in Carson and Lounsbury
(eds), *Chesapeake House*, p. 90. And see
Lebsock, *Virginia Women*, pp. 17–18.

47. Ralph Hamor, *A True Discourse of the
Present Estate of Virginia, London 1615*
(Amsterdam, Da Capo Press, 1971),
p. 19.

48. Carson and Lounsbury (eds),
Chesapeake House, pp. 94–5.

49. Kingsbury, *Records*, vol. 2, p. 383.

50. Bowen, 'Foodways', p. 95; and Lois
Green Carr, 'Emigration and the
Standard of Living: The Seventeenth
Century Chesapeake', *Journal of
Economic History*, vol. 52 no. 2, June
1992, pp. 271–91.

51. Kingsbury (ed.), *Records*, vol. 3,
pp. 455–8; and FP 251.

52. Kingsbury (ed.), *Records*, vol. 3,
pp. 417–18.

53. Carville Earle, *Geographical Inquiry and
American Historical Problems* (Stanford,
Calif., Stanford University Press,
1992), pp. 25–58.

54. See Sarah Hand Meacham, '"They
will be adjudged by their Drinke…"',
in Debra Meyers and Melanie
Perreault (eds), *Colonial Chesapeake:
New Perspectives* (Lanham, Lexington
Books, 2006), pp. 201–26. For
Thorpe's corn beer, see Kingsbury
(ed.), *Records*, vol. 3, p. 417.

55. FP 145; and *William and Mary
Quarterly*, second series, vol. vi, no. 2,
April 1926, p. 118.

56. https://www.dgif.virginia.gov/wildlife/
information/canebrake-rattlesnake/.

57. George Gardyner of Peckham, *A
Description of the New World. OR,
America Islands and Continent* (London,
1651), pp. 99–100.

58. Louis B. Wright and Virginia Freund
(eds), *The Historie of Travell into Virginia
Britania (1612) By William Strachey, gent.*
(London, Hakluyt Society,

1953), second series, no. 103,
pp. 70–6.

59. H. R. McIlwaine (ed.), *Journals of
the House of Burgesses of Virginia,
1619–1658/59* (Richmond, Va., 1915),
pp. 9–10.

60. Kingsbury, *Records*, vol. 3, p. 446.

61. Ibid. vol. 3, p. 305; and see Martha
W. McCartney, 'George Thorpe's
Inventory of 1624: Virginia's Earliest
Known Appraisal' in Robert Hunter
(ed.), *Ceramics in America 2016.*

62. FP 247.

63. Kingsbury (ed.), *Records*, vol. 3, p. 584.

64. See Helen C. Rountree, *Pocahontas,
Powhatan, Opechancanough: Three
Indian Lives Changed by Jamestown*
(Charlottesville, Va., University of
Virginia Press, 2005), pp. 208–15.

Chapter 13: Catastrophe

1. Patrick Copland, *Virginia's God be
Thanked, or A Sermon of Thanksgiving
for the happie successe of the affayres in
Virginia this last yeare* (London, 1622),
p. 24.

2. My source is: http://5ko.free.fr/en/
easter.php?y=17.

3. See Carole Shammas, 'The Domestic
Environment in Early Modern
England and America' in *Journal of
Social History*, vol. 14, no. 1, autumn
1980, pp. 3–24.

4. Except where stated, the details of
the Indian attack and all quotations
are taken from Edward Waterhouse's
account for the Virginia Company
in Susan Myra Kingsbury (ed.),
*The Records of the Virginia Company
of London* (4 vols, Washington,
Library of Congress, 1906–35), vol.
3, pp. 541–71. A company official,
Waterhouse was not an eyewitness to
the attack.

5. Philip L. Barbour, *The Complete Works
of Captain John Smith (1580–1631)* (3
vols, Chapel Hill, University of North
Carolina Press, 1986), vol. 2, p. 120.

6. Kingsbury (ed.), *Records*, vol. 3, p. 612.

7. http://www.history.org/foundation/journal/winter07/A%20Trewe%20Relation.pdf; and Bernard W. Sheehan, *Savagism and Civility: Indians and Englishmen in Colonial Virginia* (Cambridge, Cambridge University Press, 1980), p. 169.

8. Barbour (ed.), *Complete Works*, vol. 1, p. 166. See Helen C. Rountree, *Pocahontas, Powhatan, Opechancanough, Three Indian Lives Changed by Jamestown* (Charlottesville, Va., University of Virginia Press, 2005), pp. 150–1.

9. Martha W. McCartney, *Virginia Immigrants and Adventurers, 1607–1635: A Biographical Dictionary* (Baltimore, Genealogical Publishing Company, 2007), p. 634; and Kingsbury (ed.), *Records*, vol. 2, p. 93 and vol. 1, p. 166.

10. For the story of Waters, see Barbour (ed.), *Complete Works*, vol. 2, pp. 308–9.

11. Barbour (ed.), *Complete Works*, vol. 2, p. 295.

12. Ibid. vol. 2, pp. 295–6.

13. Ibid. vol. 2, p. 309. Kingsbury (ed.), *Records*, vol. 4, p. 98 refers to 'aboute twenty' English prisoners.

14. Aside from those listed among the dead at Martin's Hundred and Edward Bennett's plantation, just one other 'maid' appears in the list of those killed, at the house of Master Waters, together with a boy and a child. Waters and his wife were in fact taken prisoner and later escaped but no mention is made of a maid escaping with them (Barbour (ed.), *Complete Works*, vol. 2, pp. 308–9).

15. Ivor Noël Hume and Audrey Noël Hume, *The Archaeology of Martin's Hundred, Part I Interpretive Studies* (Philadelphia, University of Pennsylvania Museum of Archaeology and Anthropology, 2001); and see these articles by Ivor Noël Hume in *National Geographic*: 'First Look at a Lost Virginia Settlement', vol. 155, no. 6 of June 1979, pp. 734–67; and 'New Clues to an Old Mystery', vol. 161 no. 1 of January 1982, pp. 52–77.

16. Noël Hume, 'First Look', p. 762.

17. Hume and Hume, *The Archaeology of Martin's Hundred*, Part 1, pp. 65–7, 70–84 and *passim*.

18. Hume, 'New Clues', pp. 72–6.

19. Conversation with Nicholas Luccketti at Martin's Hundred/Carter's Grove, Sunday 2 April 2017.

20. Hume and Hume, *The Archaeology of Martin's Hundred*, Part 1, p. 71.

21. Barbour (ed.), *Complete Works*, vol. 2, pp. 297–8; Kingsbury, *Records* vol. 3. pp. 555–6; and Rountree, *Pocahontas*, p. 213.

22. Kingsbury (ed.), *Records*, vol. 3, p. 554.

23. Ferrar Papers, Magdalene College Cambridge Old Library, FP 309.

24. Kingsbury (ed.), *Records*, vol. 4, pp. 515–16.

25. McCartney, *Virginia Immigrants*, pp. 545–7.

26. H. R. McIlwaine (ed.), *Minutes of the Council and General Court of Colonial Virginia, 1622–1632, 1670–1676* (Richmond, Va., Virginia State Library, 1924), p. 131; and Kingsbury (ed.), *Records*, vol. 3, p. 570.

27. Ibid. vol. 3, pp. 609–12.

28. Ibid. vol. 3, pp. 611–15.

29. Ibid. vol. 3, p. 656.

30. Norman Egbert McClure (ed.), *The Letters of John Chamberlain* (2 vols, Philadelphia, American Philosophical Society, 1939), vol. 2, p. 446.

31. Kingsbury (ed.), *Records*, vol. 3, pp. 666–73.

32. Kingsbury (ed.), *Records*, vol. 3, pp. 666–73 and 541–71.

Chapter 14: The End of the Affair

1. Beverly A. Straube, '"Unfitt for any moderne service"? Arms and Armour from James Fort', *Post-Medieval Archaeology*, vol. 40, no. 1, 2006, pp. 33–61.

2. Edmund S. Morgan, *American Slavery, American Freedom: The Ordeal of Colonial*

Endnotes

Virginia (New York, W. W. Norton & Company Inc., 1975), p. 106.

3. Susan Myra Kingsbury (ed.), *The Records of the Virginia Company of London* (4 vols, Washington, Library of Congress, 1906–35), vol. 3, p. 494.

4. John Camden Hotten, *The Original Lists of Persons of Quality, 1600–1700* (London, Chatto & Windus, 1874), pp. 175, 174.

5. Martha W. McCartney, *Jamestown People to 1800* (Baltimore, Genealogical Publishing Company, 2012), p. 11.

6. Philip L. Barbour (ed.), *The Complete Works of Captain John Smith (1580–1631)* (3 vols, Chapel Hill, University of North Carolina Press, 1986), vol. 3, p. 218.

7. See Morgan, *American Slavery*, pp. 117–23.

8. Martha W. McCartney, *Virginia Immigrants and Adventurers, 1607–1635: A Biographical Dictionary* (Baltimore, Genealogical Publishing Company, 2007), p. 140.

9. Hotten, *Original Lists*, pp. 174–5.

10. Martha W. McCartney, *Documentary History of Jamestown Island* (3 vols, Williamsburg, Va., Colonial Williamsburg Foundation, 2000), vol. 1, pp. 78–81; and see discussion of landownership in vol. 2, Study Unit 1; and land patents in Nell Marion Nugent, *Cavaliers and Pioneers: Abstracts of Virginia Land Patents and Grants 1623–1800* (5 vols, Richmond, Va., Dietz Printing Co., 1934), vol. 1, pp. 3 and 10.

11. Kingsbury (ed.), *Records*, vol. 3, p. 570.

12. Ibid. vol. 4, p. 98 and 473.

13. In January 1623/4, when Blaney testified in court about a bargain he had witnessed, he gave his age as 'about 28 yeares'. H. R. McIlwaine (ed.), *Minutes of the Council and General Court of Colonial Virginia, 1622–1632, 1670–1676* (Richmond, Va., Virginia State Library, 1924), p. 9.

14. Kingsbury, *Records*, vol. 4, p. 111.

15. Martha W. McCartney, *Virginia Immigrants*, p. 140. McIlwaine (ed.), *Minutes*, pp. 39–40 and 46.

16. Morgan, *American Slavery*, p. 120, and n.53. Nugent's *Cavaliers* (p. 10) mentions Blaney only once in Dr Pott's 1628 patent, as lately having 'tenure' of ground adjacent to Pott's.

17. 'Virginia in 1626–7' in *Virginia Magazine of History and Biography*, vol. 16, 1908, pp. 30–1.

18. See letter from George Sandys to John Ferrar in Kingsbury (ed.), *Records*, vol. 4, pp. 106–7.

19. McIlwaine, *Minutes*, p. 121, and see p. 93.

20. Norman Egbert McClure (ed.), *The Letters of John Chamberlain* (2 vols, Philadelphia, American Philosophical Society, 1939), vol. 2, p. 492.

21. For a full discussion of the Virginia Company's disintegration, see Wesley Frank Craven, *Dissolution of the Virginia Company: The Failure of a Colonial Experiment* (Gloucester, Mass., Peter Smith, 1964).

22. These are the closing words to James I's *A Counterblaste to Tobacco*, published in 1604 (Amsterdam, Da Capo Press, 1969).

23. See Kingsbury, *Records*, vol. 4, pp. 228–39; and Emily Rose, 'The Politics of Pathos: Richard Frethorne's Letters Home' in Robert Appelbaum and John Wood Sweet, *Envisioning an English Empire: Jamestown and the Making of the North Atlantic World* (Philadelphia, University of Pennsylvania Press, 2005), pp. 105–8.

24. Kingsbury (ed.), *Records*, vol. 4, pp. 232–3.

25. Rose, 'The Politics of Pathos', pp. 92–108.

26. Kingsbury (ed.), *Records*, vol. 4, 41–2.

27. Ibid. vol. 4, pp. 58–62.

28. Hotten, *Original Lists*, p. 193. Listed among the dead at Martin's Hundred between April 1623 and February 1624 was 'Richard Frethram' – Richard Frethorne, perhaps?

29. http://www.virtualjamestown.org/exist/cocoon/jamestown/fha/J1042.
30. Craven, *Dissolution*, p. 206.
31. Ibid. p. 304.
32. See 'Harvey's Declaration: A Briefe Declaration of the State of Virginia at my comminge from thence in February 1624', *Collections of the Massachusetts Historical Society*, Fourth Series (Boston, 1871) vol. 9, pp. 60–73.
33. Theodore K. Rabb's biography of Sandys in *Oxford Dictionary of National Biography*, consulted online 22 July 2016.
34. From: http://www.britishlistedbuildings.co.uk/101264324-church-of-st-augustine-northbourne#.WeDPBIZrxE4.
35. Joyce Ransome, *The Web of Friendship: Nicholas Ferrar and Little Gidding* (Cambridge, James Clarke & Co., 2011), pp. 46–9.
36. Kingsbury (ed.), *Records*, vol. 4, p.14.
37. Ibid. vol. 3, p. 530.
38. Ibid. vol. 3, pp. 648–9.
39. Ibid. vol. 4, p. 15.
40. At the 'official' rate of three shillings per pound of tobacco, this represents just £300. In fact the actual market value was very much less.
41. Kingsbury (ed.), *Records*, vol. 4, pp. 264–6.
42. Ibid. vol. 4, p. 453.
43. See Peter Wilson Coldham, *The Complete Book of Emigrants 1607–1660* (Baltimore, Genealogical Publishing Co. Ltd, 1987), pp. 47 and 48.
44. McIlwaine (ed.), *Minutes*, p. 121; Kingsbury (ed.), *Records*, vol. 3, p. 505.
45. Ibid. vol. 4, pp. 564–5.
46. McIlwaine (ed.), *Minutes*, p. 57.
47. Ibid. p. 59.
48. The deed is quoted in full in R. J. Eldridge, *Newport Isle of Wight in Bygone Days* (Newport, Isle of Wight County Press, 1952), pp. 30 and 82.
49. William Bullock, *Virginia Impartially Examined* (London, 1649), pp. 53–4.

Chapter 15: The Crossbow Maker's Sister

1. See Chapter 4 for more on the links between Erasmus Finch, George Thorpe and other inhabitants of the Strand.
2. H. R. McIlwaine (ed.), *Minutes of the Council and General Court of Colonial Virginia, 1622–1632, 1670–1676* (Richmond, Va., Virginia State Library, 1924), p. 36.
3. Philip L. Barbour (ed.), *The Complete Works of Captain John Smith (1580–1631)* (3 vols, Chapel Hill, University of North Carolina Press, 1986), vol. 2, p. 295.
4. McIlwaine (ed.), *Minutes*, p. 47.
5. See https://www.nps.gov/jame/learn/historyculture/jamestown-and-plymouth-compare-and-contrast.htm.
6. Susan Myra Kingsbury (ed.), *The Records of the Virginia Company of London* (4 vols, Washington, Library of Congress, 1906–35), vol. 3, p. 567.
7. Barbour (ed.), *Complete Works*, vol. 2, p. 303; and Kingsbury, *Records*, vol. 3, pp. 611–15.
8. John Camden Hotten, *The Original Lists of Persons of Quality, 1600–1700* (London, Chatto & Windus, 1874), p. 171.
9. My source for much of the detail about Jordan's Journey comes from Martha W. McCartney, *Jordan's Point, Virginia: Archaeology in Perspective, Prehistoric to Modern Times* (Richmond, Va., Virginia Department of Historic Resources, 2011).
10. Martha W. McCartney, *Virginia Immigrants and Adventurers 1607–1635: A Biographical Dictionary* (Baltimore, Genealogical Publishing Company, 2007), pp. 59–60.
11. See McIlwaine (ed.), *Minutes*, p. 31; and Chapter 16.
12. McCartney, *Jordan's Point*, pp. 5–8.
13. See Helen C. Rountree, *Pocahontas, Powhatan, Opechancanough: Three*

Indian Lives Changed by Jamestown (Charlottesville, Va., University of Virginia Press, 2005), pp. 54, 199–201.

14. Jeremy Boulton, 'The poor among the rich: paupers and the parish in the West End, 1600-1724' in Paul Griffiths and Mark S. R. Jenner (eds), *Londinopolis: Essays in the Cultural and Social History of Early Modern London* (Manchester, Manchester University Press, 2000), p. 207.

15. Hotten, *Original Lists*, pp. 209–13.

16. McCartney, *Virginia Immigrants*, pp. 193–4.

17. Barbour (ed.), *Complete Works*, vol. 2, p. 295.

18. See Kingsbury (ed.), *Records*, vol. 4, pp. 218-20; and McCartney, *Virginia Immigrants*, pp. 290-1, 433-4 and 566.

19. See McIlwaine (ed.), *Minutes*, pp. 41–2.

20. Ibid. pp. 88–9, court hearing of 9 January 1625/6.

21. McCartney, *Jordan's Point*, pp. x–xii.

22. Ibid. pp. 61–81, amplified by a visit to the Virginia Department of Historic Resources at Richmond.

23. Kingsbury (ed.), *Records*, vol. 4, p. 233.

24. Details refined in personal correspondence with Beverly Straube, 2 January 2018.

25. See Cary Carson et al., 'New World, Real World: Improvising English Culture in Seventeen-Century Virginia', *The Journal of Southern History*, vol. 74, no. 1 (February 2008), p. 88.

26. H. R. McIlwaine (ed.), *Journals of the House of Burgesses of Virginia, 1619–1658/59* (Richmond, Va., 1915), p. 13.

Chapter 16: The Planter's Wife

1. Ferrar Papers, Magdalene College Cambridge Old Library, FP 309.

2. Email from Steven Hobbs FSA, archivist at the Wiltshire and Swindon archives, 20 October 2015, confirming that Bridgett, daughter of John Croft, was baptized on 12 November 1601 in the church of St Peter at Britford, Wiltshire.

3. Much of my information on John Wilkins comes from an unpublished but meticulously referenced manuscript by W. E. Wilkins, *John Wilkins of Northampton County, c. 1599 -1650*, shown to me on 6 April 2017 by Nancy Harwood Garrett.

4. John Frederick Dorman (ed.), *Adventurers of Purse and Person, Virginia 1607-1624/5*, fourth edition (3 vols, Baltimore, Genealogical Publishing Co., 2007), vol. 3, pp. 573–4.

5. Susan Myra Kingsbury (ed.), *The Records of the Virginia Company of London* (4 vols, Washington, Library of Congress, 1906–35), vol. 3, pp. 609–11.

6. Helen C. Rountree, *Pocahontas, Powhatan, Opechancanough: Three Indian Lives Changed by Jamestown* (Charlottesville, Va., University of Virginia Press, 2005), p. 209.

7. Kingsbury (ed.), *Records*, vol. 3, pp. 656–7.

8. John Camden Hotten (ed.), *The Original Lists of Persons of Quality, 1600- 1700* (London, Chatto & Windus, 1874) , pp. 189, 265.

9. See Nell Marion Nugent, *Cavaliers and Pioneers, Abstracts of Virginia Land Patents and Grants 1623-1666* (Richmond, Va., 1934), vol. 1, p. 46.

10. Susie M. Ames (ed.), *County Court Records of Accomack-Northampton, Virginia, 1632-1640* (Washington, American Historical Association, 1954), p. 56.

11. Susie M. Ames, *Studies of the Virginia Eastern Shore in the Seventeenth Century* (Richmond, Va., Dietz Press, 1940), p. 2.

12. Philip L. Barbour (ed.), *The Complete Works of Captain John Smith (1580-1631)* (3 vols, Chapel Hill, University of North Carolina Press, 1986), vol. 1, pp. 224–6.

13. For the settlement's history see James R. Perry, *The Formation of a Society on Virginia's Eastern Shore, 1615-1655*

(Chapel Hill, University of North Carolina Press, 1990).

14. Samuel Purchas, *Hakluytus Posthumus or Purchas his Pilgrimes* (20 vols, Glasgow, James MacLehose, 1906), vol. 19, pp. 90–5.

15. Kingsbury (ed.), *Records*, vol. 3, p. 304.

16. Perry, *Formation of a Society*, p. 24.

17. Appendix V in William Meade (ed.), *Old Churches, Ministers and Families of Virginia*, facsimile of 1861 edition (Baltimore, Genealogical Publishing Company, 1966), vol. 2, pp. 430–3.

18. See Martha W. McCartney, 'An Early Virginia Census Reprised' in *Quarterly Bulletin of the Archeological Society of Virginia*, vol. 54, no. 4, December 1999, pp. 178–196.

19. Ralph T. Whitelaw, *Virginia's Eastern Shore: A History of Northampton and Accomack Counties* (Gloucester, Mass., Peter Smith, 1968), vol.1, pp. 167–80, and 214–21.

20. Nell Marion Nugent, *Cavaliers and Pioneers, Abstracts of Virginia Land Patents and Grants 1623–1666* (Richmond, Va., 1934), vol. 1, p. 84.

21. Ames (ed.), *County Court Records, 1632–1640*, p. 31.

22. http://www.virtualjamestown.org/ Muster/muster24.html.

23. William Waller Hening, *The Statutes at large… Laws of Virginia* (New York, 1823), vol. 1, p. 203. Wilkins is wrongly recorded as John Wilkinson; and see Ames, *County Court Records, 1632–1640*, p. 2.

24. Ames (ed.), *County Court Records, 1632–1640*, p. 8.

25. Susie M. Ames (ed.), *County Court Records of Accomack-Northampton, Virginia, 1640–1645* (Charlottesville, Va., University Press of Virginia, 1973), pp. 275–6; and Wilkins, *John Wilkins*, pp. 8–9.

26. Hotten, *Original Lists*, pp. 188–9; and 262–5.

27. See Nugent, *Cavaliers*, vol. 1, p. 9.

28. H. R. McIlwaine (ed.), *Minutes of the Council and General Court of Colonial Virginia, 1622–1632, 1670–1676* (Richmond, Va., 1924), p. 50.

29. Martha W. McCartney, *Virginia Immigrants and Adventurers 1607–1635: A Biographical Dictionary* (Baltimore, Genealogical Publishing Company, 2007), pp. 282–3; and Edmund S. Morgan, *American Slavery, American Freedom: The Ordeal of Colonial Virginia* (New York, Norton, 1975), pp. 119–20.

30. Kingsbury (ed.), *Records*, vol. 3, p. 242.

31. See http://www.virtualjamestown.org/ Muster/muster24.html; and Wilkins, *John Wilkins*, p. 6.

32. McIlwaine (ed.), *Minutes*, p. 50.

33. Ibid. pp. 139–40, and pp. 141–2.

34. Ibid. p. 148.

35. Ibid. p. 142.

36. McCartney, *Virginia Immigrants*, p. 283. From Virginia he moved on to the West Indies.

37. http://espl-genealogy.org/MilesFiles/ site/p133.htm#i13289.

38. Nugent, *Cavaliers*, p. 84, 46, 56, 152 (the Surry land was at first mistakenly recorded as lying in Accomack County); and Whitelaw, *Virginia's Eastern Shore*, vol. 1, pp. 161–3; Ames (ed.), *County Court Records*, vol. 1, p. 170.

39. Nugent, *Cavaliers*, p. 46 (his negro); and Ames, *County Court Records, 1632–1640*, p. xxxiii (windmill).

40. Ames (ed.), *County Court Records, 1632–1640*, pp. xxxiii–iv.

41. Ibid. *1640–1645*, pp. 7 and 51–2.

42. Ibid. *1640–1645*, pp. 5 and 19; and see Wilkins, *John Wilkins*, pp. 44–5.

43. Ames (ed.), *County Court Records, 1640–1645*, pp. 165–7.

44. Ibid. *1632–40*, pp. 20–2. The original manuscript can be found at the court house in Eastville, Va., *Northampton County Orders, Wills, Deeds* etc., Book 1, *1632–1640*, p. 35, Accawmack County, 8 September 1634.

45. Ames (ed.), *County Court Records, 1640–1645*, p. 292.

46. Ibid. *1640–1645*, pp. 22, 26.

47. Dorman (ed.), *Adventurers*, vol. 3, p. 574.

48. Ames (ed.), *County Court Records, 1640–1645*, p. 326.

49. Northampton County Orders, Deeds & Wills etc, 1645–1651, Manuscript volume, Eastville, Va., f. 239.

50. Wilkins, *John Wilkins*, pp. 47–8.

51. Personal communication with the author, 29 September 2017.

52. Ames (ed.), *County Court Records, 1640–1645*, p. 202.

Chapter 17: The Cordwainer's Daughter

1. I draw heavily on David R. Ransome, 'Village Tensions in Early Virginia: Sex, Land, and Status at the Neck of Land in the 1620s', *Historical Journal*, vol. 43 no. 2, June 2000, pp. 365–81.

2. Centre for Buckinghamshire Studies, Aylesbury, Will of Thomas Hoare, 31 January 1626/7, D/A/Wf/26/299.

3. Philip L. Barbour (ed.), *The Complete Works of Captain John Smith (1580–1631)* (3 vols, Chapel Hill, University of North Carolina Press, 1986), vol. 2, pp. 35–7.

4. See for instance H. R. McIlwaine (ed.), *Minutes of the Council and General Court of Colonial Virginia, 1622–1632, 1670–1676* (Richmond, Va., 1924), p. 106. Even when appointed as a commissioner of the upper parts in 1626, he appears as plain Thomas Harris, unlike the other five who are referred to as 'Mr' or given military titles.

5. John Camden Hotten, *The Original Lists of Persons of Quality, 1600–1700* (London, Chatto & Windus, 1874), pp. 170, 203.

6. McIlwaine (ed.), *Minutes*, p. 129; and see Ransome, 'Village Tensions', pp. 371–2 and 378.

7. Martha W. McCartney, *Virginia Immigrants and Adventurers 1607–1635: A Biographical Dictionary* (Baltimore, Genealogical Publishing Company, 2007), pp. 761–2.

8. John F. Dorman (ed.), *Adventurers of Purse and Person: Virginia, 1607–1624/5*, fourth edition (3 vols, Baltimore, Genealogical Publishing Inc., 2004–7), vol. 2, pp. 264–7.

9. The history of Bermuda Hundred is taken from E. Randolph Turner III and Antony F. Opperman, *Searching for Virginia Company Period Sites: An Assessment of Surviving Archaeological Manifestations of Powhatan–English Interactions, A.D. 1607–1624*, draft prepared for the Virginia Department of Historic Resources' Survey and Planning Report Series, 10/1/95 version, pp. 5.17–5.19.

10. Martha W. McCartney, 'An Early Virginia Census Reprised', *Quarterly Bulletin of the Archeological Society of Virginia*, vol. 54, no. 4, December 1999, pp. 182 and 184.

11. Susan Myra Kingsbury (ed.), *The Records of the Virginia Company of London* (4 vols, Washington, Library of Congress, 1906–35), vol. 3, pp. 609 and 611.

12. Ibid. vol. 4, p. 259.

13. I have assumed that these refer to the same ship, which arrived in August 1620.

14. David Ransome speculates that she might have gone to the College Land in Henricus as the wife of Ezekiel Raughton, but Margaret Bourdman sailed by the *Marmaduke*, not the *Warwick*: Ransome, 'Village Tensions', p. 377.

15. Margaret Bourdman was baptized on 4 February 1599/60 at Bilton Ainsty, York, England. Her father was Addam Bourdman. I have found two sisters with the same father: Elsabeth Bourdman, baptized at Bilton

Ainsty on 13 June 1602 and Esabell Bordman, baptized 1 Sept 1605 at Bilton Ainsty.

16. See John Nichols, *The Progresses, Processions, and Magnificent Festivities of King James the First* (4 vols, London, Society of Antiquaries, 1828), vol. 2, p. 126.

17. Ferrar Papers, Magdalene College Cambridge Old Library, FP 309.

18. http://www.virtualjamestown.org/ Muster/muster24.html. The two exceptions were Margarett Pilkinton, living in the muster of Treasurer George Sandys, and Thomas Graye's wife, living with him at James City.

19. McIlwaine (ed.), *Minutes*, p. 36.

20. Ibid. p. 47.

21. H. R. McIlwaine (ed.), *Journals of the House of Burgesses of Virginia, 1619–1658/9* (Richmond, Va., 1915), pp. viii, xv and xix.

22. McIlwaine (ed.), *Minutes*, p. 106.

23. Ibid. p. 151.

24. Ibid. p. 476.

25. McIlwaine (ed.), *Minutes*, pp. 96–7.

26. Ibid. p. 129.

27. Nell Marion Nugent, *Cavaliers and Pioneers, Abstracts of Virginia Land Patents and Grants 1623–1666* (Richmond, Va., 1934), vol. 1, pp. 33, 37, 60 and 101; and McCartney, *Virginia Immigrants*, p. 58.

28. Nugent, *Cavaliers*, p. 60.

29. Ibid. pp. 33 and 101.

30. Ibid. p. 33.

31. No patent survives in William Vincent's name and there is no record of precisely when he died, but his lands feature in two patents for the area: see Nugent, *Cavaliers*, pp. 87 and 111.

32. We know she was not the mother of Mary Harris (see Thomas Hoare's will, discussed later) and she would have been at least forty-six when William Harris was born.

33. Dorman, vol. 2, pp. 264–7.

34. McIlwaine (ed.), *Journals*, p. xxii. Thomas Lyggon and William Harris both represented Henricus at the 1656 assembly, Lyggon's only appearance as a burgess.

35. Ibid. p. 101. For his election as burgess, see pp. xxi, xxii, xxiii and 99.

36. Personal communication with the author, 30 June 2017.

37. Personal communication with the author, 24 June 2017.

38. Centre for Buckinghamshire Studies, Aylesbury, Will of Thomas Hoare, 31 January 1626/7, D/A/Wf/26/299. The scribe throws in many spare vowels, some of which I have omitted.

Chapter 18: Captured by Indians

1. Ferrar Papers, Magdalene College Cambridge Old Library, FP 306.

2. H. R. McIlwaine (ed.), *Minutes of the Council and General Court of Colonial Virginia, 1622–1632, 1670–1676* (Richmond, Va., 1924), p. 181.

3. But see J. Frederick Fausz, 'The missing women of Martin's Hundred', *American History*, vol. 33, no. 1, March 1998, p. 56, http://www.historynet. com/powhatan-uprising-of-1622.htm.

4. All my quotations are taken from *A Narrative of the Captivity and Removes of Mrs Mary Rowlandson* (Fairfield, Washington, Ye Galleon Press, 1974), first published in 1682.

5. Helen C. Rountree, *Pocahontas's People: The Powhatan Indians of Virginia Through Four Centuries* (Norman, University of Oklahoma Press, 1990), p. 110.

6. Ibid. p. 12.

7. Susan Myra Kingsbury (ed.), *The Records of the Virginia Company of London* (4 vols, Washington, Library of Congress, 1906–35), vol. 4, p. 238.

8. Philip L. Barbour (ed.), *The Complete Works of Captain John Smith (1580–1631)* (3 vols, Chapel Hill, University of North Carolina Press, 1986), vol. 2, pp. 309–10.

9. Kingsbury (ed.), *Records*, vol. 2, pp. 115–16.
10. Ibid. vol. 2, p. 311.
11. *A Narrative of the Captivity*, p. 31.
12. Barbour (ed.), *Complete Works*, vol. 2, pp. 310–15.
13. Ibid. vol. 2, p. 319.
14. Helen C. Rountree, *Pocahontas, Powhatan, Opechancanough: Three Indian Lives Changed by Jamestown* (Charlottesville, Va., University of Virginia Press, 2005), pp. 239–40; Sylvia R. Frey and Marian J. Morton, *New World, New Roles: A Documentary History of Women in Pre-Industrial America* (New York, Greenwood, 1986), pp. 49–51; Rountree, *Pocahontas's People*, pp. 3–14.
15. See chapter 8, 'The "Pamunkey": the York River Drainage' in Helen C. Rountree, Wayne E. Clark and Kent Mountford, *John Smith's Chesapeake Voyages, 1607–1609* (Charlottesville, Va., University of Virginia Press, 2007), pp. 164–84.
16. *A Narrative of the Captivity*, p. 57.
17. Ibid. pp. 104–5.
18. Ibid. p. 73.
19. Barbour (ed.), *Complete Works*, vol. 1, pp.161–2.
20. Louis B. Wright and Virginia Freund (eds), *The Historie of Travell into Virginia Britania (1612) By William Strachey, gent.* (London, Hakluyt Society, 1953), pp. 174–207.
21. For a full appreciation of the cultural differences between English settlers and their Indian hosts, see Helen C. Rountree's chapter 'Merging into the Indian World', taken from her forthcoming book, *Roanokes and Others: The Algonquian-speaking Indians of the Carolina Sounds*. I am extremely grateful to the author for letting me read the chapter in draft.
22. Kingsbury (ed.), *Records*, vol. 4, p. 238.
23. Barbour (ed.), *Complete Works*, vol. 1, p. 175.
24. Kingsbury (ed.), *Records*, vol. 4, pp. 98–9.
25. Ibid. vol. 2, p. 483. For a clear account of these events, see Rountree, *Pocahontas*, pp. 218–20.
26. Kingsbury (ed.), *Records*, vol. 4, pp. 221–2.
27. Ibid. vol. 4, pp. 102–3.
28. Ibid. vol. 4, p. 473.
29. Ibid. vol. 1, p. 516.
30. Ibid. vol. 4, p. 110.
31. The character assessment of Pott comes from Martha W. McCartney, *Land Ownership Patterns and Early Development in Middle Plantation* (Williamsburg, CWF Research report series 1724, 2010), pp. 6–7.
32. Library of Virginia, Richmond, Va., letter of Gov. John Harvey 1630, 36138, Box 142 (Folder 1), 1168988. Pott and Harvey were declared enemies.
33. Kingsbury (ed.), *Records*, vol. 2, pp. 519–28.
34. See John Camden Hotten, *The Original Lists of Persons of Quality, 1600–1700* (London, Chatto & Windus, 1874), pp. 181 and 239.
35. FP 569. See Ivor Noël Hume and Audrey Noël Hume, *The Archaeology of Martin's Hundred, Part I, Interpretative Studies* (Philadelphia, University of Pennsylvania Museum of Archaeology and Anthropology, 2001), pp. 40–2.
36. See Martha W. McCartney, *Virginia Immigrants and Adventurers, 1607–1635: A Biographical Dictionary* (Baltimore, Genealogical Publishing Company, 2007), p. 13. The 1624 census omitted some 227 names and the 1625 muster at least 44.
37. McIlwaine (ed.), *Minutes*, p. 128.
38. Ibid. p. 172.
39. Ibid. p. 181.
40. *A Narrative of the Captivity*, pp. 108–9.
41. See Rountree, *Roanokes*.
42. Rountree, *Pocahontas's People*, p. 8.
43. McIlwaine (ed.), *Minutes*, p. 70.

44. Ibid. p. 153.
45. Rountree, *Roanokes.*
46. Wright and Freund (eds), *The Historie of Travell*, pp.112–13.
47. See Canny, 'The permissive frontier', pp. 30–4.
48. Records for St Margaret's parish, Westminster, from findmypast.co.uk, which also record the burials of William Jacksons in 1634 and 1636. A number of John Jacksons were buried here around this time, including one in 1632.

Endnote: Return to Jamestown

1. Ivor Noël Hume and Audrey Noël Hume, *The Archaeology of Martin's Hundred, Part I, Interpretative Studies* (Philadelphia, University of Pennsylvania Museum of Archaeology and Anthropology, 2001), p. 122; and pp. 5–6, 39–44, 122–6.
2. Artefacts from Virginia's Department of Historic Resources, 44PG300 and 44PG307.
3. Philip L. Barbour, *The Complete Works of Captain John Smith (1580–1631)* (3 vols, Chapel Hill, University of North Carolina Press, 1986), vol. 1, pp. 224.
4. See http://www.virtualjamestown.org/ajohnsonRP.html.
5. See Carville V. Earle, 'Environment, Disease, and Mortality in Early Virginia' in Thad W. Tate and David L. Ammerman (eds), *The Chesapeake in the Seventeenth Century* (Chapel Hill, University of Carolina Press, 1979), p. 125.
6. Susan Myra Kingsbury (ed.), *The Records of the Virginia Company of London* (4 vols, Washington, Library of Congress, 1906–35), vol. 4, pp. 236–7.
7. H. R. McIlwaine (ed.), *Minutes of the Council and General Court of Colonial Virginia, 1622–1632, 1670–1676* (Richmond, Va., 1924), p. 80.
8. Kingsbury (ed.), *Records*, vol. 4, p. 235.
9. Anon, 'A Market for young Men', 1695–1703?, English Broadside Ballad Archive, http://ebba.english.ucsb.edu/ballad/21894/image.

Illustrations

p. ix *Ciuis Londinensis Filia* by Wenceslaus Hollar (*University of Toronto Wenceslaus Hollar Digital Collection*); p. 11 Detail from the 'Agas' map of London, *c*.1560; p. 17 East Cowes, Isle of Wight, sketched by Lambert Doomer; p. 26 Map of the Isle of Wight engraved by Jodocus Hondius, 1611; p. 29 Map from: *A Mapp or Description of the River of Thames from Westminster to the Sea ...* by Jonas Moore, 1662 (© *The British Library Board*); p. 39 *View of Gravesend from the river in 1662,* from Robert Peirce Cruden's *The History of the Town of Gravesend in the County of Kent* (London, 1843); p. 46 Illustration from 'Fill Gut, & Pinchbelly', a broadside ballad of 1620; p. 51 *The kitchen-maid* by Wenceslaus Hollar (*University of Toronto Wenceslaus Hollar Digital Collection*); pp 60–1 *Long View of London from Bankside* by *Wenceslaus Hollar*, 1647 (*Wikimedia Commons*); p. 66 *Tothill Fields* by Wenceslaus Hollar (*University of Toronto Wenceslaus Hollar Digital Collection*); p. 71 *The Englishman's Arrival in Virginia: 1590*, engraving by Theodore de Bry, after John White (*Universal History Archive/Getty Images*); p. 81 Virginia Company broadside of 1616 (*Library of Virginia*); p. 97 Illustration depicting the kidnap of Pocahontas, 1619 (© *John Carter Brown Library*); p. 101 Portrait of Pocahontas by Simon de Passe, 1616 (*Hulton Archive/ Getty Images*); p. 107 Portrait of Sir Thomas Smythe (*Florilegius/Alamy Stock Photo*); p. 109 Portrait of Sir Edwin Sandys (*Granger Historical Picture Archive/Alamy Stock Photo*); p. 119 Virginia Company coat of arms (*MPI/Getty Images*); p. 127 Illustration from the title page of the Virginia Company's 'Nova Britannia', 1609 (*Granger Historical Picture Archive/ Alamy Stock Photo*); p. 144 *A yacht and three warships in a storm* by Wenceslaus Hollar (*University of Toronto Wenceslaus Hollar Digital Collection*); p. 150 John Ferrar's map of Virginia, 1651 (© *John Carter Brown Library*); p. 159 'Their Dances at Their Great Feasts', engraving by Theodor de Bry, after John White (*Science History Images/Alamy Stock Photo*); p. 163 'Shipload of Wives' (*Bettman/Getty Images*); p. 169 Engraving depicting Jamestown in 1622 (*Fotosearch/Stringer/Getty Images*); p. 177 *A Marriage Ceremony,* an illustration from 'A Book of Roxburghe Ballads' (woodcut) (b/w photo), English School, 17th century (*Private Collection/Bridgeman Images*); p. 189 Native fishing scene as depicted by John White, *c*.1585 (*Granger Historical Picture Archive/Alamy Stock Photo*); p. 206 Illustration of a rattlesnake by Mark Catesby, 1743 (*The Picture Art Collection/ Alamy Stock Photo*); p. 213 Illustration depicting the Jamestown Massacre, from 1634 (*MPI/Getty Images*); p. 221 An illustration of Captain John Smith taking Chief Opechancanough prisoner, published in *The Generall Historie of Virginia, New-England, and the Summer Isles* by John Smith, 1624 (*Bettman/Contributor/Getty Images*); p. 228 Map of Jamestown *c*.1624, from Samuel H. Yonge's *The Site of Old 'James Towne' 1607–1698* (Richmond, Hermitage Press, 1907); p. 233 'Two broad-sides against tobacco', 1672 (*Folger Shakespeare Library*); p. 245 Detail from a mid-eighteenth-century map of Virginia and Maryland by Joshua Fry and Peter Jefferson (*Library of Congress*); p. 252 *Woman with a bodkin in her hair* by Wenceslaus Hollar (*University of Toronto Wenceslaus Hollar Digital Collection*); p. 259 Detail from Captain John Smith's original map of Virginia, 1612 (*Library of Congress*); p. 267 Illustration of a woman on a ducking stool (*Culture Club/Getty Images*); p. 273 *The lacemaker* by Wenceslaus Hollar (*University of Toronto Wenceslaus Hollar Digital Collection*); p. 282 Map titled 'Dale's Settlements on the Upper James', from *Virginia Under the Stuarts* by Thomas J. Wertenbaker (Princeton: Princeton University Press, 1914); p. 291 The Algonquian village of Pomeiooc as depicted by John White, *c*.1585 (*Granger Historical Picture Archive/ Alamy Stock Photo*); p. 299 *Mulier ex Virginia* by Wenceslaus Hollar (*University of Toronto Wenceslaus Hollar Digital Collection*); p. 303 Undated engraving entitled 'Site of Jamestown, Virginia' (*Time Life Pictures/Mansell/The LIFE Picture Collection/Getty Images*); p. 311 *Young woman with side curls* by Wenceslaus Hollar (*University of Toronto Wenceslaus Hollar Digital Collection*)

Index

Index

Index